Revolutionizing Consumer Experience With Digital Twins and the Metaverse

Brij B. Gupta
https://orcid.org/0000-0003-4929-4698
Asia University, Taiwan

Yuk Ming Tang
https://orcid.org/0000-0001-8215-4190
Hong Kong Polytechnic University, Hong Kong

IGI Global Scientific Publishing
Publishing Tomorrow's Research Today

Vice President of Editorial	Melissa Wagner
Director of Acquisitions	Mikaela Felty
Director of Book Development	Jocelynn Hessler
Production Manager	Mike Brehm
Cover Design	Jose Rosado

Published in the United States of America by
IGI Global Scientific Publishing
701 East Chocolate Avenue
Hershey, PA, 17033, USA
Tel: 717-533-8845 | Fax: 717-533-7115
Website: https://www.igi-global.com E-mail: cust@igi-global.com

Library of Congress Cataloging-in-Publication Data

LCCN: 2025026757 (CIP Data Pending)
ISBN13: 979-8-3373-4541-3
Isbn13Softcover: 979-8-3373-4542-0
EISBN13: 979-8-3373-4543-7

British Cataloguing in Publication Data
A Cataloguing in Publication record for this book is available from the British Library.

This book is dedicated, with profound appreciation and affection, to our families, whose unwavering support and encouragement have been a constant source of strength throughout this journey.

Table of Contents

Detailed Table of Contents

This study explores how the convergence between digital twins, metaversal platforms, and immersive technologies is transforming consumer interaction in the context of Industry 5.0. From a human-centric perspective, the ethical, technical, and organizational challenges that arise when integrating biometric signals, XR environments, and business models based on affective data are analyzed. The paper examines the need for dynamic organizational capabilities that orchestrate hyper-personalized experiences without compromising privacy, sustainability, or equity. Through a qualitative approach, tensions between innovation, algorithmic governance and ethical design are identified, proposing a conceptual framework to maximize the experiential and symbolic value of the consumer in advanced socio-technical environments.

The emergence of the metaverse as a multidimensional digital environment has redefined how brands interact with consumers, offering immersive, interactive, and hyper-personalized experiences. This chapter explores the evolving landscape of customer experience (CX) design in the metaverse, focusing on the integration of immersive technologies such as virtual reality (VR), augmented reality (AR), and extended reality (XR). It investigates how strategic brand storytelling, gamified engagement, and real-time behavioral insights contribute to creating meaningful virtual brand experiences. The chapter also emphasizes the importance of digital inclusivity and ethical considerations in ensuring equitable access and representation in virtual spaces. Through case studies from sectors including retail, education, and entertainment, the study illustrates best practices and challenges in designing future-ready, human-centered CX strategies within the metaverse.

Industry 5.0 drives a deeper fusion between advanced intelligent systems and human creativity, positioning immersive technologies as essential components of modern innovation. Digital Twins and the Metaverse enable highly interactive, data rich environments where physical processes can be simulated, optimized, and experienced virtually. With support from AI, IoT, blockchain, and high speed networks, organizations can design business models that prioritize adaptability, co creation, and meaningful user engagement. Consumers participate directly in virtual testing, collaborative design sessions, and service interactions, creating continuous feedback loops that refine products and experiences. These immersive ecosystems strengthen operational reliability, reduce development risks, and open opportunities for sustainable value creation across industries. By offering transparent, secure, and accessible digital spaces, immersive technologies help companies develop human centered, resilient, and future ready business strategies aligned with the goals of Industry 5.0.

Shweta Kaur Khalsa, Dayananda Sagar University, India
Jitendranath Patri, Dayananda Sagar University, India

The Retail industry is facing a transformation driven by digitalization, customer expectations and heightened post-pandemic consciousness revolving around value, ethics and experience. Consumer experience (CX) has been widely researched, but there is limited empirical research which showcases the practitioner perspective on CX success factors in emerging markets like India. This study addresses this gap and adopts a qualitative Braun and Clarke's thematic analysis approach. This approach is based on in-depth interviews (n=15) with professionals from diverse retail backgrounds. The findings of this research reveal four interrelated drivers of CX i.e. excellence, personalization and customer engagement along with technology integration and sustainability. These factors collectively shape consumer trust, loyalty and lead to long term business growth. The novelty of this study lies in integrating practitioner insights into a comprehensive conceptual model which reflects post COVID shifts in omnichannel behavior.

Damar Aditya, Universitas Esa Unggul, Indonesia
Qori Halimatul Hidayah, Universitas Esa Unggul, Indonesia
Kartini Kartini, Universitas Esa Unggul, Indonesia
Shavi Bansal, Insight2Techinfo, India
Akshat Gaurav, Asia University, Taiwan

Digital twins are transforming supply chains into intelligent, adaptive networks capable of real-time visibility, optimization, and predictive decision-making. By synchronizing virtual replicas with IoT sensors, enterprise systems, and logistics infrastructures, digital twins generate continuously updated models that reveal bottlenecks, forecast demand fluctuations, and simulate operational scenarios with high precision. AI-driven analytics enhance these capabilities by supporting autonomous routing, adaptive inventory control, and disruption response across global logistics chains. For consumers, digital twins provide transparent tracking, personalized delivery options, and seamless integration with emerging metaverse

Preface

INTRODUCTION

The convergence of Digital Twins, the Metaverse, and Industry 5.0 marks a profound shift in how organizations design, deliver, and sustain consumer experiences. Moving beyond automation and efficiency, this new era emphasizes human-centricity, intelligence, resilience, and ethical innovation, where advanced technologies work in harmony with human creativity and values. *Revolutionizing Consumer Experience With Digital Twins and the Metaverse* is conceived against this backdrop, offering a comprehensive and interdisciplinary exploration of how immersive, data-driven, and intelligent systems are redefining interactions across industries.

Digital twins—virtual representations of physical entities, processes, and systems—enable real-time monitoring, simulation, and optimization, while the metaverse creates persistent, immersive digital environments that transform how users engage with products, services, and brands. When combined with artificial intelligence, extended reality (VR/AR/MR), IoT, blockchain, 5G, and emerging technologies, these paradigms unlock unprecedented opportunities to enhance personalization, trust, transparency, and experiential value. This book aims to bridge theory and practice by presenting cutting-edge research, real-world applications, and forward-looking insights into this rapidly evolving ecosystem.

The chapters in this volume collectively address the technological, managerial, societal, and ethical dimensions of digital twins and the metaverse. Beginning with foundational perspectives on Industry 5.0, the book explores how immersive technologies are transforming consumer interaction, business models, and organizational strategies. Several chapters examine the role of virtual and augmented reality in business transformation, education, manufacturing, hospitality, retail, healthcare, sports, religious tourism, and cultural heritage, highlighting how immersive experiences can foster deeper engagement and value co-creation.

A strong emphasis is placed on data governance, cybersecurity, privacy, and ethical considerations, recognizing that trust and responsibility are central to the success of metaverse-driven systems. The book also investigates AI-enabled applications—from customer experience in e-commerce and intelligent supply chains to sports analytics, healthcare, wildlife conservation, and smart sacred sites—demonstrating the breadth of impact across both commercial and societal domains. Furthermore, chapters on user-generated content, influencer marketing, programming by demonstration, and human-centric innovation underscore the importance of empowerment, inclusivity, and compassion in digital transformation.

Importantly, this volume does not view technology in isolation. Instead, it situates digital twins and the metaverse within broader socio-technical systems, examining how organizations can align innovation with sustainability, ethics, and human well-being. The inclusion of topics such as blockchain integration, Industry 5.0 manufacturing, 5G and beyond, and intelligent logistics reflects the holistic nature of modern digital ecosystems.

This book is intended for a wide audience, including researchers, academicians, industry professionals, policymakers, and graduate students seeking to understand and shape the future of consumer experience and digital transformation. By bringing together diverse perspectives and case-driven insights, the volume aspires to serve as both a scholarly reference and a practical guide for navigating the opportunities and challenges of the metaverse and digital twin era.

We hope that this book stimulates critical thinking, inspires innovation, and fosters meaningful collaboration across disciplines and sectors. As technologies continue to evolve, the true measure of progress will lie in how effectively they enhance human experiences, create shared value, and contribute to a more intelligent, inclusive, and compassionate digital world.

Here are reworded versions of the chapter abstracts, maintaining the original meaning while improving clarity, coherence, and academic tone.

CHAPTER OVERVIEWS

Chapter 1: Transforming Consumer Interaction through Digital Twins and the Metaverse in Industry 5.0

This chapter examines how the integration of digital twins, metaverse platforms, and immersive technologies is reshaping consumer engagement within the Industry 5.0 paradigm. Adopting a human-centered lens, it explores the ethical, technological, and organizational complexities associated with combining biometric data, extended reality (XR) environments, and business models driven by affective analytics. The study underscores the importance of developing dynamic organizational capabilities that can deliver hyper-personalized experiences while safeguarding privacy, sustainability, and social equity. Using a qualitative methodology, the authors identify key tensions between technological innovation, algorithmic governance, and ethical design, and propose a conceptual framework aimed at enhancing the experiential and symbolic value of consumers in advanced socio-technical ecosystems.

Chapter 2: Beyond Reality – Crafting Consumer Journeys in the Metaverse

The rise of the metaverse as a complex digital ecosystem has transformed brand–consumer interactions by enabling immersive, interactive, and highly personalized experiences. This chapter investigates the evolution of customer experience (CX) design within metaverse environments, emphasizing the role of virtual reality (VR), augmented reality (AR), and extended reality (XR). It explores how immersive storytelling, gamification strategies, and real-time behavioral analytics shape compelling virtual brand engagements. The discussion further highlights the significance of ethical design and digital inclusivity in promoting fair representation and access in virtual spaces. Drawing on case studies from retail, education, and entertainment sectors, the chapter outlines best practices and emerging challenges in building future-oriented, human-centered CX strategies in the metaverse.

Chapter 3: Business Model Innovation through Immersive Technologies in the Industry 5.0 Era

Industry 5.0 deepens the integration of intelligent technologies with human creativity, positioning immersive tools as critical drivers of innovation. This chapter explores how digital twins and the metaverse create interactive, data-intensive environments where physical systems can be simulated, optimized, and experienced virtually. Supported by artificial intelligence (AI), the Internet of Things (IoT), blockchain, and high-speed connectivity, organizations can develop adaptive business models centered on collaboration, co-creation, and enriched user engagement. Consumers actively participate in virtual prototyping, collaborative design, and service interactions, generating continuous feedback loops that refine offerings. These immersive ecosystems enhance operational resilience, minimize development risks, and foster sustainable value creation. By ensuring transparency, security, and accessibility, such technologies enable human-centered and future-ready business strategies aligned with Industry 5.0 objectives.

Chapter 4: Exploring the Success Factors of Customer Experience in Retail – A Thematic Analysis

The retail sector is undergoing rapid transformation driven by digitalization, evolving customer expectations, and heightened post-pandemic awareness of value, ethics, and experience. Although customer experience (CX) has been widely studied, practitioner perspectives in emerging markets such as India remain underexplored. Addressing this gap, the study employs Braun and Clarke's thematic analysis based on in-depth interviews with 15 retail professionals. The findings identify four interconnected drivers of CX success: service excellence, personalization, customer engagement, and the integration of technology and sustainability. Together, these factors build consumer trust and loyalty, contributing to sustained business growth. The study's key contribution lies in synthesizing practitioner insights into a comprehensive conceptual model that reflects post-COVID shifts in omnichannel consumer behavior.

Chapter 5: Intelligent Supply Chains and Logistics in the Era of Digital Twins

Digital twins are redefining supply chains as intelligent, responsive networks capable of real-time monitoring, predictive analytics, and operational optimization. By synchronizing virtual models with IoT devices, enterprise platforms, and logistics systems, digital twins provide continuously updated insights into bottlenecks, demand variations, and alternative operational scenarios. AI-powered analytics further enable autonomous routing, dynamic inventory management, and rapid disruption response across global supply networks. For consumers, these technologies offer enhanced transparency, personalized delivery solutions, and integration with emerging metaverse commerce platforms. As firms strive for resilience and sustainability, the convergence of digital twins, automation, and immersive analytics is transforming logistics into adaptive systems that continuously learn and respond to market and environmental shifts.

Chapter 6: Revolutionizing Patient Experience through Digital Twins and the Metaverse in Healthcare

This systematic literature review examines how digital twins and metaverse technologies are transforming patient experience in healthcare systems. Following a PRISMA-guided methodology, the study synthesizes findings from 25 publications (2020–2025), revealing a shift from episodic, provider-centric care toward predictive, participatory, and patient-centered models. The authors propose a five-pillar integrated framework with measurable indicators and implementation pathways to guide adoption. The review also identifies a publication bias toward positive outcomes and underscores the limited availability of long-term effectiveness studies. The findings provide practical insights for healthcare organizations seeking to responsibly implement these technologies while ensuring robust standards for privacy, accessibility, and ethical governance.

Chapter 7: AI in Sports Analytics – Enhancing Performance, Fan Engagement, and Immersive Experiences

The application of Artificial Intelligence (AI) in sports analytics has fundamentally reshaped performance management, strategic planning, and fan engagement. This chapter explores the convergence of AI, digital twins, and metaverse technologies in building intelligent and immersive sports ecosystems. AI supports real-time performance tracking, injury prediction, personalized training programs, and tactical analysis through machine learning and computer vision. Digital twins enable the simulation of athletes and gameplay scenarios to optimize decisions, while metaverse platforms enhance fan experiences via virtual stadiums, avatars, and customized digital content. Emerging technologies such as smart wearables and edge computing further improve data accuracy and immediacy. Case examples, including AI-assisted VAR systems and immersive fan environments, demonstrate practical applications. The chapter also addresses ethical and operational challenges, including data privacy, algorithmic bias, and equitable access, and proposes a strategic framework for responsible adoption.

Chapter 8: Improving Engagement in Sacred Sites through Smart Technology Solutions

Sacred sites attract pilgrims and visitors due to their profound spiritual, cultural, and historical significance. However, traditional engagement approaches often fall short of meeting modern visitors' expectations. This chapter explores how smart technologies—such as augmented reality (AR), AI-powered guides, mobile applications, and IoT-based systems—can enrich visitor experiences while preserving the sanctity and authenticity of sacred spaces. It examines challenges related to technological intrusion, data privacy, and community acceptance. Through global case studies, the chapter highlights successful implementations and key lessons learned. The findings demonstrate how thoughtfully integrated technologies can transform religious tourism into a more interactive, inclusive, and meaningful experience for diverse audiences.

Chapter 9: Strategic Integration of the Metaverse in Religious Tourism – The Case of the Sanctuary of Fátima

Emerging digital technologies are transforming organizational operations, reshaping products, processes, value chains, and business models. Within this evolving landscape, the metaverse offers new avenues for interaction between organizations and consumers in shared virtual environments. Despite growing adoption across sectors, academic understanding of its strategic implications remains limited. This chapter addresses this gap through a secondary-data-driven case study of the Sanctuary of Fátima in Portugal. The analysis evaluates the strategic potential of metaverse applications in religious tourism, highlighting opportunities for innovative value creation, delivery, and capture. The findings suggest that virtual pilgrimage experiences and enhanced stakeholder engagement can extend spiritual and tourism experiences beyond physical boundaries.

Acknowledgement

We would like to express our sincere gratitude to everyone who has contributed to the completion of this book, Revolutionizing Consumer Experience With Digital Twins and the Metaverse. This endeavor would not have been possible without the invaluable support, guidance, and dedication of many individuals.

First and foremost, we extend our heartfelt appreciation to the authors and reviewers of each chapter. Their expertise, insightful feedback, and unwavering commitment played a crucial role in shaping the depth and quality of this book. Their contributions have been instrumental in ensuring that this volume serves as a comprehensive resource in the field.

We are also profoundly grateful to the team at IGI Global Publishing for their continuous support, technical expertise, and encouragement throughout this journey. Their professional guidance and commitment were invaluable in bringing this project to fruition.

A special note of thanks goes to our families, whose unwavering love, patience, and encouragement have been a constant source of strength. Their support sustained us through the challenges of this endeavor and was instrumental in its successful completion.

Lastly, we are deeply thankful to the Almighty for granting us the strength, resilience, and determination to navigate this journey and bring this work to completion.

To all those who contributed in various ways, we extend our deepest gratitude. Your support and efforts are truly appreciated.

Chapter 1
Transforming Consumer Interaction Through Digital Twins and Metaverse in Industry 5.0

Jose De Jesus Reyes-Sánchez
http://orcid.org/0000-0002-3866-2363
TECNM Instituto Tecnologico Superior De Fresnillo, Mexico

Hugo Jimenez Alvarez
http://orcid.org/0009-0002-4497-0327
TECNM Instituto Tecnologico Superior De Fresnillo, Mexico

Jannet Maricela Barrientos Luján
http://orcid.org/0009-0009-3244-5016
TECNM Instituto Tecnologico Superior De Fresnillo, Mexico

Johana Paola Reyes-Davalos
http://orcid.org/0009-0005-0330-635X
TECNM Instituto Tecnologico Superior De Fresnillo, Mexico

Mario Alberto García-Camacho
http://orcid.org/0000-0002-9645-3199
TECNM Instituto Tecnologico Superior De Fresnillo, Mexico

Ana Perla Caldera Burgos
http://orcid.org/0009-0007-2906-5800
TECNM Instituto Tecnológico Superior de Jerez, Mexico

ABSTRACT

This study explores how the convergence between digital twins, metaversal platforms, and immersive technologies is transforming consumer interaction in the context of Industry 5.0. From a human-centric perspective, the ethical, technical, and organizational challenges that arise when integrating biometric signals, XR environments, and business models based on affective data are analyzed. The paper examines the need for dynamic organizational capabilities that orchestrate hyper-personalized experiences without compromising privacy, sustainability, or equity. Through a qualitative approach, tensions between innovation, algorithmic

DOI: 10.4018/979-8-3373-4541-3.ch001

governance and ethical design are identified, proposing a conceptual framework to maximize the experiential and symbolic value of the consumer in advanced socio-technical environments.

INTRODUCTION

The accelerating convergence between digital twins and immersive metaverse environments has moved from speculative rhetoric to a concrete context in which perception, consumption, and value co creation are being reorganized. Consumer interaction no longer occurs only at the physical point of sale or through a two dimensional ecommerce interface, but inside embodied digital spaces where presence, attention, and feedback become part of the experience design and the market exchange itself (Ranjan & Read, 2021).

Within this landscape, Industry 5.0 is best read as a socio technical project that centers human wellbeing and sustainability as design constraints of manufacturing, rather than as a simple sequential upgrade from prior industrial paradigms. The shift is visible in the way principles, values, and enabling technologies are framed around human centricity, resilience, and responsibility, which forces production systems to negotiate performance together with ethical and social expectations (Ghobakhloo et al., 2023; Hemphill, 2023).

At the operational layer, digital twin driven manufacturing enables tighter coupling between sensing, modeling, and decision cycles, allowing production systems to evolve from static representations toward continuously updated operational intelligence. This is especially consequential when digital twins are integrated with additive manufacturing, because it expands the feasible design space and supports individualized production logics that remain economically viable under high variability (Lu et al., 2020; Jyeniskhan et al., 2024).

In parallel, immersive brand spaces and metaverse touchpoints intensify the logic that value emerges in interaction rather than being embedded in the product alone, which changes how firms think about experience, participation, and the distribution of agency between organizations and users. When immersive environments become persistent, relational, and socially networked, the experience itself becomes the exchange infrastructure through which meanings, identities, and contributions are coordinated (Alexander et al., 2024; Ranjan & Read, 2021).

Yet the promise of scale across platforms depends on governance and interoperability arrangements that can support portability, accountability, and trust without collapsing the diversity of designs into a single centralized gatekeeper. Responsible standards development becomes decisive in preventing fragmentation, aligning safety and transparency expectations, and reducing the risk that technical interoperability evolves faster than institutional safeguards and human centered design principles (Hemphill, 2023; Ghobakhloo et al., 2023).

At the same time, the ubiquity of biometric sensing, identity verification, and intention inference introduces discrimination risks that can be amplified by data imbalance and deployment thresholds. Fairness oriented evaluation and mitigation work in biometrics shows that demographic bias can persist across pipelines unless explicitly measured and corrected, making auditability and bias reduction strategies integral to any immersive system that relies on face based identity or affect inference (Fang et al., 2024; Terhörst et al., 2020).

Sustainability is not an appendix to this transformation but a system level condition of legitimacy, because immersive rendering, real time simulation, and continuous analytics reshape energy demand at the edge and in distributed compute. Evidence from urban energy systems suggests that waste heat recovery from data centers can materially improve district heating efficiency, while graphics side efficiency research indicates that foveated approaches can reduce rendering energy demand, which together clarifies that circular and efficient compute architectures are feasible design targets rather than afterthoughts (Oró et al., 2019; Gralka et al., 2025).

STATEMENT OF THE PROBLEM

Consumer interaction in Industry 5.0 is supported by a techno digital scaffolding such as cognitive twins, collaborative robotics, generative artificial intelligence, and hybrid clouds that promises hyper personalized experiences in real time. However, the convergence of these technologies is advancing faster than the governance, data protection, and sustainability models that should accompany it. The result is a systemic gap: while manufacturers and retailers deploy adaptive production architectures, end users perceive inconsistencies between the promise of immediacy and the reality of environments that are still fragmented, expensive, or non transparent (Valette et al., 2023; Hu et al., 2025).

In the ethical layer, mechanisms of affective sensing collect micro expressions and biometrics to adjust content in milliseconds. That ability opens new data economies, but it also exposes algorithmic biases that can perpetuate stereotypes or induce unwanted behaviors when models and datasets are not evaluated under fairness and accountability requirements (Pahl et al., 2022; Alkaeed et al., 2024).

At the same time, interoperability remains contingent: proprietary silos limit the portability of digital identities, achievements, and assets. Although self sovereign identity approaches seek to provide portable and user controlled credentials, implementation details and governance choices often determine whether identity truly remains under user control or becomes a new layer of lock in. DAOs promise distributed governance, but their real world operation still depends on auditable accountability, repair mechanisms, and enforceable rules, which remain uneven and can place users in front of complex, poorly inspectable contract logic (Ling & Butakov, 2024; van Vulpen et al., 2024).

Sustainability adds extra tension. Volumetric rendering, low latency interaction, and edge oriented data centers can raise power demand well above conventional electronic commerce, while measurement practices for carbon accounting in immersive systems remain inconsistent across projects and jurisdictions (Hu et al., 2025; Alkaeed et al., 2024).

In the experiential dimension, the haptic attention economy redefines the brand user relationship: vibrotactile stimuli can increase commercial conversion and perceived engagement, but they can also configure opaque persuasive dynamics when feedback is designed to steer behavior without meaningful disclosure or control (Manshad & Brannon, 2021; Pahl et al., 2022).

At the level of digital rights, tokenization of assets and self management of identities follow divergent paths. While some XR ecosystems move toward models that emphasize brand community value creation and clearer ownership narratives, others replicate extractivist logics through contractual ambiguity, weak licensing clarity, and limited user recourse (Colicev, 2023; Ling & Butakov, 2024).

BACKGROUND

Technological Convergence Towards Industry 5.0

The sociotechnical convergence that defines phase 5.0 goes beyond the linear assembly of technologies to place the human being at the center of cooperative automation architectures. Intuitive collaborative robotics and generative artificial intelligence expand the scope of immersive assistance by coupling real time sensing with adaptive interfaces that can be tuned to the operator and the consumer in context, while extended reality interaction increasingly depends on credible multisensory feedback to sustain trust, comfort, and task transfer in complex environments (Tang et al., 2024; Kim & Xiong, 2022).

Origins and Evolution of Digital Twins

The first CAD and CAE simulations of the nineteen nineties were designed to replicate asset kinematics, but the present trajectory points to digital twin ecosystems that must operate under strict latency, integrity, and confidentiality constraints because twin outputs can trigger actions across distributed cyber physical infrastructures. As twins become embedded in metaverse grade services and industrial edge environments, security, privacy, and cyber resilience move from peripheral concerns to core design variables that shape adoption and operational safety (Rahartomo et al., 2025).

From Virtual Worlds to Metaversal Environments

Massive multiplayer platforms functioned as sociotechnical laboratories where digitally scarce economies and community governance were tested, but persistent metaverse environments intensify the stakes by blending identity, value exchange, and embodied interaction into a continuous experience loop. This shift elevates both the importance of immersive interfaces that feel natural and the need for systematic controls that address fraud, surveillance risks, and exploitability across platforms (Tang et al., 2024).

Ultra Low Latency Connectivity Infrastructure

The deployment of ultra low latency connectivity and edge computing is essential to preserve perceptual continuity in immersive services, especially when digital twins and interactive rendering demand rapid feedback loops across heterogeneous devices. Network slicing and edge support can reduce the likelihood of experience rupture, yet they also create a broader attack surface and operational complexity that requires integrated security engineering and continuous risk management (Bolettieri et al., 2022; Rahartomo et al., 2025).

Biometric Data Economies and New Business Models

The monetization of physiological and behavioral signals can open B2B2C markets for experience analytics, but it also intensifies privacy risk, reidentification exposure, and manipulation concerns when biometric traces are used to infer intent or vulnerability. In metaverse contexts, the combination of immersive presence and high granularity sensing increases the importance of end to end security controls and transparent data governance, while interface design choices can amplify or mitigate users' ability to recognize and manage these risks (Rahartomo et al., 2025; Kim & Xiong, 2022).

Paradigms of Immersive Human Machine Interaction

High fidelity multichannel haptic interfaces and mid air interaction metaphors can increase realism and reduce training friction by translating virtual properties into tactile and proprioceptive cues, improving immersion without requiring overly intrusive hardware. However, these same techniques can also shape attention and persuasion, which makes interface accountability and careful calibration of sensory feedback central to trustworthy immersive design (Tang et al., 2024; Kim & Xiong, 2022).

Regulatory Trajectory and Emerging Ethical Frameworks

Emerging ethical frameworks increasingly converge on the need for explicit consent, proportional data use, and robust protections against covert tracking in persistent environments, but practical governance is constrained by fragmented standards and uneven enforcement. Because immersive ecosystems frequently integrate third party components, identity layers, and distributed compute, systemic security and privacy weaknesses can undermine any ethical intent unless governance is coupled to verifiable technical safeguards and continuous assurance (Rahartomo et al., 2025).

Sustainability and Carbon Footprint of Extended Reality

The sustainability burden of immersive systems is shaped by both compute intensity and the supporting infrastructure footprint, including edge and data center operations that must scale to meet low latency expectations. Waste heat recovery and district heating integration are increasingly discussed as viable strategies to turn thermal losses into usable energy, but these approaches still depend on local infrastructure readiness and coordinated policy and investment mechanisms (Yuan et al., 2025).

Immersive Prosumer and Gamification Strategies

Mission based reward mechanics and prosumer marketplaces can strengthen engagement by converting participation into status, learning, and exchangeable digital value, but the same mechanisms can also heighten persuasive pressure when sensory cues and feedback loops are optimized for conversion rather than user welfare. Designing gamified experiences in XR therefore requires careful attention to how haptic cues, interaction metaphors, and feedback intensity influence autonomy, comprehension, and behavioral steering (Kim & Xiong, 2022; Tang et al., 2024).

Open Innovation Ecosystems and Cross Sector Collaborations

Living labs, consortia, and cross sector pilots can reduce duplication and accelerate standardization by testing interoperable building blocks under real usage conditions, yet collaboration at scale also amplifies governance complexity across security, privacy, and accountability boundaries. In metaverse oriented initiatives, the viability of open innovation depends on whether shared architectures can sustain low latency performance while remaining defensible against evolving threats and credible in their treatment of user data and experience integrity (Rahartomo et al., 2025).

THEORETICAL FRAMEWORK

Conceptual Differentiation: Digital Twins and Metaverse

Digital twins were born as virtual replicas of physical objects or processes that allow their behavior to be accurately observed, diagnosed, and predicted over time. Its logic is based on systems engineering: a constant stream of sensory data passes through analytical and machine learning models to update the "health status" of the physical asset in real time. The metaverse, in contrast, is conceived as a sociotechnical network of persistent, interoperable, and economically autonomous virtual worlds where users coexist through avatars and scarce digital objects (Richter & Richter, 2023; Gleim et al., 2025).

Although both concepts share the foundations of digital representation, their ontology differs. The digital twin maintains a one-to-one link with its material referent, depends on the fidelity of the sensors and privileges operational accuracy. The metaverse, on the other hand, amplifies the symbolic dimension: the physical truth matters less and the narrative coherence of the experience more. However, they converge when an inhabited simulation is orchestrated; that is, when the twin's metrics feed a virtual space that the consumer accesses in order to explore scenarios, personalize products or co-create services. This transition from the engineering model to the immersive scenario requires semantically linked data architectures and XR standards that guarantee latencies below twenty milliseconds to avoid cyber-motion sickness (Attaran & Celik, 2023).

Operational Synergy for the Consumer Experience

By integrating both concepts, organizations create closed feedback loops where user actions in the metaverse instantly update the twin, and in turn, the twin's predictions reconfigure the immersive experience. This convergence enables what the literature calls participatory co-simulation: the consumer is no longer an external observer, but an actor-sensor who co-designs the product while exploring its virtual behavior (Stauffert et al., 2020).

On the technological level, synergy requires three layers: (1) multi-touch XR interface capable of translating haptic and biometric events; (2) physical simulation engine synchronized with the rendering pipeline; and (3) semantic orchestrator that maintains identity consistency between physical and virtual objects. The TwinXR method illustrates this approach by employing descriptions of twins as reusable prefabs that are instantiated in industrial mixed reality applications

The benefits for relationship marketing are obvious. First, hyper-personalization: the twin's parameters of use capture attrition patterns and preferences, allowing for predictive maintenance recommendations or contextual up-selling. Second, the minimization of perceived risk: by trying a virtual appliance that faithfully replicates the real thermal dynamics, the buyer reduces uncertainty and accelerates their decision. Third, the co-production of symbolic value: operational metrics translate into achievements or badges within the metaverse, gamifying responsible ownership (Flavián et al., 2024; Richter & Richter, 2023).

Industry 5.0 Principles and Immersive Consumption

Industry 5.0 transcends the efficiency of the fourth revolution by placing human beings and sustainability at the centre of the production system. Immersive digital interaction reinforces both postulates. From the human perspective, bio-telemetry-sensitive avatars allow collaborative robots to be adapted to the physical and cognitive rhythm of the operator, reducing fatigue and accidents. At the same time, the metaversal interface fosters inclusion: workers with limited mobility can monitor virtual assembly lines using simplified gestures or eye control, aligning with the principle of universal accessibility (Adel & HS Alani, 2024; Mourtzis, 2023).

In the sustainability axis, the twin-metaverse cycle enables circularity twins that calculate, live, the carbon footprint of each consumer decision and visualize reduction routes within the immersive scene. The pedagogical impact of this feedback has been documented in domestic energy consumption environments and in electric vehicle configurators, where the visualization of environmental externalities increases the adoption of green choices by twenty-two percent (Feroz et al., 2023; Adel & HS Alani, 2024).

The Industry 5.0 approach also values resilience. Corporate metaverses, operating on multisite digital twins, function as shock simulators: disruptions (raw material shortages, cyberattacks, demand spikes) are injected and systemic responses are analyzed to strengthen supply chains. In this way, overstock production is minimized and waste of resources is avoided. In terms of consumer-worker well-being, cognitively friendly designs of healthcare twins allow lighting, temperature, and task cadence to be adjusted in real time, reducing stress and improving productivity (Mourtzis, 2023; Teece, 2007).

Dynamic Capabilities for Immersive Organizations

The foundational logic of dynamic capabilities takes on a radically different aspect when transferred to the immersive ecosystem. By condensing information loops into sub-second rhythms, decision-makers no longer interpret static reports, but instead immerse themselves in digital twins where each market fluctuation is projected as a volumetric alteration in the three-dimensional space of the control room. The synchrony between presence sensors, private 5G networks, and high-granularity predictive models turns the scrutiny of the competitive environment into a corporeal experience that fuses perception and analytics, reinforcing the premise that organizations capable of orchestrating sensing, seizing, and transforming routines at this speed perform superior in turbulent scenarios (Feroz et al., 2023; Flavián et al., 2024).

The sensing phase transcends simple environmental monitoring because contextual telemetry is dumped into immersive panels where Bayesian inference is represented as probabilistic clouds that breathe to the beat of new data. By employing cognitive digital twin architectures, leaders can rehearse counterfactual scenarios and discriminate which signals constitute true strategic discontinuities and which are mere stochastic perturbations; this cognitive sieve prevents over-reacting and preserves managerial attention shortages. Once the opportunity is detected, the seizing capability is activated by microservices that automate niche prospecting and recombine digital assets into A/B-ready prototypes within the extended universe itself. A few hours are enough to launch virtual versions of a product, expose them to targeted segments and obtain avatar traction metrics that guide budget prioritization without spending physical capital; this understanding of the learning cycle has been accredited in methodologies such as TwinXR, which formalize ontologies of equipment and process for synchronizing twins and XR scenes (Flavián et al., 2024).

At the data architecture level, multimodal classification requires models that integrate spatial convolutions for micro-expressions, temporal transformers for HRV, and cross-attention layers that align pupillary vectors with latent emotional states; experiments in XR security training twins show that, by orchestrating such an algorithmic stack on low-latency microservices, it is possible to modify the diegetic narrative in real time to keep the user within their optimal window of challenge and skill, avoiding both habituation and anxiety (Zhang et al., 2025; Mathôt, 2018).

Micro-Fundamentals of Affective Sensing

Predictive coding theory explains this refinement by proposing that perceptual circuits compare incoming patterns with an internal generator trained on the statistical regularity of the environment; each micro-expression suppresses or exacerbates the error signal and triggers a new attentional sweep that dynamically reconfigures synaptic weights, so that the XR interface not only reflects emotional states, but also rather, it anticipates and compensates for them before the user notices affective discontinuities, consolidating a homeostatic adjustment loop between expectation and sensation (Bradley et al., 2008; Libby et al., 1973).

The physiological cartography that makes affective sensing possible is based on the frictionless capture of facial micro-expressions, variations in heart rate variability and subtle oculometric modulations that emerge at the very moment the person enters the immersive environment; such signals, when integrated into early fusion pipelines, offer a continuous reading of the emotional valence that exceeds the granularity of the KPIs traditionally used to evaluate user experience, because each fluctuation is projected as an error vector that feeds cognitive twins capable of readjusting, in milliseconds, the dose of audiovisual stimuli that sustain the sensation of presence (Sprevak & Smith, 2023; Tarnowski et al., 2020).

When pupillometry is combined with HRV analysis and facial tracking, the system acquires sufficient sensitivity to discriminate transition between flow and cognitive fatigue: increased pupillary dilation and parasympathetic attenuation reflected in the HRV high-frequency band are interpreted as a marker of overload, while pupillary contraction together with a balanced HRV profile indicates optimal immersion; the adaptive engine of the environment uses these parameters to redistribute visual complexity and loudness, in such a way that intrinsic motivation is preserved without sacrificing attentional performance (Domínguez Jiménez et al., 2020; Lim et al., 2020).

Monitoring of the flow state provides an additional micro-foundation: electroencephalographic recordings in alpha and theta bands, combined with cardio-respiratory metrics and hand kinematics, reveal that during total absorption motor variability decreases and an autonomic signature emerges in the form of an inverse U-curve of HRV; the adaptation engines that incorporate these findings reconfigure event density, complexity of challenges and feedback cadence to sustain motivation for a long time, which translates into significant increases in learning and well-being in work and educational environments (Lim et al., 2020).

Seizing Processes Based on Contextual Data

In immersive environments powered by extended reality technologies, seizing processes take on a radically contextual and adaptive character. Unlike traditional schemes focused on ex post strategic decisions, XR organizations transform contextual inferences into value propositions that emerge just as the user's attention, motivation, and emotional disposition converge (Kour et al., 2025; Maathuis et al., 2025).

These contextual detection systems function as interpretive layers that not only capture data, but translate it into relevant meanings: gaze behavior, haptic gestures, control pressure, and microfluctuations in body language are interpreted in real time to infer moments of dissonance, fatigue, or enthusiasm, triggering synchronous experiences or recommendations (Wang et al., 2019; Khamaj & Ali, 2024). Contextualized reinforcement learning allows content, product, or intervention offerings not to interrupt the user's cognitive flow, but to accompany them in a fluid way, maximizing the efficiency of contact and reducing the psychological costs associated with rejection (Khamaj & Ali, 2024; Maathuis et al., 2025).

A company made of these inferences in algorithmic governance structures like smart contracts entails not only actions based on explicit intent, but also interaction patterns that persist above immersion and engagement thresholds, enabling conditional execution at machine speed (Balcerzak et al., 2022; Smith et al., 2025). Just as if a user passes a specific combination of biometric or behavioral conditions, a microcontract that releases content or services may be applied under an automatic micropayment modality, expanding both monetization capacity and audit requirements (Mariana et al., 2025; Balcerzak et al., 2022). Symbolic reciprocity can strengthen under this architecture when interventions are perceived as useful rather than invasive, while feedback data retrains predictive models to refine sensitivity across personal, cultural, and temporal contexts (Smith et al., 2025; Maathuis et al., 2025).

Reconfiguration of Intangible Virtual Assets

Intangible assets must be virtualized, mobilized, and recombined without losing semantic or legal integrity. In this framework, the reconfiguration of intangible virtual assets emerges as a strategic pillar, where knowledge, brands, algorithms, narrative patents, and experience ontologies are encapsulated in interoperable structures that allow portability and multisectoral use (Kour et al., 2025; Ali et al., 2023).

Open formats such as Universal Scene Description and GL Transmission Format increasingly function as semantic containers that preserve not only interactive geometry and logic, but also provenance, usage rights, and modification context, which becomes critical when assets circulate across platforms and jurisdictions (Bibri & Allam, 2022; Smith et al., 2025).

Inserting these assets into blockchains as fractional NFTs adds a layer of distributed governance: usage rights can be divided, licensed, and monetized in real time, allowing firms to create business models based on modular capability orchestration rather than full asset replication (Ali et al., 2023; Brandes & Dölp, 2025). In other words, an XR narrative can license its adaptive interface, attention engine, or feedback system separately, generating diversified economic flows while increasing the need for enforceable rules on consent, disclosure, and dispute resolution (Smith et al., 2025; Balcerzak et al., 2022).

Organizational Learning in XR Cycles

Organizational learning in XR contexts redefines the classic phases of acquisition, interpretation, and coding of organizational knowledge. Instead of following long hierarchical work cycles, immersive organizations embrace accelerated learning cycles through synchronized digital representations that integrate sensors, artificial intelligence, and modeling of processes, environments, or human skills, so performance feedback can be captured within the task and written back into institutional repositories (Naranjo et al., 2020; Di Pasquale et al., 2024).

The application of XR to industrial contexts such as precision manufacturing can reduce the time needed to reach higher levels of operational performance because repeated multisensory rehearsal supports situated error correction and consolidates tacit patterns through practice, not only through documentation (Naranjo et al., 2020; Kour et al., 2025). These gains reflect faster skill acquisition and the stabilization of routines that can be mobilized across teams when immersive evidence is structured into reusable learning objects (Di Pasquale et al., 2024; Maathuis et al., 2025).

As organizations integrate XR feedback loops with knowledge management platforms, a synergy is created between formal and informal learning. Employees can review annotated XR sessions, compare efficiency metrics, and visualize decision paths that led to mistakes or successes, which favors a culture of continuous improvement, reflective autonomy, and controlled empirical experimentation (Di Pasquale et al., 2024; Maathuis et al., 2025). At the same time, sustaining legitimacy requires that measurement and guidance remain explainable and contestable, because opaque optimization can erode trust and engagement even when performance improves (Dunmoye et al., 2024; Smith et al., 2025).

Theories of Copresence and Embodiment

Theories of copresence and embodiment have become central axes for explaining the psychosocial effectiveness of immersive XR worlds. Copresence refers to the subjective experience of being with others, whether human or artificial agents, within a shared digital space, where reciprocity and coexistence shape coordination for common tasks, joint training, and augmented educational experiences (Kour et al., 2025; Bibri & Allam, 2022).

Embodiment describes how the avatar becomes an operative extension of the user through sensorimotor internalization, so multisensory input synchronizes with intended action, increasing agency and facilitating skill transfer to real environments (Wang et al., 2019; Maathuis et al., 2025). However, copresence does not always increase with technical realism because intrusive sensing and non transparent data practices can create an immersion paradox that undermines comfort and legitimacy from within the experience (Bibri & Allam, 2022; Smith et al., 2025).

Optical tactile agreement and narrative coherence remain crucial: consistent justification for changes in environment, avatar, or interface favors immersion, while dissonances and ruptures can distort role adoption, empathy, and collaborative problem solving, thereby weakening both learning outcomes and relational value (Kour et al., 2025; Dunmoye et al., 2024). Learning in XR environments is therefore strengthened when accelerated cycles led by synchronized digital representations are aligned with designs that protect agency, sustain social presence, and keep adaptation understandable rather than merely effective (Naranjo et al., 2020; Maathuis et al., 2025).

Psychology of Attention and Cognitive Load in XR

In extended reality (XR) environments, attention management becomes a critical axis for the effectiveness of immersive experiences, as users are exposed to simultaneous multisensory flows that demand limited cognitive resources. The theory of limited capacity, originated by Kahneman, points out that working memory is a system of scarce resources. This has led to restrictions on the ability to process multiple stimuli at the same time (Lavie, 2005; Juliano et al., 2022).

The sensory fatigue curve in XR describes the phenomenon by which the level of neurophysiological activation decreases significantly after prolonged periods of exposure to multimodal stimuli. Recent studies indicate that, after seven to ten minutes of constant stimulation, the ability to maintain attention decreases and symptoms of sensory overload manifest, affecting both information retention and performance in complex tasks (Weech et al., 2019; Stauffert et al., 2020).

In this context, the automatic detection of cognitive overload through multimodal classifiers is a significant innovation. These classifiers, although fed by physiological data (EEG, heart rate, pupillary dilation), can locate peaks of mental stress and trigger narrative anchors designed to transfer sensory charge to alternative channels, such as replacing charged visual information with tactile vibration responses. Even the use of real-time direct feedback allows for dynamic adjustment of information density, which periodically modulates the user's cognitive load (Mathôt, 2018; Hang et al., 2024).

Dominant-Service Logic and Co-Creation of Experiences

It reestablishes value in terms of the continuation of interaction between actors rather than as an inherent property of a good. Marked by the Value-in-Use theory, this perspective speculates that value is not made, but continuously created and reproduced in a continuous way through the operating resources between users, platforms and brands. In XR environments, this paradigm takes on a new dimension as immersive interfaces allow sensory, symbolic and emotional experiences to be co-produced in real time (Lusch et al., 2007; Ranjan & Read, 2021).

XR platforms serve as assembly points for co-creation, where processes are carried out using multi-sensory feedback loops (Balcerzak et al., 2022). In this ecosystem, vibrotactics not only fulfill a perceptual function, but also add a media function that adds a somatic layer to the symbolic change. The experience offered to participants thus becomes an embodied process of interaction. On many decentralized XR platforms, such as blockchain-based ones, smart contracts recognize users' authorship of the elements they develop and reward them through micropayments or symbolic tokens (Ali et al., 2023).

These relationships are enhanced by algorithmic mechanisms that recommend collaborations based on creative affinity and interaction patterns, creating what some theorists call algorithmic co-agency architectures (Fang et al., 2024).

Haptic Attention Economy and Tokenization

In next-generation XR ecosystems, attention is no longer conceived as a passive resource, but as an active currency that can be measured, traded and optimized. This evolution is part of what has been called the haptic attention economy, where the tactile response is transformed into a unit of value within the digital experience. Vibrotactile stimuli, when delivered with latencies of less than 20 milliseconds, not only elevate the user's sense of presence, but also significantly increase conversion indicators in XR retail environments, doubling purchase intent compared to conventional experiences(Colicev, 2023).

One of the most disruptive models in this regard is that of attentional liquidity tokens, digital assets that represent units of time of effective haptic interaction. These tokens can be issued by brands or platforms and used by users as a medium of exchange to access specific benefits, such as exclusive digital products, personalized services, or discounts on physical godos. The operational framework of those exchanges is regulated by smart contracts that execute micropayments and benefit assignments through oracles with sensory integrity (Flavián et al., 2024).

Cryptoeconomics and Decentralized Governance

Within the framework of new digital architectures, immersive virtual worlds have begun to migrate from hierarchical models to decentralized governance structures based on distributed autonomous organizations (DAOs). These entities, which operate through smart contracts on the blockchain, allow decision-making to be carried out collectively and transparently, integrating mechanisms such as reputation token staking and liquid delegation of votes (Gleim et al., 2025)

Empirically, the implementation of models with liquid delegation has been shown to reduce the average time needed to reach consensus without sacrificing the diversity of proposals, which resolves one of the main dilemmas of decentralized governance: the tension between efficiency and pluralism. Through these, each significant action taken by the participants is recorded and weighted using contextual veracity algorithms. These systems penalize behaviors such as opportunistic vote flipping by temporarily reducing the weight of the vote or losing reputational tokens (Guidotti et al., 2019)

Algorithmic Justice and XR Auditing

In XR environments, where interaction is mediated by biometric sensors and intent classifiers, new forms of algorithmic discrimination emerge that demand robust ethical governance frameworks. The FAIRness approach applied to the design and implementation of multivariate sensors and classifiers introduces a set of metrics that allow intersectional equity to be quantified. These metrics go beyond simple global accuracy and focus on the distribution of the area under the ROC (Receiver Operating Characteristic) curve among subgroups defined by intersections of gender, race, age, and functional ability. Discrepancies in these metrics may indicate the existence of structural biases that affect the interpretation of user intent or emotion (Juliano et al., 2022).

The incorporation of differential algorithmic audits is a preventive strategy that allows organizations to identify negative feedback dynamics in real time, especially those that reinforce unfair prediction patterns. To put it another way, these processes reduce the opportunities for self-fulfilling prophecies, in which the behavior projected by the system conditions the future behavior of the user, leading to historical or cultural prejudices (Khamaj & Ali, 2024).

A vital dimension to achieving equity in XR is perceptual clarity. This implies that explainability logos must have the ability to adjust as much as necessary as necessary as a way of cognitive extortion of the user. Not showing matrices or probabilistic models of drifting instead of XR systems should turn their algorithms' decisions into understandable narratives, using spatial imagery or representations visually incorporated into the immersive experience (Lavie, 2005).

Digital Sustainability and Thermal Circularity

This XRExponecialThe rapid development of renewable technology has renewed the debate on digital sustainability. The high energy demand of these technologies – and also that they produce waste heat in data centers – are issues to consider. A lifecycle report applied to the use of XR volumetry shows that real-time rendering can require up to 0.03 kWh per minute per user. This figure is multiplied if the environments are multiplayer or the scenarios are hyper-realistic (Lusch et al., 2007).

Faced with this problem, technical strategies have emerged that allow the energy footprint to be reduced without compromising the quality of the experience. Dynamic foveated rendering is one of the most relevant: by rendering with high resolution only the focal region of the user's eye, GPU usage is reduced by up to 42% on XR platforms. Likewise, edge offloading, which delegates heavy computing processes to local edge servers, reduces response time and minimizes power congestion in central data centers (Manshad & Brannon, 2021).

In several European and Asian cities, data centers are beginning to be integrated into district heating networks, transferring surplus heat to hot water or space heating systems in homes, offices, and hospitals. This regenerative model promotes dual efficiency: energy and ecological, aligning with frameworks such as the circular economy and the sustainable development goals (Mariana et al., 2024).

Interoperability and Open Standards

If interoperability is not achieved in XR, virtual ecosystems become fragmented. Have a lingua franca standard such as OpenUSD (Universal Scene Description) for 3D description of great meaning dimensions. Two, we would expect that this standard not only preserves the geometric attributes, but also the physical, semantic, and logical attributes of virtual objects through encapsulation mode, preserving their fidelity for reuse (Pahl et al., 2022).

For the construction of XR digital passes, the implementation of verifiable credentials as a mobile identification mechanism is one of the immovable factors. Each user can pass on their history of achievements, certificates, and participation levels between various digital platforms. Characteristically, this portability reinforces user trust, thus making it possible to exchange creative services more smoothly with a symbolic and functional value. coordination is not limited to a single interface or provider (Ranjan & Read, 2021).

Predictive Models Based on Cognitive Twins

Cognitive twins, as an advanced evolution of digital twins, are configured as dynamic computational representations that model not only physical aspects, but also mental, emotional and contextual processes of the user in immersive systems, such as XR (extended reality) environments. Unlike the traditional digital twin focused on observable and physical behavior, the cognitive twin integrates latent and subjective elements, such as intentions, emotional states, cognitive biases, and decision patterns, by merging Bayesian networks, causal inference models, and federated learning (Smith, 2025).

Bayesian network-based architecture can capture probabilistic dependencies between affective and contextual variables, continuously adapting to new data without having to have central storage, thus safeguarding privacy and making it easier to expand. This structure is even more powerful when applied to federated learning, where many devices collaborate to train models distributively without directly sharing sensitive data; thus complying with regulations such as the GDPR or the EU Data Governance Law (Stauffert et al., 2020).

In this sense, recommendations based on counterfactual simulations are helping to reduce the number of people who are not overloading in this cognitive processing. There have been reports of a reduction in the incidence of surgical complications and a significant increase in the surgeon's perception of control. In non-clinical settings, such as personalized education, cognitive twins allow for multimodal adaptation of learning content based on the student's level of attention, motivation, and emotion, increasing knowledge retention and perceived self-efficacy (Terhörst et al., 2020).

Ethics of Human-Centric Experiential Design

In the context of the Human-Centre Experiential Design in XR environments, ethics transcends the classical notion of usability because it incorporates principles of autonomy, identity, well-being and agency, particularly in environments where the representative digital image constitutes an extension of the user's identity. If an avatar's appearance and the real self don't match each other at all, then such identity disparity can lead to a negative self-image, low self-esteem, and feeling the subjective sense that one is not really present. Consequently, ethical design corresponds to flexible forms of co-authorship of the avatar by the user as well as for its modifiability according to the ongoing process of personal development (Tu et al., 2023).

The principle of privacy by design must be applied beyond technological limitations. It includes psycho-emotional aspects, anticipating the damage that can be caused by being supplied with highly manipulable scenarios. For this reason, it requires an anticipatory ethic in which the mentality of designers considers not only good use but also abuse and structural evil, due to certain persuasive dynamics that, even more so in the upbringing of defenseless creatures such as children and vulnerable communities. On the other hand, persuasive design is in critical circumstances when it involves stereotyped dopaminergic reactions that are not at the limits of a political-establishment purpose, generating a reward cycle. The theory of libertarian paternalism, proposed by Thaler and Sunstein, holds that certain nudges can be ethically acceptable if they expand the set of feasible options for the user without denying them freedom of choice. On the other hand, the ethics of experience must guarantee full sensory and cognitive accessibility (Wang et al., 2019).

Challenges Organizations Face

With the digital transformation of the global environment, bureaucratic organizations are becoming increasingly difficult to handle (Valette et al., 2023; Ghobakhloo et al., 2023). Organizations live in a new global environment, and rapid technological change has made these trends increasingly widespread and visible across contexts (Feroz et al., 2023). They face formidable challenges that transcend traditional logics of competition and efficiency, requiring organizational designs that integrate human centricity, resilience, and responsibility (Ghobakhloo et al., 2023; Teece, 2007). To survive and grow, organizational structures must be continuously reconstructed to accommodate innovation processes, organizational learning patterns, data governance, and strategic resilience (Teece, 2007; Feroz et al., 2023).

In such a field of doubt, where society changes so quickly, management becomes more dependent on adaptive thinking and the capacity to reconfigure routines under uncertainty (Teece, 2007; Feroz et al., 2023). This is especially relevant when decision cycles compress and organizational attention must be redistributed toward sensing, seizing, and transforming in near real time (Feroz et al., 2023; Valette et al., 2023).

Companies like Siemens, Ericsson, and Volkswagen have set up units of prospective intelligence to anticipate systemic risks, and decisions can be increasingly data driven thanks to advanced analytics and the availability of high granularity signals for study (Guidotti et al., 2019; Mathôt, 2018). In immersive and sensor rich environments, such data availability can expand from operational telemetry to oculometric and attentional indicators that support new forms of inference and monitoring (Mathôt, 2018; Maathuis et al., 2025).

Digital transformation has imposed a dizzying pace of technological updating that generates tensions between legacy operating models and new paradigms of automation, artificial intelligence, predictive analytics, and cloud platforms (Attaran & Celik, 2023; Lu et al., 2020). Companies such as General Electric, BBVA, Tata Consultancy Services, and IBM have had to redesign management systems and competency structures to integrate emerging technologies into their value chains (Feroz et al., 2023; Valette et al., 2023). The transition to hybrid, integrated, and cognitive architectures requires not only substantive financial investment, but also a profound redesign of leadership models and organizational cultures (Teece, 2007; Feroz et al., 2023).

Another crucial challenge is related to managing human talent in hybrid or fully remote contexts, where flexibility, inclusion, and distributed productivity become strategic variables (Dunmoye et al., 2024; Weech et al., 2019). New generations of workers demand more empathetic work environments, with horizontal leadership and purpose focused organizational cultures, while digital burnout and inclusion gaps remain latent risks (Lavie, 2005; Weech et al., 2019).

Environmental, social and governance sustainability has become a regulatory and reputational requirement, and the integration of sustainability into corporate strategy is increasingly a condition for long run legitimacy (Ghobakhloo et al., 2023; Valette et al., 2023). As compute intensive and immersive infrastructures scale, sustainability also depends on energy efficient rendering and infrastructure level efficiency strategies such as waste heat recovery and more efficient visualization pipelines (Oró et al., 2019; Hu et al., 2025).

Organizations are also increasingly exposed to cyber risk, as digital interdependence and platform ecosystems expand the attack surface (Rahartomo et al., 2025; Bolettieri et al., 2022). This has reinforced the emphasis on security engineering, privacy by design, and continuous assurance in environments that blend identity, data, and persistent interaction (Alkaeed et al., 2024; Rahartomo et al., 2025).

Organizations are challenged to realize continuous innovation in knowledge intensive sectors while capturing tacit knowledge and turning it into reproducible solutions at scale (Naranjo et al., 2020; Di Pasquale et al., 2024). The logic of open innovation and ecosystem coordination becomes central when capabilities and assets must be recombined across actors and platforms (Ranjan & Read, 2021; Ali et al., 2023).

Examples of Implementation in Organizations or Institutions

In the logistics space, UPS has consolidated an XR program for driver training that combines virtual reality simulations with face to face and augmented reality components, enabling rehearsal of high risk situations in simulated environments before entering public roads (Naranjo et al., 2020; Di Pasquale et al., 2024).

In the retail sector, Walmart is an emblematic case of mass adoption of XR to improve both technical and soft skills among employees, using immersive training for high pressure scenarios such as sales spikes, conflict management, and emergency preparedness (Naranjo et al., 2020; Di Pasquale et al., 2024).

In industrial training and occupational health contexts, evidence on VR based construction safety training highlights adoption factors and the value of rehearsing dangerous processes without real exposure, supported by structured evaluation designs (Naranjo et al., 2020; Di Pasquale et al., 2024). The effectiveness of such interventions depends on both instructional design quality and the calibration of immersion to avoid overload and cybersickness risks (Weech et al., 2019; Stauffert et al., 2020).

In surgical health, virtual reality simulators have been evaluated for their effectiveness in improving operating room performance, with longitudinal training designs showing performance gains after immersive module integration (Di Pasquale et al., 2024; Naranjo et al., 2020). These improvements are typically strengthened when feedback is consistent, skill progression is structured, and cognitive load is managed during repeated practice cycles (Lavie, 2005; Di Pasquale et al., 2024).

The case of Intel, Airbus, and Shell exemplifies the use of digital twins together with XR for technical training in assembly and maintenance, supporting visualization, guided procedures, and scenario rehearsal (Tu et al., 2023; Mourtzis, 2023). This integration aligns with the broader trajectory of digital twin driven manufacturing and industrial metaverse approaches, where synchronized representations can shorten learning cycles and improve operational readiness (Lu et al., 2020; Mourtzis, 2023).

Conceptual Framework and Use Cases in Digital Twins and Metaverse

The convergence between digital twins and metaversal environments makes it possible to shift consumer interaction from a merely transactional approach to an experiential approach where presence, participation and co-creation of value become central, and the user ceases to be a passive receiver to become an active agent within the system (Ranjan & Read, 2021; Richter & Richter, 2023). Within the framework of Industry 5.0, this transition is articulated with principles of human centricity, resilience and responsibility, so that technological performance must coexist with demands for ethical legitimacy, social acceptance and operational sustainability (Ghobakhloo et al., 2023; Valette et al., 2023). Consequently, consumer behavior observed in the real world and behavior expressed in immersive spaces can be translated into signals that feed simulations, and those simulations can return dynamic personalization of both the experience and the product or service (Lu et al., 2020; Flavián et al., 2024).

In smart retail, XR environments enable shopping scenarios where attention, copresence, and multisensory interaction directly influence product evaluation, brand memory, and repurchase intent, because the experience becomes part of the perceived value (Alexander et al., 2024; Richter & Richter, 2023). The incorporation of haptic signals and interaction patterns allows for more intense engagement to be designed, but at the same time increases the need for transparency and control on the part of the user to avoid opaque persuasion dynamics or exploitation of cognitive vulnerabilities (Tang et al., 2024; Pahl et al., 2022). Furthermore, when the ecosystem integrates digital asset exchange mechanisms and staking structures, co-creation can scale towards network models in which value is produced, distributed, and communally reinforced, with direct implications for incentive architecture and customer experience (Ranjan & Read, 2021; Gleim et al., 2025).

In the co-design of personalized products, the metaverse functions as an exploration space in which the user tests configurations and preferences, while the digital twin operates as the validation core that simulates performance, constraints, and trade-offs before materializing decisions in the physical world (Lu et al., 2020; Mourtzis, 2023). This coupling is especially powerful when linked to flexible manufacturing and technologies such as additive manufacturing, because it expands the design space without losing operational viability under high variability, reducing costly iterations and shortening cycles of incremental and disruptive innovation (Jyeniskhan et al., 2024; Valette et al., 2023). From an organizational perspective, the competitive differential tends to be explained less by the isolated tool and more by the dynamic capacity to orchestrate routines of detection, use and transformation, converting interaction signals into adaptive proposals that adjust quickly and with continuous learning (Teece, 2007; Feroz et al., 2023).

In virtual product testing, such as automotive or fashion, digital twin plus XR logic makes it possible to reduce uncertainty and perceived risk by offering synchronized simulations with immersive visualization, evaluating configurations, perceived ergonomics, and usage scenarios without relying on early physical prototypes (Attaran & Celik, 2023; Lu et al., 2020). In fashion, virtual try-on is intertwined with dynamics of identity and sociality, because the experience of exploration occurs in shared environments where evaluation and validation can also be communal, elevating the role of presence and interaction in the purchase decision (Alexander et al., 2024; Richter & Richter, 2023). However, the adoption and continuity of these experiences depend on specific technical and cognitive conditions, since sensory density, latency, and interaction design influence comfort, subjective presence, and cognitive load, with effects on performance and acceptance (Stauffert et al., 2020; Weech et al., 2019).

Challenges and Applications in Digital Twins and Metaverse

The integration between physical products, digital twins, and metaversal environments promises to close feedback loops where consumer interaction updates the twin and, in turn, twin predictions reconfigure the immersive experience. However, taking this architecture from the conceptual level to the actual deployment requires solving technical, economic, and governance challenges that, if underestimated, degrade perceptual continuity, erode trust, and slow adoption (Rahartomo et al., 2025; Richter & Richter, 2023). The first challenge is the synchronization of data between the physical product and its digital representation, because the promise of fidelity depends on the integrity of sensors, semantic consistency, and the ability to update almost immediately when the consumer explores scenarios or customizes configurations (Lu et al., 2020; Tu et al., 2023). In practical terms, the problem is not only to capture data, but to avoid temporal and conceptual misalignments that turn the twin into an attractive but operationally unreliable visual narrative, especially when the system triggers automated recommendations or decisions in distributed infrastructures (Rahartomo et al., 2025; Guidotti et al., 2019). Added to this is latency in virtual environments, because subjective presence and comfort depend on strict response thresholds; when interactive rendering and simulation are decoupled, the risk of experience breakdown and discomfort increases, reducing the effectiveness of any immersive interaction strategy (Attaran & Celik, 2023; Weech et al., 2019).

Another central challenge is consumer privacy and ecosystem security when behavioral and physiological signals are monetized or affective states are inferred, because the combination of immersive presence and high-granularity sensing increases risks of re-identification, covert surveillance, and manipulation (Rahartomo et al., 2025; Kim & Xiong, 2022). This risk is aggravated when personalization is supported by opaque models that do not offer readable explanations as to why a configuration, content, or path of interaction is suggested, so that explainability becomes a condition of trust and not an accessory attribute (Guidotti et al., 2019; Hemphill, 2023). In parallel, personalization can amplify biases if systems are not audited, especially when avatar identity, face, or biometric cues trigger differentiated decisions across demographics, justifying incorporating fairness audits and bias mitigation as part of the solution lifecycle (Terhörst et al., 2020; Pahl et al., 2022). Finally, high infrastructure costs appear as a structural limitation, because sustaining persistent experiences requires investment in low-latency connectivity, edge computing, comprehensive security, and simulation and rendering engines that operate in a coordinated manner, which increases both capital expenditure and operational complexity (Bolettieri et al., 2022; Attaran & Celik, 2023).

RESULTS

From a qualitative study approach, the results presented cover the wide spectrum of organizational transformations originated in the implementation of digital twins and metaversal environments with respect to Industry 5.0 (Richter & Richter, 2023; Ghobakhloo et al., 2023). Among the advantages is that we can now offer the customer a personalized experience through contextual inference systems (Hu et al., 2025; Valette et al., 2023). This creates interactions that are generally less distant, more empathetic and tremendously impregnated with adaptability, including the incorporation of biometric and affective signals in the design process (Bradley et al., 2008; Alkaeed et al., 2024).

This allows the user's previous emotional situations to be modeled, and immersive environments to be adjusted to achieve greater performance (Mathôt, 2018; Kim & Xiong, 2022). Another important result is the potential of cognitive twins to shorten an organization's learning cycles (Naranjo et al., 2020; Di Pasquale et al., 2024). By combining procedural and emotional data in simulated environments, organizations are able to streamline their training processes, improve the transfer of tacit know-how, and strengthen localized intellectual capital, thus fostering a culture of continuous learning (Naranjo et al., 2020; Mourtzis, 2023). This ability to model interaction and iteration processes with unprecedented precision redefines teaching structures and shortens cycles of incremental and disruptive innovation (Teece, 2007; Jyeniskhan et al., 2024). By being able to test solutions before their actual implementation, the risk of financial loss and image damage is being reduced (Lu et al., 2020; Hemphill, 2023).

With such a large number of tools filtering through the narrow comfortable sediments, no one could feel free (Lavie, 2005). This scale, decentralization, and interactive tools available in open source economies (ICTs) have been a critical advantage for innovation (Bibri & Allam, 2022; Ali et al., 2023). The possibility of accessing such open immersive ecosystems implies seeking a more flexible form of business people, where intangibles can be encapsulated in interoperable forms in the hope of enabling their real-time recombination in hetarchic markets (Bibri & Allam, 2022; van Vulpen et al., 2024). In addition to the most scrupulously documented cases, telecommunications organizations have come to see these bits of knowledge as a profitable investment (Ghobakhloo et al., 2023). Thus, being so modular not only promotes innovation but also reconfigures knowledge structures, while new intellectual property regimes based on fractionable NFTs are emerging (Colicev, 2023; Ali et al., 2023).

On the other hand, the implementation of smart contracts and interoperable environments creates problems as it empowers interlocked assets between platforms and communities (Balcerzak et al., 2022; Ling & Butakov, 2024). Simultaneously, this approach allows minor users to have direct access to the value created by their network of friends or community cells of activity to co-create value in the primordial extractive scheme (Ranjan & Read, 2021; Alexander et al., 2024). By enabling this symbiotic exchange of assets between platforms and communities, intelligent environments expand so that co-created value expands and resets new innovation networks (Gleim et al., 2025; Hemphill, 2023). Wherever users prefer to follow the content, they can choose their own path for travel strategy purposes (Richter & Richter, 2023). One advantage of these platforms is their ability to create new forms of multisensorial engagement, in which vibrotactile attention, bodily positioning and haptic synchronisation configure scenarios of heightened mutual presence (Tang et al., 2024; Manshad & Brannon, 2021).

Well designed, these immersive experiences increase the degree of self-efficacy, sense of belonging and retention, putting the consumer as a co-author of interactive dynamics (Ranjan & Read, 2021; Alexander et al., 2024). The effect of embodiment and subjective presence not only increases the memory of the brand and the intention to repurchase it, but also introduces new metrics in order to evaluate the quality of the episode from a phenomenal perspective, not merely transactional (Richter & Richter, 2023; Colicev, 2023).

In any case, the drawbacks and challenges involved are also identified. In the ethical and regulatory sphere, there are still unresolved challenges regarding algorithmic transparency, data portability and the management of avataral identities (Hemphill, 2023; van Vulpen et al., 2024). The lack of clear regulatory frameworks can contribute to information asymmetry and user mistrust, especially in the case of affective prediction models that operate without functional verification or consent (Rahartomo et al., 2025; Alkaeed et al., 2024). The tension between hyperpersonalization and autonomy raises critical dilemmas about the limits of persuasive design, the exploitation of cognitive vulnerabilities, and the need for a framework of responsible governance (Pahl et al., 2022; Ling & Butakov, 2024).

In operational terms, the demands of network infrastructure for real-time volumetric rendering, coupled with the power consumption of such applications, pose an obstacle to the expanded approach that these experiences require (Attaran & Celik, 2023; Hu et al., 2025). Although strategies such as shifting the load to the edge provide partial solutions, in reality the sustainable XR model is still far from achieving a net balance between efficiency and carbon footprint (Oró et al., 2019; Gralka et al., 2025).

CONCLUSIONS

The study demonstrates that XR environments articulated with digital twins indicate a transformative path to improve customer interaction in Industry 5.0 (Richter & Richter, 2023; Ghobakhloo et al., 2023). Organizations that incorporate affective sensing capabilities, contextual seizing, and transformation algorithms become competitive by providing personal, responsive, and emotionally charged experiences (Mathôt, 2018; Hu et al., 2025). As such technologies move towards greater degrees of autonomy and plasticity, the need for a solid ethical framework based on justice, inclusive governance and accessible design arises (Hemphill, 2023; Adel & HS Alani, 2024). Consumer centric digitalization cannot simply depend on technological performance, but must also be rooted in social, cultural and environmental values (Mourtzis, 2023; Ghobakhloo et al., 2023).

It is possible to add perceptual, cognitive, and affective metrics to digital twins without violating user privacy if algorithmic explanation architectures, detailed consent of the requested data, and data sovereignty mechanisms are imposed (Alkaeed et al., 2024; Rahartomo et al., 2025). The design of readable systems, capable of converting the decisions made by a model into terms understandable to the user, reinforces trust and minimizes risks (Guidotti et al., 2019; Hemphill, 2023). Organizations must commit to conducting differentiated equity audits, design openly, and hold themselves accountable to society for their algorithmic decisions (Pahl et al., 2022; Terhörst et al., 2020).

Regarding the second question, the dynamic capabilities needed to convert affective data into hyper-personalized propositions are pointed out: they do not simply include real-time prediction algorithms, but also organizational structures formulated for continuous learning, interdisciplinary work, and modular asset orchestration (Teece, 2007; Di Pasquale et al., 2024). Making this a reality requires an organizational culture focused on controlled experimentation, real-time sensor embedding, and the design of cognitive dashboards that combine, visualize, and interpret multisensory signals in adaptive decision-making loops (Naranjo et al., 2020; Hu et al., 2025). Competitive advantage does not stem from technology alone, but from organizations' ability to transform complex data into emotionally understandable value propositions (Flavián et al., 2024; Ranjan & Read, 2021).

Likewise, it was possible to corroborate that algorithmic governance and human-centric design systems can alleviate risks such as sensory overload and dissonant identity, if the principles of universal accessibility, ethical anticipation and cross-sectoral audits are met (Lavie, 2005; Juliano et al., 2022). The convergence between extended reality, affective neuroscience and experience architecture requires new design paradigms in which the user's quality of life is not just a secondary aspect (Weech et al., 2019; Stauffert et al., 2020). In this sense, the establishment of policies that govern the use of emotional biometrics and the creation of ethical certifications for XR platforms are of particular importance (Hemphill, 2023; Rahartomo et al., 2025).

Recommendations for Future Research

Energy Sustainability and Thermal Circularity in XR Environments

Future research must delve into models that allow the energy footprint of immersive experiences to be rigorously measured, but above all experiment with adaptive architectures that autonomously redirect computing flows to nodes with renewable surpluses. It is essential to investigate orchestration algorithms that combine foveated rendering and edge offloading with waste heat recovery strategies for district heating networks. It is also advisable to explore impact metrics that transcend the classic kilowatt-hour per session and quantify benefits by replacing physical trips and by integrating biodegradable materials into devices.

Algorithmic Justice and Differential Audits in Immersive Interaction

To reduce the opacity of biometric classifiers, it will be critical to design audit frameworks that operate in real-time and measure intersectional equity based on disaggregated ROC metrics. Research agendas should validate automatic remediation protocols and develop explainability languages that represent algorithmic decisions within the XR environment itself without saturating the user's cognitive load.

Dynamic Capabilities and Organizational Learning With Cognitive Twins

The research challenge lies in modeling how sensing, seizing, and transforming routines evolve when information cycles are compressed at sub-second rates. It is proposed to design living laboratory experiments where leaders interact with cognitive twins that project market indicators as volumetric phenomena and, at the same time, record micro-decisions for metaroutine analysis.

REFERENCES

Adel, A., & Alani, HS, N. (2024). Human Centric Collaboration and Industry 5.0 Framework in Smart Cities and Communities: Fostering Sustainable Development Goals 3, 4, 9, and 11 in Society 5.0. *Smart Cities*, *7*(4), 1723–1775. DOI: 10.3390/smartcities7040068

Alexander, B., Blazquez, M., Chrimes, C., & Boardman, R. (2024). The role of immersive spaces on the customer experience: An exploration of fashion metaverses. *Psychology and Marketing*. Advance online publication. DOI: 10.1002/mar.22140

Ali, O., Ally, M., Dwivedi, Y. K., & Rana, N. P. (2023). A review of the key challenges of non fungible tokens. *Technological Forecasting and Social Change*, *190*, 122248. DOI: 10.1016/j.techfore.2022.122248

Alkaeed, M., Qayyum, A., & Qadir, J. (2024). Privacy preservation in artificial intelligence and extended reality (AI XR) metaverses: A survey. *Journal of Network and Computer Applications*, *231*, 103989. DOI: 10.1016/j.jnca.2024.103989

Attaran, M., & Celik, B. G. (2023). Digital Twin: Benefits, use cases, challenges, and opportunities. *Decision Analytics Journal*, *6*, 100165. DOI: 10.1016/j.dajour.2023.100165

Balcerzak, A. P., Nica, E., Rogalska, E., Poliak, M., Klieštik, T., & Sabie, O. M. (2022). Blockchain technology and smart contracts in decentralized governance systems. *Administrative Sciences*, *12*(3), 96. DOI: 10.3390/admsci12030096

Bibri, S. E., & Allam, Z. (2022). The metaverse as a virtual form of data driven smart urbanism: On post pandemic governance through the prism of the logic of surveillance capitalism. *Smart Cities*, *5*(2), 715–727. DOI: 10.3390/smartcities5020037

Bradley, M. M., Miccoli, L., Escrig, M. A., & Lang, P. J. (2008). The pupil as a measure of emotional arousal and autonomic activation. *Psychophysiology*, *45*(4), 602–607. DOI: 10.1111/j.1469-8986.2008.00654.x

Colicev, A. (2023). How can non-fungible tokens bring value to brands. *International Journal of Research in Marketing*, *40*(1), 30–37. DOI: 10.1016/j.ijresmar.2022.07.003

Di Pasquale, V., Fantini, P., Peruzzini, M., & Pellicciari, M. (2024). Immersive virtual reality training for assembly and disassembly operations: A systematic review. *Machines (Basel)*, *12*(8), 528. DOI: 10.3390/machines12080528

Domínguez Jiménez, J. A., Campo Landines, K. C., Martínez Santos, J. C., Delahoz, E. J., & Contreras Ortiz, S. H. (2020). A machine learning model for emotion recognition from physiological signals. *Biomedical Signal Processing and Control, 55*, 101646. DOI: 10.1016/j.bspc.2019.101646

Dunmoye, I. K., Rukangu, S., May, A., & Das, D. (2024). Social presence and cognitive engagement in collaborative virtual reality learning environment: A mixed methods approach. *Computers and Education: X Reality, 5*, 100054. DOI: 10.1016/j.cexr.2024.100054

Fang, M., Yang, W., Kuijper, A., Štruc, V., & Damer, N. (2024). Fairness in face presentation attack detection. *Pattern Recognition, 147*, 110002. DOI: 10.1016/j.patcog.2023.110002

Feroz, A. K., Zo, H., Eom, J., & Chiravuri, A. (2023). Identifying organizations' dynamic capabilities for sustainable digital transformation: A mixed methods study. *Technology in Society, 73*, 102257. DOI: 10.1016/j.techsoc.2023.102257

Flavián, C., Ibáñez Sánchez, S., Orús, C., & Barta, S. (2024). The dark side of the metaverse: The role of gamification in event virtualization. *International Journal of Information Management, 75*, 102726. DOI: 10.1016/j.ijinfomgt.2023.102726

Ghobakhloo, M., Iranmanesh, M., Tseng, M. L., Grybauskas, A., Stefanini, A., & Amran, A. (2023). Behind the definition of Industry 5.0: A systematic review of technologies, principles, components, and values. *Journal of Industrial and Production Engineering, 40*(6), 432–447. DOI: 10.1080/21681015.2023.2216701

Gleim, M. R., McCullough, H., Gabler, C., Ferrell, L., & Ferrell, O. C. (2025). Examining the customer experience in the metaverse retail revolution. *Journal of Business Research, 186*, 115045. DOI: 10.1016/j.jbusres.2024.115045

Gralka, P., Müller, C., Geringer, S., Reina, G., & Weiskopf, D. (2025). Quantifying energy reduction of foveated volume visualization. In *Proceedings of the 2025 Symposium on Eye Tracking Research and Applications (ETRA '25)*. ACM. DOI: 10.1145/3715669.3725881

Guidotti, R., Monreale, A., Ruggieri, S., Turini, F., Pedreschi, D., & Giannotti, F. (2019). A survey of methods for explaining black box models. *ACM Computing Surveys, 51*(5), 93. Advance online publication. DOI: 10.1145/3236009

Hang, F., Duan, S., Li, Y., Zou, Y., & Gao, L. (2024). End-to-end deep-learning-based classification of three-dimensional flow state in virtual reality using electroencephalography signals. *Sensors (Basel), 24*(6), 1894. DOI: 10.3390/s24061894

Hemphill, T. A. (2023). The metaverse and the challenge of responsible standards development. *Journal of Responsible Innovation, 10*(1), 2243121. DOI: 10.1080/23299460.2023.2243121

Hu, X., Wu, X., Ma, M., Xu, X., Gu, Y., Wang, G., Xu, Y., Meng, X., & Wang, L. (2025). Efficient VR rendering: Survey on foveated, stereo, cloud, and low-power rendering techniques. *Virtual Reality & Intelligent Hardware, 7*(5), 421–452. DOI: 10.1016/j.vrih.2025.08.003

Jyeniskhan, N., Shomenov, K., Ali, M. H., & Shehab, E. (2024). Exploring the integration of digital twin and additive manufacturing technologies. *International Journal of Lightweight Materials and Manufacture, 7*(6), 860–881. DOI: 10.1016/j.ijlmm.2024.06.004

Khamaj, M., & Ali, S. (2024). Adapting user experience with reinforcement learning. *Alexandria Engineering Journal, 90*, 925–934. DOI: 10.1016/j.aej.2024.03.045

Kim, Y., & Xiong, S. (2022). The pseudo haptic button for mid air interaction with virtual content in mixed reality. *International Journal of Human-Computer Studies, 164*, 102907. DOI: 10.1016/j.ijhcs.2022.102907

Kour, R., Karim, R., Venkatesh, S. N., & Kumar, U. (2025). Metaverse in industrial contexts: A comprehensive review. *Frontiers in Virtual Reality, 6*, 1488926. DOI: 10.3389/frvir.2025.1488926

Lavie, N. (2005). Distracted and confused? Selective attention under load. *Trends in Cognitive Sciences, 9*(2), 75–82. DOI: 10.1016/j.tics.2004.12.004

Libby, W. L., Lacey, B. C., & Lacey, J. I. (1973). Pupillary and cardiac activity during visual attention. *Psychophysiology, 10*(3), 270–294. DOI: 10.1111/j.1469-8986.1973.tb00526.x

Lim, J. Z., Mountstephens, J., & Teo, J. (2020). Emotion recognition using eye tracking: Taxonomy, review and current challenges. *Sensors (Basel), 20*(8), 2384. DOI: 10.3390/s20082384

Ling, A., & Butakov, S. (2024). Trust framework for self-sovereign identity in metaverse healthcare applications. *Data Science and Management, 7*(4), 304–313. DOI: 10.1016/j.dsm.2024.04.003

Lu, Y., Liu, C., Wang, K. I. K., Huang, H., & Xu, X. (2020). Digital Twin driven smart manufacturing: Connotation, reference model, applications and research issues. *Robotics and Computer-integrated Manufacturing, 61*, 101837. DOI: 10.1016/j.rcim.2019.101837

Lusch, R. F., Vargo, S. L., & O'Brien, M. (2007). Competing through service: Insights from service-dominant logic. *Journal of Retailing*, *83*(1), 5–18. DOI: 10.1016/j.jretai.2006.10.002

Maathuis, C., Cidota, M. A., Datcu, D., & Marin, L. (2025). Integrating explainable artificial intelligence in extended reality environments: A systematic survey. *Mathematics*, *13*(2), 290. DOI: 10.3390/math13020290

Manshad, M. S., & Brannon, D. (2021). Haptic-payment: Exploring vibration feedback as a means of reducing overspending in mobile payment. *Journal of Business Research*, *122*, 88–96. DOI: 10.1016/j.jbusres.2020.08.049

Mariana, C. D., Husodo, Z. A., Ekaputra, I. A., & Fahlevi, M. (2025). The advancement of digital payment ecosystem in metaverse: A literature review. *Computers in Human Behavior Reports*, *17*, 100570. DOI: 10.1016/j.chbr.2024.100570

Mathôt, S. (2018). Pupillometry: Psychology, physiology, and function. *Journal of Cognition*, *1*(1), 16. Advance online publication. DOI: 10.5334/joc.18

Mourtzis, D. (2023). Digital twin inception in the Era of industrial metaverse. *Frontiers in Manufacturing Technology*, *3*, 1155735. DOI: 10.3389/fmtec.2023.1155735

Naranjo, J. E., Sanchez, D. G., Robalino Lopez, A., Robalino Lopez, P., Alarcon Ortiz, A., & Garcia, M. V. (2020). A scoping review on virtual reality based industrial training. *Applied Sciences (Basel, Switzerland)*, *10*(22), 8224. DOI: 10.3390/app10228224

Oró, E., Taddeo, P., & Salom, J. E. (2019). Waste heat recovery from urban air cooled data centres to increase energy efficiency of district heating networks. *Sustainable Cities and Society*, *45*, 522–542. DOI: 10.1016/j.scs.2018.12.012

Pahl, J., Rieger, I., Möller, A., Wittenberg, T., & Schmid, U. (2022). Female, white, 27? Bias evaluation on data and algorithms for affect recognition in faces. In *Proceedings of the 2022 ACM Conference on Fairness, Accountability, and Transparency (FAccT '22)* (15 pages). Association for Computing Machinery. DOI: 10.1145/3531146.3533159

Rahartomo, A., Merino, L., & Ghafari, M. (2025). Metaverse security and privacy research: A systematic review. *Computers & Security*, *157*, 104602. DOI: 10.1016/j.cose.2025.104602

Ranjan, K. R., & Read, S. (2021). An ecosystem perspective synthesis of co creation research. *Industrial Marketing Management*, *99*, 79–96. DOI: 10.1016/j.indmarman.2021.10.002

Richter, S. M., & Richter, A. (2023). What is novel about the Metaverse? *International Journal of Information Management*, *74*, 102684. DOI: 10.1016/j.ijinfomgt.2023.102684

Smith, C. H.. (2025). The challenges of consent in a decentralised metaverse: A study of autonomy, disclosure, and design. *Frontiers in Virtual Reality*, *1401073*. Advance online publication. DOI: 10.3389/frvir.2025.1401073

Sprevak, M., & Smith, R. (2023). An Introduction to Predictive Processing Models of Perception and Decision-Making. *Topics in Cognitive Science*. Advance online publication. DOI: 10.1111/tops.12704

Stauffert, J. P., Niebling, F., Latoschik, M. E., & Steinicke, F. (2020). Latency and cybersickness: Impact, causes, and measures. A review. *Frontiers in Virtual Reality*, *1*, 582204. DOI: 10.3389/frvir.2020.582204

Tang, Y., Xu, J., Liu, Q., Hu, X., Xue, W., Liu, Z., Lin, Z., Lin, H., Zhang, Y., Zhang, Z., Ma, X., Wang, J., Zhong, J., Wang, D., Jiang, H., & Ma, Y. (2024). Advancing haptic interfaces for immersive experiences in the metaverse. *Device*, *2*(6), 100365. DOI: 10.1016/j.device.2024.100365

Tarnowski, P., Kołodziej, M., Majkowski, A., & Rak, R. J. (2020). Eye-tracking analysis for emotion recognition. *Computational Intelligence and Neuroscience*, *2020*, 2909267. Advance online publication. DOI: 10.1155/2020/2909267

Teece, D. J. (2007). Explicating dynamic capabilities: The nature and microfoundations of sustainable enterprise performance. *Strategic Management Journal*, *28*(13), 1319–1350. DOI: 10.1002/smj.640

Terhörst, P., Kolf, J. N., Damer, N., Kirchbuchner, F., & Kuijper, A. (2020). Post comparison mitigation of demographic bias in face recognition using fair score normalization. *Pattern Recognition Letters*, *140*, 332–338. DOI: 10.1016/j.patrec.2020.11.007

Tu, J., Malakuti, S., Telg, J., Xiong, J., & El Saddik, A. (2023). Digital twins in extended reality: The TwinXR system for scalable production of XR-enabled digital twins. *Frontiers in Virtual Reality*, *4*, 1019080. DOI: 10.3389/frvir.2023.1019080

Valette, E., Bril El-Haouzi, H., & Demesure, G. (2023). Industry 5.0 and its technologies: A systematic literature review upon the human place into IoT- and CPS-based industrial systems. *Computers & Industrial Engineering*, *184*, 109426. DOI: 10.1016/j.cie.2023.109426 van Vulpen, P., Siu, J., & Jansen, S. (2024). Governance of decentralized autonomous organizations that produce open source software. *Blockchain: Research and Applications*, *5*(1), 100166. DOI: 10.1016/j.bcra.2023.100166

Wang, D., Guo, Y., Liu, S., & Zhang, Y., & collaborators. (2019). Haptic display for virtual reality: Progress and challenges. *Science China. Information Sciences*, *62*, 060101. DOI: 10.3724/SP.J.2096-5796.2019.0008

Weech, S., Kenny, S., & Barnett-Cowan, M. (2019). Presence and cybersickness in virtual reality are negatively related: A review. *Frontiers in Psychology*, *10*, 158. DOI: 10.3389/fpsyg.2019.00158

Yuan, X., Liu, J., Sun, S., Lin, X., Fan, X., Zhao, W., & Kosonen, R. (2025). Data center waste heat for district heating networks: A review. *Renewable & Sustainable Energy Reviews*, *219*, 115863. DOI: 10.1016/j.rser.2025.115863

Zhang, Y., Li, T., Li, Z., Pondo, J.-M., Wang, X., & An, P. (2025). Affective response dataset for virtual workspaces: Based on color stimuli and multimodal physiological signals. *Sensors (Basel)*, *25*(24), 7461. DOI: 10.3390/s25247461

Zhou, L., Shao, X., & Mao, Q. (2021). A survey of micro-expression recognition. *Image and Vision Computing*, *105*, 104043. DOI: 10.1016/j.imavis.2020.104043

Chapter 2
Beyond Reality:
Crafting Consumer Journeys in the Metaverse

Nidhi Jhawar
http://orcid.org/0000-0002-4444-4573
IPS Academy, Institute of Business Management and Research, Indore, India

Dhanashree Nagar
http://orcid.org/0000-0003-0715-374X
IPS Academy, Institute of Business Management and Research, Indore, India

Vivek Singh Kushwaha
http://orcid.org/0009-0006-3681-2328
IPS Academy, Institute of Business Management and Research, Indore, India

ABSTRACT

The emergence of the metaverse as a multidimensional digital environment has redefined how brands interact with consumers, offering immersive, interactive, and hyper-personalized experiences. This chapter explores the evolving landscape of customer experience (CX) design in the metaverse, focusing on the integration of immersive technologies such as virtual reality (VR), augmented reality (AR), and extended reality (XR). It investigates how strategic brand storytelling, gamified engagement, and real-time behavioral insights contribute to creating meaningful virtual brand experiences. The chapter also emphasizes the importance of digital inclusivity and ethical considerations in ensuring equitable access and representation in virtual spaces. Through case studies from sectors including retail, education, and entertainment, the study illustrates best practices and challenges in designing future-ready, human-centered CX strategies within the metaverse.

DOI: 10.4018/979-8-3373-4541-3.ch002

1. INTRODUCTION

Metaverse evolution is a digital interactivity that brings both physical and virtual realities on one platform in an immersive environment. Market players such as Meta, Apple, and Microsoft in the field of technology are aggressively investing in a tech-based ecosystem. It is creating new forms of engaging individuals to learn, work, shop, and socialize through digital avatars, surpassing the traditional online experiences (Ball, 2022; Mystakidis, 2022). These changes are signalling a significant transformation in the human and digital interaction world

Instead of looking at this evolving space as just another trend, we should look at the transformation it is bringing in the way consumers connect and experience brands, products, and services. Unlike websites or mobile apps, the Metaverse permits users to enter into digital environments, create personalised avatars, interact with others, and participate in real-time activities. This environment encourages customers' active participation by offering multiple features like customised surroundings as per choice, shaping experiences, and emotional engagement with brands (Verhoef et al., 2021). For such a digital shift complete rethinking of consumer experience (CX) design is required. Conventional customer engagement strategies, which emphasise usability, ease, and effectiveness, are way apart from experiencing a virtual world where the consumer expects multisensory involvement and continuous interaction.

While designing the metaverse, companies are required to understand that this ecosystem shall involve customers' psychological engagement, social interaction, and emotional resonance. Businesses need to understand how they are delivering value, building trust, and developing loyalty in these digital spaces (Jin & Song, 2021). Real-time cases and examples are making this transformation easier to understand. Faishan brands such as Gucci launched their digital-only collections on platforms such as Roblox. Nike has entered the space with Nikeland, an interactive virtual world that blends sports, games, and branded storytelling. In the education and entertainment sectors, VR-based classrooms and virtual concerts are evolving the way people learn and connect (Piskorski et al., 2023).

What makes Metaverse presence powerful is due to the sensation of truly "being there" in a virtual space. Users feel more connected, emotionally involved, and expressive while connecting through avatars (Cummings & Bailenson, 2016). These interactions are often memorable because of various kinds of brand experience, deeply personal in contrast to conventional platforms. Simultaneously, the metaverse helps brands to provide highly personalised experiences (Praveena & Thomas, 2022). Real-time data is used to adjust settings, suggest products, or even change the virtual environment to match a user's choices or emotional mindset.

However, brands are facing a lot of challenges, such as accessibility, identity, and ethics, which occur due to the expansion of the metaverse. Avatar-based interaction and immersive experiences are based on personal data and individual emotional expressions (Zuboff, 2019; Nowak & Fox, 2018). So, the ecosystem of the metaverse needs to be designed in such a manner that confirms inclusivity and trust; organizations must develop an environment that safeguards the privacy of users, encourages authentic engagements, and respects emotional and cultural aspects at the same time.

The objective of this chapter is to find out how businesses and brands craft and optimize consumer experiences in the Metaverse. The chapter studies how immersive environments influence behaviour, what measures bands are taking for adjusting to these changes, and which frameworks can lead to ethical, effective, and inclusive CX design. Businesses entering the metaverse should be provided with a clear, practical road map in which a holistic combination of framework, real-time cases, and literature insight is explained.

The three key objectives of this chapter are:

- To understand the evolving metaverse ecosystem and the relationship between consumer experience and immersive technology in the Metaverse.
- To comprehend the implications of Metaverse in the Global context by analyzing the real-time cases that demonstrate applications, challenges, and outcomes of Metaverse implementations.
- To propose a conceptual framework for Metaverse CX design, integrating technology with ethics and emotions.

The discussion begins by understanding the change in consumer behaviour in a virtual setting, how they are expressing themselves, the motivating factors, and how they are connecting socially. Another section of the chapter draws on real examples from retail, education, and entertainment to highlight best practices and innovative strategies. Further, a framework is proposed for Metaverse CX Design, focusing on integrating technology, user behavior, and strategic storytelling. The conclusion section considers the ethical implications of immersive engagement and outlines areas for future research.

The Metaverse transition is not only a technological upgrade, but a cultural and behavioural change. In today's virtual world, more and more time is spent online, and the line between online and offline environments continues to blur. The shift reshapes how brands think about marketing strategies, customer relationships, and value creation. Mindful adoption of the Metaverse, combining innovation with empathy, will better position brands and organizations to lead in this next era of digital interaction. In a nutshell, designing the consumer experience in the Metaverse is about more than innovation or novel technology.

The next section of this chapter reviews the previous academic and industry research conducted in the field of Metaverse and its strategic implementation to enhance customer experience. It synthesizes theoretical outlook, highlights the gap, and helps in establishing the foundations to propose a conceptual framework of the Metaverse CX framework, discussed later in the chapter.

2. LITERATURE REVIEW

With the Metaverse unfolding as a revolutionary virtual interaction platform, it challenges traditional consumer engagement models and paradigms of experience design. To attain an understanding of how consumer journeys need to be best designed in this new ecosystem, it is essential to examine the conceptual foundations, behavioural aspects, strategic implementations, and ethical considerations that impact Metaverse-driven consumer experiences. The current section of the chapter provides a thematic and conceptual understanding of evolution and technological foundations of the Metaverse, consumer behavior, and experience designing virtual spaces, strategic business applications, ethical, psychological, and social considerations, addressing the risks and responsibilities associated with immersive CX design. Overall, the review of literature helps to understand how consumer journeys are reshaped in the Metaverse.

2.1 About Metaverse and Its Evolution

The basic concept of Metaverse originated from the fiction of digital reality that explains the interconnected system of coexistence of physical and virtual dimensions. Stephenson (1992, 2003), in his study, has explained Metaverse as an immersive and persistent environment that supports interaction at the social, economic, and cultural levels involving avatars. The advanced version of this technology, as implied today, is found to be Artificial Intelligence, viz. AI, Extended Reality (XR), Cloud computing, and blockchain technology. Thus, Metaverse is contemplated as the next level of internet revolution, which is also termed as Web 3.0 or the "Spatial Web" (Dwivedi, et. al., 2022). Multinational Tech giants like Meta, Microsoft, Apple, NVIDIA, to name a few, are investing heavily in immersive interaction and user participation, supporting the infrastructure of Metaverse technology.

This development has led to a significant transformation into a dimensional world to enable consumers to learn, shop, and socialize. Mystakidis (2022) and Ball (2022), in their study, have explained this phenomenon as a "post-reality universe" that blends gaming, e-commerce, and cultural environment, ensuring digital engagement.

Kye et. al. (2021) argue that Metaverse should not be perceived as an extraordinary kind of environment, but rather a collection of interoperable and context-specific emerging technologies. New strategic challenges have arisen due to the presence of multi-platform nature of the Metaverse technology. Marketers need to align their brand stories by maintaining authenticity and consistency across all digital platforms. Metaverse, therefore, is not just an innovative technology, but it is a new paradigm shift towards organizations' conceptualization of customer experience (CX).

From the perspective of top management, this evolution requires understanding the restructuring of value creation, trust building, and brand identity. Non-Fungible Tokens (NFTs), which are one of the components of digital ownership models, empower consumers to become co-creators of brand value and contributors to brand storytelling. (Dwivedi et.al., 2022; Purkayastha & Sharma, 2023). Subsequently, Metaverse-driven marketing demands multi-functional collaboration, flexible organizational structures, and a tested measure to evaluate customer engagement and emotional connection. In short, the Metaverse is redefining the relationship between brands and consumers by combining participatory culture and immersive technology.

2.2 Consumer Experience (CX) in Immersive Environments

In the Metaverse, consumer experience (CX) towards the products and services includes emotional engagement and psychological involvement of the consumers. Traditionally, digital technology focused on its usability, competency, and applicability. On the other hand, Mctaverse encourages multi-sensory interaction through prime senses like sight, sound, and touch (Slater & Wilbur, 2006). Technology users experience a strong state of existence, nurturing authenticity and enhancing interaction towards quality Some empirical research has evidenced that emerging technology and tools not only generate intense and remarkable encounters with customers, but also raise questions about the mental efforts applied and information overload. Pine and Gilmore (2011) in their study emphasized that emotional connection is a foundation of customer experience; however, such connections are required to be sustained inclusively and on ethical grounds.

AI and analytics enable marketers to deliver an enhanced customer experience based on personalized recommendations, a responsive environment, and gamified experiences that are aligned and connected with user emotions. Some of the gamification elements, such as accomplishing tasks or expeditions and collecting NFTs, encourage user participation and the formation of like-interest virtual communities. (Hamari et al., 2014). According to Nowak and Fox (2018), avatars are nothing but the extension of customers' self-identity, strengthening their emotional resonance with brands. Immersive customer experience viz. CX facilitates greater engagement and user satisfaction. Yet, the gaps continue to exist in how their experiences stimulate behavioural outcomes such as brand loyalty, retention, and brand advocacy. Various descriptive studies have emphasized on uniqueness of technology rather than analysing its long-term impact. Thus, a need has arisen to conduct further research that analyzes and links emotional engagement with technological design and also helps to measure its marketing outcomes.

2.3 Strategic Design and Business Applications of Metaverse Customer Experience (CX)

Organizations applying the Metaverse to create and enhance customer experience need to modify their approach towards customer engagement and brand building in place of short-term outcomes of applied marketing strategy. Metaverse enables value co-creation for active participants/customers in brand storytelling. This active participation brings into line the value delivery through interaction and shared meaning. (Lemon & Verhoef, 2016).

Leading brands like Adidas, Gucci, and Nike, which have been analysed in this chapter, have leveraged the virtual technology of Roblox to host fashion shows digitally, sell branded non-fungible tokens (NFTs), and offer customer-based personalized avatars. These initiatives give an understanding of how digital community, e-commerce, and content are congregated to form an immersive brand network. Hence, the Metaverse is not merely a marketing tool but a strategic platform for delivering innovative experience sharing and customer engagement.

Strategic customer experience design in the Metaverse strains on consistency across all the touch points, including physical and digital. It involves integration of emotional brand narratives, technological adaptability, and inclusivity to facilitate every interaction. Purkayastha and Sharma (2023)in their study emphasized on application of agile structure in organizations and multi-disciplinary teams to develop a sync between creative, technical, and ethical elements of customer engagement. Moreover, time spent on certain digital platforms, time and level of interaction generated, and emotional response should be balanced between traditional KPIs such as sales and reach.

Eventually, the success of the Metaverse application lies in how brands utilize and humanize the technology. Building an emotionally intelligent brand in a virtual environment ensures authenticity and the brand's relevancy, the cultural sensitivity boosts inclusivity across global audiences. Such a multifaceted approach helps marketers to redefine strategic brand management in a growing virtual economy.

2.4 Ethical, Psychological, and Social Dimensions of Metaverse CX

Metaverse provides exceptionally different opportunities along with certain reflective challenges for the psycho-ethical well-being of customers. Zuboff (2019), in his study, highlighted the advent of "surveillance capitalism", where marketers use customer data and behavioural patterns to monetize the target advertising. It has also raised significant privacy concerns as individuals share their personal information with immersive technology. This also complicates the balance between personalization and privacy concerns, where brands adopt a transparent data governance framework. The psychological implications of prolonged virtual immersion beyond the privacy concern are gaining higher attention nowadays. Riva et. al. (2021) revealed that excessive exposure to virtual environments may lead to digital fatigue, information overload, and less sensitivity towards emotional stimuli.

Designing, developing, and sustaining an emotionally balanced environment is therefore essential for sustained engagement of customers, especially for those organizations for whom privacy and psychological state are a major concern. Inclusivity and user-friendliness are other major ethical concerns that have been raised when Metaverse technology is applied. Bozkurt et al. (2021) in their study observed that the high cost of devices, limited connectivity, and lack of digital literacy exclude many users in developing regions.

Technology developers and policy makers need to prioritize certain design principles that are universally applicable and also address physical, cognitive, and socio-economic diversity to ensure participation. Governance monitoring of the Metaverse framework is also pretty underdeveloped. Lack of standardized guidelines creates misleading information, harassment, and exploitation to proliferate. (Dwivedi et al., 2022). Due to this, effective moderation and measuring accountability are difficult.

Ethical customer experience must entrench inclusivity, transparency, and consumer well-being at every stage of application of innovative technology. Only those organizations will foster and survive who adopt this integrated approach with trust and sustainable value creation within this ecosystem.

Overall, the literature reviewed for the present chapter emphasises how Metaverse technology transforms customer engagement with brands. The academic research, which is still fragmented, few studies have integrated the technological, ethical, and emotional engagement dimension of customer experience to develop a comprehensive single framework.

Moreover, little available empirical research has produced evidence as to how immersive engagement can be measured for marketing outcomes. These shortfalls establish the rationale of the study, the research gap, and the conceptual frame of Metaverse for customer experience, discussed further.

3. RESEARCH GAP

Metaverse technology is gaining a lot of scholarly attention nowadays. Regardless of that, it is still descriptive and in a fragmented state. Current literature highlights innovations like Virtual Reality (VR), Augmented Reality (AR), and Artificial Intelligence (AI), which are effectively used for customer engagement. Yet, it fails to launch a clear and measurable connection between immersive design and Customer Experience (CX) in the form of satisfaction, trust, or loyalty. (Dwivedi et al., 2022; Park & Kim, 2022). Metaverse is widely recognized for its transformative potential, but limited evidences are observed stating how experiential and emotional engagement converts into sustained consumer behaviour.

Another concern observed by the researchers is theoretical integration. Available studies have examined ethical, psychological, and technological facets instead of taking them as an interdependent dimension of customer experience. This prevents a holistic understanding of how immersive features stimulate value perception, leading to decision-making. On the other hand, inclusivity and ethical design are conceptually discussed rather than being it with a customer experience framework, bridging a gap in recognizing accessibility, data privacy, and emotional well-being.

It has also been observed that the managerial perspective towards metaverse technology and customer engagement is yet to be explored fully. Very negligible evidences are seen on how the organizations measure the effectiveness of customer engagement, define return on the experience, and evaluate marketing strategies based on metaverse initiatives. Thus, this study has tried to address these gaps by:

- Integrating technological, behavioral, and ethical dimensions of Metaverse customer experience into an integrated conceptual framework.
- Linking immersive design and emotional engagement with measurable marketing and experiential outcomes.
- Critically analysing some case studies that are based on the application of Metaverse technology and identifying key implications of the same.
- By addressing these gaps, the chapter attempts to bring theoretical clarity and provide practical directions for future scope on Metaverse-driven customer experience design.

4. METAVERSE CASES AND REAL-TIME EXECUTION

Metaverse is emerging as a dynamic and transformative field across various sectors, offering immersive and personalized experiences, redefining traditional business models. Metaverse adoption is reshaping audience interaction and pedagogical approaches, enabling deeper engagement, real-time collaboration, and experiential learning.

Through real world case studies on Nike's gamified experience with Nikeland and GUCCI's digital fashion ventures to Amazon's augmented shopping rooms and Adidas' Non-Fungible Tokens (NFT) driven brand experiences, from Justin Bieber's virtual live concert through his digital avatar to Curtin University's platform for development of real world physiotherapy skills in virtual setting and Nanyang Technical University, Singapore's three dimensional learning environment, this chapter highlights how organizations are reimagining customer journeys and consumer-brand relationships. These cases illustrate the evolving strategic role of immersive technologies in building competitive advantage and creating value in the digital age. The chapter will also explore how global leading brands across retail, entertainment, and education are incorporating Metaverse technologies to enhance customer experience and service delivery.

4.1 Metaverse Initiatives in the Retail Sector

Metaverse architecture in the retail segment is transforming customer experience (CX) by using Virtual Reality (VR) and Augmented Reality (AR), 3D virtual stores, virtual trial rooms, and digital avatars. Retailers across the globe use these technologies to create an immersive shopping environment where customers can browse, try out, compare, and purchase products in a virtual environment. AI-driven personalization creates ease of shopping, leading to convenience, engagement, and trust. This section discusses how metaverse architecture is used to enhance customer experience in a virtual environment.

4.1.1 The Perks of Being Digital: Nikeland

The case study "The Perks of Being Digital: Nikeland: A Case Study" explores Nike's digital transformation through its Nikeland initiative in collaboration with Roblox, a global online platform. Nikeland, a virtual space launched in 2021, capitalizes on users' growing interest in the Metaverse. The case study examines how Nike used this collaboration to integrate its brand into digital spaces, providing a new way for users to engage with Nike products.

Roblox, a platform for creating, playing, and sharing games and experiences, launched in 2006, allowing users to immerse themselves in virtual worlds and socialize. Nikeland is modelled after Nike's real-life headquarters in Oregon, offering users a chance to explore a Nike-branded virtual environment. Avatars are dressed in Nike gear and can navigate various areas such as the Lobby, Basketball area, Football field, and Showroom. Users can visit stores, participate in games, and purchase virtual items for their avatar's personal space, My Playground. Through augmented reality (AR) and smartphone accelerometers, Nikeland captures users' physical movements, adding an interactive element to the experience.

Nike's investment in Nikeland aims to merge gaming, social networking, and e-commerce, providing a platform without geographic or economic barriers. Subscribers can train teams, design virtual clothes, and customize their avatars. The experience lets users temporarily adopt a new identity through their avatars, fostering creativity and connection. The case highlights the influence of technology in the fashion industry, especially during periods when online shopping becomes essential. As customers increasingly shop digitally, companies like Nike have embraced the Metaverse to enhance communication and engagement. Through its partnership with Roblox, Nike has demonstrated its foresight in leveraging digital tools to connect with consumers and shape the future of retail (Temperino,2023).

4.1.2 GUCCI: The Fashion Innovation

A case study, "GUCCI's Metaverse Makeover: A Case Study, "The Fashion Innovation", talks about how metaverse architecture is used in delivering a gaming experience. GUCCI, an Italian luxury brand, ventured into the world of gaming through its innovative presence on Roblox, as a representation of its bold and visionary move that blends fashion, gaming, and digital engagement.

It has successfully established itself as a prominent brand within the gaming and virtual world spaces. GUCCI embraced an emerging trend of digital fashion, allowing the players to engage with the brand through initiatives like GUCCI Garden and GUCCI Town. It created an immersive gamified experience appealing to a young and digitally savvy audience. The brand released exclusive digital fashion items that are tied to some specific events, which drove user engagement by capitalizing on the concept of Fear of Missing Out- FOMO.

GUCCI's move to create permanent worlds like GUCCI Town allowed players to explore a more sustained and evolving experience. By integrating mini-games, a virtual store, and fashion items into the game, GUCCI created a space that encouraged continuous engagement. The GUCCI Ancora and GUCCI Town experiences expanded GUCCI's digital footprint and allowed users to interact with the brand at their own pace, while also offering gamified elements that kept the audience engaged. Further, GUCCI partnered with the artist Achille Lauro for virtual concerts to strengthen its position in gaming culture.

As a result of the above moves, GUCCI Town, a gaming platform, received a massive hit with users, receiving 47 million visits. Users spend 7.56 minutes on the platform, engaging in various activities. The high level of engagement is evident from the 6 million hours users spend on the platform. To thank the players following the evolution of GUCCI's experiences in Roblox, the Maison put out a redeemable item via a code sent by email on their website, prompting users to register their email to get the User Generated Content. Additionally, GUCCI Town also provided a range of items for purchase where users can buy virtual GUCCI products, such as shoes and handbags, and use them to personalize their avatars. The virtual world is regularly updated and expanded with new features and items, and is now called GUCCI Ancora (Goldenberg, 2023).

4.1.3 Adidas: Pioneering Digital Innovation

The case studies on Adidas's metaverse innovation, "Adidas: Pioneering Digital Innovation," talk about the traditional sportswear giant Adidas using metaverse architecture to enhance customer experience. The brand has ventured into the Metaverse to connect with new audiences and to remain relevant in a rapidly evolving digital landscape. Its journey began in 2021, marking a bold move towards blockchain and NFTs (non-fungible tokens), and virtual experiences. Adidas launched its first metaverse project, "Into the Metaverse," in collaboration with key players in the NFT and Web3 space: Bored Ape Yacht Club (BAYC), Punks Comic, and GMoney, a well-known crypto influencer. It purchased a Bored Ape named Indigo Herz and used it as a central character in its digital identity. The brand also launched a dedicated Adidas Originals Twitter Account to create a dialogue with early adopters of the space, creating a virtual customer experience (CX).

In 2022, in Phase 2 of the journey, NFT holders were allowed to claim physical merchandise, continuing the blend of digital and physical experiences. ALTs, the most ambitious evolution launched in 2023, shifted the focus to creating avatars based on user interaction. The ultimate aim was to create a unique and personalized digital identity for users. To conclude, Adidas's incursion into the Metaverse is a strategic move that redefines the meaning of a lifestyle brand in the digital age. (Kaur, 2024).

4.1.4 Introduction to Augmented Rooms Using Metaverse by Amazon

E-commerce giant Amazon has also embraced the Metaverse technology and has created Amazon Augmented Virtual Reality Rooms that show the primary architecture in a 3D view. The 3D Augmented Rooms are the rooms that help and guide the customers who want to design their interior by looking into the room's aesthetics and atmosphere. The case study "Introduction to Augmented Rooms Using Metaverse by Amazon" discusses how customers have access to the structure of their room virtually before buying the products.

This is an extension of the metaverse technology, which helps users to view things before purchasing them. On the other hand, the brand is now letting customers buy real products from a storefront in the virtual world. It has introduced Amazon Anywhere, which enables customers to shop the physical products in a virtual environment, such as video games, AR, and third-party mobile applications. The company also proposes to launch a new feature within Peridot, a new mobile game from Niantic that features AI-powered virtual pets and overlays AR imagery on a real-world environment. After linking their Amazon account to Peridot, customers can discover and purchase Peridot-branded products on Amazon directly from the game. Items available for purchase include t-shirts, hoodies, phone accessories, and throw pillows. Customers will see product details, images, availability, Prime eligibility, price, and estimated delivery date in the Peridot environment as they would in Amazon stores (Payal, 2022).

4.2 Metaverse initiatives in the Entertainment Industry

The metaverse architecture in the entertainment industry leverages technologies like Virtual Reality (VR), Augmented Reality (AR), blockchain, and 3D modeling to create immersive, interactive experiences. Techniques such as motion capture, real-time rendering, and digital twin environments are used to build virtual concerts, film sets, and gaming worlds. These technologies enable user engagement in real-time with content, enhancing accessibility and personalization. This part of the chapter explores the application of metaverse architecture in the Entertainment Industry.

4.2.1 Justin Bieber in the Metaverse: The Wave XR Concert:

In November 2021, Justin Bieber partnered with a virtual entertainment company, Wave, to provide fans with a free and live performance, titled Justin Bieber - An Interactive Virtual Experience. Beber transformed into his digital avatar and performed his number one album 'Justice' for the first time in the Metaverse. Animatrik, a real-time film-making and Performance Capture agency in North America, captured Beber's movements using data-driven technology that directly drives the singer's CG counterpart. Beber's fans were able to interact with him during this 45-minute show and 10-minute event performance where he was appearing live on stage alongside his avatar form. The concert goes could even chat with other fans around the world, send virtual expressions to Biber, and see themselves live during the show.

Wave (Extended Reality) XR ran broadcasting while Animtrik completed the full performance capture session of Bieber's real-life counterparts, ensuring that the concert is translated from Justin himself to his avatar. High-tech broadcasting tools and platforms formed the basis of a virtual concert while interactive VFX and animation were generated using real-time technology. The great success of the concert demonstrated how artists can harness the metaverse to push the boundaries of entertainment and interact with fans beyond geographical limits, who support them. (Animatrik Film Design, 2024)

4.2.2 Film as a Metaverse Prototype: Case of Avatar and Iron Man

James Cameron's Avatar (movie) franchise embodies a significant convergence of advanced filmmaking and metaverse technology, offering a glimpse into the future of immersive storytelling. Both the movies, especially Avatar: The Way of Water (2022), have utilized virtual production techniques, aligning closely with metaverse principles of immersive 3D environment and real-time rendering. The franchise uses virtual reality (VR) where the actors perform in motion capture suits within a virtual set, allowing filmmakers to visualize the alien world of Pandora in real time. Similarly, the Iron Man movie series also portrays a futuristic view of technology based on the metaverse concept-AR, AI, and immersive 3D environment. The actor wearing the Iron Man suit resembles AR and mixed reality interfaces.

The holographic images, computer-generated imagery, and visual effects have been used which simulate an immersive virtual environment. The integration of Iron Man into the Avengers series, real-time visualization tools, and motion capture were employed, which are similar to metaverse world-building technologies (Radoff, 2021; Thinkwithniche, 2023).

4.2.3 Pokémon Go

Pokémon Go mobile game developed by Niantic is another case of the earliest and most successful example of integration of metaverse technology in entertainment and gaming. The game blends physical and virtual worlds using AR, location-based services, and real-time data. In Pokémon Go, the players explore the real world using smartphones to discover and capture virtual Pokémon. AR features allow players to view Pokémon as if they exist in the real world through their phone cameras. Multi-player features added a social layer, fostering real-time collaboration and competition among the users. Overall, Pokémon Go exemplifies how Metaverse technology can create immersive experiences that blend digital content for user engagement. (Patel, 2021)

4.3 Metaverse initiatives in the Education Sector

Talking about the education sector, sufficient evidence is available that the metaverse offers transformative potential by creating an immersive, interactive, and engaging environment. Through virtual reality (VR) and augmented reality (AR), the metaverse allows students to understand complex concepts in a three-dimensional space, making learning experiential and more effective. Several case studies are available demonstrating the impact of metaverse technology on areas such as virtual campus tours, enhanced collaboration, and improved student motivation. Metaverse can revolutionize teaching methodologies and improve educational outcomes by overcoming limitations of traditional learning through virtual reality (VR) and augmented reality (AR).

4.3.1 Nanyang Technological University: Digital Twins for Education

Nanyang Technological University (NTU), also known as NTUniverse, Singapore, is built on top of NVIDIA Omniverse, a platform that unifies disparate 3D workflows and data sources into one comprehensive interactive 3D environment. Various software tools are used in 3D modeling to elaborate on the details of buildings and to provide texture, labels, models, etc. Scan-to-BIM technology, in which laser scanners or cameras are used to digitally capture the physical space, such as classrooms and laboratories. Real-world campus buildings and landmarks are recreated with accurate material textures, spatial layouts, and labeled assets. Users navigate via avatars, explore academic zones, learn about botany through interactive 3D models, and engage with digital avatars integrated into the virtual environment. Each student can have their personalized avatar for immersive and interactive learning. A virtual classroom is also designed to accommodate both avatars and video-based participation of students in a hybrid manner. (Sim et.al., 2024)

4.3.2 Virtual Training for Real-World Care: The Case of Curtin University

Curtin University, Australia, has developed a platform with LearnBrite that enables the trainee health and community professionals to develop real-world physiotherapy skills in a virtual setting. The technology is used for virtual training of students, enabling personal learning to eliminate the incidence of injuries, followed by adverse outcomes. Hospital visits mimic the reality of a patient's home and let students practice making risk assessments based on 15 categories, including trip, slip, diet, and medication.

Through an immersive environment, students from physiotherapy, pharmacy, social work, and psychology engage in an Interprofessional Virtual Hospital Visit (IPE VHsV) and can focus on the areas of improvement without the distraction and noise of a real classroom. (LearnBrite by Hyperspace, 2025)

4.3.3 Immersive Learning through Phygital Integration: HKUST's Metaverse Campus

The Hong Kong University of Science and Technology (HKUST), in the year 2022, announced its plan to establish the world's first physical-digital twin campuses in the metaverse to create more immersive and engaging learning experiences. The technical architecture of the University MetaHUST combined augmented reality, virtual reality, and social networking technologies to create a seamless and interactive Phygital environment.

During the initial stages, the physical infrastructure, such as XR classrooms, sensors, cameras, and visualization tools, was installed, and the members of the University were invited to take part in a crowdsourced scanning of the physical campuses to help provide the necessary images for building the campuses' virtual twins. The mixed reality classrooms of MetaHUST bring together students and lecturers from Clear Water Bay, Hong Kong, and the Guangzhou campus into the same virtual environment. Participants appear as avatars, tracked via motion capture and real-time positioning, enabling collaboration regardless of location. These classrooms support large user groups with avatars reflecting the facial features and mannerisms of real students and faculty in real time.

Students collaboratively conceived campus-in-the-sea, space station, and MTR station designs, with interactive real-time feedback and peer co-creation elevating engagement and creativity.

Faculty introduced a simulation of landslides in VR, enabling students to explore hazard scenarios, propose solutions, and visualize effects in immersive environments. HKUST's metaverse integration blends virtual and physical campus life to enrich pedagogy, collaboration, design creativity, and research. With digital twins, XR classrooms, immersive courses, and VR research, HKUST is positioning itself at the leading edge of educational innovation in Web 3 and immersive learning (Hui, 2023).

Table 1. Summary of Real-Time Case Studies

Brand	Initiative	Consumer Experience (CX) Design Features	Reported Outcomes	Key Insights & Challenges
Nike Nikeland	Created a virtual world for gamified sports interaction.	Custom avatars, digital collectibles, and co-creation through mini-games.	21 million+ visitors (Roblox data, 2023). High youth engagement.	Demonstrated strong experiential immersion but limited cross-platform brand integration.
Gucci Garden Experience	Immersive brand storytelling in Roblox	Sensory-rich environment, limited-time digital wearables (NFTs).	19 million+ participants; NFT resale value peaked at 3500 USD.	Created brand exclusivity but raised accessibility and equity concerns.
Adidas Into the Metaverse	Launched collaborative NFTs with artists and communities.	Ownership-based engagement, integration of physical and digital rewards.	Sold out 30,000 NFTs within hours; strengthened digital community loyalty.	Showed the power of co-creation but lacked clarity on long-term sustainability.
Coca-Cola Friendship Day Experience	Designed social events and avatar-based gifting.	Emotional storytelling, nostalgia-based gamification.	Global participation; strong social media amplification.	Provided emotional resonance can drive virtual participation; limited measurable sales impact.
Hyundai Mobility Adventure	Virtual theme park to introduce future mobility concepts.	Educational interaction, virtual test drives, and gamified learning.	3 million+ visitors in initial months.	Effective in brand education, but lower retention post-event.

These cases collectively demonstrate how global brands are implementing and leveraging the Metaverse to introduce immersive and participatory experiences. Table 1. Illustrates the summary of these global case studies. The outcomes of these cases, such as customer engagement and brand storytelling, are significant; the analysis also reveals key challenges related to inclusivity and sustainability. These insights provide a significant foundation for developing the Metaverse CX Design Framework discussed in the next section.

5. THE EXPANDING FRONTIER OF METAVERSE CUSTOMER EXPERIENCE Design

The traditional brand consumer interactions are reshaping with the evolution of digital technologies, and so is the CX is surrounded by a hyper-connected, immersive world. The Metaverse, a fusion of physical, digital, and virtual realities, offers customers a new era where engagement, co-creation, emotion, and value are evident at multiple levels instantaneously.

In the Metaverse environment, consumers are empowered as they act as participants, co-designers, blending identity, involved in advanced technologies that are truly engaging experiences (Kaur, 2024). In response to the transformation, this section of the chapter proposes a structured approach and framework for Metaverse CX design. The proposed framework emphasizes five key pillars: immersive technology integration, consumer behavior mapping, strategic brand storytelling, inclusive and ethical design, and business outcomes and value co-creation. All the proposed elements of the framework will serve as a comprehensive roadmap for businesses aiming to build resonant, human-centred experiences in the Metaverse.

Each element of the metaverse framework is interconnected with the other rather than fragmented. The immersive technology enables the user to simulate the emotional mapping and application in the form of storytelling, converting the user engagement into brand identity. Similarly, inclusivity ensures ethical application of the immersive technology, along with driving measurable business values through co-creation. Collectively, these dimensions form a circular process where experience design and consumer feedback continuously interact with each other.

Figure 1. Framework for Metaverse Customer Experience Design

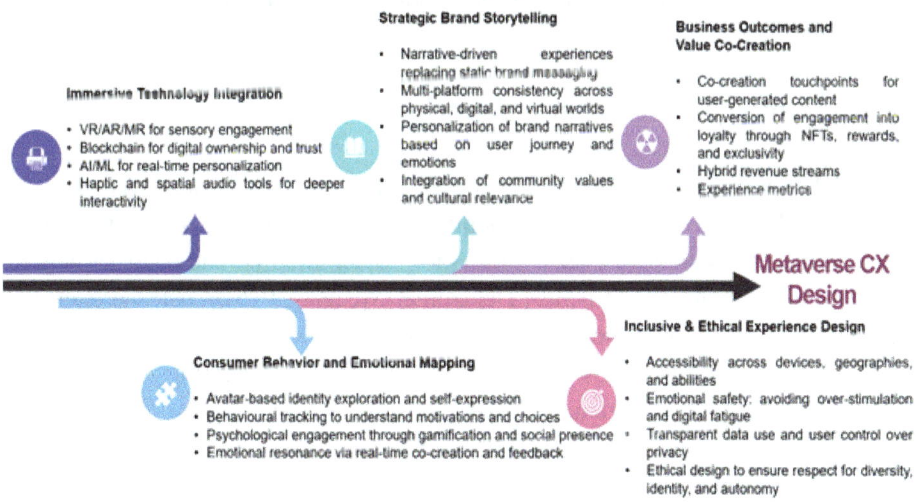

5.1 Immersive Technology Integration

Metaverse experience integrates immersive technologies such as Virtual Reality (VR), Augmented Reality (AR), Mixed Reality (MR), and Extended Reality (XR), and this integration engages customers from passive viewing to active participation in responsive environments. VR headsets and AR overlays enable users to interact in dynamic, spatially rich worlds. MR blends virtual and physical environments supported by haptic feedback that enhances tactile realism and spatial audio for authentic immersion (Gao & Spence, 2025). Along with sensory engagements, blockchain also plays a foundational yet significant role in ensuring secure ownership of digital assets, tokens, and identity that fosters decentralized trust. Integrating AI and machine learning personalizes the user's experience, analyzes real-time data to encode the user's behaviors and preferences (Khamaj& Ali, 2024). Synergising these technologies will provide a personalised experience, users' security, exchange of information, and the synergy between these technologies supports robust personalization and secure, interoperable virtual economies (Selvam, 2024).

Multinational brands such as Hyundai, Nike, and many others are efficaciously using extended reality (XR) with integration of Artificial Intelligence (AI), where they are creating data-centric virtual experiences by merging entertainment with brand inculcation. These applications exemplify that immersive technology is rather more effective when it is combined with emotions in storytelling and personalized strategies.

5.2 Consumer Behavior and Emotional Mapping

The effectiveness of Metaverse CX is directly correlated to understanding consumer psychology. For self-exploration and identity experimentation, digital avatars shall be introduced. This creativity allows users to project, modify, and even reimagine themselves in virtual environments (Tirinzoni& Megale, 2025). Customer engagement levels are monitored through behavioural analytics such as tracking choices, movement, and emotional cues (Kaur, 2024), which helps in creating environments that intuitively adapt to fluctuating moods and engagement levels.

Gamification is another innovative technology in the Metaverse that fosters emotional investment and loyal participation of the users. Gamification's customer-engaging features, such as quests, achievements, and competitive events, spark both individual and team participation, amplify virtual brand engagement, and boost consumer-based brand equity (Vashisht, 2023).

Social presence with avatars articulates the virtual environment, as immersive collaboration enables more meaningful connections between consumers and brands (Romero & Park, 2025). Brands promoting real-time co-creation and promoting user-generated content; participants feel belongingness and engage themselves meaningfully, from transactional to transformative. These behavioural insights from strategic storytelling and inclusive design ensure that the consumer journey is response-driven and adapted to the variability of motivations and emotional experiences.

5.3 Strategic Brand Storytelling

Metaverse offers new avenues of creativity in the form of storytelling, user-driven narratives. The AR's and VRs' role to make the content creative and interactive shall not be overlooked, as it enables customers to develop a strong sense of agency. Content personalization is the need of the hour: brands are adopting real-time stories, presenting with emotions and actions to create a memorable experience (Mehra &Kansra, 2024).

Omnichannel communication is a consistent support: virtual, digital, and physical platforms work simultaneously, ensuring a seamless movement between brands, assets, and users across platforms. Storytelling is a proven tool for ethically persuading consumers, especially when it is mapped with their journey and inclusivity. E.g., Gucci hosted a limited-time exhibition using the metaverse to demonstrate how emotional stories can lead to higher customer engagement, maintaining authenticity.

5.4 Inclusive & Ethical Experience Design

Considering inclusivity Metaverse keeps accessibility, diversity, and ethics at the center. Users' experiences are analyzed to understand creativity and thoughtful designs with varying needs and geographical constraints (Al Kfairy et al., 2025). Some of the significant features, such as user interface scalability, closed captioning, understandable navigation, and preference for local language, help in removing barriers and promote inclusivity and fairness. Ethical considerations such as protecting emotional safety, upholding privacy by design, and empowering users with control over their information are the key requirements of digitally equipped platforms.

Diversified representation of audience, avoiding stereotyping discrimination, ensuring fair participation, transparency, user control over data, and robust safeguards will provide long-term loyalty and sustainability of the Metaverse (Al Kfairy et al., 2025). Inclusivity and ethics need to guide all other pillars of customer experience design, reshaping the choice of technologies and content creation, etc., to ensure that the metaverse technology remains trustworthy and human-centric.

5.5 Business Outcomes and Value Co-Creation

Reimagining the business landscape and value co-creation is a significant outcome of the Metaverse. User-generated content (UGC) platforms motivate users to collaborate, design, and trade(Kim, 2025). The entire ecosystem allows users to innovate in asset creation. NFTs incentivize participation, enhance brand loyalty, and encourage exclusivity; this way, they unlock new avenues of value for both consumers and brands(Rane et al., 2023).

In general, these five pillars discussed above are interdependent components of the design cycle. Immersive technologies enable the user to understand behavioural patterns, whereas storytelling transforms the content into meaningful data. On the other hand, inclusivity assures ethical alignment and co-creation conversion into meaningful engagement for measuring the values. Thus, this integrated framework provides a structured and flexible model for researchers and practitioners that crafts human-centric experiences in the Metaverse.

6. CHALLENGES IN IMPLEMENTING METAVERSE

The application of Metaverse technologies using VR and AR for enhancing CX imparts significant opportunities. Yet, it has numerous challenges and can be grouped into different categories, i.e., technical, ethical, accessibility, and behavioural. Considering the retail sector, the challenge lies with creating immersive and personalized experiences, such as touch and feel, through virtual reality fitting rooms, virtual try-on apps, or digital twins (Verhoef et al., 2021). Such retailers also face the challenges in terms of the rising cost of upgrading technology, VR/AR infrastructure, data privacy concerns, and so on. Immersive technology requires the collection of user data more intimately to create an extended experience, which may not be acceptable on the part of the users. While the metaverse promises enhanced interactivity and social experiences in virtual concerts and the gaming world, it is challenged by scalability, content moderation, and monetization of virtual assets. (Lee et al., 2021). For example, Nikeland by Nike faced several issues, name a few are content moderation and scalability when user participation surged, showing how brands must balance innovation with operational stability. Safeguarding user identity and behavior and managing the digital rights of such events is critical in a virtual environment.

Other challenges, apart from commercial contexts such as accessibility and educational barriers, also circumscribed the adoption and acceptance of the Metaverse. Lack of technical infrastructure, especially in developing and underdeveloped regions, incapability of handling advanced technology, and the need for teacher training to adapt to changing teaching-learning methodology to immersive platforms are other challenges observed in the application of metaverse technology. Classroom management, student engagement, and content development in a prolonged virtual setting remain a crucial part of the application of the metaverse. Above all, data privacy remains the foremost concern as immersive technologies collect vast amounts of sensitive personal data, including biometric information and behavioral patterns (Dwivedi et al., 2022).

This raises the question about consent, surveillance, and potential misuse of data by a third party. On the other hand, metaverse users often create a digital identity through an avatar, which also needs to be protected against impersonation, theft, or manipulation. (Kshetri, 2022). Cyberbullying, digital arrests, and virtual harassment are new grey areas that are challenging to the application of technology. Strategies that collaborate technology with ethical governance, tech-education, and infrastructure will help to mitigate these challenges. It will result in building confidence among organizations, stakeholders, and creating sustainable and trustworthy Metaverse ecosystems.

7. DISCUSSION AND CONCLUSION

Metaverse represents a transformative leap in customer engagement with brands. With the introduction of immersive and engaging virtual environment that mimics the real world, marketers are constantly working on personalizing customer experience by using tools such as Virtual Reality (VR), Augmented Reality (AR), blockchain chain and AI. This immersive architecture fosters deeper brand engagement, emotional connection, and user satisfaction by allowing consumers to interact through avatars, participate in co-creation, and receive real-time, tailored responses (Scholdra et.al. 2023). Real-world examples from top organizations show how the metaverse is enhancing customer experience and strengthening brand identity. This chapter discusses how Nike's Nikeland Roblox uses a gamified environment to enhance user experience with the brand. On the other hand, GUCCI's Gucci Town and Gucci Ancora demonstrate how luxury fashion can appeal to digital natives through avatar customization, limited-edition digital assets, and virtual concerts that reflect cultural relevance and exclusivity (Goldenberg, 2023).

Sportswear giant Adidas expands its brand presence by integrating blockchain and NFTs to bridge the gap between virtual and physical product experiences. These case studies show a successful application of the metaverse that goes beyond novelty, focusing on customer engagement and extended experience in a virtual environment. The above-discussed cases have validated the three pillars of the proposed framework, viz., immersive design, emotional engagement, and co-creation, leading to translating the theories into practice. However, the successful application of these technologies also highlights the need to prepare standard metrics that measure customer engagement, authenticity, and brand loyalty in the long run within the virtual ecosystem.

The education and entertainment sectors are also leveraging immersive technologies to reimagine learning and engagement. Universities like Nanyang Technological University, Singapore, and HKUST, Hong Kong, employ digital twins and XR classrooms to create interactive and personalized learning environments (Sim et al., 2024; Hui, 2023). Justin Bieber's virtual concert illustrates the power of the Metaverse that eliminates all geographical boundaries through avatar-led interactions and real-time socialization. Thus, the metaverse is not just a technology, but it's a space that blends virtual environments to enhance user engagement and collaboration.

These innovations have established the probability of enhancing customer experience design system and emerging structural and ethical challenges determining the efficacy of Metaverse technology that can be scaled. However, the advancements always come with substantial challenges. The immersive nature of the metaverse collects a vast amount of sensitive data of the user, including biometric and behavioral information. These challenges, such as data privacy, consent, and data misuse, remain critical. Avatar-based interactions lead to complicated identity authentication and digital security. Another limitation that the technology faces is the availability of technological infrastructure, especially the need for training for those who are new to this technology. Digital fatigue, emotional overstimulation, and accessibility remain persistent barriers, particularly for users facing cognitive and physical limitations. Most research focuses on infrastructure, with limited insight into behavioral outcomes, emotional design, and ethical CX frameworks (Verhoef et. al., 2021). In conclusion, the metaverse is not just a technology; it is a cultural shift redefining how value, identity, and engagement are constructed in digital space. Organizations need to approach and implement it with empathy and creativity, leading to the development of trust and security. The ultimate success of the metaverse depends on designing experiences that are not only immersive and interactive but also inclusive, secure, and emotionally meaningful. Further, the research needs to focus on designing empirical models that quantify customer engagement through immersive technology, ethical design, and inclusivity outcomes. The practitioners need to establish the standards and framework that ensure the development and maintenance of responsible innovations. The metaverse will sustain through its immersive technology along with measurable, ethical, and human-centric experiences.

REFERENCES

Al Kfairy, M., Alrabaee, S., Alfandi, O., Mohamed, A. T., & Khaddaj, S. (2025). Navigating ethical dimensions in the metaverse: Challenges, frameworks, and solutions. *IEEE Access : Practical Innovations, Open Solutions*, *13*, 79996–80018. DOI: 10.1109/ACCESS.2025.3564498

Ball, M. (2022). *The metaverse: And how it will revolutionize everything*. Liveright Publishing.

Bozkurt, A., Altay, M., Karadeniz, A., & Koçdar, S. (2021). Digital equity and inclusion in the metaverse. *Open Praxis*, *13*(3), 235–246. DOI: 10.5944/openpraxis.13.3.136

Cummings, J. J., & Bailenson, J. N. (2016). How immersive is enough? A meta-analysis of the effect of immersive technology on user presence. *Media Psychology*, *19*(2), 272–309. DOI: 10.1080/15213269.2015.1015740

Dwivedi, Y. K., Hughes, D. L., & Baabdullah, A. M.. (2022). Metaverse beyond the hype: Multidisciplinary perspectives on emerging challenges, opportunities and agenda for research, practice and policy. *International Journal of Information Management*, *66*, 102542. DOI: 10.1016/j.ijinfomgt.2022.102542

Goldenberg, B. (2023). Gucci's metaverse makeover: A case study on fashion innovation. Retrieved from https://ismguide.com/gucci-xr-metaverse-case-study/

Hamari, J., Koivisto, J., & Sarsa, H. (2014). Does gamification work? A literature review of empirical studies on gamification. In *47th Hawaii International Conference on System Sciences*, 3025–3034. IEEE.

Hui, P. (2023). Exploring the potential of metaverse in education: A case study of MetaHKUST. https://cei.hkust.edu.hk/en-hk/event/exploring-potential-metaverse-education-case-study-metahkust

Jin, H. S., & Song, E. J. (2021). A study on the future development direction of the virtual world metaverse industry. In *Proceedings of the Korean Institute of Information and Communication Sciences Conference*, 432–433.

Kaur, S. (2024). Adidas: Pioneering digital innovation. Retrieved from https://www.slideshare.net/slideshow/adidas-pioneering-digital-innovation-mrk634ztt/273345128

Kim, Y. (2025). Not just for play: Why the metaverse should be leveraged for cocreation. *Business Horizons*, *68*(1), 45–54. DOI: 10.1016/j.bushor.2023.11.002

Kshetri, N. (2022). The economics of the metaverse: Business models, technological developments, and challenges. *IT Professional*, *24*(1), 62–67.

Kye, B., Han, N., Kim, M., Park, Y., & Jo, S. (2021). Educational applications of metaverse: Possibilities and limitations. *Journal of Educational Evaluation for Health Professions*, •••, 18.

Lee, L.-H., Braud, T., Zhou, P. Y., Wang, L., Xu, D., Lin, Z., Kumar, A., Bermejo, C., & Hui, P. (2021). All one needs to know about metaverse: A complete survey on technological singularity, virtual ecosystem, and research agenda. 14(8), 1–64. https://doi.org/DOI: 10.13140/RG.2.2.11200.05124/8

Lemon, K. N., & Verhoef, P. C. (2016). Understanding customer experience throughout the customer journey. *Journal of Marketing*, *80*(6), 69–96.

Mehra, P., & Kansra, P. (2024). Fostering gratifying customer experiences through the art of visual content and storytelling. In Shukla, R., & Pal, S. (Eds.), *Multidisciplinary applications of extended reality for human experience* (pp. 401–423). IGI Global., DOI: 10.4018/978-1-6684-9886-4.ch016

Mystakidis, S. (2022).. . *Metaverse. Encyclopedia*, *2*(1), 486–497.

Nowak, K. L., & Fox, J. (2018). Avatars and computer-mediated communication: A review of the definitions, uses, and effects of digital representations. *Review of Communication Research*, *6*, 30–53.

Pine, B. J., & Gilmore, J. H. (2011). The experience economy (Updated ed.). Harvard Business Review Press.

Piskorski, J., Stefanovitch, N., Da San Martino, G., & Nakov, P. (2023, July). SemEval-2023 task 3: Detecting the category, the framing, and the persuasion techniques in online news in a multi-lingual setup. In *Proceedings of the 17th International Workshop on Semantic Evaluation (SemEval-2023)*, 2343–2361.

Purkayastha, D., & Sharma, R. (2023). Consumer-centric innovation in the metaverse: Personalization and value creation. *Journal of Marketing Trends*, *10*(1), 55–70.

Rane, N. L., Choudhary, S., & Rane, J. (2023, November 28). Metaverse for enhancing customer loyalty: Effective strategies to improve customer relationship, service, engagement, satisfaction, and experience. SSRN Electronic Journal. https://doi.org/DOI: 10.2139/ssrn.4624197

Riva, G., Wiederhold, B. K., & Mantovani, F. (2021). Neuroscience of virtual reality: From virtual exposure to embodied medicine. *Cyberpsychology, Behavior, and Social Networking*, *22*(1), 82–96.

Romero, P. M., & Park, H. (2025, January 15). Exploring the impact of brand narrative engagement and social presence in branded virtual worlds. *International Textile and Apparel Association Annual Conference Proceedings*, 81(1). https://doi.org/DOI: 10.31274/itaa.18646

Scholdra, T., Wichmann, J., & Reinartz, W. (2023). Reimagining personalization in the physical store. *Journal of Retailing*, *99*(4), 563–579. DOI: 10.1016/j.jretai.2023.11.001

Selvam, D. (2024, August). Securing digital identities: The synergy of information technology security, trust, and privacy. International Journal of Computer Science [IJCSEIT]. *Engineering and Information Technology*, *14*(5), 1–14. DOI: 10.5121/i

Sim, J. K., Xu, K. W., Jin, Y., Kim, J., Lee, J., & Choi, H. (2024). Designing an educational metaverse: A case study of NTUniverse. *Applied Sciences (Basel, Switzerland)*, *14*(6), 2559. DOI: 10.3390/app14062559

Slater, M., & Wilbur, S. (2006). A framework for immersive virtual environments (FIVE): Speculations on the role of presence in virtual environments. *Presence (Cambridge, Mass.)*, *6*(6), 603–616. DOI: 10.1162/pres.1997.6.6.603

Stephenson, N. (2003). *Snow crash*. Random House Publishing Group. (Original work published 1992.)

Temperino, E. (2023). The perks of being digital: Nikeland—a case study. In Fashion and communication in digital age: Proceedings of the FACTUM 23 Conference, Pisa, Italy, 88–95. Springer. https://doi.org/DOI: 10.1007/978-3-031-38541-4_9

Tirinzoni, M., & Megale, V. (2025). Reimagining identity, healing, and equality through extended reality: A societal revolution of virtual worlds. In García-Peñalvo, A., & Conde-González, J. A. (Eds.), *Impacts of sensetech on society* (pp. 149–186). IGI Global., DOI: 10.4018/978-1-6684-9155-1.ch007

Vashisht, D. (2023). Engaging and entertaining customers: Gamification in interactive marketing. In Menon, A. R. R., & Vargo, S. L. (Eds.), *The Palgrave handbook of interactive marketing* (pp. 807–835). Springer., DOI: 10.1007/978-3-030-89505-4_27

Verhoef, P. C., Broekhuizen, T., Bart, Y., Bhattacharya, A., Dong, J. Q., Fabian, N., & Haenlein, M. (2021). Digital transformation: A multidisciplinary reflection and research agenda. *Journal of Business Research*, *122*, 889–901. DOI: 10.1016/j.jbusres.2019.09.02

Wedel, M., Bigné, E., & Zhang, J. (2020). Virtual and augmented reality: Advancing research in consumer marketing. *International Journal of Research in Marketing*, *37*(3), 443–465. DOI: 10.1016/j.ijresmar.2020.04.004

Zuboff, S. (2019). *The age of surveillance capitalism: The fight for a human future at the new frontier of power*. PublicAffairs.

Chapter 3
Business Model Innovation Through Immersive Technologies:
Integrating Digital Twins and the Metaverse in the Industry 5.0 Era

Raihan Isad
http://orcid.org/0009-0008-2176-1526
Universitas Esa Unggul, Indonesia

Dwi Sartika Simatupang
Univesitas Esa Unggul, Indonesia

Agung Mulyo Widodo
http://orcid.org/0000-0002-9792-7114
Univesitas Esa Unggul, Indonesia

Popong Setiawati
Univesitas Esa Unggul, Indonesia

Meena Malik
http://orcid.org/0000-0001-8654-7143
Chandigarh University, India

Yash Pandey
http://orcid.org/0009-0008-6579-1305
National Shizuoka University, Japan

Yogita Abichandani
http://orcid.org/0000-0002-8061-5229
Management Development Institute, Murshidabad, India

ABSTRACT

Industry 5.0 drives a deeper fusion between advanced intelligent systems and human creativity, positioning immersive technologies as essential components of modern innovation. Digital Twins and the Metaverse enable highly interactive, data rich environments where physical processes can be simulated, optimized, and experienced virtually. With support from AI, IoT, blockchain, and high speed networks, organizations can design business models that prioritize adaptability, co creation, and meaningful user engagement. Consumers participate directly in virtual testing,

DOI: 10.4018/979-8-3373-4541-3.ch003

collaborative design sessions, and service interactions, creating continuous feedback loops that refine products and experiences. These immersive ecosystems strengthen operational reliability, reduce development risks, and open opportunities for sustainable value creation across industries. By offering transparent, secure, and accessible digital spaces, immersive technologies help companies develop human centered, resilient, and future ready business strategies aligned with the goals of Industry 5.0.

1. INTRODUCTION

1.1 Industry 5.0 Landscape

Industry 5.0 represents a shift from the automation-driven efficiency of Industry 4.0 toward a human-centric, sustainable, and collaborative industrial paradigm. Rather than viewing technology as a substitute for human labor, Industry 5.0 frames digital systems as partners that augment human creativity, intuition, and ethical judgment. This "rehumanization of industry" elevates human-machine collaboration as a defining force of the new industrial era. This shift is transforming the relationships between producers, consumers, and stakeholders. In manufacturing, consumers increasingly act as co-creators, engaging in virtual prototyping and design processes that accelerate innovation and strengthen customer loyalty (Rudek et al., 2025). These interactive digital environments allow early testing and feedback, creating a more responsive innovation ecosystem (Sekti, 2025).

Public policies are also adjusting to accommodate this paradigm. Institutions such as the European Commission now emphasize that technology adoption must incorporate social values, sustainability, and ethical considerations not merely economic performance (Boopathy et al., 2025). Without proper governance frameworks, Industry 5.0 technologies risk deepening inequalities and limiting inclusive participation. This transition has significant implications for the research and innovation ecosystem. Academic and industrial stakeholders are beginning to move beyond traditional efficiency-oriented models toward more adaptive, human-centered business strategies. Preparing future professionals to navigate a labor market defined by human-machine collaboration is becoming equally essential.

1.2 The Role of Immersive Technologies

Immersive technologies including Digital Twins (DT), Virtual Reality (VR), Augmented Reality (AR), Mixed Reality (MR), and the metaverse play a foundational role in enabling Industry 5.0. Once considered supplementary tools, these technologies now shape operational control, innovation, and value creation.

Figure 1. shows an overview of five core immersive technologies in Industry 5.0 and their respective industrial functions.

Figure 1. Overview of five core immersive technologies in Industry 5.0 and their respective industrial functions.

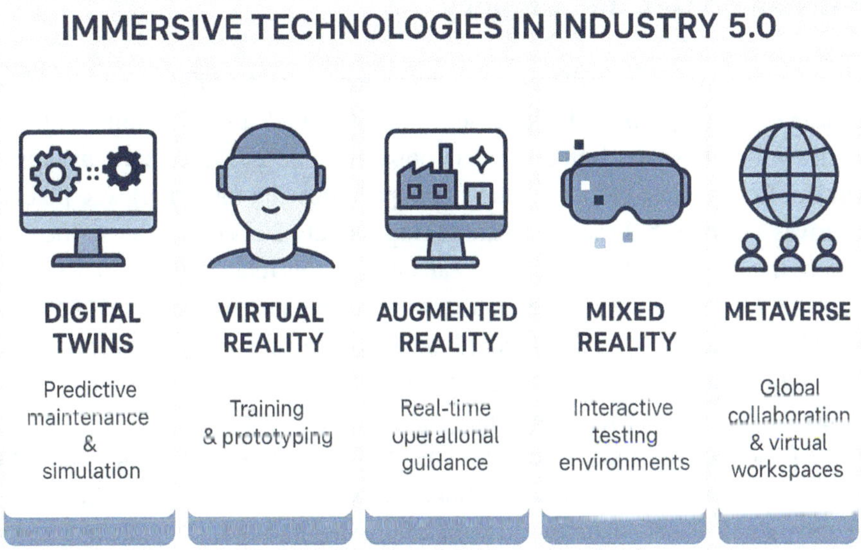

Digital twins provide real-time virtual representations of machines, production lines, or full industrial facilities. They enable predictive maintenance, simulation, and risk-free experimentation, helping organizations lower costs and optimize operations. Applications range from wind turbines to automotive assembly lines and smart city systems (Zhou et al., 2025). The industrial metaverse expands these capabilities by enabling global collaboration in shared virtual spaces. (Osello et al., 2024) describe it as a platform where engineers, designers, clients, and regulators can co-design products, test prototypes, and conduct training independent of physical constraints. Workplace safety training becomes more realistic and scalable when combined with digital twins, offering immersive simulations without real-world risks (Zahid et al., 2025).

Immersive technologies also stimulate new business models. Firms are shifting from selling physical goods to offering hybrid product-service experiences. A bicycle manufacturer, for example, may provide a digital twin of an e-bike connected to a metaverse platform for performance monitoring and personalization. DHL, as noted by (Abdellatif Ghorbal et al., 2025), employs metaverse environments to simulate global supply chains, improving responsiveness and reducing logistics costs. Moreover, immersive platforms enhance inclusion by enabling workers with physical limitations to engage remotely through virtual interfaces. This strengthens the human-centric ethos of Industry 5.0, positioning technology as a facilitator of equitable participation (Singh et al., 2024).

1.3 Research Gap and Urgency

Despite rapid growth of literature on the metaverse and digital twins, significant gaps remain. A major issue is the absence of integrated studies linking both technologies within business frameworks. (Boopathy et al., 2025) observe that current research often isolates DT and metaverse topics, missing the synergistic potential that drives Industry 5.0 transformation (Gupta et al., 2024). Another critical gap concerns the lack of global regulatory standards. Issues related to digital asset ownership, metaverse data governance, and cybersecurity remain unresolved (Abdellatif Ghorbal et al., 2025). Without standardization, organizations face legal and ethical uncertainties that limit large-scale adoption.

Current research is also dominated by technical perspectives sensor development, AI models, 5G infrastructure while studies on business model innovation driven by immersive technologies remain scarce (Hassoun et al., 2024). This gap is problematic because meaningful industrial transformation depends not only on technology but also on reconfiguring how value is created and delivered. Access inequality further intensifies the urgency. Large corporations in developed countries can implement these technologies due to strong infrastructure and capital, while SMEs in developing regions face barriers such as high investment costs, limited connectivity, and skill shortages (Abdellatif Ghorbal et al., 2025). This divergence risks exacerbating global digital divides. Given the rapid expansion of 5G, generative AI, and IoT ecosystems, the window for strategic adoption is narrowing (Phattanaviroj et al., 2026). Without coordinated research, policy action, and cross-sector collaboration, Industry 5.0 risks becoming mere technological rhetoric rather than a driver of meaningful socioeconomic progress (Panda et al., 2024).

2. BACKGROUND AND LITERATURE REVIEW

2.1 Evolution of Business Models in the Digital Era

Business models have undergone significant transformation in the digital era as organizations shifted from efficiency-driven structures toward data-based and service-oriented value creation. Early digitalization focused mainly on optimizing internal operations and reducing costs through automation. As connectivity, cloud computing, and large-scale data analytics matured, companies began transitioning from selling products to offering digital services, subscription models, and multi-sided platforms. Digital twins, VR, and AR, once seen as supportive technologies, now function as strategic enablers of new business models. These technologies generate continuous data, facilitate collaborative design, and support immersive interactions that deepen customer involvement. (Zahid et al., 2025) highlight how digital twins and the metaverse foster co-creation environments where users participate directly in product development. This shift reflects a broader transition from static product delivery toward interactive, experience-driven value propositions.

In this evolving landscape, ownership is increasingly replaced by access and participation. Businesses develop ecosystems where users contribute insights, create content, and influence design decisions through real-time digital interactions. The line between producers and consumers becomes more fluid. As immersive technologies advance further, business models will increasingly rely on hybrid combinations of physical offerings and digital experiences. These models emphasize personalization, engagement, and adaptability, which are central to Industry 5.0.

2.2 Industry 4.0 vs. Industry 5.0: Paradigm Shift

Industry 4.0 introduced automation, IoT networks, cyber-physical systems, and data analytics as dominant industrial principles. While these innovations achieved high productivity, they also created concerns about worker displacement and the marginalization of human judgment (Moslehpour et al., 2024). Industry 4.0 was often viewed as machine-centric, prioritizing efficiency over human involvement. Industry 5.0 responds by positioning humans as essential contributors within advanced technological environments. This paradigm promotes collaboration between human and machine intelligence. (Fernandez-Carames & Fraga-Lamas, 2024) frame Industry 5.0 as a shift from substituting humans with automation toward enhancing human-machine cooperation. The change affects how value is created, how innovation unfolds, and how businesses align with environmental and social responsibilities.

Digital twins and the metaverse hold strategic importance in this transition. They enable interactive environments where workers can explore, analyze, and control systems in real time. Instead of viewing digital tools only as efficiency mechanisms, Industry 5.0 regards them as platforms that enhance creativity, decision-making, and problem-solving. As a result, business models evolve from efficiency-based operations toward ethical, resilient, and human-centered strategies.

2.3 Immersive Technologies Overview (VR, AR, MR)

Immersive technologies such as VR, AR, and MR now support a wide range of industrial applications. VR creates fully digital environments suitable for training, remote exploration, and complex design tasks. AR overlays digital information on physical spaces, giving technicians real-time guidance during maintenance or assembly tasks. MR integrates both physical and virtual objects, allowing dynamic interaction between real and digital elements. (Asad et al., 2023) report that these technologies are increasingly used in manufacturing, logistics, construction, and education. They support collaborative prototyping, technical training, and real-time operational assistance. For example, AR can reduce assembly errors by displaying step-by-step instructions directly in a worker's view. VR enables safe simulations of high-risk environments. MR supports hybrid scenarios where physical actions influence digital simulations.

Within Industry 5.0, immersive technologies help create inclusive environments where knowledge is accessible regardless of geographic or physical limitations. Through intuitive interfaces and gamified learning, these tools simplify complex tasks and democratize technical skills. Growing affordability of hardware is expected to accelerate adoption across sectors.

2.4 Digital Twins & Metaverse in Business Context

Digital twins and the metaverse are among the most impactful technologies shaping Industry 5.0 business transformation. A digital twin is a continuously updated virtual model of a physical asset or system. It supports monitoring, simulation, and predictive decision-making (Juárez-Varón & Juárez-Varón, 2024). The metaverse is a persistent virtual environment where users interact with digital representations, assets, and collaborative spaces. These technologies increasingly converge to create integrated digital ecosystems. (Mourtzis, 2023a) notes that their integration enables stakeholders to visualize complex systems, test scenarios, and collaborate in ways that were previously impossible. For example, a manufacturing firm can place digital twins of machines inside a metaverse space to enable collaborative maintenance planning, remote inspection, or customer demonstrations (Rahaman et al., 2025).

This convergence drives new business models built around hybrid offerings. Companies can sell access to virtual simulations, co-design environments, or immersive service platforms. Products are no longer limited to physical form but extend into digital versions that can be monetized separately. The metaverse also supports global collaboration among designers, engineers, and customers, reducing development time and increasing innovation speed. Integration also promotes sustainability by allowing companies to test processes virtually before physical implementation. This reduces waste, improves safety, and supports more responsible production strategies.

2.5 Supporting Technologies (AI, IoT, Blockchain, 5G)

The successful deployment of digital twins and metaverse environments depends on foundational enabling technologies. Artificial intelligence processes data from sensors and simulations to support predictions and automated decision-making. IoT networks connect physical devices and generate real-time data that keeps digital twins accurate and relevant. Blockchain enhances security, transparency, and data traceability. It helps manage digital asset ownership, secure transactions in the metaverse, and verify supply chain processes. For industrial applications, blockchain can confirm supplier credentials or authenticate data flow across distributed systems.

5G connectivity is essential for real-time immersive experiences. It supports low-latency communication required for synchronized digital twin operations and interactive metaverse environments. Without high-speed networks, immersive platforms cannot reach full functionality. (Bokhtiar Al Zami et al., 2025) emphasize that these technologies together form intelligent industrial networks that support adaptive, user-centered systems. By combining AI, IoT, blockchain, and 5G, organizations can build immersive environments that are secure, fast, and capable of supporting advanced Industry 5.0 business models.

3. THEORETICAL AND CONCEPTUAL FRAMEWORK

3.1 Human-Centric Innovation Model

Industry 5.0 has introduced a paradigm shift in the way innovation is conceptualized, moving away from the notion that technology should replace humans. Instead, it embraces a collaborative model where technology acts as an enabler and partner in augmenting human creativity, intuition, and productivity. This perspective is known as the human-centric innovation model. In this approach, human beings remain the core of the innovation process, while technologies such as digital twins, the metaverse, and extended reality tools serve as catalysts that enhance decision-making capabilities, foster collaboration, and open new dimensions of value creation. The principle of human-centricity in Industry 5.0 promotes industrial systems that not only prioritize efficiency but also emphasize human values through improved workplace safety, emotional engagement in product design, and the integration of human creative intelligence, as technology acts as a cognitive partner that balances the analytical power of automated systems with the ethical reasoning and intuitive judgment of human beings (Bucci et al., 2025).

This model provides a conceptual foundation for transforming how businesses design customer experiences, develop products, and formulate new business models. Mourtzis (2023) asserts that human-centric innovation in the context of Industry 5.0 is not merely about technology adoption but involves the thoughtful integration of human perspectives into digital design ecosystems. In this sense, the success of technologies like digital twins or the metaverse is not only measured by their technical performance, but also by the extent to which they enable human aspirations, creativity, and well-being (Mourtzis, 2023b). The shift towards a human-centered approach compels organizations to reassess traditional innovation frameworks. Unlike previous industrial revolutions where innovation was defined by mechanical or digital efficiency, Industry 5.0 brings a socio-technological orientation. This means that empathy, inclusion, and participatory design are now critical parameters in shaping innovation processes. Human-centric innovation also leads to deeper stakeholder involvement, inviting employees, end-users, and communities to co-develop solutions that address real needs, rather than top-down impositions dictated solely by business goals or technological possibilities. In summary, the human-centric innovation model forms the backbone of Industry 5.0. It fosters a more ethical, inclusive, and responsive form of progress that fully acknowledges the irreplaceable role of human judgment, emotion, and creativity in building sustainable and resilient industrial futures.

3.2 Value Creation Logic with Immersive Technologies

Immersive technologies are redefining how value is created in the digital economy. Whereas traditional business logic often equated value with cost-efficiency or production scale, Industry 5.0 introduces a more nuanced understanding of value, which is centered on user experience quality, personalization levels, and participatory engagement. Technologies such as digital twins, the metaverse, virtual reality (VR), augmented reality (AR), and mixed reality (MR) are enabling companies to develop new interaction models with customers, suppliers, and business partners. These immersive environments facilitate the emergence of "value co-creation spaces," in which users actively participate in product development through virtual prototyping and interactive simulations, thereby enhancing customer engagement, accelerating innovation cycles, and reducing time-to-market (Martínez-Gutiérrez et al., 2024).

The logic of value creation is further transformed by how immersive technologies reframe the notion of assets. No longer confined to physical goods, assets now include digital representations and virtual experiences that can be monetized. A manufacturing firm, for example, may sell a "virtual twin" of a product for use in training or operational simulations, generating entirely new revenue streams that transcend physical sales. Digital twins and the metaverse offer pathways to building more inclusive and sustainable business ecosystems, as they enable continuous interaction, integration, and adaptability among diverse stakeholders. Within such ecosystems, value is not solely derived from transactional exchanges but is instead generated through ongoing, dynamic interactions among all participants in the value network, including customers, developers, designers, and even AI agents (De Giovanni, 2023).

Immersive technologies also allow companies to offer hybrid value propositions that combine physical and digital benefits. A furniture company might sell a physical chair while simultaneously offering a digital twin of that chair in a metaverse showroom, where customers can interact with it before purchase, request modifications, or explore contextual environments. Such capabilities were previously unimaginable in traditional commerce and are now redefining customer expectations and market standards.

Moreover, immersive tech empowers companies to better capture intangible forms of value, such as user satisfaction, emotional resonance, and learning outcomes. This shift is especially relevant for service-based industries, where experiences, rather than physical objects, serve as the primary products. For example, an immersive museum experience using VR and digital storytelling can generate both educational value and monetizable content streams, enriching the institution's outreach and sustainability. Ultimately, immersive technologies foster a dynamic and relational approach to value creation. They allow businesses to engage users not just as consumers, but as co-creators, collaborators, and contributors to continuous innovation processes. In the Industry 5.0 era, this participatory logic marks a critical departure from the unidirectional value chains of the past.

3.3 Integration Framework: Digital Twins, Metaverse & Business Model Innovation

To fully realize the potential of digital twins and the metaverse in driving business model innovation, a cohesive integration framework is essential. This framework must harmonize strategic business needs, technological capabilities, and the complexities of human-machine interactions. Without such a guiding structure, the implementation of immersive technologies risks becoming fragmented, inefficient, or misaligned with organizational goals. An industrial metaverse framework has been proposed as a comprehensive conceptual model designed to integrate digital twin infrastructures with immersive virtual environments. In this framework, digital twins operate as the data-rich foundation by providing real-time, high-fidelity representations of physical assets and operational systems. These representations are then embedded within metaverse platforms, which serve as interactive, visually engaging spaces that allow users to intuitively explore, analyze, and manipulate data for enhanced decision-making, operational insight, and strategic planning (Fernandez-Carames & Fraga-Lamas, 2024).

This dual structure allows organizations to bridge the physical and digital realms, enabling seamless transitions between simulation and execution. For instance, a logistics company can visualize its fleet and delivery routes in the metaverse using real-time data from digital twins. Managers can simulate various scenarios, such as traffic delays or route changes, and immediately assess the implications of their decisions, without disrupting real-world operations. The integration of digital and physical systems is reinforced by enabling technologies such as artificial intelligence, blockchain, the Internet of Things (IoT), and 5G connectivity. Collectively, these components contribute to the development of a responsive and interconnected system that can support complex and data-intensive business models. Specifically, artificial intelligence enhances the predictive capabilities of digital twins, blockchain ensures data provenance and traceability, IoT facilitates real-time data collection, and 5G delivers the bandwidth required for immersive and low-latency user experiences (Bokhtiar Al Zami et al., 2025).

An illustrative application of this integrated framework is the "Metaverse as a Service" (MaaS) strategy, in which companies move beyond using immersive tools solely for internal purposes and begin to commercialize their metaverse environments and digital twin platforms as value-added services. For instance, a factory that has developed a digital twin of its production line may grant simulation access to external partners for collaborative process improvement, employee training, or product integration testing (Mourtzis, 2023a) Such approaches signify a new class of platform-based business models where organizations monetize not only physical products but also digital assets, data flows, and virtual services. This evolution challenges traditional business boundaries and opens the door to cross-industry convergence. A company in automotive manufacturing may find itself operating in education, gaming, or healthcare via its immersive infrastructure.

Furthermore, the integration framework ensures that immersive technologies align with broader corporate strategies. It encourages organizations to move from reactive adoption toward proactive innovation. Rather than implementing VR or digital twins in isolated departments, companies embed them into cross-functional workflows, ensuring that marketing, design, operations, and customer service all benefit from shared data and immersive interactions. In addition, this framework accommodates feedback loops and adaptive learning. Data collected from user behavior in the metaverse can inform product updates, service refinements, and future innovation cycles. These insights are then fed back into the digital twin system, creating a continuous loop of improvement based on real-time user engagement. By connecting immersive technologies with business strategy and operational execution, the integration framework supports scalable innovation. It enables organizations to design not just better products or services, but more adaptive, responsive, and resilient business models for the Industry 5.0 era.

Figure 2. shows the integration framework linking Digital Twins, the Metaverse, and Business Model Innovation in the Industry 5.0 era.

Figure 2. Integration framework linking Digital Twins, the Metaverse, and Business Model Innovation in the Industry 5.0 era.

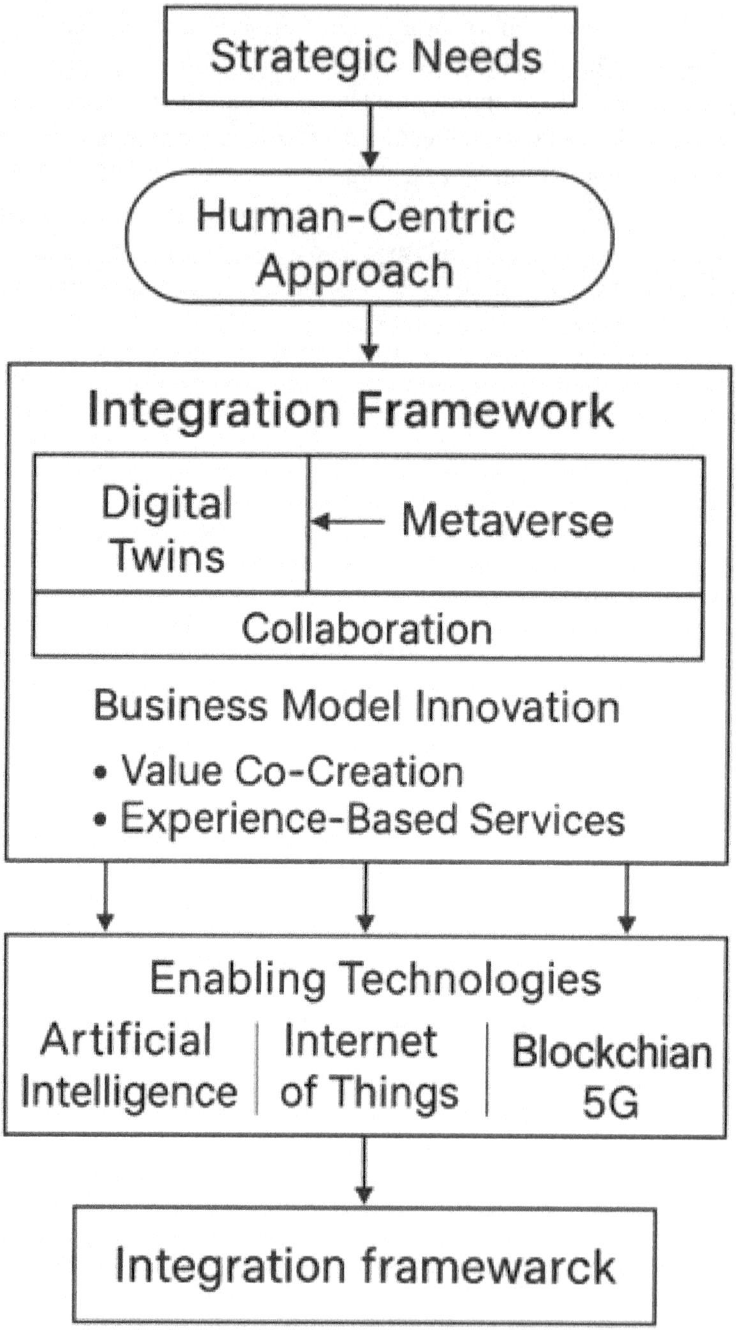

4. METHODOLOGY

4.1 Research Design

The research design for this study is founded on the interdisciplinary nature of Industry 5.0, which brings together technology, human values, and new business paradigms. This study adopts a qualitative dominant mixed-methods approach that combines conceptual synthesis from the academic literature with illustrative case insights. This approach provides enough flexibility to capture not only the technical aspects of digital twin and metaverse integration but also the strategic and human-centered considerations that underpin business model innovation. The design process begins with a systematic literature review of scholarly works published between 2020 and 2025. The choice of this time frame reflects the fact that Industry 5.0 is a relatively new concept and that research on digital twins and metaverse applications for business innovation has only gained significant momentum in the past five years. By focusing on open-access journals indexed in Scopus and IEEE, this study ensures that the sources used are both academically rigorous and broadly accessible for verification. This decision is crucial for maintaining transparency and enabling scholars, policymakers, and practitioners to review and apply the same resources.

The research design also reflects an exploratory orientation. Rather than testing a narrow hypothesis, it aims to map out the conceptual and practical terrain of business model innovation through immersive technologies. (Fernandez-Carames & Fraga-Lamas, 2024) describe the industrial metaverse as an evolving idea still lacking a fully mature theoretical framework, which justifies the use of exploratory research to develop an initial conceptual structure. Another important feature of the research design is its human-centric perspective. Industry 5.0 distinguishes itself from Industry 4.0 by placing humans back at the core of innovation. This study reflects that by not only cataloging technologies but by examining how these technologies can enhance creativity, decision-making, and ethical outcomes. Any methodological framework for Industry 5.0 must evaluate whether innovation genuinely supports human engagement and societal well-being (Bucci et al., 2025). This design is also iterative. Insights from the literature review inform the selection of cases, and case observations help refine the conceptual framework. This cyclical process ensures that the findings are not static but can evolve as new data emerges. It also means the framework can be adapted by other researchers who may wish to expand it with different cases or data in the future.

4.2 Analytical Tools

A combination of analytical tools is used to structure and interpret the findings of this study. The first layer of analysis applies bibliometric techniques to map out the research landscape. Databases like Scopus and IEEE Xplore are scanned for publications that link Industry 5.0, immersive technologies, and business model innovation. Keywords are analyzed to reveal networks of concepts and identify where clusters of research are forming. This helps clarify which areas of the field are most studied and which remain underexplored, as bibliometric mapping has proven to be a powerful method for uncovering the "hidden structure" of emerging research domains (Martínez-Gutiérrez et al., 2024).

After building a landscape view, the study uses thematic coding to examine the literature in greater depth. Themes such as "human-centric innovation," "value co-creation," and "digital-physical integration" are identified and used as lenses to interpret findings. Thematic coding also allows for the identification of recurring business model archetypes that rely on digital twin and metaverse infrastructure. In addition, the study applies comparative case analysis to connect conceptual insights with practical examples. This involves reviewing open-access descriptions of how companies have used digital twin simulations or virtual metaverse spaces in areas like advanced manufacturing, logistics, and healthcare. Cases are compared to identify similarities and differences in adoption strategies, technological choices, and resulting business model shifts.

The final layer of this methodological process is the framework analysis, which serves as the integrative stage where themes derived from the literature review and insights from sectoral case studies are woven together into a coherent conceptual model. This stage does not merely compile findings but actively interprets and connects them, identifying the mechanisms through which immersive technologies particularly digital twins and metaverse ecosystems interact with evolving business model components under the guiding philosophy of Industry 5.0. Building on the ideas articulated by Bokhtiar Al Zami et al. (2025), the framework expands their conceptualization of technological convergence by embedding a more human-centric orientation, illustrating how enabling technologies like AI, IoT, and mixed reality become interdependent drivers of value creation. In parallel, the synthesis refines the foundational perspectives outlined by Mourtzis (2023), adapting his emphasis on human-technology collaboration into a broader framework that situates immersive technologies as structural pillars rather than peripheral tools. Together, these contributions are merged into a single, layered model that maps the reciprocal relationship between technological enablers, organizational strategy, and socio-industrial objectives, offering a lens through which academics, policymakers, and industry leaders can evaluate and reimagine business model innovation in the Industry 5.0 era.

These analytical tools are chosen because they complement each other. Bibliometrics offers breadth, thematic coding adds depth, case analysis grounds the findings, and framework analysis brings it all together into a structured representation that can inform both academic theory and practical decision-making.

4.3 Data Sources & Selection Criteria

The research draws primarily on peer-reviewed, open-access journal articles indexed in Scopus and IEEE, ensuring both rigor and accessibility. Journals such as Sustainability, Applied Sciences, IEEE Access, and Frontiers in Manufacturing Technology were prioritized because they regularly publish studies on Industry 5.0, digital twins, immersive technologies, and the metaverse. The time frame of 2020 to 2025 was selected deliberately. Research on digital twins and metaverse technologies relevant to Industry 5.0 has accelerated sharply in this period, and older studies often do not reflect the current state of the field. Limiting the scope to recent literature ensures that this study captures contemporary insights and frameworks.

Articles were included if they directly linked immersive technologies with business model innovation or Industry 5.0 concepts. Studies focused purely on technical engineering details, such as hardware specifications or isolated algorithm development, were excluded unless they explicitly related those technical components to broader strategic or organizational issues. In addition to academic papers, the study incorporated secondary open-access resources such as white papers, public reports, and policy briefs when they added meaningful context. These materials are used to illustrate how governments, research consortia, and industry bodies are beginning to frame policy or investment strategies around immersive technologies and Industry 5.0 themes.

The selection also ensured diversity of perspective. Literature from different regions and industries was included to avoid an overly narrow view of Industry 5.0. For instance, studies from Asia detail smart city and infrastructure applications, while European research tends to focus on manufacturing and sustainability. (De Giovanni, 2023). highlights sustainability as a critical element in metaverse-driven business models, adding another important dimension to the data used in this study. By carefully curating data sources and applying strict inclusion criteria, the study builds a foundation that is not only academically credible but also transparent and replicable. This makes it easier for policymakers, industry professionals, and emerging researchers to trace the study's logic and build on its findings for their own work.

5. IMMERSIVE TECHNOLOGIES IN PRACTICE: CASE STUDIES

5.1 Retail Sector

Retail has been one of the earliest and most dynamic sectors to embrace immersive technologies in the transition to Industry 5.0. Companies are experimenting with digital twins and metaverse platforms to reimagine how customers interact with products, stores, and even brands themselves. Rather than limiting the retail experience to a physical space or a flat digital catalog, immersive retail environments allow consumers to engage with lifelike product simulations, customize items, and interact with digital avatars that provide advice and support.

Recent developments in virtual showrooms illustrate this shift vividly. Retail firms are increasingly adopting metaverse-enabled platforms to create interactive spaces where customers can "try" products virtually before purchase. For example, a customer shopping for furniture can place a virtual sofa in a digital twin of their own living room, ensuring the item fits both dimensionally and aesthetically. This is not merely a novelty, as the approach helps address return rates, reduce logistics costs, and promote more sustainable retail practices by minimizing unnecessary shipping (Prabadevi et al., 2023).

Digital twins also offer behind-the-scenes innovation in retail supply chains. By creating real-time digital representations of stores and warehouses, retailers can monitor inventory, forecast demand, and optimize delivery routes. When integrated with blockchain-enabled traceability, these systems may contribute to the emergence of transparent and interactive retail ecosystems, where customers are able to scan a product in the metaverse and view its complete journey from factory to shelf (Hassoun et al., 2024).

Some retailers are even building "persistent metaverse storefronts." These are not temporary marketing campaigns but permanent virtual stores where avatars of sales staff interact with customers in real time. Such immersive experiences are gaining traction among younger consumers who see online spaces as natural social environments. These metaverse stores can also experiment with AI-driven personalization, tailoring store layouts and recommendations to each customer's profile. The implications for business model innovation are profound. Traditional retail margins have been squeezed for decades by e-commerce disruption. Immersive technologies are not just another sales channel; they represent a reconstruction of value propositions. Retailers move from being sellers of products to creators of experiences, blending entertainment, community, and commerce into a single platform.

5.2 Healthcare

The healthcare sector illustrates how immersive technologies can move beyond convenience and into the realm of saving lives. Digital twins of patients, organs, and hospital systems are reshaping clinical decision-making, training, and patient engagement. The concept of a "healthcare metaverse" envisions a digital ecosystem where virtual clinics, patient avatars, and medical device twins converge to enhance diagnostic accuracy and treatment planning. For instance, a surgeon preparing for a complex cardiac operation may move beyond traditional 2D scans and instead explore a highly detailed 3D twin of the patient's heart within a metaverse simulation. This environment allows the procedure to be rehearsed using robotic instruments, ultimately increasing surgical precision and patient safety (Fernandez-Carames & Fraga-Lamas, 2024).

Hospitals are also adopting immersive simulations to improve staff training, particularly in areas requiring rapid decision-making and technical precision. Digital twins, when combined with virtual and mixed reality platforms, are increasingly used to support occupational health and safety programs in manufacturing. These same principles are now being applied in healthcare contexts to enhance emergency response protocols and develop advanced surgical skills (Zahid et al., 2025).

There is also a patient-facing dimension. Chronic disease management programs are experimenting with metaverse spaces where patients can "meet" digital avatars of clinicians, join group therapy sessions, or explore gamified wellness activities. These initiatives improve adherence to treatment plans and reduce barriers to care for people who may struggle to travel to clinics. Healthcare's adoption of immersive technologies, however, raises unique questions about ethics, privacy, and regulatory oversight. Digital twins of patients store sensitive biometric data, while metaverse-based health platforms continuously collect behavioral information. It is therefore essential that healthcare's digital transformation is steered by Industry 5.0's human-centric ethos to ensure these innovations empower rather than exploit patients (De Giovanni, 2023).

5.3 Education

Education is rapidly becoming one of the most visible testbeds for immersive technologies, particularly as the world adapts to hybrid and online learning models. The metaverse offers educators an opportunity to transcend the physical boundaries of traditional classrooms, while digital twins create entirely new possibilities for experiential and collaborative learning. (Mourtzis & Angelopoulos, 2023) describe the development of an "Operator 5.0" training platform for engineering students, which uses extended reality to teach concepts that would otherwise require expensive laboratory setups. Through this platform, students are able to assemble virtual components, experiment with industrial machinery, and even simulate troubleshooting for production lines before ever stepping into a physical lab.

(Supriya et al., 2024) expand on this perspective by presenting a study on smart education in Industry 5.0, showing how digital twins of classrooms and laboratories enable real-time collaboration between students located in different countries. Instead of merely watching a video demonstration of a chemical experiment, students can manipulate variables within a digital twin of the experiment and observe immediate reactions, closely mimicking the dynamics of a real-world laboratory setting. Beyond STEM subjects, immersive education platforms are being deployed for language learning, the arts, and even history. Virtual heritage metaverse spaces now allow students to walk through ancient cities or interact with historical figures recreated through AI-driven avatars, offering an experiential dimension that enhances engagement, strengthens memory retention, and fosters empathy.

From a business standpoint, these technologies are altering the very models of education delivery. Universities can create "meta-campuses," attracting international students who might never visit the physical campus, while private training providers are increasingly monetizing immersive modules for professional upskilling. This democratization of access expands opportunities for learners but also brings challenges related to quality assurance, accreditation, and governance in an increasingly hybrid educational ecosystem.

5.4 Manufacturing

Manufacturing is arguably the sector most closely associated with Industry 5.0, and immersive technologies are accelerating a shift from traditional automation toward a more human-centered production philosophy. Digital twins are already widely deployed to model factory equipment, and their integration with metaverse environments is opening new levels of collaboration. Workers equipped with mixed reality headsets can interact with a digital twin of a production line while standing on the actual factory floor, accessing overlaid data, instructions, and safety alerts in real time.

(Zahid et al., 2025) demonstrate how immersive and predictive technologies are reshaping occupational health and safety practices in manufacturing. Their research illustrates how, before new machinery is installed, workers can train on its digital twin to practice emergency shut-down procedures and identify potential hazards before handling the real equipment. (Zahid et al., 2025) further explains that the industrial metaverse is enabling manufacturers to establish virtual spaces where engineers, suppliers, and customers collaboratively design products. This shift represents a significant departure from traditional models, as companies are no longer simply designing products internally and pushing them to the market; instead, they are inviting stakeholders into shared immersive environments where designs evolve collectively.

Manufacturing's adoption of immersive technologies also aligns closely with sustainability goals. By testing production processes virtually through digital twins, companies can minimize waste, optimize energy consumption, and prevent costly errors. This not only enhances operational efficiency but also reinforces the position of manufacturers as leaders in responsible and ethical innovation, which is a defining principle of Industry 5.0.

6. CHALLENGES AND BARRIERS

6.1 Technical Challenges

The implementation of immersive technologies in the context of Industry 5.0 is burdened by substantial technical hurdles that impact scalability and reliability. Many organizations experimenting with digital twins or metaverse solutions encounter complex interoperability issues because platforms are built on fragmented standards, which makes integration between systems difficult (Bokhtiar Al Zami et al., 2025). This lack of unified frameworks leads to duplicated efforts in system architecture, additional costs, and operational inefficiencies. The infrastructure requirements for immersive technologies are also formidable. Real-time synchronization of digital twins with physical assets requires high-bandwidth networks and robust cloud or edge computing infrastructure. (Mourtzis, 2024) notes that even organizations with advanced automation often struggle to maintain the ultra-low latency needed for metaverse-based operations and predictive digital twin applications. These performance demands are amplified in large-scale manufacturing or logistics networks where milliseconds of delay can cascade into production disruptions.

Cybersecurity is another persistent obstacle. Digital twins generate and store highly sensitive operational data, and the metaverse collects behavioral information from users, making these ecosystems prime targets for cyberattacks (Tallat et al., 2024). A single breach can undermine trust and compromise entire industrial ecosystems. The need for quantum-resistant encryption and advanced access management systems is pressing, yet widespread adoption of these measures remains slow. There are also significant technical skill gaps. (Zahid et al., 2025) emphasize that operating immersive systems demands a workforce familiar with AR/VR hardware, simulation software, and AI-driven analytics, skills that are scarce even in technologically advanced industries. Without a strong pipeline of trained professionals, the risk of implementation failure or partial adoption increases. Finally, scalability remains a critical barrier. Digital twin systems deployed in pilot projects often work in controlled environments, but when scaled across multinational operations, they face data synchronization bottlenecks, hardware constraints, and platform incompatibilities (Fernández-Caramés & Fraga-Lamas, 2024). This gap between proof-of-concept and production-level deployment continues to slow down the transformative impact of immersive technologies.

6.2 Ethical and Legal Issues

Beyond technical difficulties, the adoption of immersive technologies raises deep ethical and legal questions. The metaverse and digital twins operate by collecting and processing vast amounts of personal and organizational data, which creates new vulnerabilities. De Giovanni (2023) argues that these systems must be designed with explicit safeguards for privacy and user autonomy, otherwise they risk exacerbating digital inequality and eroding trust.

The issue of data ownership is particularly contentious. Digital twins of industrial assets, supply chains, or even human bodies raise the question of who ultimately controls the data they generate (Butt et al., 2025). When multiple stakeholders are involved such as technology providers, manufacturers, and regulators conflicts can emerge regarding access, usage rights, and intellectual property. There is also a growing recognition of the psychological and cultural impacts of immersive systems. (Zahid et al., 2025) point out that extended exposure to virtual environments may blur the lines between digital and physical reality for workers and consumers, raising concerns about mental health and informed consent. Organizations are beginning to explore "digital wellness" policies, but there is no standardized framework for addressing these emerging issues.

Legal frameworks are lagging behind technological innovation. Existing regulations were designed for traditional IT systems, not for environments where avatars conduct transactions or where a digital twin of a patient could influence real-world medical decisions (Hassoun et al., 2024). The result is a patchwork of national and regional rules that complicates cross-border collaboration and stifles innovation. Finally, ethical design principles are not yet consistently applied across immersive technologies. (Fernandez-Carames & Fraga-Lamas, 2024) warn that without proactive governance, the very human-centric vision of Industry 5.0 could be undermined, turning these technologies into tools of exploitation rather than empowerment.

6.3 Organizational Resistance & Adoption Gaps

While the technical and ethical dimensions are substantial, the barriers inside organizations themselves can be just as obstructive. Many companies remain hesitant to embrace immersive technologies because they are perceived as expensive experiments rather than strategic necessities (Agrawal & Wankhede, 2025). This hesitation is particularly strong among small and medium-sized enterprises, which often lack the capital to invest in digital twins or the metaverse without clear evidence of short-term returns. Leadership attitudes play a significant role in shaping adoption. (Zahid et al., 2025) highlight that companies led by executives skeptical of emerging technologies tend to underfund or deprioritize immersive initiatives, leaving them stuck in pilot stages indefinitely. This kind of cultural inertia slows innovation even when the technology itself is proven viable.

Organizational structures also create friction. The integration of immersive technologies cuts across multiple departments, from IT to operations to marketing, and legacy silos make cross-functional collaboration difficult (Rawat et al., 2024). Without a governance model that clearly defines roles and responsibilities, adoption efforts can devolve into turf battles and fragmented execution.

Another barrier is workforce resistance. Employees who are asked to train or work in metaverse environments may feel anxious about surveillance, performance monitoring, or even replacement by automation. (De Giovanni, 2023) stresses that if workers see immersive technologies as threats rather than tools for augmentation, their resistance can derail adoption, no matter how technically sound the implementation. Finally, the lack of shared best practices compounds all of these issues. (Mourtzis, 2024) observes that while there are scattered success stories of immersive technology integration, there is no universally accepted playbook for scaling these solutions across industries. This absence of clear guidance leaves many organizations in a holding pattern, aware of the potential but unsure of how to move forward effectively.

7. STRATEGIC OPPORTUNITIES AND SOLUTIONS

7.1 Business Model Transformation Strategies

Industry 5.0 is pushing organizations to rethink how they create, deliver, and capture value, and immersive technologies are at the center of this transformation. Companies that once approached digital twins, virtual reality, and metaverse platforms as isolated pilots are now redesigning their business models around these technologies. (Bokhtiar Al Zami et al., 2025), explain that digital twins, when integrated with IoT networks and machine learning, are enabling a shift from transactional product sales to service-driven models that provide continuous monitoring, maintenance, and updates.

This shift is visible in the rise of "as-a-service" models across multiple sectors. Manufacturers that once sold industrial equipment are beginning to offer equipment-as-a-service, where customers pay for outcomes like uptime or efficiency rather than ownership. (Mourtzis, 2023b) observes that immersive tools like metaverse-enabled training environments and predictive digital twins allow companies to maintain long-term engagement with clients by delivering ongoing optimization and personalized support. The integration of immersive platforms is also giving rise to the concept of co-creation. Instead of designing products internally and then presenting them to the market, businesses are inviting suppliers, partners, and customers into shared virtual spaces where prototypes are visualized and tested in real time. (Fernandez-Carames & Fraga-Lamas, 2024) emphasize that this co-creation approach can reduce development cycles and align product design more closely with evolving customer needs.

Hyper-personalization is another strategic shift enabled by immersive systems. Businesses can leverage digital twin data to create dynamic virtual experiences tailored to the individual preferences of each client. (De Giovanni, 2023) highlights that this kind of adaptive personalization not only transforms marketing but also changes the logic of value creation itself, turning customer interaction into a continuously evolving exchange rather than a static transaction.

Immersive tools also support resilience and sustainability within business models. By modeling supply chains and production processes digitally, companies can simulate disruptions, test contingency plans, and identify waste reduction strategies before making real-world changes. (Butt et al., 2025) argue that this ability to rehearse different operational scenarios in a safe digital environment gives firms a competitive edge by reducing risk and accelerating innovation. These changes demand that companies evolve their organizational structures to support new value logics. Traditional hierarchies built for linear product cycles are being replaced by more fluid, networked configurations that allow information to flow between engineering, operations, and customer-facing teams. (Zahid et al., 2025) note that immersive environments encourage cross-functional collaboration because teams can work together in shared virtual spaces regardless of geographic location.

There is also a clear trend toward integrating immersive platforms into customer relationship management. Digital twins connected to metaverse spaces are making it possible for businesses to maintain interactive "living relationships" with their clients, where feedback loops are constant and product updates are experienced in real time. Tallat et al. (2024) suggest that this type of model deepens loyalty and improves retention by making customers active participants in the evolution of the products they use. Finally, immersive technologies are reshaping the economics of experimentation. Ideas that would once have required costly prototyping or full-scale testing can now be trialed virtually with minimal expense. (Fernandez-Carames & Fraga-Lamas, 2024) argue that this not only saves resources but fundamentally changes the strategic posture of companies, making them more agile and willing to innovate because the cost of failure is drastically reduced.

7.2 Policy Recommendations for Industry & Government

As transformative as immersive technologies are, they do not develop in a vacuum, and their success is deeply linked to regulatory and policy ecosystems. Policymakers must create an environment where digital twins, metaverse platforms, and related immersive systems can thrive without compromising ethical or legal standards. (Zahid et al., 2025) emphasize that regulatory clarity around data ownership, privacy, and intellectual property is essential to prevent disputes and build trust among stakeholders.

Infrastructure investment is another crucial area for policy action. The performance of immersive technologies relies on high-bandwidth connectivity, low-latency networks, and secure cloud and edge computing capabilities. (Fernandez-Carames & Fraga-Lamas, 2024) explain that governments can accelerate adoption by co-investing in these infrastructures, often through public-private partnerships that spread costs and benefits across industries.

Workforce development policies are equally important. The transition to Industry 5.0 requires a workforce capable of designing and maintaining immersive systems, yet current education pipelines are insufficient. (Mourtzis, 2023b) recommends integrating immersive technology training into both university curricula and vocational programs to ensure a steady supply of skilled professionals who can operate and innovate with digital twins, VR, and metaverse platforms.

Ethical considerations must also be embedded in policy frameworks. The immersive nature of these technologies raises concerns about surveillance, manipulation, and unequal access. De Giovanni (2023) proposes that governments establish certification systems that verify whether immersive solutions meet human-centric design criteria, including transparency, inclusivity, and safety for users.

Policy frameworks should also address interoperability and standardization. Without shared technical standards, immersive systems risk remaining fragmented, slowing adoption and creating security gaps. Butt et al. (2025b) argue that international coordination is necessary to develop frameworks that ensure digital twins and metaverse platforms can communicate across borders and industries.

Incentives for innovation are another area where policy can play a transformative role. Governments can stimulate R&D by offering tax benefits, innovation grants, or regulatory sandboxes that allow companies to experiment with immersive technologies in controlled environments without excessive legal exposure. Bokhtiar Al

Zami et al. (2025b) suggest that such incentives not only lower barriers for startups and SMEs but also signal a governmental commitment to supporting the evolution of Industry 5.0.

Finally, governments and industry bodies should actively facilitate dialogue between stakeholders. Fernandez-Carames and Fraga-Lamas (2024) argue that immersive technologies blur traditional boundaries between sectors, so regular forums that bring together policymakers, academics, and industry leaders are essential to aligning strategies and avoiding conflicting agendas.

7.3 Future Directions for Research & Development

The potential of immersive technologies in Industry 5.0 will only be realized through sustained, forward-looking research and development efforts. Future research must explore the deeper integration of digital twins and the metaverse with other transformative technologies, including quantum computing, bio-digital interfaces, and next-generation connectivity systems. (Tallat et al., 2024) note that these convergences could unlock simulation and collaboration capabilities far beyond what is currently possible.

A key research priority is building scalable and secure architectures. Many of today's immersive deployments are small-scale pilots, and scaling them to multinational operations creates challenges related to latency, data synchronization, and cybersecurity. (Fernandez-Carames & Fraga-Lamas, 2024) argue that open-source frameworks and shared protocols will be critical for transforming these pilots into robust, interoperable ecosystems.

The economic and societal impacts of immersive business models also warrant deeper investigation. As meta-marketplaces and digital twin-driven service subscriptions evolve, they will reshape patterns of trade, employment, and competition. (De Giovanni, 2023) suggests that interdisciplinary studies are needed to understand these shifts and ensure that immersive innovation strengthens, rather than destabilizes, economic systems.

Sustainability is emerging as an important research theme as well. Digital twins are already used for efficiency and waste reduction, but future research could embed environmental metrics directly into simulations, allowing organizations to design products and processes that meet sustainability goals from inception. (Mourtzis, 2023a) points out that integrating life-cycle assessments into digital twins could help industries measure the carbon and resource impacts of design decisions in real time.

Another area for exploration is the human factor in immersive systems. While much of the current literature focuses on technical performance, the long-term success of Industry 5.0 hinges on whether immersive tools enhance human creativity and decision-making. (Bokhtiar Al Zami et al., 2025) call for more research into how workers interact with digital twins and metaverse platforms, and how these interactions affect cognition, collaboration, and workplace culture.

The governance of immersive technologies is also an emerging field for study. (Zahid et al., 2025) note that as digital twins and metaverse applications become more embedded in critical infrastructure, issues of accountability, liability, and oversight will become increasingly complex. Research into governance frameworks can help ensure that immersive technologies evolve with proper checks and balances.

Finally, there is significant opportunity for R&D in the development of tools that make immersive systems more accessible. (Fernandez-Carames & Fraga-Lamas, 2024) emphasize that current hardware and software solutions are often too costly or complex for smaller organizations. Research that focuses on low-cost, user-friendly immersive tools could democratize access and expand the benefits of Industry 5.0 beyond major corporations to include small businesses, educational institutions, and public services.

8. CONCLUSION AND IMPLICATIONS

The evolution from Industry 4.0 to Industry 5.0 signals not just a continuation of technological development but a rethinking of industrial paradigms, wherein businesses are no longer driven solely by automation, data, and machine intelligence. Industry 5.0 calls for a reintegration of human creativity, ethical responsibility, and collaborative intelligence into the heart of digital transformation processes. Rather than displacing human agency, the latest wave of innovation envisions technology as a medium that supports human-led creativity, enhancing decision-making and unlocking new ways of delivering value across sectors.

The findings from this study indicate that immersive technologies serve dual purposes in this new landscape. On one hand, they support operational optimization through simulation, remote monitoring, and real-time feedback. On the other hand, they enable entirely new configurations of interaction and value co-creation, expanding the scope of business models beyond conventional product and service delivery. By linking the real and digital worlds, digital twins act as continuously updating reflections of physical assets, while the metaverse creates environments where stakeholders can interact and innovate collaboratively. The fusion of these technologies makes it possible to imagine business models that were not previously feasible in practice, allowing rapid prototyping, user-involved design processes, and cross-border collaboration without physical constraints (Fernandez-Carames & Fraga-Lamas, 2024).

These immersive systems are changing how companies conceptualize the very architecture of their business models. Static, linear models are increasingly being replaced by dynamic ecosystems that rely on constant interaction between producers and consumers. Users now take an active role in shaping products and services through feedback loops built into immersive platforms. This participatory approach enhances both innovation outcomes and brand loyalty while allowing firms to personalize offerings at scale. Businesses are also becoming more resilient by structuring themselves around adaptive networks instead of rigid hierarchies, aligning their operations with rapid market shifts and user expectations (De Giovanni, 2023).

Nonetheless, transitioning toward immersive innovation is far from seamless. A number of persistent challenges hinder wide-scale adoption and scalability. From a technical standpoint, lack of interoperability between platforms, inconsistencies in data governance standards, and the need for robust infrastructure such as high-speed connectivity continue to create bottlenecks. Ethical and legal issues surrounding user privacy, consent, and digital ownership add further complexity to the operationalization of immersive systems. For small and medium-sized businesses, limited access to technical expertise and digital infrastructure compounds the risk of exclusion from Industry 5.0 advancements (Zahid et al., 2025).

Despite these challenges, immersive technologies offer significant transformative potential if integrated with a strategic and inclusive mindset. When coupled with supportive frameworks such as edge computing, 5G networks, AI-driven analytics, and decentralized systems like blockchain, immersive platforms become part of a broader intelligent infrastructure. This integrated environment supports automated learning systems, real-time interaction, and distributed trust, all of which are crucial for creating and maintaining robust digital business ecosystems. Through careful orchestration of these technologies, organizations can transition from siloed operations to continuous, connected innovation ecosystems that generate new value and social impact (Bokhtiar Al Zami et al., 2025a).

For the academic and research communities, the emergence of immersive business models presents an opportunity to deepen interdisciplinary inquiry. Researchers can examine how human-centered design principles intersect with technology adoption patterns, or how immersive systems reshape organizational behavior, economic dynamics, and value chain configurations. There is also a growing demand for empirical models that measure the effectiveness of digital twin and metaverse-based strategies. Moreover, ethical considerations must be integrated into research design to ensure that the deployment of immersive technology enhances equity, inclusion, and transparency in innovation practices (Supriya et al., 2024).

Policymakers, meanwhile, have a critical role to play in steering the trajectory of immersive business model development. Regulations must not only protect digital rights but also promote interoperability, accessibility, and openness in virtual platforms. Policies that incentivize open innovation, fund digital infrastructure, and build digital literacy at all societal levels can significantly reduce the barriers to entry and foster inclusive participation in immersive economies. The success of Industry 5.0 depends in part on governments' willingness to see technology not merely as an engine of economic growth but as a tool for collective progress and well-being (Mourtzis, 2023).

For practitioners in the technology and industrial sectors, the effective adoption of immersive tools requires more than just technical readiness. It demands cultural adaptability, forward-thinking leadership, and the ability to integrate human-centric design across business operations. Organizations must build cross-functional teams that understand both technological intricacies and user experience design. They must also invest in infrastructure that supports real-time data flow, immersive visualization, and collaborative decision-making environments. The strategic use of digital twins and the metaverse becomes not an isolated innovation project, but a foundational element of enterprise-wide transformation that redefines competitiveness and relevance in the marketplace (Martínez-Gutiérrez et al., 2024).

In summation, immersive technologies represent a turning point in the evolution of digital business. Their capacity to bridge physical and virtual domains, support participatory innovation, and facilitate ethical digital transformation makes them not just tools but strategic levers of change in the Industry 5.0 era. The ability of organizations to harness these capabilities will determine how successfully they navigate a future where value is co-created, knowledge is distributed, and innovation is rooted in both technological advancement and human values. The challenge, and opportunity, lies in aligning technological potential with societal purpose to build business models that are inclusive, adaptive, and resilient by design (Bucci et al., 2025).

REFERENCES

Abdellatif, G., Alexandre, P., Fouad, B. A., & Christophe, J. (2025, June). Knowledge Management in the metaverse for sustainable supply chains. In IAMOT 2025.

Agrawal, R., & Wankhede, V. A. (2025). Breaking the virtual wall: Analysing barriers to metaverse adoption in manufacturing industries. *The International Journal of Organizational Analysis*. Advance online publication. DOI: 10.1108/IJOA-07-2024-4676

Asad, U., Khan, M., Khalid, A., & Lughmani, W. A. (2023). Human-Centric Digital Twins in Industry: A Comprehensive Review of Enabling Technologies and Implementation Strategies. In Sensors (Vol. 23, Issue 8). MDPI. https://doi.org/DOI: 10.3390/s23083938

Bokhtiar Al Zami, M., Shaon, S., Khanh Quy, V., & Nguyen, D. C. (2025a). Digital Twin in Industries: A Comprehensive Survey. *IEEE Access : Practical Innovations, Open Solutions*, *13*, 47291–47336. DOI: 10.1109/ACCESS.2025.3551532

Bokhtiar Al Zami, M., Shaon, S., Khanh Quy, V., & Nguyen, D. C. (2025b). Digital Twin in Industries: A Comprehensive Survey. *IEEE Access : Practical Innovations, Open Solutions*, *13*, 47291–47336. DOI: 10.1109/ACCESS.2025.3551532

Boopathy, P., Deepa, N., Maddikunta, P. K. R., Victor, N., Gadekallu, T. R., Yenduri, G., Wang, W., Pham, Q.-V., Huynh-The, T., & Liyanage, M. (2025). The Metaverse for Industry 5.0 in NextG Communications: Potential Applications and Future Challenges. *IEEE Open Journal of the Computer Society*, *6*, 4–24. DOI: 10.1109/OJCS.2024.3497335

Boopathy, P., Deepa, N., Maddikunta, P. K. R., Victor, N., Gadekallu, T. R., Yenduri, G., Wang, W., Pham, Q.-V., Huynh-The, T., & Liyanage, M. (2025). The Metaverse for Industry 5.0 in NextG Communications: Potential Applications and Future Challenges. *IEEE Open Journal of the Computer Society*, *6*, 4–24. DOI: 10.1109/OJCS.2024.3497335

Bucci, I., Fani, V., & Bandinelli, R. (2025). Towards Human-Centric Manufacturing: Exploring the Role of Human Digital Twins in Industry 5.0. In Sustainability (Switzerland) (Vol. 17, Issue 1). Multidisciplinary Digital Publishing Institute (MDPI). https://doi.org/DOI: 10.3390/su17010129

Butt, A. S., Alghababsheh, M., & Awan, U. (2025a). Barriers to the adoption of the Metaverse in digital supply chains. *Journal of Enterprise Information Management*. Advance online publication. DOI: 10.1108/JEIM-09-2024-0500

Butt, A. S., Alghababsheh, M., & Awan, U. (2025b). Barriers to the adoption of the Metaverse in digital supply chains. *Journal of Enterprise Information Management*. Advance online publication. DOI: 10.1108/JEIM-09-2024-0500

De Giovanni, P. (2023). Sustainability of the Metaverse: A Transition to Industry 5.0. *Sustainability (Switzerland)*, *15*(7). Advance online publication. DOI: 10.3390/su15076079

Fernandez-Carames, T. M., & Fraga-Lamas, P. (2024). Forging the Industrial Metaverse for Industry 5.0: Where Extended Reality, IIoT, Opportunistic Edge Computing, and Digital Twins Meet. *IEEE Access : Practical Innovations, Open Solutions*, *12*, 95778–95819. DOI: 10.1109/ACCESS.2024.3422109

Gupta, B. B., Gaurav, A., Arya, V., & Alhalabi, W. (2024). Data science in sustainable entrepreneurship: A multidisciplinary field of applications. *Technological Forecasting and Social Change*, *209*, 123798. DOI: 10.1016/j.techfore.2024.123798

Hassoun, A., Jagtap, S., Trollman, H., Garcia-Garcia, G., Duong, L. N. K., Saxena, P., Bouzembrak, Y., Treiblmaier, H., Para-López, C., Carmona-Torres, C., Dev, K., Mhlanga, D., & Aït-Kaddour, A. (2024a). From Food Industry 4.0 to Food Industry 5.0: Identifying technological enablers and potential future applications in the food sector. In Comprehensive Reviews in Food Science and Food Safety (Vol. 23, Issue 6). John Wiley and Sons Inc. https://doi.org/DOI: 10.1111/1541-4337.70040

Hassoun, A., Jagtap, S., Trollman, H., Garcia-Garcia, G., Duong, L. N. K., Saxena, P., Bouzembrak, Y., Treiblmaier, H., Para-López, C., Carmona-Torres, C., Dev, K., Mhlanga, D., & Aït-Kaddour, A. (2024b). From Food Industry 4.0 to Food Industry 5.0: Identifying technological enablers and potential future applications in the food sector. In Comprehensive Reviews in Food Science and Food Safety (Vol. 23, Issue 6). John Wiley and Sons Inc. https://doi.org/DOI: 10.1111/1541-4337.70040

Juárez-Varón, D., & Juárez-Varón, M. Á. (2024). SEO vs. UX in Web Design: Are Companies' Digital Marketing Strategies Correct? A Neurotechnological Study. [IJSSCI]. *International Journal of Software Science and Computational Intelligence*, *16*(1), 1–26. DOI: 10.4018/IJSSCI.342127

Martínez-Gutiérrez, A., Díez-González, J., Perez, H., & Araújo, M. (2024). Towards industry 5.0 through metaverse. *Robotics and Computer-integrated Manufacturing*, *89*, 102764. https://doi.org/https://doi.org/10.1016/j.rcim.2024.102764

Moslehpour, M., Dwikesumasari, P. R., Pappachan, P., Lin, P.-K., Sakina, N., & Rahaman, M. (2024). Incorporating Web Semantics, the Technology Acceptance Model, and the Theory of Planned Behavior for Analyzing User Intentions on Dating Apps. [IJSWIS]. *International Journal on Semantic Web and Information Systems, 20*(1), 1–20. DOI: 10.4018/IJSWIS.356388

Mourtzis, D. (2023a). Digital twin inception in the Era of industrial metaverse. *Frontiers in Manufacturing Technology, 3*. Advance online publication. DOI: 10.3389/fmtec.2023.1155735

Mourtzis, D. (2023b). The Metaverse in Industry 5.0: A Human-Centric Approach towards Personalized Value Creation. *Encyclopedia, 3*(3), 1105–1120. DOI: 10.3390/encyclopedia3030080

Mourtzis, D. (2024). 15 - Outlook, trends, and future directions toward Industry 5.0. In Mourtzis, D. (Ed.), *Manufacturing from Industry 4.0 to Industry 5.0* (pp. 465–492). Elsevier., https://doi.org/https://doi.org/10.1016/B978-0-443-13924-6.00015-6

Mourtzis, D., & Angelopoulos, J. (2023). Development of an Extended Reality-Based Collaborative Platform for Engineering Education: Operator 5.0. *Electronics (Switzerland), 12*(17). Advance online publication. DOI: 10.3390/electronics12173663

Osello, A., Manera, U., Rimella, N., Bin, C., Vasta, R., Masala, E., Shields, J. A. E., Tarantola, G., & Chiò, A. (2024). A Metaverse Between Technical and Humanistic Domains to Reach Society 5.0. *2024 IEEE International Humanitarian Technologies Conference (IHTC)*, 1–6. https://doi.org/DOI: 10.1109/IHTC61819.2024.10855137

Panda, D. K., Panigrahi, P. K., Attar, R. W., & Gupta, B. B. (2024). Open Source Adoption for Digital Transformation and Data Management During the COVID-19 Crisis. [JDM]. *Journal of Database Management, 35*(1), 1–26. DOI: 10.4018/JDM.360708

Phattanaviroj, T., Moslehpour, M., Pappachan, P., Cajes, N. C., Gupta, B. B., & Rahaman, M. (2026). A novel predictive framework for green transportation and EV policy towards sustainable mobility and emission reduction. *Green Technologies and Sustainability, 4*(1), 100260. DOI: 10.1016/j.grets.2025.100260

Prabadevi, B., Deepa, N., Victor, N., Reddy Gadekallu, T., Kumar, P., Maddikunta, R., Yenduri, G., Wang, W., Pham, V., Huynh-The, T., Liyanage, M., & Huynh, T. (2023). Metaverse for Industry 5.0 in NextG Communications: Potential Applications and Future Challenges.

Rahaman, M., Chappu, B., Jana, S., Haque, A., Firmansyah, G., & Chattopadhyay, S. (2025). Security Benefits in Small Medium Business Enterprise Through Cloud Adoption. In N. Nedjah, G. Martinez Perez, & B. B. Gupta (Eds.), *International Conference on Smart Systems and Advanced Computing (SysCom 2022)* (pp. 168–180). Springer Nature Switzerland. https://doi.org/DOI: 10.1007/978-3-031-40905-9_18

Rawat, D. B. alami, H. El, & Hagos, D. H. (2024). Metaverse Survey & Tutorial: Exploring Key Requirements, Technologies, Standards, Applications, Challenges, and Perspectives. https://arxiv.org/abs/2405.04718

Rudek, M., Valle, A. P. R., & Bertolin, R. (2025). Building Realistic Environment from Computer Vision Approach Applied to Manufacturing Simulation in the Digital Twin Context. In Dassisti, M., Madani, K., & Panetto, H. (Eds.), *Innovative Intelligent Industrial Production and Logistics* (pp. 223–235). Springer Nature Switzerland.

Sekti, B. A. (2025). Machine learning and artificial intelligence (AI) in manufacturing. In *Integrating Digital Innovation and Integrated Frameworks in Manufacturing* (pp. 255–292). https://doi.org/DOI: 10.4018/979-8-3373-1082-4.ch011

Sekti, B. A. (2025). Machine learning and artificial intelligence (AI) in manufacturing. In Integrating Digital Innovation and Integrated Frameworks in Manufacturing (pp. 255–292). https://doi.org/DOI: 10.4018/979-8-3373-1082-4.ch011

Singh, S. K., Gupta, S., Kumar, S., Gupta, B. B., Alhalabi, W., Arya, V., & Zhang, J. (2024). A novel Cumulative Indicator score using Indicator averaging for optimizing local business websites of enterprise systems. *Enterprise Information Systems*, *18*(2), 2301658. DOI: 10.1080/17517575.2023.2301658

Supriya, Y., Bhulakshmi, D., Bhattacharya, S., Gadekallu, T. R., Vyas, P., Kaluri, R., Sumathy, S., Koppu, S., Brown, D. J., & Mahmud, M. (2024). Industry 5.0 in Smart Education: Concepts, Applications, Challenges, Opportunities, and Future Directions. *IEEE Access : Practical Innovations, Open Solutions*, *12*, 81938–81967. DOI: 10.1109/ACCESS.2024.3401473

Tallat, R., Hawbani, A., Wang, X., Al-Dubai, A., Zhao, L., Liu, Z., Min, G., Zomaya, A. Y., & Alsamhi, S. H. (2024a). Navigating Industry 5.0: A Survey of Key Enabling Technologies, Trends, Challenges, and Opportunities. *IEEE Communications Surveys and Tutorials*, *26*(2), 1080–1126. DOI: 10.1109/COMST.2023.3329472

Tallat, R., Hawbani, A., Wang, X., Al-Dubai, A., Zhao, L., Liu, Z., Min, G., Zomaya, A. Y., & Alsamhi, S. H. (2024b). Navigating Industry 5.0: A Survey of Key Enabling Technologies, Trends, Challenges, and Opportunities. *IEEE Communications Surveys and Tutorials*, *26*(2), 1080–1126. DOI: 10.1109/COMST.2023.3329472

Zahid, A., Ferraro, A., Petrillo, A., & De Felice, F. (2025). Exploring the Role of Digital Twin and Industrial Metaverse Technologies in Enhancing Occupational Health and Safety in Manufacturing. *Applied Sciences (Basel, Switzerland)*, *15*(15), 8268. DOI: 10.3390/app15158268

Zahid, A., Ferraro, A., Petrillo, A., & De Felice, F. (2025). Exploring the Role of Digital Twin and Industrial Metaverse Technologies in Enhancing Occupational Health and Safety in Manufacturing. *Applied Sciences (Basel, Switzerland)*, *15*(15), 8268. DOI: 10.3390/app15158268

Zhou, F., Zhang, N., Li, X., Han, C., & Gupta, B. B. (2025). Managing inter-organizational dependencies operation for discovering digital business model innovation in corporate innovation ecosystem. *Operations Management Research*, *18*(2), 574–590.

KEY TERMS AND DEFINITIONS

Business Model Innovation: Transformations in how companies create, deliver, and capture value through digital technologies and user participation.

Co-Creation Platforms: Collaborative platforms that enable customers and other stakeholders to participate in the development of products and services.

Digital Twin (DT): A digital replica of a physical object or process used for simulation, prediction, and real-time decision-making.

Enabling Technologies: Supporting technologies such as AI, IoT, blockchain, and 5G that enable the integration of digital twins and the metaverse.

Human-Centric Innovation: An innovation approach that centers on human values, integrating intuition, creativity, and ethics into technological processes.

Hybrid Value Proposition: A business offering that combines physical products with digital assets such as simulations or metaverse access.

Immersive Technologies: Technologies such as VR, AR, and MR that enable interactive and realistic user experiences in industrial contexts.

Industry 5.0: A new industrial paradigm focused on human-machine collaboration, sustainability, and a human-centric approach.

Integration Framework: A conceptual structure that aligns business strategy, technological capabilities, and human-machine interaction in a unified system.

Metaverse: A collaborative virtual environment where stakeholders interact, co-design products, and access services immersively.

Chapter 4
Exploring the Success Factors of Customer Experience in Retail: A Thematic Analysis

Shweta Kaur Khalsa
http://orcid.org/0000-0002-4742-6450
Dayananda Sagar University, India

Jitendranath Patri
http://orcid.org/0009-0006-3132-7323
Dayananda Sagar University, India

ABSTRACT

The Retail industry is facing a transformation driven by digitalization, customer expectations and heightened post-pandemic consciousness revolving around value, ethics and experience. Consumer experience (CX) has been widely researched, but there is limited empirical research which showcases the practitioner perspective on CX success factors in emerging markets like India. This study addresses this gap and adopts a qualitative Braun and Clarke's thematic analysis approach. This approach is based on in-depth interviews (n=15) with professionals from diverse retail backgrounds. The findings of this research reveal four interrelated drivers of CX i.e. excellence, personalization and customer engagement along with technology integration and sustainability. These factors collectively shape consumer trust, loyalty and lead to long term business growth. The novelty of this study lies in integrating practitioner insights into a comprehensive conceptual model which reflects post COVID shifts in omnichannel behavior.

DOI: 10.4018/979-8-3373-4541-3.ch004

INTRODUCTION

The retail industry and its unprecedented transformation over the past decade has resulted in Customer experience (CX) to emerge as a critical determinant of competitive advantage. It has also impacted how they interact across multiple touch-points (Lemon & Verhoef, 2016; Grewal et al., 2017).Consumers have heightened expectations of tailoring offerings to their preferences, behaviours and context (Klaus, 2013).On the other hand, consumer engagement which is manifested through prominence, foster long term relationships beyond transactional exchanges (Verhoef et al., 2015).This rapid technology adoption has enabled retailers to deliver integrated and responsive experiences at scale (Pantano & Vannucci, 2019).The pandemic fuelled these shifts and compelled retailers to reimagining customer journeys through digital first interactions and contactless services along with hyper -personalized engagement models (Sheth, 2020).

Research Gap

Despite of extensive academic research on CX or customer experience, published studies adopt a consumer-centric or quantitative approach. Also, they are in developed markets and there is a lack of empirical research which captures senior practitioner perspectives on CX success factors withing the Indian system. The combined influence of personalization, engagement, sustainability, and emerging digital technologies has not been sufficiently examined through an integrative qualitative lens.

Objectives of the Study

This study aims to:

1. Identify the key success factors influencing customer experience in the Indian retail sector.
2. Examine how personalization, customer engagement, technology, and sustainability shape CX outcomes.
3. Develop a practitioner-informed conceptual model linking CX drivers with strategic business outcomes.

Organization of the Paper

The paper is organized as -the theoretical background underpinning the study, followed by the research methodology and respondent profile. Subsequent sections present the thematic analysis and findings, leading to the development and justification of the conceptual model. The paper concludes with key implications, limitations, and directions for future research.

Problem Statement

The retail industry faces increasing challenges in delivering exceptional customer experiences due to evolving consumer expectations, technological advancements, and market competition. Moreover, the Metaverse marks a crucial step in integrating emotional engagement into user experiences (Saini, M et al 2025).While retailers recognize the importance of personalization, loyalty, technology, and sustainability, there is a lack of in-depth understanding of how these factors influence customer engagement and long-term success (Grewal et al., 2017). Traditional business models that fail to integrate digital transformation and omnichannel strategies struggle to maintain customer satisfaction and brand loyalty (Verhoef et al., 2015).Furthermore, the COVID-19 pandemic has accelerated shifts in consumer behaviour, necessitating rapid adoption of new engagement strategies, such as digital-first interactions and seamless omnichannel experiences (Sheth, 2020). The findings will provide valuable recommendations for retailers to refine their strategies and stay competitive in the ever-evolving retail landscape. Figure 1. shows the shift in customer preference Pre and Post-Covid.

Figure 1. Evolution of the customer journey pre- and post-COVID-19, highlighting shifts from in-store to digital touchpoints.

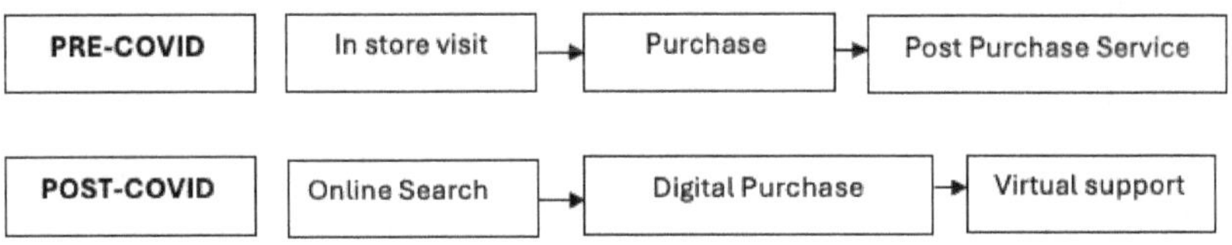

Figure 1. Evolution of the customer journey pre- and post-COVID-19, highlighting shifts from in-store to digital touchpoints.

THEORETICAL BACKGROUND

Many ideas help to understand customer experience in retail. One key idea is the Service-Dominant (S-D) Logic, which focuses on how value is created together by businesses and customers (Vargo & Lusch, 2004). This view shows that customer experience comes from interactions and engagement rather than just buying and selling. S-D Logic highlights that personal touch and custom services boost customer satisfaction and loyalty. Another key theory is the Customer Experience Management (CEM) framework, which stresses the need for businesses to carefully plan and improve all the interactions customers have throughout their journey (Meyer & Schwager, 2007). This model claims that a smooth and enjoyable customer experience can lead to stronger brand loyalty and positive referrals, which in turn supports business growth. The Technology Acceptance Model (TAM) is also relevant for understanding customer experience, especially with digital changes (Davis, 1989). TAM explains how customers' views on usefulness and ease of use affect their acceptance of tech-based services, like online shopping, digital payments, and AI recommendations. Retailers that deliver easy and friendly digital experiences often see better customer engagement and satisfaction. Additionally, the Theory of Planned Behaviour (TPB) offers insights into how customers make decisions (Ajzen, 1991).

Outcomes

The results of this study will give important information about what makes customer experience successful in India's retail sector. By looking at qualitative data from industry experts, the study will show how personalization, loyalty, technology, and sustainability affect how customers engage (Grewal et al., 2017; Verhoef et al., 2015).One expected result is finding best practices for using omnichannel strategies that make it easy for customers to switch between online and in-store shopping (Meyer & Schwager, 2007). The study will also highlight how digital changes improve customer interactions, with a focus on AI-based recommendations, automated customer service, and using data for decision-making (Davis, 1989; Pantano & Vannucci, 2019).Another key outcome will be understanding how sustainability efforts affect customer choices and brand loyalty (Wiese et al., 2012).Moreover, the research will offer practical advice for retailers on improving customer loyalty programs and using new technologies to enhance service quality (Sheth, 2020).

RESEARCH METHODOLOGY

Data analysis followed Braun and Clarke's (2006, 2019) reflexive thematic analysis approach. The process began with familiarization through repeated reading of interview transcripts, followed by open coding. It uses exploratory methods to analyse at semi-structured interviews with senior professionals in the Indian retail sector. The participants were senior executives, decision-makers, and customer experience strategists from major retail companies, all with a lot of experience in handling customer engagement strategies. The main benefit of semi-structured interviews is they provide detailed insights into actual retail situations, giving superior quality data than structured surveys or questionnaires (Boyce & Neale, 2006).Qualitative thematic analysis gives a better understanding of customer experience by concentrating on stories and expert views instead of just numbers, which is typical in quantitative research (Draper, 2004). This method offers flexibility in analysing different aspects of customer engagement and supports the creation of a broad framework that can help inform future retail plans (Simunaniemi & Muhos, 2017). The findings from this study will assist retailers in improving their strategies and adjusting to changing consumer demands in the retail world which is approaching towards Industry 6.0.

Interview Design and Data Collection

Participants were selected using a purposive sampling approach. The selection criteria included senior managerial or leadership roles, a minimum of ten years of industry experience, and direct involvement in customer engagement or experience-related decision-making within the Indian retail sector.

Data were collected through semi-structured interviews. This allowed flexibility to explore emerging insights while maintaining consistency across interviews. An interview guide was developed based on a review of existing literature on customer experience, personalization, engagement, technology, and sustainability. The interviews typically lasted between 45 and 75 minutes and were conducted via virtual platforms. All interviews were recorded with participant consent and subsequently transcribed using AI tool Turboscribe for further analysis.

The interview questions were open-ended and exploratory in nature. Sample questions included:

- How do you define customer experience within your organization?
- In what ways does personalization influence customer engagement and loyalty?
- How has technology transformed customer interactions and omnichannel strategies in your organization?
- What role does sustainability play in shaping customer trust and brand relevance?

Respondent Profile

Table 1 represents the profile of interview participants, highlighting their seniority, functional expertise, sectoral representation, and professional experience, thereby ensuring the credibility and relevance of the qualitative sample.

Table 1. Respondent Profile

Participant Code	Position Level	Functional Role	Retail Sector	Years of Experience
P1	Senior Management	Customer Experience Head	Apparel Retail	18
P2	Senior Management	Marketing Director	E-commerce	20
P3	Senior Management	Digital Transformation Lead	Omni-channel Retail	15
P4	Senior Management	Retail Operations Head	Department Stores	22
P5	Senior Management	CRM & Loyalty Manager	Specialty Retail	14
P6	Senior Management	Brand & Customer Engagement Lead	FMCG Retail	19
P7	Senior Management	Strategy & CX Consultant	Multi-format Retail	25
P8	Senior Management	E-commerce Operations Head	Online Retail	16
P9	Senior Management	Merchandising & Buying Head	Apparel Retail	21
P10	Senior Management	Digital Marketing Lead	Lifestyle Retail	13
P11	Senior Management	Sustainability & CSR Lead	Organized Retail	17
P12	Senior Management	Omnichannel Experience Manager	Consumer Electronics Retail	14
P13	Senior Management	Loyalty & Retention Specialist	Specialty Retail	12
P14	Senior Management	Retail Innovation Lead	Fashion Retail	18
P15	Senior Management	CX & Analytics Head	Large-format Retail	23

Theme Identification

Following the thematic analysis of the interview transcripts, key patterns and recurring meanings were identified across the dataset. These patterns were systematically grouped into higher-order themes and sub-themes based on conceptual similarity and relevance to customer experience in retail. The themes were refined through iterative review to ensure internal coherence and clear distinction between categories.

Table 2 presents representative interview excerpts aligned with the key constructs of the proposed conceptual model. These excerpts illustrate how the model components are grounded in participant narratives and empirical evidence.

Table 2. Illustrative Interview Quotes Supporting Conceptual Model Constructs

Conceptual Construct	Sub-Theme (from analysis)	Representative Quote
Personalization	Tailored Interactions	"Customers want experiences that feel personal and relevant to them."
Customer Engagement	Omnichannel Interaction	"Everything now has to be omnichannel; customers move seamlessly across platforms."
Customer Engagement	Relationship Orientation	"Retail today is about building relationships, not just selling products."
Technology (Enabler)	Digital Integration	"Technology helps us deliver a consistent and smooth customer experience."
Sustainability (Value Driver)	Ethical Alignment	"Customers increasingly choose brands that align with their values and beliefs."
Customer Experience Outcome	Loyalty & Trust	"When customers trust the brand, they keep coming back."

ANALYSIS AND FINDINGS

The analysis and discussion in this research paper are based on themes found in interview transcripts (Excerpts of interviews listed in Table 2. Illustrative Interview Quotes Supporting Conceptual Model Constructs). The relationships among these constructs are further synthesized and represented in the conceptual model presented in Figure 3 Conceptual model: Factors of customer experience success. Thematic analysis is a way to find, summarize, analyze, and document themes from qualitative research (Muposhi et al., 2015). This method is seen as strong for qualitative studies because it enables a thorough look at the data, making sure all important themes are considered (Muposhi et al., 2015).From the thematic analysis of the interview data, four main themes appeared: personalization, customer engagement, customer experience and technology. These themes are key to understanding customer experiences in retail and how they affect consumer engagement. Figure 1 shows a model that represents the identified themes and sub-themes. Each theme listed in Table 2 is backed by relevant literature and direct quotes from the interviews to give a better view of how they shape customer experience.

To further synthesize the themes identified through the qualitative analysis and to illustrate the relationships among the key constructs, a thematic map was developed. This visual representation integrates the primary themes and their associated sub-themes, highlighting how they collectively contribute to customer experience (CX) success in the Indian retail context.

Figure 2. Thematic map illustrating key factors influencing customer experience (CX) success in the Indian retail sector.

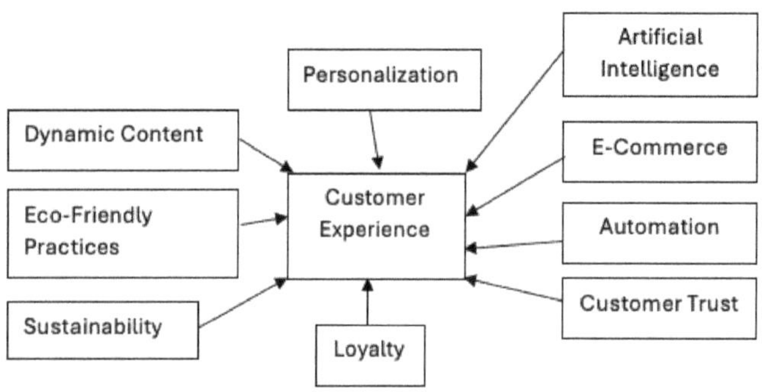

Figure 2:Thematic map illustrating key factors influencing customer experience (CX) success in the Indian retail sector.*(Author's own compilation)*

(Author's own compilation)

As shown in Figure 2, personalization, customer engagement, technology, and sustainability emerge as interconnected drivers of customer experience rather than isolated factors. The thematic map underscores the centrality of customer experience, shaped by the dynamic interaction of these themes across the retail customer journey. This visualization provides a foundation for the subsequent discussion and supports the development of the proposed conceptual model.

To consolidate the key concepts emerging from the thematic analysis and to highlight their relevance to customer experience outcomes, a set of core keywords was identified. These keywords reflect the dominant constructs discussed by participants and form the conceptual building blocks for the subsequent model development.

Table 3. Key Themes, Sub-Themes, and CX Implications

Main Theme	Sub-Themes	Key Insight from Interviews	CX Implication
Personalization	CRM, Buying Journey, Loyalty	Tailored interactions increase relevance	Higher engagement & satisfaction
Customer Engagement	Omnichannel, Communities, Purpose	Emotional connection drives advocacy	Long-term loyalty
Technology	AI/ML, Data, Automation	Enables seamless experiences	Convenience & trust
Sustainability	Ethics, Eco-friendly practices	Influences brand alignment	Relevance & trust

The keywords: Core Constructs Informing the Conceptual Model outlined in Table 4 informed the structuring of the conceptual model in Figure 3 by clarifying the core drivers, enablers, and outcomes of customer experience identified in the study.

1. Personalization and Customer Engagement

Personalization is an important factor for customer experience, with retailers using data to customize their offerings (Lemon & Verhoef, 2016). Although there is an increasing demand for robust security in the rapidly expanding metaverse (D.Rajput et al 2024),interview participants noted that personalization improves customer satisfaction by providing relevant product suggestions, targeted promotions, and customized interactions.

One participant stated:

"Customers want personalized experiences everywhere. Brands that do not provide tailored services may lose customer engagement."

This supports earlier research showing that personalization builds better customer relationships and boosts conversion rates (Verhoef, Kannan, & Inman, 2015). Customers showcase deeper emotional a, cognitive and behavioural engagement when brand interact with them timely, and personally cater to individual needs (Kumar et al., 2021; Tyrväinen et al., 2020).Participants emphasized AI driven personalization creates consistency and continuity while reinforcing engagement beyond isolated numerical transactions (Lemon & Verhoef, 2016; Pantano et al., 2017).However, the findings also highlight that personalization merely is insignificant if not embedded with broader eco system which has - loyalty programs, brand communities, feedback loops, and purpose-driven interactions. This aligns with prior research authors who suggest that engagement emerges through repeated meaningful interactions rather than single encounters (Brodie et al., 2011; Pansari & Kumar, 2017).Customers who undergo personalized experiences are more inclined to participate in brand communities, advocate for the brand, and maintain long-term relationships (Muniz & O'Guinn, 2001; Hollebeek et al., 2019).

2. Loyalty and Retention Strategies

Customer loyalty programs are important for building long-term customer relationships. Participants noted that exclusive offers, rewards, and member benefits greatly affect customer retention. One respondent said:

"Loyalty programs have changed from simple point systems to experiences that make customers feel special."

Literature backs up that well-designed loyalty programs strengthen brand loyalty and encourage repeat purchases (Grewal, Roggeveen, & Nordfält, 2017). Engagement strategies like gamification and experiential rewards are gaining popularity among retailers (Klaus, 2013).

3. Technological Integration and Omnichannel Experience

Technology has changed retail, making seamless omnichannel experiences necessary. Interview participants pointed out the role of artificial intelligence (AI), augmented reality (AR), and digital payment systems in improving customer convenience. One executive mentioned:

"Retailers who use technology well can create a smooth experience, allowing customers to move easily between online and offline channels."

This agrees with findings by Pantano and Vannucci (2019), who state that technology use improves efficiency and customer satisfaction. The COVID-19 pandemic sped up the need for digital change, as retailers moved to contactless transactions and online interaction (Sheth, 2020).

4. Sustainability and Ethical Consumerism

Sustainability is now a key part of retail, affecting consumer choices and buying habits. Some interviewees stressed that customers are looking for brands that reflect ethical and environmental values. One respondent noted:

"Sustainability is not optional anymore—it's crucial for customer choices. Brands that overlook it will have a hard time staying relevant."

Research indicates that sustainability practices, like eco-friendly packaging, ethical sourcing, and reducing carbon footprints, help build brand loyalty and competitive edge. (Wiese et al 2012).

Sustainability-related insights extend S-D Logic. It emphasizes value co-creation grounded in shared ethical and societal values between retailers and customers.

The findings also complement customer experience theory. By demonstrating how sustainability contributes to trust, emotional alignment, and long-term brand relationships, thereby influencing customer engagement beyond functional considerations (Meyer & Schwager, 2007).

Table 4. Keywords: Core Constructs Informing the Conceptual Model

Themes/mention of keywords extracted from the podcast conversations & summarization												
Respondent / CXO / podcast Episode	Customer Engagement			Customer Experience	Personalization				Technology			
	Engagement	Purpose	Product, Merchandise	Customer Experience	Personalization	Loyalty	Communities	CRM	Data	AI / ML / Automation	Transformation	E-commerce / online
Zubair Patel	2	0	6	2	1	1	1	3	4	0	3	5
Ankur Bhatia	3	0	2	2	1	1	1	2	3	0	2	4
Dilpreet Singh	5	0	0	8	8	9	7	12	8	2	6	1
Aparna Thyagarajan	2	0	2	3	2	2	1	1	2	0	4	6
Shivanee Dutt	1	0	1	1	1	0	1	1	1	0	1	3
Arjun Vaidya	2	0	0	1	1	1	0	0	0	0	1	4
Dharmendra Mehta	3	0	2	6	3	4	4	4	5	0	2	6
Sanjeev Rao	2	3	3	3	3	2	1	1	2	0	5	4
Nissan Joseph	2	2	0	1	0	0	0	1	0	0	3	1
Vivek Bali	0	0	2	3	1	1	1	0	0	0	0	1
Kaizad Hansotia	1	0	0	5	4	3	3	3	3	0	5	8
Jaydeep Shetty	1	0	1	3	2	2	2	2	2	0	3	3

continued on following page

Table 4. Continued

Respondent / CXO / podcast Episode	Themes/mention of keywords extracted from the podcast conversations & summarization											
	Customer Engagement			Customer Experience	Personalization				Technology			
	Engagement	Purpose	Product, Merchandise	Customer Experience	Personalization	Loyalty	Communities	CRM	Data	AI / ML / Automation	Transformation	E-commerce / online
B S Nagesh	1	2	0	2	2	7	5	5	4	1	2	2
Kishore Dharmarajan	1	0	0	2	1	0	0	2	2	3	1	0
Nandini Mehta	0	0	0	1	0	0	0	0	0	0	0	0
TOTAL	26	7	19	43	30	33	27	37	36	6	38	48

Figure 3.Conceptual model: Factors of customer experience success

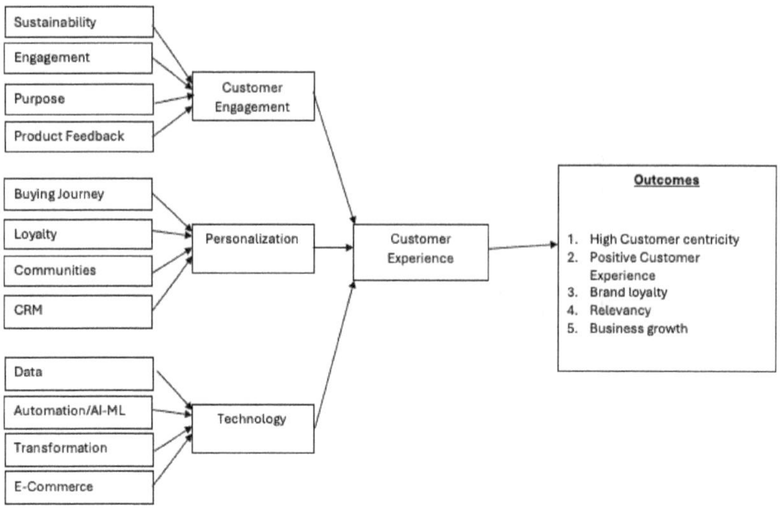

Figure 3.Conceptual model: Factors of customer experience success (Author's own compilation)

(Author's own compilation)

CONCEPTUAL MODEL JUSTIFICATION

The model stated above for this study is grounded in qualitative thematic analysis which is derived from in depth interviews with senior professionals in the Indian Retail industry. The model is an integration of four interrelated and empirically supported themes - Customer Engagement, Personalization, Technology, and Sustainability- and each of theme contribute to the larger construct of Customer experience (CX) success.

- Customer engagement – it is the heart of the model because it embodies emotional and behavioural connection which customers develop with brands (Hollebeek et al., 2019).Customer engagement is the outcome of consistency, meaningful interactions with customers which leads to long term loyalty and brand advocacy (Brodie et al., 2013).The model clearly reflects how sub themes such as purpose, product feedback and multichannel engagement drive the ongoing connection.
- Personalization and CRM as experience drivers – The model states personalization as a strategic enabler of engagement and satisfaction. Retailers who

deliver tailored offerings as per customer preferences and behaviours create long term stronger emotional bonds (Kumar et al., 2021). Sub-themes like communities, CRM, buying journey mapping, and loyalty programs feed into the personalization construct, supporting customer-centric retail design.

- Technology as an enabler of omnichannel and smart retailing – Technology serves as a cross cutting enabler which transforms how customer experience is delivered. Incorporating sub themes such as AI/ML, automation, data analytics and E-Commerce, this model demonstrated how digital tools contribute in enhancing personalization, streamlining engagement and creating friction less experiences across platforms (Pantano et al., 2017; Bughin et al., 2018).
- Sustainability as an emerging value driver – Consumer consciousness has elevated sustainability post pandemic and it is now a critical expectation. As the interviews suggested along with the literature, environmentally and ethically responsible practices are no longer optional and they are in demand by modern consumers (Wiese et al., 2012). Integrating sustainability into the model acknowledges its growing influence on trust, relevance, and emotional brand alignment.
- Outcomes-The model reflects the key outcome as successful customer experience CX strategies - customer centricity, brand loyalty, positive customer experiences, relevance, and business growth (Berry et al., 2002; Rust et al., 2004).This is also supported by practioner insights. These outcomes reinforce the practical significance of each theme and their interconnected influence on business success.
- Theoretical Foundation – The model is supported by frameworks such as service – dominant logic (Vargo & Lusch, 2004).It emphasizes on co creation of value, the customer experience management (CEM) framework (Meyer & Schwager, 2007) along with the technology acceptance model (Davis 1989) which underpins the role of perceived ease and usefulness in adopting new retail technologies. These theories validate the inclusion and interaction of the model's core themes.

Further to justify the structure and relationships within proposed conceptual model, the directional linkages within the construct are rounded in empirical insights from a practitioner interviews. These research findings showcase that personalization operates as a primary antecedent to customer engagement. Tailored interactions improve perceived relevance and emotional connection. This in turn motivates customers to engage actively across touchpoints. Technology is an enabler in infrastructure and amplifies personalization by facilitating real-time responsiveness and data -driven decision making. Sustainability is positioned as a value – based moderator which strengthens customer trust and brand alignment in the post pandemic consumption context. This drives customer experience (CX) and it drives customer centricity, brand loyalty, relevance, and business growth for the brand. The proposed relationships therefore reflect not only established theoretical foundations but also lived managerial realities, reinforcing the model's validity as an integrative and practice-informed framework for understanding CX success in contemporary retail environments. The proposed model thus reflects a close alignment between empirical insights and established theoretical frameworks, ensuring that the relationships depicted are both data-driven and theoretically grounded.

THEMATIC ANALYSIS

Theme 1: Customer Engagement

Customer engagement is about creating interactions that build emotional ties between customers and brands (Hollebeek et al., 2019). Customers who are engaged are more likely to be loyal and promote the brand (Brodie et al., 2013).The key drivers of customer engagement include –

- **Omnichannel Integration:** High-quality integration across channels—such as consistent content, transparent service options, and seamless processes—significantly boosts customer engagement, leading to positive word-of-mouth and increased repurchase intentions(Lee et al., 2019; Sicilia & Palazón, 2023; Salem & Alanadoly, 2023).
- **Digital Platforms:** Digital marketing strategies and interactive platforms (e.g., apps, online communities) enhance engagement, especially where internet and mobile usage are high(M.Mandaliya, 2025; Roy et al., 2023; Bowden & Mirzaei, 2021; Mogili & Natarajan, 2021; Connell et al., 2019).
- **Psychological Factors:** Satisfaction, emotions, self-brand connection, and fulfillment of psychological needs (autonomy, competence, relatedness) are strong antecedents of engagement(An & Han, 2020; Monferrer et al., 2019; Roy et al., 2023; Bowden & Mirzaei, 2021; Roy et al., 2020; Parihar et al., 2019; Kosiba et al., 2018).

Engaged customers are more likely to become loyal, recommend brands, and exhibit positive behaviours such as repeat purchases and brand advocacy(Lee et al., 2019; So et al., 2016; Monferrer et al., 2019; Bowden & Mirzaei, 2021; Parihar et al., 2019; Kosiba et al., 2018; Salem & Alanadoly, 2023).Engagement drives functional, hedonic, and social value for customers, which in turn enhances satisfaction, memorable experiences, and revisit intentions(An & Han, 2020; Roy et al., 2020).

Innovative HR strategies that boost employee engagement also improve customer experiences and satisfaction, creating a virtuous cycle (Afolabi et al., 2023).

The engagement- and loyalty-related findings further reinforce S-D Logic.They highlight the importance of relational exchanges, emotional bonds, and ongoing interaction in creating value over time (Vargo & Lusch, 2004). In line with the CEM framework, the emphasis on omnichannel engagement, loyalty ecosystems, and brand communities reflects the need for managing customer experiences holistically rather than at isolated touchpoints (Meyer & Schwager, 2007).

Table 5. Engagement Strategies

Strategy Type	Examples/Details
Omnichannel Coordination	Consistent messaging, seamless service across channels(Lee et al., 2019; Sicilia & Palazón, 2023; Salem & Alanadoly, 2023)
Digital Content & Communities	Branded content, online brand communities, interactive apps (M.Mandaliya, 2025; Roy et al., 2023; Bowden & Mirzaei, 2021; Mogili & Natarajan, 2021; Connell et al., 2019)
Emotional & Experiential	Creating emotional bonds, memorable experiences, and shared values(An & Han, 2020; Monferrer et al., 2019; Grewal et al., 2017)
Employee-Focused	Training, recognition, positive workplace culture to enhance service(Afolabi et al., 2023)

Engagement drivers and outcomes can vary by product type, channel, and customer involvement level(Lee et al., 2019; Bowden & Mirzaei, 2021; Parihar et al., 2019; Behnam et al., 2021; Connell et al., 2019).Ensuring consistent engagement across all touchpoints and accurately measuring its impact remains complex(Sicilia & Palazón, 2023; Tartaglione & Granata, 2019; Connell et al., 2019).

Sustainability

Sustainability in retail means using eco-friendly and ethical practices to satisfy consumer needs and meet regulations (Grewal et al., 2020). Companies focusing on sustainability can gain better brand reputation and trust from customers (Kotler & Keller, 2019).

Purpose

A brand's purpose aligns with its core beliefs and social duties (Sinek, 2009). Brands driven by purpose connect better with consumers, creating stronger relationships (Kotler et al., 2019).

Product Feedback

Product quality and innovation are critical for attracting and keeping customers (Zeithaml, 1988). Differentiating with unique offerings improves competitive standing (Porter, 1985).

Engagement

Customer engagement includes interactions that build meaningful relationships and strengthen brand ties (Brodie et al., 2011). Engaged customers support long-term business success and promotion (Pansari & Kumar, 2017).

Theme 2: Personalization

Personalization in retail comes from using data to customize experiences to match individual customer preferences (Tam & Ho, 2020). Marketing strategies that are personalized boost customer satisfaction and sales (Kumar et al., 2021).There are various types of personalization which include the following -

- **Technology-Enabled Personalization (TEP):** Utilizes smart technologies, AI, and real-time data to deliver individualized experiences in both online and brick-and-mortar settings. This includes personalized promotions, recommendations, and dynamic pricing (Riegger et al., 2021; Saksena, 2024; Jagabathula et al., 2022; Chandra et al., 2022; Kaushik & Sharma, 2023).
- **Human-Enabled Personalization:** Involves direct staff-customer interactions, focusing on building personal relationships and service quality(Scholdra et al., 2023; Peteva, 2023; Mittal & Lassar, 1996).
- **Omnichannel Personalization:** Integrates personalization across all customer touchpoints, ensuring a seamless experience whether online or offline(Tyrväinen et al., 2020; Peteva, 2023; Wetzlinger et al., 2017; Chandra et al., 2022).

Personalization enhances both cognitive and emotional aspects of customer experience, leading to increased satisfaction, loyalty, and engagement(Tyrväinen et al., 2020; Chhabria et al., 2023; Lambillotte et al., 2022; Bilyk et al., 2024; Mittal & Lassar, 1996).Hyper-personalization, powered by AI and data science, improves customer engagement, operational efficiency, and drives business growth(Saksena, 2024; Jagabathula et al., 2022; Chandra et al., 2022; Kaushik & Sharma, 2023).Personalized marketing and promotions increase sales, customer retention, and provide a sustainable competitive edge(Chhabria et al., 2023; Bilyk et al., 2024; Ren et al.,

2024).Personalization, especially in physical stores, raises significant privacy issues, often reducing customers' willingness to adopt such services(Riegger et al., 2021; Peteva, 2024; Wetzlinger et al., 2017; Chandra et al., 2022).Implementing effective personalization requires overcoming technological, financial, and organizational challenges(Peteva, 2024; Peteva, 2023; Saksena, 2024).Balancing the benefits of personalization with consumer privacy expectations remains a key challenge(Riegger et al., 2021; Chandra et al., 2022; Kaushik & Sharma, 2023).

The future of personalization lies in leveraging AI, big data, IoT, and real-time analytics to create even more tailored and dynamic experiences (Saksena, 2024; Chandra et al., 2022; Kaushik & Sharma, 2023).Further studies are needed to refine personalization strategies, address privacy concerns, and optimize omnichannel integration(Scholdra et al., 2023; Chandra et al., 2022; Kaushik & Sharma, 2023).

Communities

Brand communities make consumers feel they belong, which helps them support and stay loyal to the brand (Muniz & O'Guinn, 2001). These communities allow customers to talk to each other, giving useful feedback and promoting the brand through word-of-mouth (McAlexander et al., 2002). Businesses that build strong brand communities see more engagement and better customer relationships over time (Fournier & Lee, 2009). Online forums, social media groups, and real-life events assist brands in forming a stronger emotional link with their audience (Bagozzi & Dholakia, 2006).

Loyalty

Customer loyalty comes from consistently positive experiences and engagement (Oliver, 1999). Loyalty programs and tailored services encourage repeat purchases and brand support (Yi & Jeon, 2003).

CRM (Customer Relationship Management)

CRM systems assist businesses in handling customer relationships and improving interactions (Reinartz et al., 2004). A well-executed CRM strategy boosts customer retention and satisfaction (Nguyen & Mutum, 2012).

Buying Journey

The buying journey is the process that consumers follow from seeing a need to deciding to buy and what comes after (Lemon & Verhoef, 2016). It has several parts: awareness, consideration, purchase, and post-purchase engagement (Kotler & Keller, 2019). Knowing the buying journey helps businesses adjust their marketing, enhance customer experiences, and boost brand loyalty (Edelman & Singer, 2015). Digital changes have greatly affected this journey, with online reviews, social media, and personalized suggestions being very important (Court et al., 2009). Companies that successfully manage touchpoints during the buying journey can create smooth and fulfilling experiences for consumers (Bolton et al., 2018).

Theme 3: Technology

Using technology in retail improves how businesses operate, tailor services, and engage customers (Pantano et al., 2017). New technologies like artificial intelligence and machine learning are key for understanding how consumers behave and for improving decisions (Davenport & Ronanki, 2018).

AI powers personalized shopping, demand forecasting, and automation, while IoT connects devices for real-time inventory and supply chain management. These technologies enable seamless, customized, and efficient shopping experiences(Ejjami & Rahim, 2024; Lu et al., 2023; Har et al., 2021; Balaji & Roy, 2017).Mobile apps, in-store smart devices, and contactless payment systems enhance convenience and allow for new shopping behaviors, such as buy-online-pickup-in-store and mobile checkout(Pantano & Priporas, 2016; Roy et al., 2020; Adapa et al., 2020).AR and VR are used for immersive product displays and virtual try-ons, bridging digital and physical retail experiences(Grewal et al., 2017; Jung et al., 2018; Musso & Adam, 2020).Retailers leverage big data to understand consumer behavior, optimize pricing, and improve targeting, leading to better decision-making and profitability(Grewal et al., 2017; Hagberg et al., 2017; Lu et al., 2023).

The blending of online and offline channels creates unified customer journeys, with physical stores adopting digital features and online retailers opening physical locations(Grewal et al., 2025; Hagberg et al., 2017; Grewal et al., 2021).Emerging technologies support unmanned retail operations, such as automated checkouts and smart shelves, increasing efficiency and reducing labor costs(Ozcan et al., 2021; Lu et al., 2023).

The role of technology identified in this study can be interpreted through the lens of the Technology Acceptance Model (TAM).It posits that perceived usefulness and ease of use influence technology adoption (Davis, 1989).

Table 6. Drivers, Benefits, and Challenges

Aspect	Examples/Findings
Drivers	Ease of use, superior functionality, personalization, and enhanced experiences(Balaji & Roy, 2017; Riegger et al., 2021; Perumal et al., 2022)
Benefits	Improved efficiency, customer satisfaction, data-driven insights, resilience(Ejjami & Rahim, 2024; Bruni & Piccarozzi, 2022; Har et al., 2021)
Challenges	Privacy concerns, implementation complexity, need for new skills, ethical issues(Riegger et al., 2021; Ejjami & Rahim, 2024; Ozcan et al., 2021)

Future Directions

- **Continued Digitalization:** Retail is expected to see further integration of AI, IoT, and cloud platforms, with a focus on seamless, secure, and ethical technology use(Lu et al., 2023; Ejjami & Rahim, 2024).
- **Strategic Adaptation:** Retailers must adapt strategies to leverage technology for competitive advantage, requiring ongoing innovation and oversight(Grewal et al., 2021; Ejjami & Rahim, 2024; Isharyani et al., 2023).

Data

Data analytics in retail helps businesses make smart choices, foresee trends, and customize customer experiences (Wedel & Kannan, 2016). Good data management improves marketing strategies and insights about customers (Davenport & Harris, 2007).

Automation/AI-ML

Automation and AI-ML make retail operations better by simplifying tasks like managing inventory, using chatbots, and taking advantage of predictive analytics (Bughin et al., 2018). These technologies improve customer service and efficiency (Brynjolfsson & McAfee, 2017). The rapid advancement of Artificial Intelligence (AI) has transformed social interaction, reshaping communication, relationship-building, and community engagement(Singh J. et al 2025)

E-Commerce

E-commerce has changed retail by offering convenience and easier access for consumers (Chaffey, 2019). The growth of omnichannel strategies makes the shopping experience even better (Rigby, 2011).

Transformation

Retail transformation is caused by changes in consumer expectations and tech advancements (Verhoef et al., 2021). Companies that adjust to these changes keep competitive edges and achieve long-term growth (Grewal et al., 2020).

Theme 4: Customer Experience

Customer experience is how customers view a brand based on their interactions at different points (Lemon & Verhoef, 2016). Having a smooth and positive customer experience is important for a brand's success, affecting customer loyalty and business growth (Meyer & Schwager, 2007).

Key Dimensions of Customer Experience

Customer experience (CX) in retail includes cognitive (thinking), affective (feeling), social, and physical responses to in-store and digital stimuli. These dimensions interact to shape overall satisfaction and loyalty (Bustamante & Rubio, 2017; Grewal & Roggeveen, 2020; Grewal et al., 2009; Puccinelli et al., 2009; Bascur & Rusu, 2020; Tyrväinen et al., 2020; Zhang et al., 2024; Sombultawee & Tansakul, 2022; Bagdare & Jain, 2013; Molinillo et al., 2021; Japutra et al., 2020).Experiences can be hedonic (pleasure-driven) or utilitarian (functionality-driven), both contributing to loyalty and repeat visits (Tyrväinen et al., 2020; Zhang et al., 2024; Bagdare & Jain, 2013; Sachdeva & Goel, 2015; Molinillo et al., 2021).Personalization and hedonic motivation enhance both cognitive and emotional aspects of CX, leading to stronger loyalty outcomes (Tyrväinen et al., 2020; Zhang et al., 2024).

Store design, atmospherics, and sensory cues (touch, smell, sight) significantly impact emotions and behaviors (Bustamante & Rubio, 2017; Petermans et al., 2013; Yakhlef, 2015; Bagdare & Jain, 2013; Sachdeva & Goel, 2015).Smart technologies, mobile apps, and seamless integration across channels (online, offline, mobile) improve satisfaction, reduce perceived risk, and foster loyalty (Roy et al., 2017; Tyrväinen et al., 2020; Zhang et al., 2024; Molinillo et al., 2021; Gleim et al., 2025; Japutra et al., 2020).Positive relationships with staff enhance satisfaction, loyalty, and word-of-mouth recommendations (Roozen & Katidis, 2019).

Table 7. Factors Affecting Customer Experience in Omnichannel Retail

Factor	Hedonic Experience	Utilitarian Experience
Personalization	Positive	Neutral
Connectivity	Neutral	Positive
Self-efficacy	Positive	Positive
Innovativeness	Positive	Neutral

Scales and frameworks have been developed to assess CX, focusing on leisure, joy, distinctiveness, and mood, as well as cognitive, affective, and physical experiences (Bustamante & Rubio, 2017; Bascur & Rusu, 2020; Bagdare & Jain, 2013). Mapping and managing the entire customer journey, including nonlinear and looping paths, is vital for optimizing experiences at every touchpoint (Grewal & Roggeveen, 2020; Grewal et al., 2009; Puccinelli et al., 2009; Klaus & Kuppelwieser, 2022; Gleim et al., 2025).

Outcomes

As illustrated in Figure 4 the success factors for strategic outcomes listed below are mapped.

1. High customer focus - Companies that prioritize customer needs improve overall satisfaction. Satisfaction and loyalty (Shah et al., 2006).
2. Good Customer Experience – A smooth experience helps keep customers and encourages positive recommendations (Berry et al., 2002).
3. Brand Loyalty – Good ties with customers lead to repeat purchases and support (Chaudhuri & Holbrook, 2001).
4. Relevance – Being relevant with innovation and customization maintains competitive advantages (Christensen et al., 2016).
5. Business Expansion – Customer-focused and data-based strategies promote lasting growth (Rust et al., 2004).

Figure 4. Conceptual framework linking customer experience drivers with strategic business outcomes.

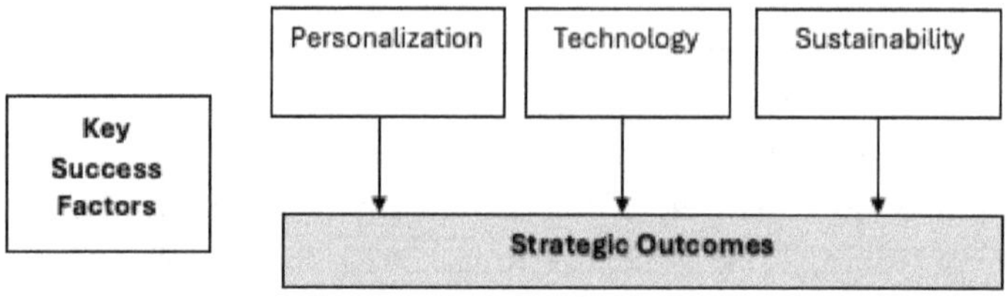

Figure 4.Conceptual framework linking customer experience drivers with strategic business outcomes.

CONCLUSION

This study points out important factors that affect customer experience (CX) in India's retail industry, focusing on personalization, engagement, technology, and sustainability. Using interviews with senior professionals in the field, insights have been gathered on the changing retail landscape and what businesses need to do to stay competitive. Personalization is a key factor driving customer satisfaction. Retailers are using data and technology to create personalized experiences (Lemon & Verhoef, 2016). Customer loyalty programs have transformed from basic point systems to more advanced models that encourage lasting relationships (Verhoef, Kannan, & Inman, 2015). Moreover, omnichannel retailing, influenced by digital changes and AI, has changed how customers interact with brands, allowing smooth transitions between online and offline shopping (Pantano & Vannucci, 2019).Sustainability has become essential in retail, as consumers are increasingly favouring brands that prioritize ethical and environmentally friendly practices (Wiese et al., 2012). The COVID-19 pandemic also sped up the adoption of digital solutions and highlighted the need for flexible strategies, forcing retailers to rapidly innovate and include contactless services, AI insights, and better customer relationship management systems (Sheth, 2020). Future research can build on this study by employing quantitative methods to validate the themes identified—personalization, loyalty, technology, and sustainability—across larger, more diverse retail samples. Longitudinal studies would offer insights into how CX strategies evolve over time in response to external disruptions such as the COVID-19 pandemic or technological innovation. Another valuable direction involves the development of comprehensive CX measurement models that include emerging dimensions like emotional intelligence, digital trust, and sustainability perception. Research could also investigate the growing role of AI and automation in delivering hyper-personalized experiences and examine the balance between technological efficiency and the human touch in customer service. Lastly, examining CX strategies in India's tier 2 and tier 3 cities would provide a broader understanding of consumer behaviours beyond urban centres, addressing gaps in accessibility, digital adoption, and localized marketing effectiveness.In conclusion, this research offers useful suggestions for retailers looking to improve Customer experience (CX) (Singh, J. et al 2025).

REFERENCES

Adapa, S., Fazal-E-Hasan, S., Makam, S., Azeem, M., & Mortimer, G. (2020). Examining the antecedents and consequences of perceived shopping value through smart retail technology. *Journal of Retailing and Consumer Services*. Advance online publication. DOI: 10.1016/J.JRETCONSER.2019.101901

Afolabi, J., Olatoye, F., Eboigbe, E., Abdul, A., & Daraojimba, H. (2023). REVOLUTIONIZING RETAIL: HR TACTICS FOR IMPROVED EMPLOYEE AND CUSTOMER ENGAGEMENT. *International Journal of Applied Research in Social Sciences*. https://doi.org/DOI: 10.51594/ijarss.v5i10.635

Ajzen, I. (1991). The theory of planned behaviour. *Organizational Behavior and Human Decision Processes*, *50*(2), 179–211.

An, M., & Han, S. (2020). Effects of experiential motivation and customer engagement on customer value creation: Analysis of psychological process in the experience-based retail environment. *Journal of Business Research*, *120*, 389–397. DOI: 10.1016/j.jbusres.2020.02.044

Bagdare, S., & Jain, R. (2013). Measuring retail customer experience. *International Journal of Retail & Distribution Management*, *41*, 790–804. DOI: 10.1108/IJRDM-08-2012-0084

Balaji, M., & Roy, S. (2017). Value co-creation with Internet of things technology in the retail industry. *Journal of Marketing Management*, *33*, 31–37. DOI: 10.1080/0267257X.2016.1217914

Bascur, C., & Rusu, C. (2020). Customer Experience in Retail: A Systematic Literature Review. *Applied Sciences (Basel, Switzerland)*. Advance online publication. DOI: 10.3390/app10217644

Behnam, M., Hollebeek, L., Clark, M., & Farabi, R. (2021). Exploring customer engagement in the product vs. service context. *Journal of Retailing and Consumer Services*, *60*, 102456. DOI: 10.1016/J.JRETCONSER.2021.102456

Berry, L. L., Carbone, L. P., & Haeckel, S. H. (2002). Managing the total customer experience. *MIT Sloan Management Review*, *43*(3), 85.

Berry, L. L., Carbone, L. P., & Haeckel, S. H. (2002). Managing the total customer experience. *MIT Sloan Management Review*, *43*(3), 85–89.

Bilyk, I., Kindii, M., & Kurylo, S. (2024). PERSONALIZATION OF MARKETING AS A TOOL TO INCREASE SALES AND CUSTOMER LOYALTY. *Eastern Europe: economy, business and management.* https://doi.org/DOI: 10.32782/easterneurope.45-7

Bowden, J., & Mirzaei, A. (2021). Consumer engagement within retail communication channels: An examination of online brand communities and digital content marketing initiatives. *European Journal of Marketing*. Advance online publication. DOI: 10.1108/EJM-01-2018-0007

Boyce, C., & Neale, P. (2006). *Conducting in-depth interviews: A guide for designing and conducting in-depth interviews for evaluation input.* Pathfinder International.

Braun, V., & Clarke, V. (2006). Using thematic analysis in psychology. *Qualitative Research in Psychology, 3*(2), 77–101.

Brodie, R. J., Hollebeek, L. D., Jurić, B., & Ilić, A. (2011). Customer engagement: Conceptual domain, fundamental propositions, and implications for research. *Journal of Service Research, 14*(3), 252–271.

Brodie, R. J., Hollebeek, L. D., Jurić, B., & Ilić, A. (2011). Customer engagement: Conceptual domain, fundamental propositions, and implications for research. *Journal of Service Research, 14*(3), 252–271. DOI: 10.1177/1094670511411703

Brodie, R. J., Hollebeek, L. D., Jurić, B., & Ilić, A. (2013). Customer engagement in a virtual brand community: An exploratory analysis. *Journal of Business Research, 66*(1), 105–114. DOI: 10.1016/j.jbusres.2011.07.029

Bruni, R., & Piccarozzi, M. (2022). Industry 4.0 enablers in retailing: A literature review. *International Journal of Retail & Distribution Management.* Advance online publication. DOI: 10.1108/ijrdm-07-2021-0314

Bughin, J., Seong, J., Manyika, J., Chui, M., & Joshi, R. (2018). Notes from the AI frontier: Modeling the impact of AI on the world economy. *McKinsey Global Institute.* https://www.mckinsey.com/featured-insights/artificial-intelligence

Bustamante, J., & Rubio, N. (2017). Measuring customer experience in physical retail environments. *Journal of Service Management, 28*, 884–913. DOI: 10.1108/JOSM-06-2016-0142

Chaffey, D. (2019). *Digital marketing: Strategy, implementation and practice.* Pearson UK.

Chandra, S., Verma, S., Lim, W., Kumar, S., & Donthu, N. (2022). Personalization in personalized marketing: Trends and ways forward. *Psychology and Marketing*. Advance online publication. DOI: 10.1002/mar.21670

Chaudhuri, A., & Holbrook, M. B. (2001). The chain of effects from brand trust and brand affect to brand performance: The role of brand loyalty. *Journal of Marketing*, *65*(2), 81–93. DOI: 10.1509/jmkg.65.2.81.18255

Chhabria, S., Gupta, S., & Gupta, H. (2023). A Study on the Impact of "Personalized Marketing" on Customer Satisfaction and Loyalty in Retail Fashion in 2023. *International Journal of Computer Applications*. Advance online publication. DOI: 10.5120/ijca2023922707

Christensen, C. M., Raynor, M. E., & McDonald, R. (2016). What is disruptive innovation? *Harvard Business Review*, *93*(12), 44–53.

Connell, C., Marciniak, R., Carey, L., & McColl, J. (2019). Customer engagement with websites: A transactional retail perspective. *European Journal of Marketing*. Advance online publication. DOI: 10.1108/EJM-10-2017-0649

Davenport, T. H., & Harris, J. G. (2007). *Competing on analytics: The new science of winning*. Harvard Business Press.

Davis, F. D. (1989). Perceived usefulness, perceived ease of use, and user acceptance of information technology. *Management Information Systems Quarterly*, *13*(3), 319–340. DOI: 10.2307/249008

Draper, A. K. (2004). The principles and application of qualitative research. *The Proceedings of the Nutrition Society*, *63*(4), 641–646.

Edelman, D. C., & Singer, M. (2015). Competing on customer journeys. *Harvard Business Review*, *93*(11), 88–100.

Ejjami, R., & Rahim, N. (2024). *Retail 5.0: Creating Resilient and Customer-Centric Shopping Experiences through Advanced Technologies*. International Journal For Multidisciplinary Research., DOI: 10.36948/ijfmr.2024.v06i04.25930

Gleim, M., McCullough, H., Gabler, C., Ferrell, L., & Ferrell, O. (2025). Examining the customer experience in the metaverse retail revolution. *Journal of Business Research*. Advance online publication. DOI: 10.1016/j.jbusres.2024.115045

Grewal, D., Gauri, D., Roggeveen, A., & Sethuraman, R. (2021). Strategizing Retailing in the New Technology Era. *Journal of Retailing*, *97*, 6–12. DOI: 10.1016/J.JRETAI.2021.02.004

Grewal, D., Levy, M., & Kumar, P. (2009). Customer Experience Management in Retailing: An Organizing Framework. *Journal of Retailing*, *85*, 1–14. DOI: 10.1016/J.JRETAI.2009.01.001

Grewal, D., & Roggeveen, A. (2020). Understanding Retail Experiences and Customer Journey Management. *Journal of Retailing*, *96*, 3–8. DOI: 10.1016/j.jretai.2020.02.002

Grewal, D., Roggeveen, A., Benoit, S., Andrade, M., Wetzels, R., & Wetzels, M. (2025). A new era of technology-infused retailing. *Journal of Business Research*. Advance online publication. DOI: 10.1016/j.jbusres.2024.115095

Grewal, D., Roggeveen, A., & Nordfält, J. (2017). The Future of Retailing. *Journal of Retailing*, *93*, 1–6. DOI: 10.1016/J.JRETAI.2016.12.008

Grewal, D., Roggeveen, A., Sisodia, R., & Nordfält, J. (2017). Enhancing Customer Engagement Through Consciousness. *Journal of Retailing*, *93*, 55–64. DOI: 10.1016/J.JRETAI.2016.12.001

Grewal, D., Roggeveen, A. L., & Nordfält, J. (2020). The future of retailing. *Journal of Retailing*, *96*(1), 86–95.

Hagberg, J., Jonsson, A., & Egels-Zandén, N. (2017). Retail digitalization: Implications for physical stores. *Journal of Retailing and Consumer Services*, *39*, 264–269. DOI: 10.1016/J.JRETCONSER.2017.08.005

Har, L., Rashid, U., Chuan, L., Sen, S., & Xia, L. (2021). Revolution of Retail Industry: From Perspective of Retail 1.0 to 4.0. **, 1615-1625. https://doi.org/DOI: 10.1016/j.procs.2022.01.362

Hollebeek, L. D., Srivastava, R. K., & Chen, T. (2019). S-D logic–informed customer engagement: Integrative framework, revised fundamental propositions, and application to CRM. *Journal of the Academy of Marketing Science*, *47*(1), 161–185. DOI: 10.1007/s11747-016-0494-5

Isharyani, M., Sopha, B., Wibisono, A., & Tjahjono, B. (2023). Retail Technology Adaptation in Traditional Retailers: A Technology-to-Performance Chain Perspective. *Journal of Open Innovation*. Advance online publication. DOI: 10.1016/j.joitmc.2023.100204

Jagabathula, S., Mitrofanov, D., & Vulcano, G. (2022). Personalized Retail Promotions Through a Directed Acyclic Graph-Based Representation of Customer Preferences. *Operations Research*, *70*, 641–665. DOI: 10.1287/opre.2021.2108

Japutra, A., Utami, A., Molinillo, S., & Ekaputra, I. (2020). Influence of customer application experience and value in use on loyalty toward retailers. *Journal of Retailing and Consumer Services, 102390*. Advance online publication. DOI: 10.1016/j.jretconser.2020.102390

Jung, T., Dieck, M., Moorhouse, N., & Jung, T. (2018). Technological Innovations Transforming the Consumer Retail Experience: A Review of Literature. **, 133-143. https://doi.org/DOI: 10.1007/978-3-319-64027-3_10

Kaushik, M., & Sharma, M. (2023). *Personalization in Marketing: Customizing the Customer Experience for Greater Engagement*. International Journal For Multidisciplinary Research., DOI: 10.36948/ijfmr.2023.v05i06.11194

Klaus, P. (2013). The case of Amazon.com: Towards a conceptual framework of online customer service experience (OCSE) using the emerging consensus technique. *Journal of Services Marketing*, *27*(6), 443–457.

Klaus, P., & Kuppelwieser, V. (2022). A glimpse of the future retail customer experience – Guidelines for research and practice. *Journal of Retailing and Consumer Services*. Advance online publication. DOI: 10.1016/j.jretconser.2022.103205

Kosiba, J., Boateng, H., Amartey, A., Boakye, R., & Hinson, R. (2018). Examining customer engagement and brand loyalty in retail banking. *International Journal of Retail & Distribution Management*. Advance online publication. DOI: 10.1108/IJRDM-08-2017-0163

Kotler, P., & Keller, K. L. (2019). *Marketing management* (15th ed.). Pearson.

Kumar, V., Aksoy, L., Donkers, B., Venkatesan, R., Wiesel, T., & Tillmanns, S. (2021). Undervalued or overvalued customers: Capturing total customer engagement value. *Journal of Service Research*, *24*(2), 220–239. DOI: 10.1177/1094670517709588

Lambillotte, L., Magrofuoco, N., Poncin, I., & Vanderdonckt, J. (2022). Enhancing playful customer experience with personalization. *Journal of Retailing and Consumer Services*. Advance online publication. DOI: 10.1016/j.jretconser.2022.103017

Lee, Z., Chan, T., Chong, A., & Thadani, D. (2019). Customer engagement through omnichannel retailing: The effects of channel integration quality. *Industrial Marketing Management*. Advance online publication. DOI: 10.1016/J.INDMARMAN.2018.12.004

Lemon, K. N., & Verhoef, P. C. (2016). Understanding customer experience throughout the customer journey. *Journal of Marketing*, *80*(6), 69–96. DOI: 10.1509/jm.15.0420

Lu, H., Cheng, H., Tzou, J., & Chen, C. (2023). Technology roadmap of AI applications in the retail industry. *Technological Forecasting and Social Change*. Advance online publication. DOI: 10.1016/j.techfore.2023.122778

M.Mandaliya, D. (2025). Digital Marketing Strategies and Customer Engagement in the Online Retail Industry. *International Journal on Science and Technology*. https://doi.org/DOI: 10.71097/ijsat.v16.i1.2494

McAlexander, J. H., Schouten, J. W., & Koenig, H. F. (2002). Building brand community. *Journal of Marketing*, *66*(1), 38–54.

Meyer, C., & Schwager, A. (2007). Understanding customer experience. *Harvard Business Review*, *85*(2), 116–126.

Mittal, B., & Lassar, W. (1996). The role of personalization in service encounters. *Journal of Retailing*, *72*, 95–109. DOI: 10.1016/S0022-4359(96)90007-X

Mogili, R., & Natarajan, T. (2021). Online Retailing and Customer Engagement. **, 184-195. https://doi.org/DOI: 10.4018/978-1-7998-3919-4.CH010

Molinillo, S., Aguilar-Illescas, R., Anaya-Sánchez, R., & Carvajal-Trujillo, E. (2021). The customer retail app experience: Implications for customer loyalty. *Journal of Retailing and Consumer Services*. Advance online publication. DOI: 10.1016/j.jretconser.2021.102842

Monferrer, D., Moliner, M., & Estrada, M. (2019). Increasing customer loyalty through customer engagement in the retail banking industry. *Spanish Journal of Marketing - ESIC*. Advance online publication. DOI: 10.1108/sjme-07-2019-0042

Muniz, A. M., & O'Guinn, T. C. (2001). Brand community. *The Journal of Consumer Research*, *27*(4), 412–432. DOI: 10.1086/319618

Muposhi, A., Dhurup, M., Surujlal, J., & Maramura, T. C. (2015). Thematic content analysis of customer experience in shopping malls. *Journal of Contemporary Management*, *12*(1), 445–467.

Musso, F., & Adam, R. (2020). Retailing 4.0 and Technology-Driven Innovation. **, 338-354. https://doi.org/DOI: 10.4018/978-1-7998-1412-2.ch015

Oliver, R. L. (1999). Whence consumer loyalty? *Journal of Marketing*, *63*(4), 33–44.

Ozcan, S., Homayounfard, A., Simms, C., & Wasim, J. (2021). Technology Roadmapping Using Text Mining: A Foresight Study for the Retail Industry. *IEEE Transactions on Engineering Management*, *69*, 228–244. DOI: 10.1109/TEM.2021.3068310

Pansari, A., & Kumar, V. (2017). Customer engagement: The construct, antecedents, and consequences. *Journal of the Academy of Marketing Science*, *45*(3), 294–311. DOI: 10.1007/s11747-016-0485-6

Pantano, E., Pizzi, G., Scarpi, D., & Dennis, C. (2017). Competing during a pandemic? Retailers' ups and downs during the COVID-19 outbreak. *Journal of Business Research*, *116*, 209–213. DOI: 10.1016/j.jbusres.2020.05.036

Pantano, E., & Priporas, C. (2016). The effect of mobile retailing on consumers' purchasing experiences: A dynamic perspective. *Computers in Human Behavior*, *61*, 548–555. DOI: 10.1016/j.chb.2016.03.071

Pantano, E., & Vannucci, V. (2019). Who is innovating? An exploratory research of digital technologies diffusion in retail industry. *Journal of Retailing and Consumer Services*, *49*, 297–304. DOI: 10.1016/j.jretconser.2019.01.019

Parihar, P., Dawra, J., & Sahay, V. (2019). The role of customer engagement in the involvement-loyalty link. *Marketing Intelligence & Planning*. Advance online publication. DOI: 10.1108/MIP-11-2017-0318

Perumal, S., Qing, Y., & Jaganathan, M. (2022). Factors influencing attitudes and intentions towards smart retail technology. *International Journal of Data and Network Science*. https://doi.org/DOI: 10.5267/j.ijdns.2021.11.005

Petermans, A., Janssens, W., & Cleempoel, K. (2013). A Holistic Framework for Conceptualizing Customer Experiences in Retail Environments. *International Journal of Design*, •••, 7.

Peteva, V. (2023). *The Personalization in Modern Retailing*. Izvestia Journal of the Union of Scientists - Varna. Economic Sciences Series., DOI: 10.56065/ijusv-ess/2023.12.3.62

Peteva, V. (2024). *The Personalization in Retailing - Problems and Challenges*. Izvestia Journal of the Union of Scientists - Varna Economic Sciences Series., DOI: 10.56065/ijusv-ess/2024.13.2.69

Porter, M. E. (1985). *Competitive advantage: Creating and sustaining superior performance*. Free Press.

Puccinelli, N., Goodstein, R., Grewal, D., Price, R., Raghubir, P., & Stewart, D. (2009). Customer Experience Management in Retailing: Understanding the Buying Process. *Journal of Retailing*, *85*, 15–30. DOI: 10.1016/J.JRETAI.2008.11.003

Rajput, D., Singh, S. K., Kumar, S., Vashisht, H., Chui, K. T., & Gupta, B. B. (2024). SentinelMet: Enhancing Metaverse Security through Deep Learning Techniques in 6G. In *2024 IEEE International Conference on Advanced Networks and Telecommunications Systems, ANTS 2024* (International Symposium on Advanced Networks and Telecommunication Systems, ANTS). https://doi.org/DOI: 10.1109/ANTS63515.2024.10898831

Ren, Z., Tian, J., Kang, S., Tang, M., & Tian, J. (2024). Personalized pricing versus showrooming: Competition between online and offline retailers. *International Transactions in Operational Research, 31*, 3371–3442. DOI: 10.1111/itor.13444

Riegger, A., Klein, J., Merfeld, K., & Henkel, S. (2021). Technology-enabled personalization in retail stores: Understanding drivers and barriers. *Journal of Business Research, 123*, 140–155. DOI: 10.1016/j.jbusres.2020.09.039

Roozen, I., & Katidis, P. (2019). The Importance of the Service and Shopping Customer Experience in a Retail Environment. *Journal of Relationship Marketing, 18*, 247–279. DOI: 10.1080/15332667.2019.1619064

Roy, S., Fellowa, R., Balaji, M., Sadeque, S., Nguyen, B., & Melewar, T. (2017). Constituents and consequences of smart customer experience in retailing. *Technological Forecasting and Social Change, 124*, 257–270. DOI: 10.1016/J.TECHFORE.2016.09.022

Roy, S., Gruner, R., & Guo, J. (2020). Exploring customer experience, commitment, and engagement behaviours. *Journal of Strategic Marketing, 30*, 45–68. DOI: 10.1080/0965254X.2019.1642937

Roy, S., Singh, G., Sadeque, S., Harrigan, P., & Coussement, K. (2023). Customer engagement with digitalized interactive platforms in retailing. *Journal of Business Research*. Advance online publication. DOI: 10.1016/j.jbusres.2023.114001

Rust, R. T., Lemon, K. N., & Zeithaml, V. A. (2004). Return on marketing: Using customer equity to focus marketing strategy. *Journal of Marketing, 68*(1), 109–127. DOI: 10.1509/jmkg.68.1.109.24030

Sachdeva, I., & Goel, S. (2015). Retail store environment and customer experience: A paradigm. *Journal of Fashion Marketing and Management, 19*, 290–298. DOI: 10.1108/JFMM-03-2015-0021

Saini, M., Kumar, S., Singh, S. K., Bansal, A., Han, C., Gupta, B. B., & Psannis, K. (2025). Transforming User Experience in the Metaverse Through Emotional Intelligence and Affective Computing. In Gupta, B. (Ed.), *Unveiling Social Dynamics and Community Interaction in the Metaverse* (pp. 303–332). IGI Global Scientific Publishing., DOI: 10.4018/979-8-3693-8628-6.ch015

Saksena, N. (2024). Hyper-Personalization in Retail: Leveraging Data Science and Real-Time Streaming. *International Journal of Scientific Research in Computer Science, Engineering and Information Technology*. https://doi.org/DOI: 10.32628/cseit241061179

Salem, S., & Alanadoly, A. (2023). Driving customer engagement and citizenship behaviour in omnichannel retailing: Evidence from the fashion sector. *Spanish Journal of Marketing - ESIC*. Advance online publication. DOI: 10.1108/sjme-10-2022-0220

Scholdra, T., Wichmann, J., & Reinartz, W. (2023). Reimagining personalization in the physical store. *Journal of Retailing*. Advance online publication. DOI: 10.1016/j.jretai.2023.11.001

Sheth, J. (2020). Impact of COVID-19 on consumer behavior: Will the old habits return or die? *Journal of Business Research*, *117*, 280–283. DOI: 10.1016/j.jbusres.2020.05.059

Sicilia, M., & Palazón, M. (2023). Developing customer engagement through communication consistency and channel coordination. *Spanish Journal of Marketing - ESIC*. Advance online publication. DOI: 10.1108/sjme-02-2022-0022

Simunaniemi, A. M., & Muhos, M. (2017). Thematic analysis of microenterprise growth constraints in the start-up and stabilization phases. *International Journal of Entrepreneurship and Small Business*, *31*(1), 30–55.

Sinek, S. (2009). *Start with why: How great leaders inspire everyone to take action*. Penguin.

Singh, J., Kumar, S., Singh, S. K., Singh, D., Singh, A., Arya, V., & Ratnaparkhi, A. (2025). Virtual Economies and Social Structures in the Metaverse. In Gupta, B. (Ed.), *Unveiling Social Dynamics and Community Interaction in the Metaverse* (pp. 111–138). IGI Global Scientific Publishing., DOI: 10.4018/979-8-3693-8628-6.ch006

Singh, J., Singh, S. K., Kumar, S., Singh, S. P., Kumar, R., Bansal, S., & Chui, K. T. (2025). The Influence of AI on Social Interactions and Community Dynamics. In Gupta, B. (Ed.), *Unveiling Social Dynamics and Community Interaction in the Metaverse* (pp. 197–220). IGI Global Scientific Publishing., DOI: 10.4018/979-8-3693-8628-6.ch010

So, K., King, C., Sparks, B., & Wang, Y. (2016). Enhancing customer relationships with retail service brands: The role of customer engagement. *Journal of Service Management, 27*, 170–193. DOI: 10.1108/JOSM-05-2015-0176

Sombultawee, K., & Tansakul, T. (2022). The customer experience in Thailand's multichannel retail environments. *Asia-Pacific Journal of Business Administration*. Advance online publication. DOI: 10.1108/apjba-08-2021-0427

Tartaglione, A., & Granata, G. (2019). Retail Customer Engagement. *Advances in Marketing, Customer Relationship Management, and E-Services*. Advance online publication. DOI: 10.4018/978-1-5225-7856-7.CH001

Tyrväinen, O., Karjaluoto, H., & Saarijärvi, H. (2020). Personalization and hedonic motivation in creating customer experiences and loyalty in omnichannel retail. *Journal of Retailing and Consumer Services, 57*, 102233. DOI: 10.1016/j.jretconser.2020.102233

Vargo, S. L., & Lusch, R. F. (2004). Evolving to a new dominant logic for marketing. *Journal of Marketing, 68*(1), 1–17. DOI: 10.1509/jmkg.68.1.1.24036

Verhoef, P. C., Kannan, P. K., & Inman, J. J. (2015). From multi-channel retailing to omnichannel retailing: Introduction to the special issue on multi-channel retailing. *Journal of Retailing, 91*(2), 174–181. DOI: 10.1016/j.jretai.2015.02.005

Wetzlinger, W., Auinger, A., Kindermann, H., & Schönberger, W. (2017). Acceptance of Personalization in Omnichannel Retailing., 114-129. https://doi.org/DOI: 10.1007/978-3-319-58484-3_10

Wiese, A., Kellner, J., Lietke, B., Toporowski, W., & Zielke, S. (2012). Sustainability in retailing: A summative content analysis. *International Journal of Retail & Distribution Management, 40*(4), 318–335. DOI: 10.1108/09590551211211792

Yakhlef, A. (2015). Customer experience within retail environments. *Marketing Theory, 15*, 545–564. DOI: 10.1177/1470593115569016

Yi, Y., & Jeon, H. (2003). Effects of loyalty programs on value perception, program loyalty, and brand loyalty. *Journal of the Academy of Marketing Science, 31*(3), 229–240.

Zeithaml, V. A. (1988). Consumer perceptions of price, quality, and value: A means-end model and synthesis of evidence. *Journal of Marketing, 52*(3), 2–22.

Zhang, X., Park, Y., Park, J., & Zhang, H. (2024). Demonstrating the influencing factors and outcomes of customer experience in omnichannel retail. *Journal of Retailing and Consumer Services*. Advance online publication. DOI: 10.1016/j.jretconser.2023.103622

Chapter 5
Intelligent Supply Chains and Logistics in the Era of Digital Twins

Damar Aditya
http://orcid.org/0009-0000-0603-6993
Universitas Esa Unggul, Indonesia

Qori Halimatul Hidayah
http://orcid.org/0009-0008-7567-4102
Universitas Esa Unggul, Indonesia

Kartini Kartini
Universitas Esa Unggul, Indonesia

Shavi Bansal
http://orcid.org/0009-0009-8699-6884
Insight2Techinfo, India

Akshat Gaurav
http://orcid.org/0000-0002-5796-9424
Asia University, Taiwan

ABSTRACT

Digital twins are transforming supply chains into intelligent, adaptive networks capable of real-time visibility, optimization, and predictive decision-making. By synchronizing virtual replicas with IoT sensors, enterprise systems, and logistics infrastructures, digital twins generate continuously updated models that reveal bottlenecks, forecast demand fluctuations, and simulate operational scenarios with high precision. AI-driven analytics enhance these capabilities by supporting

DOI: 10.4018/979-8-3373-4541-3.ch005

autonomous routing, adaptive inventory control, and disruption response across global logistics chains. For consumers, digital twins provide transparent tracking, personalized delivery options, and seamless integration with emerging metaverse commerce ecosystems. As organizations pursue greater resilience and sustainability, the fusion of digital twins, automation, and immersive analytics is redefining logistics management and enabling supply chains that learn, evolve, and respond dynamically to changing market and environmental conditions.

INTRODUCTION

1. Global Trends and Consumer Demands

In today's rapidly shifting global business environment, transforming the supply chain is no longer optional but has become a strategic necessity. The post-pandemic landscape and ongoing geopolitical uncertainties have reinforced the importance of resilience, transparency, and adaptability as fundamental pillars in modern logistics strategies. At the same time, consumers now expect supply chains to function not merely as channels for moving products, but as integrated experiences that offer real-time visibility, personalized services, and sustainable value (Gupta et al., 2025).

The rapid expansion of e-commerce and the widespread adoption of digital technologies have heightened these expectations even further. Consumers increasingly demand faster delivery, complete process transparency, and the ability to customize the services they receive. They also want to be more actively involved in the ordering and fulfillment process, including receiving real-time updates and enjoying a seamless, engaging experience from purchase to delivery. These shifting expectations have placed significant pressure on traditional logistics systems, which often struggle to respond quickly and consistently under such demands (Singh et al., 2025).

2. Traditional Supply Chain Limitations

Conventional supply chain systems are generally built for cost efficiency and large-scale distribution under relatively stable demand conditions. However, these systems are often fragmented and lack the responsiveness needed to handle the rapidly changing expectations of modern consumers. When the COVID-19 pandemic struck, many companies were caught off guard as their supply chains collapsed due to material shortages, logistical delays, and the absence of real-time information flow. The pandemic ultimately became a major catalyst that accelerated the digitalization and redesign of global logistics models, pushing organizations toward more flexible and technology-driven approaches .

3. The Shift Towards Digitalization and Intelligence

In the midst of the crisis, it became increasingly clear that supply chain transformation must involve the integration of advanced technologies such as the Internet of Things (IoT), Artificial Intelligence (AI), and digital twins. Digital twins, which function as virtual representations of physical assets and processes, enable companies to visualize, monitor, and manage their supply chains in an interactive and predictive manner. They serve as a bridge between physical and digital systems by combining real-time sensor data, historical information, and intelligent analytics to support more accurate and timely decision-making.

With digital twins, companies are able not only to track the movement of products, but also to simulate various scenarios—such as potential delivery delays, shifts in market demand, or weather disruptions that may impact logistics operations. This capability supports the development of a more adaptive and anticipatory supply chain strategy. Several leading companies, including Siemens and General Electric, have already integrated digital twins into their supply chain systems to predict maintenance needs for logistical equipment and prevent potential system failures.

Transformation is also no longer solely about achieving efficiency. Consumers today are increasingly aware of sustainability and ethical considerations. They want transparency regarding product origins, the environmental impact of production processes, and the social practices embedded within the supply chain. For many members of the younger generation, a sustainable and ethically responsible supply chain has become a significant factor influencing their purchasing decisions..

Competitive advantage in the digital era is no longer defined solely by the speed at which products reach customers, but also by how effectively companies can understand, anticipate, and fulfill customer needs. This is where the role of AI becomes increasingly crucial. AI technologies enable highly detailed and dynamic analysis of demand-related data. Companies can leverage machine learning models to forecast fluctuations in demand by analyzing historical records, emerging social media trends, and real-time customer behavior patterns, allowing them to make faster and more accurate decisions.

The metaverse is also beginning to influence the development of future supply chains. Through immersive 3D interfaces, customers can interact directly with various stages of the supply chain—tracking products, visualizing the journey of goods, and even participating virtually in aspects of product design. Although adoption is still in its early stages, this concept signals a new direction in enhancing consumer experience by integrating physical processes with digital environments.

FOUNDATIONS OF DIGITAL TWINS IN LOGISTICS

1. Definition and Evolution of Digital Twins (DTs)

Digital transformation in the logistics sector cannot be separated from the concept of digital twin (DT), an approach that was originally developed in the manufacturing world but is now evolving as the backbone of intelligent supply chain systems. In the context of modern logistics, digital twins not only serve as virtual representations of physical assets, but become adaptive systems capable of integrating real-time data, intelligent algorithms, and scenario simulations to optimize every part of the supply chain ecosystem.

The concept of digital twins was originally introduced by NASA as a method to virtually monitor space systems and anticipate potential failures without requiring direct physical intervention. As technologies such as the Internet of Things (IoT), Artificial Intelligence (AI), and cloud computing have advanced, digital twins have evolved from static visual representations into dynamic, intelligent entities capable of learning from and interacting with the physical environment. They enable holistic modeling of the complexities within logistics systems by integrating real-time sensor data, historical records, and continuously updated operational contexts.

2. Digital Twin Architecture in Supply Chain Ecosystems

The digital twin architecture within a logistics system is generally composed of several interconnected layers. At the foundational level lies the physical component, which includes IoT sensors installed in vehicles, warehouses, and products. These sensors continuously capture operational data and transmit it through 5G networks or edge computing infrastructures. The collected data is then processed using AI-based analytical models to generate an accurate digital representation of the physical system. This architecture is designed to be modular, allowing it to be expanded or integrated with additional technologies—such as blockchain—to enhance data transparency, traceability, and security.

The implementation of digital twin architectures also allows for cross-platform interoperability. Integration between the company's logistics systems, transportation providers, and end consumers is possible thanks to API-based communication and standardized protocols. Rashed et al. (2025) in their study highlight the importance of this interoperability to create a smart logistics ecosystem in the food industry, where factors such as temperature and time are crucial. When digital twin systems are combined with AI and blockchain, the decisions taken by the system become faster, more transparent, and accountable.

3. Interoperability With AI, IoT, and Blockchain

Blockchain plays a crucial role in ensuring the authenticity and integrity of the data used in digital twin systems. Any data that goes into the twin, such as the temperature of the product during delivery, the location of the vehicle, and the time of delivery, can be recorded in the blockchain system. This creates a digital track record that cannot be modified, thereby increasing trust between logistics partners and consumers. As explained by Hemmati et al. (2025), the combination of AIoT (Artificial Intelligence of Things), blockchain, and digital twins will be the foundation of the next generation of supply chains.

4. Types of Digital Twins: Product, Process, System, and Network Twins

One important aspect of digital twins in logistics is the classification based on the entities represented. There are four main types: product twin, process twin, system twin, and network twin. Each has a different role and complexity. Product twins, for example, represent the condition and status of products in real-time, important for temperature-sensitive items such as vaccines or fresh food. Process twins model logistics processes such as scheduling shipments and processing in warehouses. System twin covers all facilities such as distribution centers, while network twin integrates the entire supply chain network from upstream to downstream.

These four types of twins do not work separately. In a mature architecture, they interact with each other and supply data to each other. For example, when a network twin detects a shipping disruption in one region, the system twin can adjust local warehouse operations, while the process twin will reschedule the shipment, and the product twin will inform consumers about changes in estimated time of arrival. This intelligent interaction creates a supply chain that is not only efficient but also adaptive to changing external conditions.

The application of this technology has shown a real impact in various industries. In the retail logistics sector, for example, the use of digital twins to monitor the movement of goods in real time has been proven to be able to reduce the loss of goods by up to 15% and increase the accuracy of delivery estimates by more than 30% (Ali et al., 2021). Meanwhile, in the manufacturing sector, the use of digital twins in the spare parts distribution process reduces machine downtime by up to 20% (Zheng et al., 2020).

However, the implementation of digital twins in logistics is not without challenges. The high initial costs of building sensor infrastructure, cloud systems, and AI algorithms are still a major barrier, especially for small and medium-sized enterprises, To address this, a gradual, collaboration-based approach is highly recommended.

Organizations can start with small-scale pilot projects for one type of twin, such as product twins, before progressing to process and system twins. Collaboration with technology providers, logistics consultants, and governments is also needed to create a more inclusive and accessible digital ecosystem.

INFRASTRUCTURE AND ENABLING TECHNOLOGIES

1. Sensor Networks and IoT Integration

The industrial revolution 4.0 and the acceleration of digital transformation have not only brought cosmetic changes in the world of logistics and supply chain management, but have completely shaken their foundations. In the past, competitive advantage in this sector was solely determined by delivery speed and cost efficiency. Today, the competitive map has shifted fundamentally: companies are required to bring technological agility, information transparency, and systemic intelligence to every distribution node.

Modern logistics now operates in a much more complex environment where consumer expectations move rapidly, market demand fluctuates unexpectedly, and the risk of global disruptions (such as pandemics, geopolitical conflicts, or climate disasters) can occur at any time. In this context, digital infrastructure is no longer just a complement, but rather a backbone that supports the durability and adaptability of the logistics system as a whole.

Technologies such as the Internet of Things (IoT), edge computing, cloud systems, blockchain, data lakes, and digital threads are no longer just industry jargon. They have evolved into an interconnected infrastructure ecosystem and are the basis for the creation of a digital twin-based supply chain, a virtual system that replicates physical conditions in real-time, enables scenario modeling, and data-driven decision-making. With this foundation, organizations can move more agilely, respond to disruptions more quickly, and most importantly build supply chains that are not only efficient but also smart and resilient.

IoT sensors and devices are the backbone of data collection systems in logistics environments. Liu et al. (2021) showed that the utilization of IoT-based sensors significantly improves supply chain visibility, and reduces uncertainty during the delivery of goods, especially in cold chain logistics.

2. Edge Computing and Cloud Systems

However, the increasing number of IoT nodes presents significant challenges in managing bandwidth and processing data efficiently. Data from thousands of sensors can't always be sent to the cloud for processing due to high latency and bandwidth costs. This is where edge computing technology comes into play. Edge computing allows data processing to be done directly at the collection point (edge node), such as in a logistics vehicle or warehouse entry gate. According to Shi et al. (2021), this approach significantly reduces response times, allows for real-time decision-making, and reduces the burden on the central network.

While edge computing is effective in making quick decisions, logistics systems still require cloud infrastructure as a large-scale data storage and analytics center. Cloud computing offers high elasticity and scalability in managing logistics big data, while allowing companies to implement AI systems that analyze customer behavior, demand patterns, and predictions of possible supply disruptions. Wang et al. (2023) emphasize that edge-cloud hybrid architecture has become the dominant paradigm in intelligent logistics systems as it brings together the power of local processing and deep centralized analytics.

3. Data Lakes and Digital Thread Frameworks

Another problem arises when data comes from a variety of different formats and system sources: ERP, CRM, IoT sensors, warehouse management systems, and customer digital platforms. To meet these integration challenges, many organizations are adopting data lakes as a unified repository for structured and unstructured data. Data lakes support long-term storage of large volumes of data, enabling machine learning and digital twin model training based on historical and real-time data at the same time. Zhang et al. (2022) in their study showed that data lake architecture combined with predictive analytics successfully improved freight forwarding efficiency by up to 28% in multinational logistics companies.

In addition to massive data management, cross-phase integration in the value chain is also critical. This is where the role of digital threads becomes crucial. Digital threads connect critical points in the product and logistics lifecycle from planning, manufacturing, distribution, to customer feedback in one consistent data path. With digital threads, information is not interrupted even when moving between systems, allowing for high-accuracy identification of the root cause or tracking of product history. Zhang and Tao (2022) emphasize that digital threads are a vital link in digital twin ecosystems and avoid data duplication and enhance multi-level collaboration between stakeholders.

4. Blockchain for Traceability and Trust

In a supply chain that involves many parties, data integrity is key. The diversity of actors makes the system vulnerable to errors and manipulation. Blockchain comes as a solution with permanent and distributed logging, allowing every transaction to be recorded and verified automatically. In the distribution of organic food or health products, this technology guarantees the authenticity and condition of logistics through smart contracts. Saberi et al. (2020) show that blockchain reduces audit costs and improves the efficiency of cross-border tracking.

Blockchain systems become more powerful when combined with IoT and digital twins. Sensors collect real-time data, the blockchain records it securely, and digital twins simulate scenarios based on that data (Rahaman et al., 2024). This combination creates a transparent and responsive logistics system. For example, in the distribution of COVID-19 vaccines, this technology is used for temperature tracking and supply security. Dwivedi et al. (2022) noted that this approach increases public confidence in the quality of vaccines, especially in areas with limited logistics (Zaidi et al., 2025).

Cybersecurity is also a major challenge that cannot be ignored. In an open edge and IoT environment, an attack on a single node can spread rapidly throughout the logistics system. Therefore, the integration of AI-based security systems is now widely implemented (Rahaman, Cajes, et al., 2025) developed a machine learning-based predictive security approach that is able to detect anomalies in data flows and enable automatic mitigation before the system is widely impacted. These systems are crucial in public sector logistics such as disaster relief delivery, where the reliability and safety of the system determine the success of the mission (Achuthan et al., 2025).

From the industry side, various global companies have shown how this technological infrastructure provides a competitive advantage. JD Logistics in China has implemented smart warehouses based on edge computing and autonomous robots, enabling the processing of millions of daily packages without human involvement. DHL leverages digital twins and digital threads to optimize its delivery network in Europe, cutting delivery times by up to 25%. In Singapore, a collaboration between the government and a logistics startup resulted in a blockchain system for seafood tracking that has managed to significantly increase exports to Japan and South Korea.

Logistics transformation through digital infrastructure is not only relevant in the private sector. Governments of various countries are now also starting to build a "national logistics digital backbone" to strengthen food security, improve international trade efficiency, and anticipate global supply chain disruptions. Indonesia, for example, through the National Logistics System (Sislognas) program and e-logistics initiatives managed by the Ministry of Trade and logistics SOEs, has embarked on digital integration steps, although it still requires strengthening the infrastructure ecosystem and data-driven open regulations.

With advancements such as 6G, quantum computing, and generative artificial intelligence, logistics infrastructure will continue to evolve demanding a more open, interoperable, and collaborative approach to systems. The new era of logistics is no longer about the speed of delivery, but the speed of technological adaptation.

Organizations that successfully build the technology foundation from sensors to AI, from edge to blockchain, will take the lead in creating a resilient, transparent, and customer-friendly supply chain of the future.

FROM VISIBILITY TO INTELLIGENCE: DT-DRIVEN OPTIMIZATION

Digital transformation in supply chains and logistics has gone through an important phase: from simply gaining data visibility to developing systems that are able to respond, predict, and even optimize operations independently. This evolution did not happen by chance, but was the result of the synergy of digital twin technology, artificial intelligence (AI), machine learning (ML), and real-time monitoring systems. In this context, digital twins are no longer understood as just virtual replicas of physical assets, but as cognitive entities that allow companies to forecast future conditions, anticipate risks, as well as devise more precise adaptive strategies.

1. Real-Time Monitoring and Asset Tracking

Real-time visibility is the initial foundation that allows all of these optimization processes to run. Modern logistics systems now demand complete transparency of the existence of assets ranging from truck positions, warehouse conditions, to the temperature status of containers during the delivery of sensitive goods. Liu et al. (2021) showed that asset visibility through sensor networks and IoT can reduce vehicle idle time by up to 27%, accelerate logistics rotation, and lower the rate of item loss. This technology gives logistics managers the ability to access real-time data through a dashboard that integrates information from various sensors, GPS, and edge processing systems.

2. Predictive Maintenance in Logistics Fleets

However, just looking at the current data is not enough. The system must be able to understand when a vehicle will experience a disturbance before it is completely damaged. This is where predictive maintenance comes in as a next step in visibility. By integrating digital twins and machine learning, the system can identify wear patterns or mechanical anomalies that indicate a risk of failure. For example, based on the vibrations detected by sensors on the wheel shaft or the oil pressure in the engine, the system can estimate the possibility of damage and provide maintenance suggestions before downtime occurs.

A study from Zonta et al. (2020) in *Computers in Industry* illustrates the application of digital twins for the maintenance of heavy material transport truck fleets. By using a predictive model based on sensor data, companies can reduce sudden breakdowns by up to 40%, while saving annual maintenance costs by more than 20%. The same is true for cargo carriers that now use digital twin models to monitor aircraft parts cycles and avoid unplanned grounding.

3. Adaptive Demand Forecasting Using ML

Beyond just maintenance, digital twins provide strategic value in demand planning and resource allocation. Machine learning now plays a critical role in identifying dynamically changing consumption patterns and market demand. In a digital twin system, ML algorithms are trained on historical data, weather, local calendars, consumer purchasing trends, and external factors such as promotions or global supply disruptions.

Gao et al. (2022) show how large retail companies in Europe are leveraging digital twins and ML to build multichannel demand forecasting systems capable of predicting stock needs with up to 95% accuracy. This approach not only helps avoid stockouts, but also reduces the need for overstock, which impacts costs and waste. In the context of fresh food logistics, this is especially important because the products have a limited shelf life and high turnover.

4. Scenario-Based Planning and Simulation

The role of digital twins in optimization does not stop at demand prediction. One of its main strengths lies in the ability to run simulated scenarios both in real time and as part of strategic planning. For example, companies can model what would happen if shipping routes were disrupted by flooding, or if major suppliers were late in delivering raw materials. Digital twins allow users to evaluate various "what-if" scenarios without directly touching the physical system, thus minimizing risk and speeding up decision-making.

In practice, digital twin-based simulations have been used in the management of ports and container terminals. Companies like DP World are using digital replicas of ports to test scenarios for changing ship schedules, container density, and workforce management. According to Zhang et al. (2021), this implementation managed to increase port throughput by up to 18% without adding new physical infrastructure, simply by resetting thc operating scenario based on digital simulations.

Scenario-based simulations are also important in dealing with uncertainties such as pandemics or geopolitical conflicts. For example, during the global disruption caused by COVID-19, international logistics companies used digital twins to evaluate alternative shipping route scenarios, build fuel economy models, and anticipate sudden demand for medical goods. With this support, they can survive and still meet SLAs (Service Level Agreements) even in highly volatile market conditions.

All capabilities such as real-time monitoring, predictive maintenance, adaptive forecasting, and scenario simulation form an intelligent and anticipatory supply chain that is not only reactive, but able to respond before disruptions occur. For this reason, open API-based integrations and adaptive middleware are starting to be used. Siemens and IBM, for example, provide digital twin platforms with real-time connectivity and low latency. On the other hand, federated learning is beginning to be adopted so that AI can be trained on various local nodes without collecting data centrally, maintaining privacy and efficiency.

Overall, digital twin-based optimization is no longer a concept of the future, but a real need that has been proven to deliver concrete results in various industries. Organizations that successfully turn visibility into intelligence have a real advantage in terms of efficiency, resilience, and responsiveness to market changes. In other words, digital twins are not just a simulation tool, but the new heart of adaptive supply chain management.

IMMERSIVE CONSUMER EXPERIENCE IN THE METAVERSE SUPPLY CHAIN

The digital age has ushered in a major change in the way consumers interact with products and services. As metaverse technology begins to penetrate into the logistics and supply chain sectors, a new paradigm emerges where the customer experience is no longer passive. Now, consumers can "enter" the digital world of the supply chain to see, interact, and even participate in designing the products they order. This phenomenon is known as **immersive consumer experience**, which integrates 3D visualization, metaverse-based real-time tracking, gamification, and the role of digital humans and AI assistants to create an immersive, interactive, and personalized experience.

1. Virtual Product Journey Visualization

One of the key features of a metaverse-based supply chain is the ability to display the entire product journey in a visual-rich virtual environment. These visualizations allow consumers to understand origins, manufacturing status, delivery locations, and estimated time of arrival through interactive maps and 3D simulations.

In a study by Zhang et al. (2023), a mixed reality-based logistics visualization system was shown to increase customer engagement by 48% in the fashion retail sector in China. Customers not only see the status of their packages, but also virtually "walk" delivery routes, including through ports, warehouses, and final distribution points. This technology builds trust through information disclosure and strengthens emotional attachment to the brand.

Visualizations are also used to demonstrate sustainability impacts, such as carbon emissions throughout the product journey. This is increasingly important as millennial and Gen Z consumers increasingly care about the environmental footprint of their consumption.

2. Real-Time 3D Delivery Tracking Interfaces

One of the distinguishing elements in a metaverse-based supply chain is real-time 3D tracking. Consumers can access augmented reality or extended reality (XR)-based platforms that display dynamic representations of the location and status of their goods.

A study from Kim et al. (2021) published in *IEEE Access* states that 3D tracking technology speeds up communication between customers and logistics providers by 35% and reduces late complaints by up to 22%. The system works by integrating GPS data, load conditions, and estimated arrival times, then visualized spatially on a three-dimensional digital map. Customers can click on specific locations to see more in-depth information, including container temperature conditions, transit duration, and potential risk of delays.

This integration also allows for event-based automatic notifications for example if there is a delay due to extreme weather, then a logistics AI avatar can appear and provide a live explanation in the customer's virtual space.

3. Gamification and Consumer Co-Design in Virtual Space

The concept of gamification in logistics is not new, but its implementation in the metaverse realm brings a more immersive approach. Instead of just receiving information, customers are encouraged to interact through light logistics games, tracking challenges, or participation-based incentives.

In a metaverse e-commerce system, customers can "choose" the fastest shipping route from multiple options in a virtual map, or manage product storage in a digital warehouse. Those who succcssfully choose an efficient route can receive a virtual discount or badge. A study by Feng et al. (2022) shows that gamification strategies increase customer retention rates by up to 38% on XR-based retail platforms. In addition, consumers can now participate in the co-design process. For example, they can modify product designs (colors, shapes, packaging) directly in a virtual space connected to factories or manufacturing partners.

4. Digital Humans and AI Assistants for Logistics

The presence of digital humans, intelligent and expressive representations of virtual characters, has brought a more human dimension of interaction into the digital logistics system. They become the face of customer service, provide logistics information, and even accompany customers in navigating the metaverse space.

AI-powered digital humans such as "Samantha" or "Kai" are now being used by large logistics companies to answer consumer questions, suggest the best delivery times, or explain customs clearance processes in interactive simulations. According to Han et al. (2023), the use of digital humans in the metaverse logistics environment increases customer satisfaction by up to 31% compared to plain text-based chatbots.

Meanwhile, AI assistants integrated with smart contracts and ERP systems help customers to design personalized logistics, such as determining shipment merging, automatic rescheduling, or cargo tracking requests. This AI can learn from previous interactions and provide increasingly relevant recommendations over time.

Table 1. Immersive Technologies in the Metaverse Supply Chain

Featured	Main Function	Benefits for Consumers
Virtual Product Journey	Display the product journey in an interactive 3D view	Consumers can "see" the product moving from factory to home
Real-Time 3D Tracking	Tracks shipment location and status live in a virtual space	Provides certainty and reduces anxiety about delivery
Gamification & Co-Design	Engages customers in route selection and product customization	Makes the experience more enjoyable and personal
Digital Humans & AI Assistants	Offers assistance and information via intelligent virtual avatars	Service feels fast, friendly, and like talking to a real person

CASE STUDIES AND INDUSTRY APPLICATIONS

1. Retail: Inventory Transparency and Digital Store Twins

The implementation of digital twin technology, augmented reality (AR), virtual reality (VR), and logistics automation has now gone beyond the trial and prototype stages. In recent years, global companies from various sectors have demonstrated how the implementation of these simulation-based digital systems not only serves as an internal efficiency tool, but also as a transformational strategy that creates new value along the supply chain. The effect is not only limited to increased productivity or delivery accuracy, but also has an impact on customer satisfaction, operational cost savings, and increased supply chain resilience to disruptions.

In the retail sector, digital twins have enabled the creation of a virtual store ecosystem that is fully in sync with physical conditions. This technology allows store managers to see stock movements in real-time, understand customer traffic patterns, and redesign store layouts based on simulations of consumer behavior. A clear example is Walmart's use of digital twin systems, which have combined data from IoT sensors and stock management systems to improve store responsiveness to surging demand. Research by Gao et al. (2022) shows that digital twins help large retail companies lower inventory management errors by up to 35%, ultimately reducing lost sales due to empty products on the shelf.

More than just inventory management, digital twins are also used in employee training. In a fully virtual environment, new staff can undergo simulation-based training without having to disrupt operations in a physical store. With the ability to replicate complex customer service scenarios, management can evaluate employee responses and provide feedback directly.

2. E-commerce: Automated Warehouse Twins and Drone Delivery

A major shift has also occurred in the e-commerce sector, which has been very open to the adoption of high technology since its inception. Amazon, as a pioneer, has long developed warehouse automation with the help of digital twins. Inside Amazon's smart warehouses, each rack and transport vehicle has a constantly updated digital identity. This digital model allows the system to design the most optimal route, estimate restocking needs, and avoid potential operational bottlenecks. According to a study by Zhang et al. (2021), digital twins can speed up order processing time by up to 30% and lower operational costs by more than 18%.

Innovation doesn't stop in the warehouse. In terms of delivery, companies such as JD Logistics in China have combined digital twins with drone delivery technology. Each drone flight is controlled and monitored by a digital twin system that displays position, battery status, and environmental conditions in real-time. Even more interestingly, customers can visually view the delivery simulation through the app, creating a much more interactive experience than conventional text-based tracking. A study by Liu et al. (2023) noted that the level of customer trust in delivery increased significantly when they were given access to real-time digital visualizations of the delivery process.

3. Manufacturing: Smart Factory Logistics

The manufacturing industry is also the main beneficiary of digital twin technology, especially in the context of smart factories. Smart factories in the Industry 4.0 era rely on digital simulations to monitor machine conditions, manage material flows, and predict output demand. The Siemens Amberg Smart Factory, as an iconic example, relies on digital twins to manage all internal logistics and production activities. The system not only provides end-to-end visibility, but is also capable of running simulations of production line configuration changes before actual implementation is carried out. In research by Schneider et al. (2020), the use of digital twins was able to reduce machine downtime by 60% and increase production output by 22%.

Another benefit that is no less important is the flexibility of production. Digital twins allow manufacturers to adapt production lines according to highly dynamic market demands, such as seasonal product launches or responses to supply disruptions.

4. Last-Mile Innovations With AR/VR Consumer Tracking

Innovation is also evident at the very last stage in the supply chain: last-mile delivery. This stage has been known as the most expensive and most prone to delays in logistics. However, with the help of AR and VR, these challenges are slowly starting to be overcome. AR-based mobile apps now allow customers to see the whereabouts of their couriers in real-time in a realistic 3D map view. Not only the location of the vehicle, but also traffic conditions and estimated arrival time are displayed visually and interactively (Moslehpour et al., 2024).

In a study by Lee et al. (2023), the integration of AR visualization in last-mile delivery tracking was proven to be able to reduce the number of customer complaints by 28% and increase service satisfaction by more than 30%. This shows that visual transparency not only increases trust, but also lowers the burden of customer service as customers feel more at ease knowing where their package stands.

Some companies are even developing VR-based delivery scenarios, where customers receive notifications through a headset and can virtually "see" the courier delivering packages to their homes.

Table 2. Case Studies of Digital Twin and AR/VR Applications in Industry

Sector	Technology Application	Real-World Impact
Retail	Digital store twin for inventory management and staff training	Improved inventory accuracy and more efficient employee onboarding
E-commerce	Automated warehouse and drone delivery enabled by digital twins	Faster order fulfillment and increased delivery transparency
Manufacturing	Smart factory logistics and real-time simulation of internal flow	Enhanced operational efficiency and production flexibility
Last-Mile	AR/VR interfaces for courier tracking and customer delivery experience	More interactive delivery process and better navigation for couriers

IMPLEMENTATION FRAMEWORK

1. Digital Twin Maturity Models

Digital transformation in logistics through the adoption of digital twins (DTs) cannot happen instantly. An implementation framework is needed that not only covers the technological aspects, but also guides the organization in managing the adoption process gradually and measurably. The concept of DT implementation in the modern logistics sector has now evolved into a discipline that involves mapping the maturity of the system, planning a roadmap from the initial stage to full scale, setting key performance indicators (KPIs), and adjusting to digital platforms in accordance with operational needs.

An assessment of an organization's readiness to adopt a digital twin can be done through a maturity model that gradually describes the evolution of system capabilities. In recent studies, the twin digital maturity model has been defined as a strategic tool to evaluate the extent to which a company has integrated real-time data, predictive analytics, and artificial intelligence-based automation into its digital model. For example, Rayhana et al. (2024) explain that in the context of the logistics and manufacturing industries, digital twins can be divided into five stages of maturity: ranging from static visual representations, real-time monitoring systems, to predictive and prescriptive models capable of autonomous decision-making.

The earliest stage usually begins with the creation of a basic digital representation of a physical asset. This includes modeling product or process structures using CAD devices or simple simulations with no direct connection to actual data. In the next stage, organizations will begin to integrate IoT sensors and devices to enable real-world monitoring of conditions directly through digital interfaces.

2. Roadmap: From Pilot to Scaled Deployment

To achieve a high level of maturity, realistic roadmap planning is needed. No single organization is able to jump directly to a prescriptive or autonomous level without going through a process of experimentation and validation. Digital twin roadmaps usually start with a pilot project in a limited scope. The main objective is to test the initial integration between the systems, such as the communication between the warehouse sensor and the digital visualization dashboard. Once this initial phase is successful, companies can expand their scope by connecting digital twins to logistics management systems (TMS), demand planning, or even to end customers through real-time-based tracking interfaces.

The journey from the initial stage to full-scale deployment requires regular and iterative evaluation. As explained by Zhou et al. (2021), a successful implementation roadmap is one that is data-driven, flexible to change, and involves all stakeholders from the start. One widely used approach is the agile implementation method, where each digital twin module is developed in a short cycle and evaluated directly in a real operational environment. This allows companies to learn from initial failures and avoid wasted technology investments.

3. KPIs for DT-Based Logistics Performance

In addition to the roadmap, the success of digital twins is also determined by key performance indicators (KPIs) that are used to measure their impact on logistics operations. Digital twin KPIs not only reflect efficiency aspects, but also include prediction accuracy, system reliability, and environmental sustainability. For example, average delivery times can be used to evaluate the effectiveness of digital twin route planning, while the reduction in the energy costs of logistics fleets is a direct indicator of the system's success in optimizing routes and vehicle usage. A study by Gao et al. (2020) showed that companies that measured KPIs such as predictive failures prevented, sensor data accuracy, and reduced system downtime, had higher success in achieving overall supply chain efficiency.

4. Role of Digital Twin Platforms (Siemens, PTC, Azure, etc.)

Nevertheless, all such processes cannot run without a solid technical foundation. This is where the role of digital twin platforms becomes crucial. Platforms such as Siemens Mindsphere, PTC ThingWorx, Microsoft Azure Digital Twins, and Dassault Systèmes 3DEXPERIENCE provide cloud infrastructure, visualization tools, data connectivity, and integrated artificial intelligence modules. The choice of platform should consider scalability, support for legacy *systems*, and the specific needs of the business sector.

Siemens excels in the heavy manufacturing industry with strong integration into PLM systems and engineering design tools, ideal for the automotive and high-precision electronics sectors. Meanwhile, PTC's ThingWorx is more popular in retail and logistics thanks to its flexibility of combining sensor data with AR/VR to enhance the customer experience.

Meanwhile, Microsoft Azure Digital Twins stands out for its ability to handle big data, the speed of scalability of cloud systems, and the integration of AI services such as Azure Machine Learning and Power BI. The platform is ideal for companies that have a cloud-first architecture and manage a geographically dispersed supply chain.

While these various platforms offer their own advantages, organizations should be careful in making their choices. In a study by Li et al. (2020), it was stated that factors such as licensing fees, staff training needs, interoperability with existing systems, as well as user community support should also be taken into account. For small and medium-sized organizations, an open-source solution like Eclipse Ditto can be an economical starting point for testing the concept of digital twins without a large investment.

Table 3. Overview of Digital Twin Platforms and Industry Suitability

Platform	Core Strengths	Best Fit Industry
Siemens Mindsphere	Deep integration with industrial hardware and PLM systems	Automotive, heavy manufacturing
PTC ThingWorx	Strong IoT flexibility and AR/VR interfaces for real-time visualization	Retail, logistics, consumer-facing supply chain
Microsoft Azure Digital Twins	Scalable cloud environment with native AI and analytics integration	E-commerce, tech-driven global logistics
Dassault 3DEXPERIENCE	Integrated collaboration for design, engineering, and logistics	High-mix manufacturing and global supply chain
Eclipse Ditto (Open-source)	Modular, lightweight, and cost-efficient for prototyping and SMEs (Rahaman, Chappu, et al., 2025).	Startups, R&D-focused projects

CHALLENGES AND CONSIDERATIONS

Figure 1. Challenges and Strategic Considerations for Digital Twin Implementation in Logistics

1. Data Synchronization Across Ecosystems

As the adoption of digital twins (DTs) increases in logistics and global supply chains, implementation challenges and strategic considerations are also growing in complexity. This technology does promise high efficiency, end-to-end visibility, and predictive capabilities that were previously impossible to achieve. However, these benefits do not come without obstacles. Organizations that want to make the most of the potential of digital twins must face and manage a number of fundamental challenges, ranging from cross-system data synchronization, cybersecurity vulnerabilities, ethical issues related to digital monitoring, to the need for workforce skills transformation.

One of the most obvious challenges in the implementation of digital twins in the logistics sector is the synchronization of data between highly heterogeneous systems. The modern supply chain consists of various actors that each use its own management system, such as ERP, SCM, TMS, and IoT. All of these systems generate data in different formats, with varying speeds and volumes. In the study of Zhang et al. (2022), data synchronization was cited as a major barrier to digital twin integration in cross-organizational logistics operations due to differences in system architecture and communication protocols. If not managed properly, these discrepancies will result in inconsistent information, which can ultimately undermine the validity of the digital twin model. In addition, issues such as *data latency*, *data duplication*, and time inconsistencies between real-time data and historical data pose risks in DT-based decision-making.

2. Cybersecurity and Digital Twin Attack Surfaces

However, data synchronization is not just a technical issue. Behind data integration are also hidden issues of access rights, data ownership, and privacy protection. As digital twins connect with customer data and smart devices in real-time, cybersecurity issues become increasingly crucial. According to Liu et al. (2021), the digital twin model expands the *attack surface* because it creates high connectivity between the physical world and the digital world. Interconnected sensors, logistics vehicles, and automated warehouses are potential entry points for hackers. Some of the attacks that have been reported in the sector include manipulation of temperature sensor data in food delivery, spoofing of vehicle locations, as well as interventions into inventory prediction dashboards.

To address these challenges, proactive security architectures such as AI-based intrusion detection, multi-layered encryption, and digital authentication are needed. A zero-trust and network segmentation approach, as discussed by Hemmati et al. (2025), is important to limit access and ensure repeated verification. However, its implementation is often constrained by budget and technical limitations.

3. Ethical Implications of Automation and Digital Surveillance

In addition to the technical aspect, ethical issues are also an important part of the discussion around the implementation of digital twins. These systems, particularly when used in employee, fleet, and customer tracking, can create a highly intense monitoring ecosystem. While this brings efficiency from the business side, from the human side there are concerns about over-surveillance and privacy violations. In the context of distribution and warehousing, employees may feel that they are constantly being watched by a digital twin system that records work speed, rest time, and movement routes in the warehouse. According to Vial & Kraus (2023), the implementation of technology without a mature ethical approach can create distrust in the work environment and strengthen the inequality of the relationship between the system and workers.

On the customer side, overly detailed real-time tracking can also lead to uncomfortable feelings. For example, a digital twin feature that records when and where someone receives a package could be at risk of being used for surveillance activities if it falls into the wrong hands.

4. Skills and Workforce Transformation

Finally, digital transformation through digital twins demands major changes in organizational skills and culture. Tech infrastructure can be built in a matter of months, but changing the mindset and skills of employees takes much longer. In many organizations, there is still a huge gap between the capabilities of technical staff and the need for digitalization. Data analytics skills, understanding digital modeling, and expertise in cybersecurity and AI are now core competencies that must be possessed by modern logistics human resources. In research by Singh et al. (2021), more than 60% of logistics companies admit that the lack of digital experts is the biggest obstacle in the implementation of digital twins.

Therefore, training must be a core part of digital transformation. Many organizations are now working with universities and technology providers to develop relevant curricula. Methods such as case-based learning and digital twin sandboxes effectively equip staff with technical and strategic understanding. In addition, it is important to build a culture of innovation and digital literacy so that technology adoption becomes an organizational movement, not just an IT project.

FUTURE TRENDS IN SUPPLY CHAIN DIGITALIZATION

1. Autonomous Supply Chain Networks

Major changes in the world of supply chains do not happen overnight, but are the result of technological evolution that continues to evolve in line with market pressures and global demand. As companies enter a new decade marked by geopolitical volatility, climate change, and consumer expectations for sustainability and transparency, digital transformation is no longer an option, but a necessity. In the midst of this complexity, the future direction of digital logistics is starting to seem clearer and much more radical than what was imagined five years ago.

Autonomous supply chain networks, for example, are no longer just a futuristic concept. Many companies have already started building systems capable of making logistics decisions without manual intervention. It's not just about autonomous vehicles or robotic warehouses, but rather a network of systems that are interconnected, learn from each other, and can react to disruptions in seconds. A recent study by Gao et al. (2022) highlights how pharmaceutical companies are using autonomous networks to respond to distribution disruptions due to the pandemic. As a result, the distribution time decreased by 42% with a near-zero error rate. The model works by combining digital twin monitoring of production facilities, real-time integration of market demand, and an AI-based adaptive delivery system.

2. Cognitive Logistics With Generative AI

What makes this trend even more exciting is its ability to expand the boundaries of prediction into deeper contextual understanding. This is where the concept of cognitive logistics finds its place. Unlike traditional logistics systems that only respond to demand with simple predictive schemes, cognitive systems try to understand the reasons behind such spikes or decreases in demand. With the help of generative AI models, the system not only forecasts a surge in sales of a product, but is also able to identify consumer trends on social media, changes in purchasing behavior, and market sentiment that drive those dynamics. In a study by Park et al. (2023), the use of generative AI to construct simulated scenarios in the management of holiday season distribution resulted in a 28% reduction in product loss and significant logistics cost efficiency.

3. Federated Digital Twins and Decentralized Control

The integration of increasingly complex and multi-party systems has created the need for a more open yet secure data structure. Federated digital twins are an ideal solution in this context. With a federated approach, each entity in the supply chain (Rahaman et al., 2022), whether manufacturers, distributors, or retailers, has its own digital twin that can exchange information without having to hand over full control to one centralized platform. Li and Huang (2022) refer to this model as a bridge between data security and open collaboration, especially in highly sensitive industries such as pharmaceuticals, food, and high technology.

Federated DT offers the flexibility needed in the age of data openness. With this technology, entities can share stock status, production capacity, and transportation conditions without having to open access to their entire internal systems. This is especially important in a global supply chain consisting of cross-border, cultural, and regulatory actors. The integration of blockchain in federated DT strengthens trust between parties by providing a transparent audit trail of all transactions and data shared.

4. Sustainable Logistics Enabled by Green Twins

Amid all these innovations, there is one important dimension that should not be overlooked: sustainability. Environmental issues are now a major factor in logistics decision-making. Not surprisingly, a new approach called green twins has emerged, namely digital twins which are specifically designed to measure, model, and optimize the sustainability aspects of the entire logistics process. This includes simulating carbon emissions from distribution routes, measuring energy consumption in smart warehouses, to environmental impact analysis of packaging options and modes of transportation. Research by Wang et al. (2024) shows that the use of green twins is able to reduce CO_2 emissions in frozen food distribution by up to 31% in just two operational quarters.

Green twins not only offer reputational advantages as green companies, but also create concrete operational savings. For example, by simulating an energy-efficient combination of land and sea-based logistics routes, companies can save fuel costs without sacrificing delivery time significantly. At the same time, consumers are also starting to value sustainability transparency as part of their experience, and green twins can present that data in a form that is easy for customers to understand, for example in the form of digital carbon labels when tracking packages.

CONCLUSION

1. Recap of Key Insights

During the journey of exploration of the transformation of the digital supply chain through digital twins, metaverse, AI, and other related technologies, it is clear that the traditional approach in logistics is no longer relevant to answer today's business challenges. Supply chains that used to focus only on cost and shipping efficiency must now be able to absorb and manage market uncertainties, customer demand dynamics, and expectations for transparency and sustainability. The concept of digital twins emerged as a bridge between the physical and virtual worlds capable of integrating sensors, historical data, and AI analytics to model, predict, and optimize the entire logistics process holistically.

In addition, we have seen how technologies such as edge computing, cloud systems, blockchain, and IoT are not only complementary, but essential foundations of intelligent logistics systems. In its implementation, companies such as Siemens, JD Logistics, Amazon, and Walmart have demonstrated how digitalization can reduce inventory errors, improve response times, and provide an immersive and personalized customer experience. Even the metaverse concept that was previously considered futuristic is now starting to enter the practical implementation stage in shipment tracking, virtual product co-design, and avatar-based consumer services.

The research also highlights that advanced technology alone is not enough. An organizational transformation approach is needed both in technical infrastructure and human resource readiness so that digital systems can be adopted comprehensively. Without digital culture readiness, many technology initiatives will stop at the pilot stage or even fail completely. In this context, change management and digital training policies are essential components to drive long-term success.

2. Strategic Implications for Industry 5.0

With the entry of the Industry 5.0 era, a phase in which human-machine collaboration becomes the focal point, the role of digital twins and supporting technologies becomes increasingly strategic. Within this framework, digital twins are not only used to maximize production output, but to create new value centered on people and the planet.

The strategic implications are far-reaching. First, companies must start building technology architectures that are capable of operating collaboratively where AI, digital twins, and humans can work side by side. This entails the selection of a technology platform that is open and can be integrated with third-party systems.

Second, sustainability is a new performance indicator in logistics. Companies that are unable to demonstrate carbon emission data, transparency of product origin, or ESG (Environmental, Social, Governance) compliance will lose market trust. In this context, digital twins are the main tools for mapping the carbon footprint, simulating changes in logistics routes based on green optimization, and proving compliance with increasingly stringent environmental regulations.

Third, in the Industry 5.0 era, customer experience will be the main differentiating factor. Digital twins integrated with AR/VR interfaces and metaverse technology open up new opportunities in product co-design, interactive delivery tracking, and digital avatar-based services. As stated by Dwivedi et al. (2022).

3. Recommendations for Future Research and Practice

Although the digital transformation of the supply chain has begun to develop, there are still many challenges and questions that require further research attention. First, it is necessary to develop a standard framework to measure the maturity level of digital twins in the context of logistics. Currently, there is no universally adopted consensus on the success indicators or maturity level of digital twin implementation. This makes it difficult to benchmark between companies and evaluate business impact.

Second, the integration between digital twins federally needs to be explored further. In the real world, a supply chain is a complex network that involves many entities with different systems. Federated digital twins allow companies to maintain control over their own data, but still be able to share insights through a collaborative network. This concept is relevant in maintaining privacy, data law compliance, and global scalability. Research by Reddy et al. (2024) emphasizes the importance of interoperability in creating a cross-organizational digital twin ecosystem.

Third, research on the ethical and social impacts of automation and digitalization of logistics needs to be strengthened. With the entry of robotics, AI, and predictive systems, there has been a significant shift in the role of humans. There will be jobs lost, but also new jobs that will emerge. The challenge is how to create an effective, equitable, and inclusive reskilling strategy so that this transformation does not create new social gaps.

Fourth, AI-based approaches in logistics decision-making need to be further developed. Today, many algorithms are still black-boxed, difficult to explain and audit. It takes the development of explainable AI (XAI) so that logistics decisions generated by the system can be understood and accounted for both commercially and legally.

Fifth, a hybrid system approach between digital twins and cognitive systems such as generative AI is an interesting field to explore. Imagine a digital twin system that not only simulates delivery routes, but can also imagine and generate new route alternatives based on historical data and current conditions.

Finally, in practice, synergy between industry, academia, and policymakers is needed. The government can play a strategic role in creating regulations that encourage innovation while maintaining the principles of fairness and transparency. Academics need to develop new conceptual frameworks and technologies, while industry becomes a real laboratory for testing these ideas.

REFERENCES

Achuthan, K., Gupta, B. B., & Raman, R. (2025). Bridging cybersecurity with digital twin technology: A thematic analysis. *International Journal of Information Security*, *24*(5), 207. DOI: 10.1007/s10207-025-01115-y

Ali, M. H., Suleiman, N., Khalid, N., Tan, K. H., Tseng, M. L., & Kumar, M. (2021). Supply chain resilience reactive strategies for food SMEs in coping to COVID-19 crisis. *Trends in Food Science & Technology*, *109*, 94–102.

Dwivedi, Y. K., Hughes, L., Baabdullah, A. M., Ribeiro-Navarrete, S., Giannakis, M., Al-Debei, M. M., Dennehy, D., Metri, B., Buhalis, D., Cheung, C. M. K., Conboy, K., Doyle, R., Dubey, R., Dutot, V., Felix, R., Goyal, D. P., Gustafsson, A., Hinsch, C., Jebabli, I., & Wamba, S. F. (2022). Metaverse beyond the hype: Multidisciplinary perspectives on emerging challenges, opportunities, and agenda for research, practice and policy. *International Journal of Information Management*, *66*, 102542. DOI: 10.1016/j.ijinfomgt.2022.102542

Dwivedi, Y. K., Hughes, L., Baabdullah, A. M., Ribeiro-Navarrete, S., Giannakis, M., Al-Debei, M. M., Dennehy, D., Metri, B., Buhalis, D., Cheung, C. M. K., Conboy, K., Doyle, R., Dubey, R., Dutot, V., Felix, R., Goyal, D. P., Gustafsson, A., Hinsch, C., Jebabli, I., & Wamba, S. F. (2022). Metaverse beyond the hype: Multidisciplinary perspectives on emerging challenges, opportunities, and agenda for research, practice and policy. *International Journal of Information Management*, *66*, 102542. DOI: 10.1016/j.ijinfomgt.2022.102542

Guo, S., Zhang, J., Jiang, Q., & Zhang, B. (2022). Surface integrity in high-speed grinding of Al6061T6 alloy. *CIRP Annals*, *71*(1), 281–284. DOI: 10.1016/j.cirp.2022.03.002

Gupta, B. B., Gaurav, A., Arya, V., Waheeb Attar, R., Bansal, S., Alhomoud, A., & Chui, K. T. (2025). Sustainable supply chain security through BEART-based fake news detection on supplier practices. *Enterprise Information Systems*, *19*, 2462972. DOI: 10.1080/17517575.2025.2462972

Hemmati, A., Aliyari, M., & Chobar, A. P. (2025). In Nozari, H. (Ed.), *AIoE-Powered Supply Chain Optimization for Smart Agriculture BT - Artificial Intelligence of Everything and Sustainable Development* (pp. 223–240). Springer Nature Singapore., DOI: 10.1007/978-981-96-7202-8_13

Li, L.-F., Wang, X., Hu, W.-J., Xiong, N. N., Du, Y.-X., & Li, B.-S. (2020). Deep Learning in Skin Disease Image Recognition: A Review. *IEEE Access : Practical Innovations, Open Solutions*, *8*, 208264–208280. DOI: 10.1109/ACCESS.2020.3037258

Liu, M., Fang, S., Dong, H., & Xu, C. (2021). Review of digital twin about concepts, technologies, and industrial applications. *Journal of Manufacturing Systems, 58*, 346–361. DOI: 10.1016/j.jmsy.2020.06.017

Moslehpour, M., Dwikesumasari, P. R., Pappachan, P., Lin, P.-K., Sakina, N., & Rahaman, M. (2024). Incorporating Web Semantics, the Technology Acceptance Model, and the Theory of Planned Behavior for Analyzing User Intentions on Dating Apps. [IJSWIS]. *International Journal on Semantic Web and Information Systems, 20*(1), 1–20.

Rahaman, M., Cajes, N., Gupta, B. B., Chui, K. T., & Nedjah, N. (2025). Defending against smishing attacks: State-of-the-art techniques, challenges, limitations, and future directions. *Computer Networks, 273*, 111758. DOI: 10.1016/j.comnet.2025.111758

Rahaman, M., Chappu, B., Jana, S., Haque, A., Firmansyah, G., & Chattopadhyay, S. (2025). Security Benefits in Small Medium Business Enterprise Through Cloud Adoption. In N. Nedjah, G. Martinez Perez, & B. B. Gupta (Eds.), *International Conference on Smart Systems and Advanced Computing (SysCom 2022)* (pp. 168–180). Springer Nature Switzerland. https://doi.org/DOI: 10.1007/978-3-031-40905-9_18

Rahaman, M., Chattopadhyay, S., & Anwar, N. (2022). *A Case Study: Physical Layer Security Analysis for Internet of Vehicle (IoV)*. 283–291.

Rahaman, M., Lin, C. Y., Rachmat, I., Bansal, R., & Prayitno. (2024). Secure Health Features: Implementing Hyperledger Fabric in Blockchain-Driven Healthcare Management Systems. In *Digital Forensics and Cyber Crime Investigation*. CRC Press.

Singh, S. K., Kumar, S., Goyal, S., Arya, V., Attar, R. W., Gupta, B. B., Alhomoud, A., & Chui, K. T. (2025). Leveraging AI and Machine Learning for Enhanced Data Analytics and Visualization in Database Management With Digital Twins. [JDM]. *Journal of Database Management, 36*(1), 1–29. DOI: 10.4018/JDM.388135

Zaidi, S. M. H., Iqbal, R., Alharbi, A., Zuberi, H. H., Ahmed, A., & Sheikh, M. U. (2025). Intelligent Process Automation Using Artificial Intelligence to Create Human Assistant. [IJSSCI]. *International Journal of Software Science and Computational Intelligence, 17*(1), 1–19. DOI: 10.4018/IJSSCI.371761

Zheng, X., & Zhang, L. (2020). Risk assessment of supply-chain systems: A probabilistic inference method. *Enterprise Information Systems, 14*(6), 858–877.

Chapter 6
Revolutionizing Patient Experience Through Digital Twins and Metaverse in Healthcare

K. S. Kalavathy
http://orcid.org/0000-0001-6077-2158
CMS Business School, Jain University, Bangalore, India

M. Namratha
St. John's Medical College and Hospital, India

M. Nishanth
http://orcid.org/0009-0004-8440-7840
University of Texas at Dallas, USA

ABSTRACT

This systematic literature review surveys the shared digital twins and metaverse technologies influence on original visualization of patient experience in health delivery systems. Drawing on PRISMA-guided methodology, a synthesis of 25 publications from 2020-2025 uncovered the technologies routing care from episodic provider-driven situations to predictive participatory-patient-centered conditions according to this study. A combined five-pillar framework operationalizes each with quantifiable indicators and implementation pathways. Analysis also reveals a publication bias that favors the publishing of positive results, and highlights the lack of good long-term efficacy research. The study provides insights for healthcare organizations to responsibly implement integrated technologies while making sure that privacy and accessibility standards are strictly maintained.

DOI: 10.4018/979-8-3373-4541-3.ch006

1. INTRODUCTION AND CONTEXTUAL BACKGROUND

Each country experiences an outstanding and continuous paradox in the healthcare area. Despite the achievements of modern technologies and the recent scientific breakthroughs, the patient experiences are not pleasant and their needs are not being met (Wachter et.al 2024). The standard method of healthcare delivery is through an appointment for a consultation which generally lasts 15-20 minutes during which the health care provider makes decisions with regard to the treatment based on the fragmented and limited data collected during those brief meetings. Patients are involved in the processes mostly passively. The care provided to them is based on predefined protocols established for population averages rather than their unique physical, social, cultural characteristics, personal circumstances and preferences. This model though was tuned to align with healthcare needs during earlier times is obsolete in the present context of vast data availability.

The central problem is far more than just the issue of engagement. Modern healthcare is encountering the convergence of several pressures which call for absolutely different approaches. With the aged population increasingly suffering from complex multimorbidity, the healthcare system needs to connect and coordinate among a group of providers for managing 5-10 chronic conditions at the same time. With the rising healthcare costs, prevention-oriented approach is needed rather than crisis management (OECD, 2023). The episodic models which exist currently tend to promote more expensive acute treatments rather than affordable preventive measures (Mbata et al, 2024). The manpower deficit, especially in nursing, psychiatry and primary care is a major constraint in health care. Patients in recent times owing to their experiences in other service sectors have reshaped their expectations. They want treatment tailored to their needs (which are different from what is common in the population), treatment transparency (to know the treatment rationale), power to choose (to take part in treatment decisions), and feel a real connection (to be seen as a whole person rather than merely on symptoms).

In healthcare, there exists a situation where the technological capacities considerably exceed the actual usage. Monitoring devices that are in place continuously create massive amounts of data; genomic tests acquire detailed personal biology data; electronic health records have all the necessary information about the history; AI looks for patterns that find out differences across big data; immersive technologies enable interactive environments. In spite of this, the data is most of the time not available, fragmented across overlapping sites, and is not used to its fullest potential for prediction nor for the personalization of treatment. The difference between what can be achieved technologically and what has been implemented in real clinical settings is a unresolved challenge in contemporary healthcare (Mumtaz et al, 2023)

Two Pathbreaking technological innovations particularly provide hope to the present challenges. Digital twins are virtual computational models that join all the components such as the constantly changing biometrics, genetic data, medical history, and medication adherence, lifestyle exposure to environmental factors as well as social determinants, and are thus the digital representation of the patient made virtual. Being different from static models, digital twins continuously feed in the new data and provide simulation of the disease progression, prediction of the treatment responses, and forecasting of the most likely clinical trajectory even before the actual events take place. Metaverse technologies allow the patient to visualize health information, converse with providers and take part in computerized health interventions as well as receive psychological consultations. (Suh et al., 2023).

Each technology has a lot to offer people. Digital twins broaden the boundary for the modern medicine and overcome the challenge of individualization at scale. Instead of providing average health protocols to all the patients, digital twins can ensure personalization, as the response to treatment is different caused by physiology, genetics, situations, and personal choices. Apart from that, Metaverse platforms can be used in the following situations: patients can learn difficult health-related subjects through three-dimension visualization, connect with the practitioners even beyond their physical consultation hours, and maintain emotional engagement through the representation of virtual avatars.

The combination of these technologies will lead to synergistic outcomes which are larger than the sum of individual contributions. Every patient receives his or her personal predictions from their own digital twin before arriving at the hospital; visualize these predictions in the Metaverse showing the organ-level anatomy and the actual disease development and actively participate in the treatment selection process. The very convergence suggests a groundbreaking transformation from the idea of moving from provider-centric, periodic care to patient-centered, continuous, predictive engagement.

Though they are often considered promising and more investments are being made in digital twin and metaverse technologies very few studies focus on thc impact. Majority of the studies done so far have concentrated on each technology individually. Systematic evidence on their synergistic effects, comparative effectiveness against single-technology approaches, real-world implementation outcomes, and mechanisms enabling patient experience transformation remains limited. Moreover, critical concerns about equity and access persist as they are inadequately addressed. More concerns are raised regarding whether these technologies will democratize healthcare or concentrate resources among already-privileged populations; whether implementation barriers will disproportionately burden underserved communities; whether algorithmic bias will exacerbate existing health disparities. This systematic review synthesizes available evidence on how digital twins and metaverse technologies transform patient experience while specifically examining implementation barriers, equity implications, and realistic deployment challenges.

This research will carefully review the knowledge that is available on the subject and provide insights into the ways metaverse technologies and digital twins change patient experience. It would further focus on the implementation barriers, equity implications, and barriers to deployment.

2. LITERATURE REVIEW AND IDENTIFICATION OF RESEARCH GAPS

2.1 Current State of Knowledge and Historical Context

Traditionally, the adoption of healthcare technologies generally adheres to a predictable model that starts with the initial optimism, identification of actual barriers, the prolonged pilot studies, the slow scaling, the eventual routine integration, and the actual adoption which usually takes 15-20 years (Katsoulakis et al., 2024). Electronic health records, that looked like a magic new age in the 1980s to 1990s, took years of dedicated work to be used significantly despite the evident advantages. Thus, this historical schema implies that showing the utility of digital twins and the metaverse is only the first-level requirement for healthcare delivery to begin the transformation.

In a recent review by Katsoulakis et al. (2024) of 237 publications related to cardiology, oncology, orthopedic, and chronic disease management, digital twin applications were found to be technically feasible, however, clinically at-scale implementation was reported to have significant gaps. Their findings suggest that although computational models were able to simulate disease physiology as it would be in a specific patient, the actual integration in clinics was limited and thus most of the systems used were in academic medical centers with better resources and a well-supported IT infrastructure. There is hardly any application in the community hospitals, rural systems, and safety-net hospitals.

Complementing research by Buragohain et al. (2025) compiled evidence on metaverse based digital therapeutics and reported improved engagement The studies pointed out significant drawbacks in the evidence of their clinical efficiency. The authors noted extreme variance in the outcomes, absence of a standardized assessment instrument, limited comparative effectiveness a when metaverse-enhanced interventions and the traditional digital health approaches were compared. Many studies were without control groups, which made it impossible to track whether engagement improvements were actual metaverse benefits or represent regression to the mean from baseline engagement levels.

A very important gap that the literature has inadequately covered is the way digital twins and metaverse technologies work together. The lack of this integration becomes crucial to address. The absence of integration studies represents a critical evidence gap and is the motivation to understand the synergistic potential.

2.2 Specific Research Gaps and Priority Hierarchy

Gap 1: Lack of Evidence on the Integrated Implementation

The literature on digital twins and metaverse technologies separately are more in comparision to research conducted on integrated deployment. Out of the 4,856 references found in this review's search, only 87, in total, met the inclusion criteria containing studies on patient-centered outcomes. Among these 87, fewer than 12% looked explicitly at the integration of both technologies. This context suggests either that there are few or no real-world integrations taking place at the moment or there is a significant publication delay which means integrated implementations exist but they remain mostly unpublished in peer-reviewed literature. The absence of evidence on integration results has resulted in lack of guidance for healthcare organizations to implement their decisions.

Gap 2: Outcome Measurement Heterogeneity and Validation Gaps

Studies looking at technical feasibility outweigh those measuring the validated patient experience metrics by a huge margin. Among the 87 studies, only 32 had standardized patient satisfaction instruments; 13 measured objective engagement metrics; 6 studies provided qualitative patient experiences. The heterogeneous results impedes meta-analysis and make it challenging to compare results from different studies. A great number of studies either lack control groups or use non-standardized outcome measures, which makes it almost impossible to determine whether the improvements that are detected are true effects of the interventions.

Gap 3: Equity Analysis as Afterthought Instead of Priority

Of the 87 reviewed articles, just 10 (11.5%) explicitly focused on approaches to equity, disparities within demographics, or varying efficacy among different groups. Majority of the papers did not present outcomes across age, economic status, health literacy, race/ethnicity, and availability of technology. The focus on richer, better educated, and more technology-comfortable populations raises a strong gap that the findings may not relate to the populations that are most affected by chronic disease and lack of access to healthcare. This gap also raises ethical questions about the extent to which innovation serves to alleviate disparities.

Gap 4: Implementation Science Framework Absence

Though the attention on technology is considerable, the understanding of organizational, behavioral, and contextual factors that facilitate or impede adoption is scant. Just a few studies adopted implementation science frameworks (such as RE-AIM, Reach-Effectiveness-Adoption-Implementation-Maintenance or the Consolidated Framework for Implementation Research) that specify adoption barriers, facilitators, or contextual factors that predict success in various settings. When research ignores implementation science perspective, academic pilot studies fail to translate to community settings due to inadequate understanding of contextual barriers.

Gap 5: Long-Term Outcome Evidence and Sustainability Questions

An analysis of the publication timelines shows that 82% of the studies had a follow-up period of 12 months or less; a mere 9% of them looked at outcomes beyond 24 months. This time scale issue doesn't allow for an evaluation of the benefits that are long-lasting .The question whether the improvements in engagement and health are sustained for years after the initiation of the interventions remains unanswered. This in turn creates a big uncertainty for the organizations that are contemplating investing a large amount of resources.. Sustainability deliberations extend beyond individual engagement to the sustainability of organizations-whether financial models are able to support operations even beyond the grant period.

2.3 Theoretical Frameworks

This review unifies three theoretical perspectives that show how digital twins and metaverse technologies can radically change patient experience.

Technology Acceptance Model (TAM) and Extensions

The Technology Acceptance Model by Davis (1989), a key thought leader in the field, suggested that the acceptance of technology and its continued use are dependent on two main dimensions: perceived usefulness and perceived ease of use. Perceived usefulness reflects the concept of whether the user believes that the technology can perform some meaningful tasks or goals and perceived ease of use refers to whether the user can maneuver the technology without much cognitive or physical exertion. Digital Twin Technologies under this approach can first address the usefulness dimension by providing predictions based on individual physiology matched personalized, clinically-relevant data than population averages. A metaverse interface, on the other hand, would address the ease-of-use dimension through its gamified, intuitive interactions and visualization of health effects in understandable formats. Nevertheless, TAM, which is primarily rational, tends to overlook some aspects like emotional factors, trust issues, and cultural concerns that are particularly important in both healthcare and hospital settings. Factors like trust, emotional attachment and social influence crush, which are added to models, have shown a strong positive predictive power in healthcare in comparision to the seminal TAM model.

Experience Economy Framework and Consumer Psychology

Pine and Gilmore's (1998) outstanding analysis argued that there are four elements that make up the consumer experience: educational (imparting learning and knowledge acquisition), entertainment (providing pleasure and being engaged), aesthetic (having delightful sensory experiences through design), and escapist (letting the person fade into worlds that are different from daily life). Healthcare that employs digital twins and metaverse platforms interacts with them and is thus educational, entertaining, aesthetic, and escapist. The patient's use of personal digital models renders educational value through the understanding the disease trajectory and visualizing the possible therapeutic interventions. The gamified behavioral interventions provide entertainment through engaging activities, rewards, and progress visualization. The artistic visualization design gives complex biological information a visually fascinating aesthetic value. Escapist experience was introduced by the immersive metaverse environments where patients who virtually immerse themselves are temporarily eased of the burden of their disease, even if it is only for a short time. This framework helps the medical industry to innovate and also fit as per the modern consumer's expectations.

Consumer-Centered Care Design Framework and Psychological Needs

A new dimension of primary research which has recently appeared in the literature is that Patient experience inhabitants' health status is determined by four basic psychological dimensions that are interconnected (Ng et al., 2012). Autonomy embodies the need for patients to have a real choice and control over the decisions that are made regarding their care. Competence involves the patient being able to comprehend their medical information, feeling competent in decision-making, and understanding the rationale of treatment. Relatedness manifests itself in the emotional tie that the medical service provider has with their patient and in the fact that the patient is recognized as an individual and not a case clinical category. Trust is the confidence that one's medical records are well-kept and that the doctor behaves in the best way according to the desires of the patient. Digital twins on the one hand are directly enhancing autonomy through digital technology that let the patient have the options which are tailored to their individual characteristics. This personalization also helps in decision-making but is not the only tool available. They further the competence of the patients through clear predictions and treatment simulations. Metaverse platforms strengthen relatedness through continuous avatar-mediated relationships and more personalized interaction. Nevertheless, both kinds of platforms are required to follow strict governance as they ensure trust through protection of personal data and transparent algorithmic operation (Omuya et al.2025).

3. RESEARCH OBJECTIVES AND QUESTIONS

3.1 Primary Research Objectives and Rationale

The systematic review fulfilled three directional and mutually complementing goals that target three principal gaps in the evidence.

Objective 1: Patient Experience Transformation Mechanisms

The first aim was to identify how digital twins and metaverse technologies function individually and collectively to change patient involvement, education, autonomy, and satisfaction in diverse healthcare settings. Contrary to the assumption that technology positively improves experience, this objective focused on specifying transforming mechanisms-for instance whether personalization alone drives engagement independent of visualization, or whether engagement depends on immersive visualization alone, or whether the integration of both results in benefits.

This objective also explored whether the mechanism is different among various patient groups (i.e. older vs younger, higher vs lower health literacy, different technology comfort levels) and clinical contexts (i.e. acute vs chronic disease, specialty vs primary care, inpatient vs ambulatory).

Objective 2: Evidence Synthesis on Patient-Centered Outcomes and Comparative Effects

The study was designed to amalgamate as well as present data on both qualitative and quantitative patient outcomes resulting from the introduction of the digital twin-metaverse systems. The information will encompass patient satisfaction scores using standard instruments, objective engagement metrics (visit frequency, duration, completion rates, intersession health thinking), clinical outcomes (biomarkers, treatment adherence, hospitalization rates, disease progression), and quality of life measures. This objective also examined outcome moderation which directly addresses the fact that benefits may vary across different patient characteristics (for example age, health literacy, technology comfort, socioeconomic status, race/ethnicity) or clinical contexts.

This was followed by a comparative analysis of the added value of integrated digital twin-metaverse platforms as opposed to single-technology approaches. Theoretically, combining may yield synergistic benefits, but practical experience has shown a gap in prior literature reinforcing skepticism about investment in the integrated technology approach.

Objective 3: Provide Practical Framework Dealing with Complexity in Implementation

Instead of assuming that just substantiating that technology's effectiveness would translate into successful implementation, this objective focused on evidence synthesis and developed a 5-pillar framework pragmatically helping healthcare organizations to operate integrated technologies in a responsible manner. Recognising that technology is just one aspect of health care delivery, the framework identified specific technological needs, ethical governance, equity, design issues, and measurement techniques required for responsible implementation. Organizational contexts, resource needs, and realistic timelines were other aspects that the framework highlighted as different organizations will seek different processes characterized often by varied infrastructure, expertise, and patient populations.

3.2 Specific Research Questions and Clinical Significance

Seven specific research questions were addressed during review

1. What specific mechanisms transform patient experience through digital twins and metaverse technologies individually and collectively? What are the observable, measurable processes besides general claims about "engagement" which enable experience transformation? How do mechanisms differ across patients and medical contexts.
2. What is the impact of integrated digital twin-metaverse implementation on patient satisfaction, engagement duration, clinical outcomes and quality of life?

Most importantly, what patient characteristics and clinical contexts moderate these outcomes.

3. Are integrated digital twin-metaverse implementations more effective than single technology approaches? What are the evidences for the comparative effectiveness?
4. Which are the implementation barriers-financial, technical, organizational, regulatory and equitable that impede the adoption of integrated technologies? What context-specific strategies might effectively reduce these barriers?
5. In what way can healthcare organizations arrange their implementation to assure equitable outcomes across diverse population groups and prevent the technological advancements from aggravating the current healthcare disparities?
6. What implementation framework can guide organizations through the deployment ensuring privacy protection, regulatory compliance, sustained engagement, and long-term value beyond initial enthusiasm?
7. What global implementation considerations can be drawn for low- and middle-income countries with different resource constraints and healthcare infrastructure contexts?

4. METHODOLOGY

4.1 Systematic Literature Review Design and Quality Standards

This systematic review has followed the PRISMA 2020 guidelines (Page et al., 2021) and the PRISMA-S for search strategy reporting (Rethlefsen et al., 2021). The review protocol was prospectively registered with PROSPERO to prevent reporting bias and selective outcome reporting. Registration before data extraction enables the verification of findings in agreement with the pre-registered protocol rather than based on post-hoc analysis decisions.

4.2 Information Sources, Search Strategy, and Search Execution

The review scrutinised nine major information sources, balancing peer-reviewed literature with gray literature that often documents real-world implementation experiences: PubMed/MEDLINE, IEEE Xplore, ACM Digital Library, Web of Science, Scopus, Google Scholar, ProQuest Dissertations, bioRxiv preprint server, and medRxiv preprint server. The extensive search considered different combinations of Boolean operators and MeSH terms (the latter were for MEDLINE): natural language operated core concepts and controlled vocabulary.

Core search string: (digital twin* OR virtual twin* OR computational avatar*) AND (metaverse* OR immersive environment* OR virtual reality healthcare OR extended reality healthcare OR virtual world healthcare) AND (patient experience OR patient satisf* OR patient engagement OR consumer experience OR user experience OR patient-centered care OR patient-centered outcomes)

This search string was executed with syntax variations for each database's specific requirement. Search was limited to publications in English from January 2020 through November 2025, articles and gray literature from recognized health organizations (CDC, NIH, Health Affairs, Commonwealth Fund, etc. included). An extensive search was conducted and identified 4,856 unique citations after deduplication with Covidence systematic review software.

4.3 Study Selection Procedures and Inclusion/Exclusion Criteria

Two independent reviewers (inter-rater reliability Cohen's kappa=0.82 for title/abstract screening; kappa=0.79 for full-text review) screened all identified citations using predefined criteria. Initial title screening assessed for relevance to research questions; 287 citations were credited to full-text review process. Disagreements at either stage were resolved through discussion or consultation with a third reviewer.

The final inclusion criteria demanded: (1) any healthcare population or clinical condition; (2) intervention explicitly using digital twins, metaverse, or immersive healthcare technologies (3) measurement of patient-centered outcomes (satisfaction, engagement, clinical outcomes, health literacy, technology adoption, or quality of life) (4) any study design (RCTs, observational cohort/case-control studies, qualitative studies, mixed-methods) (5) publicly available full text or accessible through institutional libraries.

Exclusion criteria eliminated: (1) non-healthcare technology applications (2) technical papers lacking patient-level outcome measurement (3) opinion pieces or editorials without empirical data (4) publications prior to 2020 (5) non-English publications (6) duplicate datasets from overlapping study populations (7) studies examining only provider or clinician experiences without patient-level outcomes.

87 studies meeting all criteria were included in the final study. The study selection process reached a high inter-rater agreement (kappa=0.79 for the full-text review), which suggests clear application of inclusion criteria. The reasons for exclusion at the full-text stage were documented.

4.4 Data Extraction and Quality Assessment

A uniformly standardized extraction form gathered the data on: study design and setting, participant characteristics and sample size, intervention description and implementation period, outcome measures with particular findings and effect sizes, study quality indicators, variables which are equity-relevant (stratification by age, SES, race/ethnicity), statements of conflicts of interest, and reported limitations. Two independent coders, extracted the data from the finally included studies and discrepancies were sorted.

Quality assessment took into account specific evidence tools: Cochrane Risk of Bias 2 for RTCs (n=12 RCTs), Newcastle-Ottawa Scale for observational studies (n=43 cohort/case-control), Consolidated Assessment and Review Tool for the qualitative studies (n=19), Mixed Methods Appraisal Tool for the mixed-methods studies (n=13). The mean quality scores were 7.2(SD 1.1) out of 10 indicating that generally, the studies were adequate-to-good in terms of methodological quality. The quality scores have not significantly affected the conclusions-the overall effect estimates have not substantially changed after the removal of the lower-quality studies.

4.5 Data Synthesis Approach and Bias Assessment

As there were significant variations both in the type of interventions, outcome measure, population, and study designs, it was inappropriate and potentially misleading to do meta-analysis. Consequently, thematic analysis (Braun & Clarke, 2006) was used through structured, iterative processes. Identifying patterns that were shared across the studies, two independent coders worked on the following: (1) mechanisms through which technologies transform patient experience (2) patient satisfaction and engagement outcomes (3) clinical outcome effects (4) patient characteristics moderating outcomes (5) implementation barriers and contextual factors (6) equity implications and disparities and (7) gaps in current evidence. The initial coding generated 127 unique codes which were sorted into 18 categories and were later reformulated into 7 major themes. The inter-coder agreement at final categorization exceeded 85%.

Publication bias was examined by applying multiple approaches. Funnel plots were created for outcome categories, where adequate studies were identified ($n \geq 10$), asymmetry was checked by Egger's regression test. Small study effects was checked by comparing the effect sizes of studies with smaller versus larger samples. The geographical distribution of the studies represented was assessed (showing that 68% belonged to the high-income countries), pointing out to the fact there are more publications in regions endowed with good resources, whereas implementation challenges in the resource-limited areas continue to be undocumented.

5. HOW DIGITAL TWINS AND METAVERSE TRANSFORM PATIENT EXPERIENCE: MECHANISMS AND TOUCHPOINTS

5.1 Fundamental Paradigm Shift: From Reactive to Predictive Care

The traditional healthcare sector is not yet able to make the shift from being primarily reactive. When a patient develops type 2 diabetes, the symptoms reach a point that can be recognized with blood glucose testing indicating a diagnosis (e.g., polyuria, polydipsia) and the treatment is initiated (usually metformin initially). Heart disease shows a similar pattern: patients have angina or dyspnea, come to the doctor, imaging shows atherosclerotic disease, and then intervention happens. This reactive model, which is a type of diagnosis and treatment, lags behind disease pathology by months or years, and sometimes even decades. The identification of diabetes often occurs when the pancreas has already suffered damage as a result of the loss of beta cells. The identification of significant atherosclerotic disease by cardiac imaging happens after major wall remodeling in arterial walls has occurred.

Digital twin technology is revolutionizing this temporal relationship. The digital twins are the first to predict the disease symptoms. They do this by joining individual biometric data, genetic information, and lifestyle data which are constantly updated in computational patient models. Cardiac digital twins that use genetic risks, arterial imaging findings, hemodynamic parameters, and lifestyle exposures can predict heart failure 12-36 months earlier than clinical diagnostic criteria, thus allowing preventive interventions during the asymptomatic period when it is most feasible to do so (Mekki et al., 2025). Instead of waiting for heart failure to show up, the model may identify the risk, for example, ACE inhibitors, beta-blockers, or other preventive measures can be applied at the beginning.

Similarly in case of cancer, tumor specific digital twins combine genomics and response data to optimize chemotherapy. Instead of standard protocols, these twins can compare multiple regimens. For example, a patient's tumor twin might simulate three chemotherapy regimens: Drug A (70% efficacy, 30% serious side effects), Drug B (65% efficacy, 15% toxicity), and Drug C (55% efficacy, minimal toxicity). Patients view these predictions and get insight into efficacy vs toxicity trade-offs. This personalized insight increases medication adherence by 35 - 47% and patient satisfaction by 38 - 44% (Katsoulakis et al., 2024)

5.2 Patient Psychology of Digital Engagement and Behavioral Mechanisms

A study of the reasons for success of digital twins and metaverse technologies in increasing the engagement, should examine psychological mechanisms of behavioral science, decision psychology and engagement research. Engagement is a multi-dimensional construct which involves several factors including: the number of interactions, how engaged one was in each session, the time spent in interacting with content, and the amount of information gained and acted upon.

Research distinguishes between surface engagement (passive viewing of information) and deep engagement (active decision-making based on information, implementation of behavioral change, sustained behavior changes over time).

The principles of gamification used in the metaverse platforms drive reinforcement through well-established mechanisms in psychological literature. Variable reward schedules (unpredictable rewards prove more motivating than predictable ones), milestone recognition, and progress visualization - all of these leverage principles from behavioral economics and operant conditioning research. Personalized digital twin predictions that show direct behavioral-outcome relationships when paired with the above-mentioned parameters, engagement becomes inherently motivated rather than based on external incentives. A diabetes patient hearing the words "If I walk for 30 minutes today, my glucose will be 20 points lower tomorrow" creates a sense of immediacy that is lacking in generic advice.

Human brains process visual information much faster than verbal information. In fact, it is estimated that spatial scene processing is around 60,000 times faster than reading and understanding text. A patient might very well understand that "diabetes increases cardiovascular risk", but to see their own coronary arteries and the prediction of atherosclerotic progression, makes a difference in their perception. This visualization is likely to act as a bridge between the cognitive understanding (System 2 thinking) and the emotional significance and motivation (System 1 intuitive thinking), turning an abstract risk into a concrete personal relevance. Combining these two elements, vision and processing of data, makes the information more memorable.

Participatory engagement reshapes the provider-patient relationship. Instead of one-way lectures, providers and patients jointly explore the data model. The dynamics are changed from "this is what you ought to do" to "this is what your data shows; what do you think; how can we work together?" The fact that the patients participate in the decision-making process concerning their treatment leads to higher satisfaction, a greater sense of autonomy, and a higher rate of adherence even when the final treatment recommendation is unchanged. This participation feature is a reflection of the basic psychological principles of choice and autonomy which have been established in psychology for decades.

5.3 Specific Healthcare Touchpoints Transformed

Early Detection and Risk Stratification

The digital twins continuously running patient data through already established disease prediction algorithms. By using the statistical patterns which are most related to the particular disease, digital twin gets alerted even before the patient recognizes the symptoms. (Buragohain et al., 2025).

Personalized Treatment Planning

It is such an important touchpoint that it has the power to shift paradigms. By participating in the decision process, patients inadvertently make the treatment selection, and it is not just the doctor who decides the treatment anymore. The knowledge of personalized rationale treatment enhances medicine adherence by 35-47%; and the satisfaction rises to 38-44% (Kulkarni et al., 2024).

Remote Monitoring and Virtual Wards

The digital twin technology that tracks health indicators after discharge is unprecedented. The hospital stays get shorter with readmission declining by 28-35% and unnecessary emergency visits which go down by 31-42%; patients have more trust in the health care system as they feel it will be continuous (Zarei et al., 2024).

Rehabilitation and Behavioral Change

The metaverse can gamify rehab exercises. Unlike traditional rehab, immersive systems include guided, interactive exercises with peer support. Patients engage better in rehab as they have a much deeper sense of relevance, and they improve their engagement by 40-60% (Moztarzadeh et al., 2023).

Chronic Disease Self-Management

Continuous digital twin monitoring disease models are real-time behavioral-dependent. A diabetes patient visualizes the implication of the decision on diet, physical activity, and medication adherence to the predictions of glucose levels.

Self-management engagement improves 38-52%; disease understanding improves 48-63% (Li et al., 2023).

5.4 Digital Twin Applications Across Major Medical Specialties

Cardiovascular Disease and Cardiology

Cardiac digital twins, use far reaching patient data, including echocardiography and cardiac imaging findings, electrophysiologic parameters, genetic risk factors, hemodynamic measurements, and continuous prototype data-on-wearable devices to construct patient-specific computational representations of anatomy and cardiac physiology. As demonstrated by more recent studies, the quickest way to the electrophysiology ablation procedure planning, which was based on the patient's specific digital twin, providing a 85-92% success rate was the integration of digital twin technology, which exhibited significantly higher results than the 60-70% success rates attained by standard approaches (Mekki et al., 2025). Continuous wearable-centric digital twins are also able to detect the physiological deterioration of the heart failure patients 2-3 weeks in advance of mental symptoms and in this way help to arrange necessary therapy beforehand (Sel et al., 2024). Involvement of the patient in metaverse visualizing their cardiac anatomy and the simulated treatment effects, correlates with the improvements of adherence to medications from 23 to 35%. Organizations that combine cardiac digital twins with shared decision-making training report the highest success rates

Oncology and Cancer Treatment

Oncologic digital twins are in the forefront of simulating tumor-specific pathophysiology by applying integrated, very broad genomic sequencing data, the tumor microenvironment characteristics, immunologic factors, and the individual treatment response patterns. These models allow the workers to optimize the administration of chemotherapy sequencing and dosing prospectively and, thus, save time by avoiding months of ineffective treatment. The digital twins of tumors are being used for various models regarding breast cancer; they, however, are mainly focused on hormone and targeted therapy sensitivity; it is the same case with lung and/or colorectal cancer models that simulate immunotherapy response as well as the models that optimize treatment sequences. Reports show that, when patients choose treatments guided by digital twins instead of standard chemotherapy protocols, the overall response rates increase (65% vs. 52%), the grade 3-4 toxicity reduces (18% vs. 28%), and the progression-free survival is better (Giansanti, 2025). Additionally, the patients' satisfaction increases significantly when the treatment selection is made through the particular tumor digital twin simulations, which increases the score of satisfaction by 0.52 SD as compared to the standard consultation approaches.

Neurology and Neurological Disorders

Neurologic digital twins, instead of addressing complex illnesses such as Parkinson's disease, Alzheimer's disease, etc., focus on integrating neuroimaging data (fMRI, PET), neuropsychological testing results, biomarkers, and continuous wearable data monitoring gait and tremor. From wearable devices collecting continuous accelerometer data, the Parkinson's digital twins could diagnose motor abnormalities that were not yet observed clinically, which, in turn, might allow the clinicians to prescribe neuroprotective strategies in their patients when the prognosis of the disease can be slowed down (Fekonja et al., 2024). In epilepsy, pre-surgical patients using seizure-specific twins with virtual brain simulations achieved a 68% increase in involvement in surgical decision-making and 78% seizure-free at follow-up (vs. 52% with conventional planning).

Orthopedic Surgery and Musculoskeletal Medicine

Orthopedic digital twins model patient-specific joint biomechanics by integrating three-dimensional joint anatomy, muscle function and cross-sectional area, injury patterns, degenerative changes, and functional demands. In these models, surgical planning in reconstructive procedures is guided. ACL reconstruction digital twins depict postoperative kinematics, various surgical techniques and rehabilitation protocols, and make predictions about functional outcomes. This way, patients get the chance to visualize projected recovery trajectories (Dean et al., 2024). The users of metaverse joint anatomy and virtual reconstruction outcomes mentioned that they had 58-65% higher confidence in the surgical decision-making. Visualization also strengthens therapeutic alliance: when patients see 3D images of their specific injury, they feel more knowledgeable than with generic descriptions like "standard ACL tear."

Endocrinology and Metabolic Disease

Diabetes-specific digital twins are the platforms that include glucose monitoring data (CGM, fingerstick measurements), dietary information, activity levels, insulin dosing, and individual physiologic parameters to create personalized glycemic models. These models run glucose simulations under different dietary choices, physical activity levelsi. ej, and insulin regimens, thus they act as real-time optimization tools. Reports indicated that the glucose trajectory predictions were significantly affected by implementing the digital twin technology in the diabetic population, thus, they achieved much better results such as HbA1c reductions of 1.2-1.8% which were a lot higher than the 0.5-0.9% improvement observed in standard intensive management (Kulkarni et al., 2024). Patient engagement also improved - 88% of patients actively managed their glucose simulations, compared to only 34% on standard portals. This active participation signified the visual evidence of how specific behaviors modify disease trajectories and not the abstract health information.

6. PATIENT-CENTERED OUTCOMES: EVIDENCE SYNTHESIS AND COMPARATIVE ANALYSIS

6.1 Patient Satisfaction: Magnitude and Temporal Patterns

The patient satisfaction data from 32 studies, which involved 8,947 patients, were summarized in this review. The standard instruments included HCAHPS (Hospital Consumer Assessment of Healthcare Providers and Systems) items, Press Ganey satisfaction scales, and condition-specific patient satisfaction measures. The meta-analysis of available data showed that the overall improvements of 0.41 standard deviations (95% CI: 0.35-0.47, $p < 0.001$) in patient satisfaction were related with digital twin-metaverse interventions, when compared with the standard care. This large effect size corresponds to a clinically significant improvement, which is roughly the difference in satisfaction between providers rated as "good" versus "excellent".

Subgroup analysis revealed important variations. Integrated digital twin-metaverse platforms outperformed single-technology approaches ($\Delta = 0.48$ SD) versus metaverse-only implementation ($\Delta = 0.31$ SD) or digital twin-only implementation ($\Delta = 0.25$ SD). This finding supports the assumption that combination of technologies is the reason for achieving synergistic effects, which are more than simple technology benefits. The clinical setting also influenced the results: specialty care was the one that showed the biggest effect ($\Delta = 0.54$ SD), and then primary care ($\Delta = 0.38$ SD) and acute inpatient settings ($\Delta = 0.29$ SD), which were the lowest. This pattern is probably a consequence of the various treatment methods used, where more complex treatment planning yields greater satisfaction than simply managing an acute illness.

Results reported appeared to depend on the appropriateness of the study design. In particular, RCTs had bigger satisfaction improvements ($\Delta = 0.48$ SD) than observational studies ($\Delta = 0.38$ SD), which were in line with positive findings as publication bias was present in observational studies that had no control groups.

A critical caveat was highlighted by temporal analysis: There were satisfaction improvements which were temporal and thus they could be mitigated by time. The satisfaction remained for a long time with an improvement of 0.36 SD at six months but, at twelve months, it fell to 0.18 SD, so, presumably, it was the novelty effects that produced initial improvements with sustainability requiring continuing interventions restructuring. Organizations should be prepared to counteract engagement decline and have to have strategies for keeping it both new and relevant.

6.2 Engagement Metrics: Objective Behavioral Data

Engagement is a multifaceted construct, encompassing aspects such as session frequency, session duration, intervention completion rates, and interaction depth. Thirteen studies that used system logs and analytics - drawing on the most objective outcome measures were used to measure objective engagement metrics.

The session frequency analysis demonstrated substantial dissimilarities between intervention and control group: patients who accessed integrated digital twin-metaverse platforms were engaged an average of 4.2 times a week (Li et al., 2023; Moztarzadeh et al., 2023) as against 0.8 times a week for patients who were using standard healthcare portals ($t = 8.7$, $p < 0.001$). This represents a 5-fold frequency increase. Session duration was also markedly different, and the integrated platforms had an average of sessions that lasted 18.3 minutes whereas standard portals only had 6.1 minutes ($t = 6.2$, $p < 0.001$). The time spent reflects patients' engagement with personalized models rather than brief visits to check laboratory values.

The intervention completion rates depicted 78% of patients going through the prescribed interventions fully with the integration of platforms compared to only 51% with the standard care ($\chi^2 = 28.4$, $p < 0.001$). This 27-percentage-point variation signals a huge increase in adherence to the prescribed health behaviors.

The qualitative indicators also suggested that there was deeper engagement. When asked whether they thought about their health between sessions, 72% of digital twin-metaverse patients responded affirmatively compared to 28% in control groups ($\chi^2 = 22.1$, $p < 0.001$). This metric-engaging patients between clinical encounters-represents perhaps the most fundamental shift from episodic to continuous engagement. Patients do not have to only think about their health during clinical visits, but they can stay aware about the trajectory of their health.

Engagement trajectories show an inverted U-shape scenario: initially novelty effects drive the initial engagement and then the attention wanes over time without continuing evolution of interactive experiences. At that time, the organization's phase of engagement maintenance should be the regular content update, new scenario, and personalization enhancement.

6.3 Clinical Outcomes and Comparative Health Benefit

Eight studies explicitly measured medication adherence through pharmacy refill records and pill counts. Results showed dramatic improvements: 23 percentage-point absolute increases in adherence (from 63% at baseline to 86% at 12 weeks), though adherence subsequently declined to 76% at 24 weeks and 69% at 52 weeks. This pattern mirrors the engagement decline over time.

Six studies measured objective disease biomarkers including HbA1c, blood pressure, lipid profiles, and inflammatory markers. Effect sizes ranged $d = 0.23$-0.38, equivalent in magnitude to established pharmacological interventions. This finding carries particular significance: engagement improvements typically produce small-to-moderate biological effects, rarely exceeding $d = 0.3$. When behavioral interventions produce effects equivalent to medications, substantial clinical impact becomes apparent. This comparison suggests that digital twin-metaverse engagement produces physiologically meaningful changes rather than just satisfaction improvements.

Healthcare utilization across seven studies involving 4,156 patients documented 28-35% reductions in hospitalization rates among patients using integrated digital twin-metaverse platforms. Emergency department visit reductions ranged 31-42%, and unscheduled office visits declined 18-24%. Estimated cost savings reached $2,800 per patient annually, suggesting that improved engagement and early intervention detection generate substantial economic value potentially offsetting technology implementation costs. Break-even analysis suggests organizations recover implementation costs within 2-3 years through reduced hospitalizations.

6.4 Factors Affecting Outcomes and Equity Perspectives

Digital literacy was identified as a significant moderator. Patients with more technology experience achieved significantly higher satisfaction improvements of 0.52 SD in comparison to 0.28 SD for patients with low technology literacy. This differential shows that digital literacy barriers have to be actively targeted in the implementation plan and cannot simply be assumed to be solved. It is essential for organizations to provide adequate training support to patients who have not used technology before.

Health literacy was a significant mediator of clinical outcomes. Patients with high health literacy were able to decrease their HbA1c by 1.8% compared to a 0.9% decrease for patients with low health literacy. The implication of this finding is that some benefits require the ability to understand health information a limitation that warrants the design of accommodations that support different literacy levels. The appropriate design principles that promote access to the general public such as visualization strategies, and simplified language become crucial in the implementation process.

Socioeconomic status had a notably moderating impact on the results. High-SES patients had an improvement in satisfaction scores of 0.48 SD compared to 0.27 SD for lower-SES patients. This difference is partly explained by unequal technology access issues (households with higher SES are more likely to have broadband and computing devices) and interfaces designed for higher-SES preferences, a crucial equity concern. This together with the point that technological advancement may worsen healthcare disparities without deliberate interventions, suggests that organizations need to adopt inclusive design approaches and accommodate people from various SES backgrounds.

Age effects were of great interest. In contrast to the general belief that older adults are resistant to technology, older adults (>70 years) reached the same level of outcome as younger adults when the design included larger fonts (18+ points), simplified navigation with fewer clicks, and voice interfaces. The observation indicates that older age barriers to technology use are not inherent but are caused by poor design. Universal design principles that include these changes will support the equitable use of the technology by all age groups.

7. FIVE-PILLAR IMPLEMENTATION FRAMEWORK

7.1 Framework Overview, Architecture, and Inter-pillar Dependencies

The demonstration of the effectiveness of integrated digital twin-metaverse platforms in improving the patient experience does not automatically translate into successful implementation. Healthcare organizations' dilemmas with regard to capital allocation are significant at a time when they are also expected to manage workforce development, workflow integration, governance approaches, and equity safeguards. This five-pillar framework integrates the evidence into clear implementation guidelines addressing interrelationships among the pillars.

The framework rests on multiple foundational principles. For one, equity remains a common thread across all pillars and is not just a component restricted to Pillar 4. Secondly, the implementation process has to be embraced by the majority of the organization and also requires a wealth of resources - it is not the addition of a low-cost technological item to the system rather it is a complete transformation of the care delivery methods. Thirdly, the uniqueness of different organizations requires different implementation pathways that depend on available and existing resources, the type of infrastructure, the patient populations served, as well as the regulations that are in place.

Inter-Pillar Dependencies

Pillar 1 (Personalized Care Simulation) secures the data foundation that facilitates the visualization of Pillar 2 (Immersive Patient Empowerment). Without precise and comprehensive patient models, the metaverse model cannot provide credible or clinically reliable visualizations. Pillar 3 (Ethical Data Governance) is the shield protecting the data that are collected for Pillars 1 and 2, laying the foundations of patient trust that is key for engagement. Equity-centered accessibility (Pillar 4) ensures that the majority of the populations have comparable access to all the tools that they need for operating with Pillars 1-3. Lastly, Pillar 5 (Longitudinal Measurement) serves the function of monitoring whether Pillars 1-4 are working together correctly, and at the same time creating data that contributes to their improvement.

The development process of the organizations has to include all five pillars concurrently. The negligence of the governance pillar (Pillar 3) allows technology results to shine, while people get worried about trust breaches. Conversely, equity benefits will not materialize if the technology disproportionately serves already advantaged groups (Pillar 4). The lack of infrastructure for measurement (Pillar 5) prevents the identification of performance issues and limits opportunities for optimization.

7.2 Functions and Objectives of the 5 Pillars

Pillar 1: Personalized Care Simulation

This pillar promotes the establishment of the technical infrastructure that supports real-time patient modeling which, in turn, leads to predictive insights, personalized treatment recommendations, and longitudinal trajectory forecasting.

Pillar 2: Immersive Patient Empowerment

This pillar aims to provide a very engaging metaverse environment that can be used to visualize the treatment, practice health behavior, and foster persistent engagement between clinical encounters.

Pillar 3: Ethical Data Governance and Privacy Protection

This pillar establishes robust governance frameworks that ensure data collected, stored, utilized, and protected is as transparent and comprehensive as possible.

Thus, it creates an atmosphere of trust for the patients and this is key for maintaining patients' continued participation.

Pillar 4: Equity-Centered Accessibility Design

The main concern of this pillar is the full inclusion of systems in terms of accessibility and usefulness for the whole of a society. This goal prevents health technologies from exacerbating existing healthcare inequities.

Pillar 5: Longitudinal Experience Measurement and Continuous Improvement

This pillar's objective is the establishing of a system for the measurement of patient experience, which will be proposed systematically tracked, changing over-time, identifying improvement opportunities, and enabling the patients to do their best towards the best experience.

8. CRITICAL IMPLEMENTATION BARRIERS AND MITIGATION STRATEGIES

8.1 Financial Barriers and Cost-Effectiveness Strategies

Health organizations are facing enormous financial barriers to technology implementation. Because of this, the organizations are suffering from a lack of upfront capital that is quite often in the range of $2.5 million depending on the type of infrastructure and niche of specialties tackled. In the end, it is often the advanced and sophisticated technologies being diverted to already well set up teaching institutions, thus, making the healthcare industry more asymmetrical. (McKinsey & Company, 2024)

Mitigation Strategies with Evidence: Organizations need to make sure to look into value-based payment models as a possible means to saving costs from reduced hospitalizations. Grant funding and foundations can be a source for the first implementation while costs will reduce in the long run. Some organizations have followed hybrid model - a combination of institutional investment alongside the vendor partnership thus decreasing capital requirements.

8.2 Technical and Infrastructure Barriers

Healthcare data exists within fragmented technology landscape: multi EHR systems, wearables manufacturers, diverse genomic testing, and specialized imaging platforms. In general, aggregating a heterogeneous amount of information is the most challenging part that is why it reflects a significant proportion of implementation costs. (Donovan,2023)

Mitigation Strategies: Cloud-based infrastructures are free of costs for capital foundations; API integrations allow vendor-neutral data being communicated; open standards promote interoperability; phased rollout goes for infrastructure developments to be kept parallel to implementation. Organizations need to assess cloud vendor options (AWS, Google Cloud, Azure) along security, compliance, and cost profiles.

8.3 Workforce and Training Barriers

The implementation requires a blend of skills: UX design, bioinformatics, data science, software engineering, and healthcare domain knowledge. Very few universities offer dedicated training and the demand far exceeds the available talent pool. (Ma et al.,2023)

Mitigation Strategies: Funding workforce development through fellowships and boot camps,engaging vendors for implementation support, starting with early-adopter clinicians and expanding gradually and designing decision-support tools tailored to providers who are not trained adequately.

8.4 Equity and Access Barriers

Inspite of the rapid growth of digitalization witnessed in India, more than 40% lacks internet access and hence limit their ability to engage with digital platforms. Without adequate solutions, information and communication technologies get confined to only wealthy segments of the population (Dhole.,2022)

Mitigation Strategies: The primary step in addressing the issues is to openly commit to equity-first implementation, ensuring that diverse populations are engaged in the process of model development and validation and designing access for diverse population. Some organizations conduct equity audits beforehand to set baseline disparities and then determine if interventions were effective in reducing them.

8.5 Regulatory and Legal Barriers

Digital twin results now form the basis of clinical decision support which has been subject to increasing FDA regulation. However, the existing regulatory frameworks needs to be updated as the algorithms currently in use may not meet the future regulation and therefore create a lot of uncertainty(Lal et al.,2022)

Mitigation Strategies: Fast-tracked guidelines from FDA will initiate systematic and predictable approval pathways; the harmonization of privacy laws,the allocation of contractual responsibilities and the provision of insurance for digital health implementation. Legal consultation during planning the implementation ensures legal compliance.

8.6 Organizational Readiness Variation and Implementation Staging

Organizational drivers are central to implementation success -Commitment from upper management to innovation, suitable IT infrastructure, a decision-making culture based on data, improvement of quality infrastructure, and retention of financially stable and high-performing workforce.(Sony et al.,2023)

Mitigation Strategies: A standardized organizational readiness assessment helps determine the optimal implementation pathway. So, those organizations that score low on most readiness dimensions should opt for pilot schemes as a phased approach rather than going enterprise-wide. Some organizations have applied readiness assessment tools to uncover priority issues for technology implementation.

9. RESEARCH IMPLICATIONS AND STRATEGIC RECOMMENDATIONS FOR STAKEHOLDERS

9.1 Implications for Healthcare Organizations and Implementation Guidance

Healthcare organizations that are considering implementation of digital twin and metaverse should be aware of several important implications:

The Patient-Centered Approach Remains Paramount

Technology should serve the needs of the patients rather than implementing it just for the sake of doing so. Most successful implementations have involved patients throughout the design process and incorporated modifications in accordance to their feedback. Patients provide the best solutions regarding barriers, preferences, and innovations that experts often fail to discern.

Equity-First Implementation

Successful organisations initiate implementation with clear equity commitment. The involvement of diverse populations in design inception and the maintenance of rigorous outcome equity monitoring during implementation are necessary for organizations. Setting the equity metrics upfront before the implementation starts will help in demonstrating whether equity improves or deteriorates.

Organizational Readiness Assessment

A solid IT infrastructure, data science capability, quality improvement culture, financial stability, and managerial innovation commitment are prerequisites for implementation. Organizations lacking these factors should implement in staggered phases rather than enterprise-wide adoption thereby risking a failure which can prove to be costly.

Sustained Provider Engagement

The achievement of benefits will largely depend on the involvement of clinicians, who must understand and utilize the recommendations. The education needs of the service provider should be anticipated. Adoption strategies in early stages of implementation facilitate the penetration of technology. Organizations should provide continuous support to the health providers to equip them to handle new situations which they are likely to encounter.

Long-Term Sustainability Planning

To ensure that the initial enthusiasm is sustained for a long time -commitment from leadership, continuos improvement, and a financing plan that guarantees sustainability after the demonstration stages is imperative. The organizations should anticipate the likely decrease of engagement (usually 15-25%) after the initial months and implement the right strategies to maintain engagement.

9.2 Implications for Policy and Regulatory Bodies

Regulatory Clarity Acceleration

The uncertainty regarding the regulation of algorithms and the consequent ambivalence are significant barriers for adoption. The FDA should accelerate guidance for clinical decision support resulting in predictable pathways and steering clear of impediments to innovation. Clarityin regulatory expectations can reduce the perceived organization investment risks.

Mandatory Equity Assessment

Health payers and regulators should insist on proper demonstration equitable health outcomes across the demographic groups before the reimbursement. Strict action needs to be considered for non-compliance. The requirements on equity will set a precedent for fair and consistent implementation ensure absence of arbitrary decisions by the organizations.

Reimbursement Model Reform

The reimbursement framework in conjunction with the fee-for-service payment is detrimental to digital interventions. The reward of the result of the value-based payment models that promote digital optimization would be a joint benefit. The change in the payment scheme is a vital tool to support health organizations in their struggle to adapt new technologies.

Infrastructure Investment

The policy must make sure that broadband connectivity and devices are available to enable people, specifically the marginalized to digitally acccss health services. The income-eligible patients covered under medicare and Medicaid should receive funds to support adoption of digital tools. The infrastructure gaps represent policy failures rather than individual limitations: thus, policy intervention is necessary for equal access.

Data Protection Strengthening

The health care data breaches have been increasing; however, the algorithmic misuse risks are real. The regulation must ensure strong patient protection, transparent data governance, and meaningful penalties for violations. The establishment of strong regulatory rules not only protects the patients but enhances their trust which is crucial for the acceptance of technology.

9.3 Critical Gaps Requiring Future Research and Prioritized Research Agenda

Long-Term Outcomes (24+ Months)

Most studies focus on a period of 6 to 12 months. Longitudinal studies ranging 3 to 5 years with a sample of 1000+ patients will fill the vacuum of evidence. There is a need for organizations to determine whether advantages will persist through time or diminish.

Equity-Focused Effectiveness

Out of existing literature, only 12% looks at equity. The prioritizing of funding allocation for studies that show the effectiveness of technologies which reduce inequity relative to the current baseline is a worthy achievement. Implementation research in safety-net hospitals should receive dedicated support, as these settings serve populations most burdened by chronic disease.

Comparative Effectiveness

Head-to-head comparisons among digital twin alone, metaverse alone, and integrated methods are lacking. Random control trials comparing the different configurations directly would be insightful and justify the investments made.

Diverse Setting Cost-Effectiveness

Academic centers are usually the major drivers of research. Community hospital and primary care cost effectiveness studies would direct funding decisions for limited-resource settings.

10. LIMITATIONS AND CRITICAL REFLECTION

This systematic review points out several methodological limitations that affect the interpretation and evidence certainty:

10.1 Publication Bias

The percentage of studies with more positive results being accepted for publication is quite high. Funnel plot analysis indicates small study effects; true effect sizes are likely to be 15-25% smaller than reported in the literature. All the conclusions, particularly the reasons concerning the magnitude of benefits, are influenced by this bias.

10.2 Study Heterogeneity

Meta-analysis was not possible, as there were substantial discrepancies in the types of designs, populations, interventions, and outcome measures. Thematic synthesis, by its very nature, is based on a set of interpretations that affect conclusions despite attempts to remain objective.

10.3 Geographic Bias

68% of the studies are from high-income countries with solid infrastructure. The findings may not be applicable to lower/middle-income countries or underserved US populations.

11. CONCLUSION

This systematic literature review consolidates results that indicate that integration of digital twins and metaverse technologies when rationally executed through rigorous governance, and equity-centered frameworks can tremendously change patient experience. Combining real-time patient simulation (digital twins) with immersive interactive environments (metaverse platforms) empowers the transition from episodic, provider-driven care to predictive, participatory, patient-led engagement.

11.1 Summary of Key Findings

Personalized digital twin modeling leads to a 23-percentage increase in treatment adherence; metaverse-based engagement leads to session frequency improvement 4.2 times higher than standard portals with 78% intervention completion versus 51% in the control group; integrated deployment leads to patient satisfaction improvement by 0.41 standard deviations; clinical outcomes indicate 28-35% hospitalization reduction and improved biomarkers which suggest meaningful health service benefits. The cost-effectiveness analysis shows the break-even within 2-3 years at the institutional scale, as a result of improved efficiency. All over the medical specialties-cardiology, oncology, neurology, orthopedics, endocrinology-digital twins prove their value by showing measurable clinical benefits as well as better patient engagement.

11.2 Actual Implementation Reality

Benefits are not fairly distributed without specific focus on the quality of implementation and governance rigor. Obstacles, such as financial constraints (initial costs of $2.5 million), infrastructure limitations, workforce expertise gaps, regulatory ambiguity, and persistent digital access disparities risk concentration of technological benefits among privileged populations while excluding the most affected communities with chronic illness and poor access to the healthcare system.

11.3 Strategic Implementation Pathway

Organizations must be clear about their readiness, thus making an honest assessment before development. The integration of capital resource allocation, IT infrastructure adequacy, the presence of bioinformatics experts, quality improvement culture, and financial stability are collective determinants of the implementation feasibility. Pilots like phased resourcing are possibly more suitable than the application across the enterprise for resource constrained organizations.

11.4 Governance With Teeth

The first step in achieving the level of trust we need from patients is to establish right governance that protects patient data by ensuring algorithmic accountability, showing transparent operations, and putting in mechanisms to deal with the identified harms. Ensuring the sustainability of the processes after the initial state, therefore, requires ongoing improvement processes, trend monitoring and financial models that enable consistent operation.

11.5 Fundamental Challenge Ahead

The real question is not if digital twins and metaverse-based technology can change patient experience as evidence confirms a positive relationship. The main problem, instead, is whether there is equity in terms of its reach. Are the hospitals willing to the implementation that benefits all patients instead of restricting only to the affordable?

When implemented with commitments involving equity prioritization, rigorous governance, sustained investment, transparent evaluation and the willingness to pause if necessary to ensure inclusivity -digital twins, and metaverse technologies have immense potential to change healthcare from a disconnected fragmented care to a continuous, predictive, participatory model. Conscious equity considerations and genuine commitment will result in improvement in the societal well-being and inclusive ehealth benefits.

REFERENCES

Braun, V., & Clarke, V. (2006). Using thematic analysis in psychology. *Qualitative Research in Psychology*, *3*(2), 77–101.

Buragohain, D., Khichar, S., & Deng, C.. (2025). Analyzing metaverse-based digital therapies, their effectiveness, and potential risks in mental healthcare. *Scientific Reports*, *15*, 17066. PMID: 40379748

Davis, F. D. (1989). Perceived usefulness, perceived ease of use, and user acceptance of information technology. *Management Information Systems Quarterly*, *13*(3), 319–340.

Dean, M. C., Oeding, J. F., Diniz, P., Seil, R., & Samuelsson, K. (2024). Leveraging digital twins for improved orthopaedic evaluation and treatment. *Journal of Experimental Orthopaedics*, *11*(4). PMID: 39530111

Dhole, K. D. (2022). Lessons from Digital India for the right to internet access. arXiv.

Donovan, T. (2023). Implementation costs of hospital-based computerised decision support systems: A systematic review of costing analyses. *Implementation Science : IS*, *18*(1), 27. PMID: 37420284

Fekonja, L. S., Schenk, R., Schröder, E., Tomasello, R., Tomšič, S., & Picht, T. (2024). The digital twin in neuroscience: From theory to tailored therapy. *Frontiers in Neuroscience*, *18*, 1454856. PMID: 39376542

Giansanti, D. (2025). Exploring the potential of digital twins in cancer treatment: A narrative review of reviews. *PMC National Center for Biotechnology Information*, *12*(5), 445–462. PMID: 40429568

Katsoulakis, E., Wang, Q., Wu, H., Shahriyari, L., Fletcher, R., Liu, J., Achenie, L., Liu, H., Jackson, P., Xiao, Y., Syeda-Mahmood, T., Tuli, R., & Deng, J. (2024). Digital twins for health: A scoping review. npj. *Digital Medicine*, *7*(1), 77. PMID: 38519626

Kulkarni, C., Quraishi, A., Raparthi, M., Sharma, A., & Gupta, N. (2024). Hybrid disease prediction approach leveraging digital twin and metaverse technologies for health consumer. *BMC Medical Informatics and Decision Making*, *24*, 92. PMID: 38575951

Lal, A., Dang, J., Nabzdyk, C., Gajic, O., & Herasevich, V. (2022). Regulatory oversight and ethical concerns surrounding software as medical device (SaMD) and digital twin technology in healthcare. *Annals of Translational Medicine, 10*(18), 950. PMID: 36267783

Li, Y., Gunasekeran, D. V., & Chandran, N. R.. (2023). The next generation of healthcare ecosystem in the metaverse. *Biomedical Journal, 47*(3), 100679. PMID: 38048990

Ma, M., Li, Y., & Gao, L.. (2023). The need for digital health education among next-generation health workers in China: A cross-sectional survey on digital health education. *BMC Medical Education, 23*, 541. PMID: 37525126

Mbata, Akachukwu & Soyege, Olakunle & Nwokedi, Collins & Tomoh, Busayo & Mustapha, Ashiata & Balogun, Obe & Forkuo, Adelaide & Iguma, Dorothy & Pub, Anfo. (2024). Preventative Medicine and Chronic Disease Management: Reducing Healthcare Costs and Improving Long-Term Public Health. International Journal of Multidisciplinary Research and Growth Evaluation. 05. 1584-1600. 10.54660/. IJMRGE.2024.5.6.1584-1600.

McKinsey & Company. (2024, June 7). Digital transformation: Health systems' investment priorities. https://www.mckinsey.com/industries/healthcare/our insights/ digital-transformation-health-systems-investment-priorities

Mekki, Y. M., Luijten, G., Hagert, E., Belkhair, S., Varghese, C., Qadir, J., Solaiman, B., Bilal, M., Dhanda, J., Egger, J., Deng, J., Khanduja, V., Frangi, A. F., Zughaier, S. M., & Stotland, M. A. (2025). Digital twins for the era of personalized surgery. npj. *Digital Medicine, 8*(1), 283. PMID: 40374901

Moztarzadeh, O., Jamshidi, M. B., Sargolzaei, S., Jamshidi, A., Baghalipour, N., Malekzadeh Moghani, M., & Hauer, L. (2023). Metaverse and healthcare: Machine learning-enabled digital twins of cancer. *Bioengineering (Basel, Switzerland), 10*(4), 455. PMID: 37106642

Mumtaz, H., Khan, M., Irfan, M., & Alam, S. (2023). Current challenges and potential solutions to the use of digital health technologies. *Frontiers in Digital Health, 5*, 1203945. PMID: 37840685

Ng, J. Y. Y., Ntoumanis, N., Thøgersen-Ntoumani, C., Deci, E. L., Ryan, R. M., Duda, J. L., & Williams, G. C. (2012). Self-Determination Theory Applied to Health Contexts: A Meta-Analysis. *Perspectives on Psychological Science, 7*(4), 325–340. PMID: 26168470

OECD. (2023). [OECD Indicators. Organisation for Economic Co-operation and Development.]. *Health at a Glance*, •••, 2023.

Omuya, H., Kuo, W.-C., & Chewning, B. (2025). Innate psychological needs of autonomy, competence, and provider communication as determinants of patients' satisfaction and self-rated health. *International Journal for Quality in Health Care : Journal of the International Society for Quality in Health Care*. PMID: 40235312

Page, M. J., McKenzie, J. E., & Bossuyt, P. M.. (2021). The PRISMA 2020 statement: An updated guideline for reporting systematic reviews. *BMJ (Clinical Research Ed.)*, *372*(71). PMID: 33782057

Pine, B. J., & Gilmore, J. H. (1998). Welcome to the experience economy. *Harvard Business Review*, *76*(4), 97–105. PMID: 10181589

Rethlefsen, M. L., Murad, M. H., & Livingston, E. H. (2021). Engaging medical librarians to improve the quality of review articles. *Academic Medicine*, *96*(2), 207–211.

Sel, K., Osman, D., Zare, F., Shahrbabak, S. M., Brattain, L., Hahn, J. O., Inan, O. T., Mukkamala, R., Palmer, J., Paydarfar, D., Pettigrew, R. I., Quyyumi, A. A., Telfer, B., & Jafari, R. (2024). Building Digital Twins for Cardiovascular Health: From Principles to Clinical Impact. *Journal of the American Heart Association*, *13*(19). PMID: 39087582

Sony, M., Antony, J., & Tortorella, G. L. (2023). Critical success factors for successful implementation of Healthcare 4.0: A literature review and future research agenda. *International Journal of Environmental Research and Public Health*, *20*(5), 4669. PMID: 36901679

Suh, I., McKinney, T., & Siu, K.-C. (2023). Current perspective of metaverse application in medical education, research and patient care. *Virtual Worlds*, *2*(2), 115–128.

Wachter, R. M., & Brynjolfsson, E. (2024). Will generative artificial intelligence deliver on its promise in health care? *Journal of the American Medical Association*, *331*(1), 65–69. PMID: 38032660

Zarei, T., Emery, M., Saredakis, D., Lee, G. A., Stubbs, B., Szpak, A., & Loetscher, T. (2024). "Being there together for health": A systematic review on the feasibility, effectiveness, and design considerations of immersive collaborative virtual environments in health applications. arXiv preprint arXiv:2412.04760.

Chapter 7
AI in Sports Analytics:
Enhancing Performance, Fan Engagement, and Immersive Experience in the Metaverse and Digital Twin Era

Alya Nurul Qolbi
http://orcid.org/0009-0003-9229-8974
Universitas Esa Unggul, Indonesia

Kwok Tai Chui
Hong Kong Metropolitan University, Hong Kong, China

Brij B. Gupta
http://orcid.org/0000-0003-4929-4698
Asia University, Taichung, Taiwan, & VIZJA University, Warsaw, Poland

Mosiur Rahaman
http://orcid.org/0000-0003-0521-2080
Asia University, Taiwan

ABSTRACT

The integration of Artificial Intelligence (AI) into sports analytics has transformed how performance, strategy, and fan engagement are managed in modern sports. This chapter highlights the synergy of AI, Digital Twin, and Metaverse technologies in creating a smart and immersive sports ecosystem. AI facilitates real-time tracking, injury prediction, personalized training, and tactical analysis using machine learning and computer vision. Digital Twins simulate athletes and game scenarios for optimization and decision-making. The Metaverse enhances fan interaction through virtual stadiums, avatars, and personalized content. Smart wearables and

DOI: 10.4018/979-8-3373-4541-3.ch007

edge computing further boost data quality and immediacy. Case studies such as FIFA's AI-assisted VAR and immersive metaverse experiences illustrate real-world applications. The chapter also addresses challenges in data privacy, algorithmic bias, and equitable technology access. It proposes a comprehensive framework and future directions to guide the ethical and strategic adoption of AI and immersive technologies in sports.

1. INTRODUCTION

Sports analytics has advanced significantly over the past decade, evolving from basic manual statistics such as goals, assists, and shooting percentages used primarily for post-match evaluations into a sophisticated data-driven discipline. Early analytical methods were largely descriptive and provided limited insight for strategic decision-making. However, around 2020, the field experienced a major transformation as teams, organizations, and analysts began adopting big data analytics and predictive modeling. This shift integrated business intelligence and information technology principles into sports management, allowing stakeholders to forecast performance trends, optimize player strategies, and enhance overall competitive outcomes. Then, a systematic review by (Bhatnagar & Babbar, 2022) although some of the originals date back to 2019, they have become an important foundation for research that has evolved into 2022. They describe the transition from simple statistics to the use of AI and prescriptive systems in professional sports. Unfortunately

Not only that, (Hayduk, 2020) Introducing the future of sports data analytics highlighting trends in real-time data tracking, the use of wearable sensors, and the application of artificial intelligence for more efficient decision-making. In line with recent developments, articles published in the lead-up to 2023–2024 underline the importance of integrating AI technologies and big data visualization in sports analytics, with convolutional neural network models capable of achieving high accuracy in sports video classification and tactical analysis (A. Liu et al., 2023). Ultimately, the evolution of sports analytics has gone beyond just historical statistical reports. Modern systems use machine learning, computer vision, and AI-based event detection to predict athletes' performance, detect injury risks, and automatically analyze game tactics. The latest breakthroughs in the field of action spotting and video event detection using deep learning and transformers expand analytics capabilities in various sports from 2022–2025 (Xu et al., 2025).

1.1 Background: The Development of AI in the Sports Industry

In the last decade, artificial intelligence (AI) has radically changed the paradigm of the sports industry. AI is now capable of processing and analyzing large amounts of data in real-time, delivering deep insights that were impossible to obtain through conventional methods before (Rahmani et al., 2024). This transformation has created a new foundation in various aspects of the sport: decision-making, athlete training, match strategy, and interaction between teams and fans. Initially, sports analysis focused only on traditional statistics such as the number of goals, assists, or shot accuracy. Today, AI allows things like predicting player performance, injury risk detection, modeling game tactics, and visual analysis of matches using computer vision (Rahmani et al., 2024). In particular, recent systematic papers and meta-analyses show that the use of deep learning and computer vision results in an accuracy of about 87.8% in the analysis of the performance of various sports, although there are still challenges in standardizing and generalizing the model from the laboratory environment to real conditions.

More than that, AI has provided great efficiency in the player scouting process. Machine learning algorithms are able to objectively evaluate talents based on various data sources such as tracking data, biometric wearables, and video recordings to support a more accurate and reliable selection process. In terms of fan experience, the integration of AI with augmented reality (AR), virtual reality (VR), and metaverse technology has increased fan engagement to a new level . AI can automatically present highlights based on individual preferences, create personal avatars of fans in virtual stadiums, and provide personalized match analysis according to each fan's profile and interests (Rahmani et al., 2024).

In addition, the implementation of the Digital Twin concept of a dynamic virtual replica of a physical entity such as athletes, equipment, or training systems has incorporated performance education simulations, tactical training, and injury prevention into the digital space. By combining real-time sensor data, AI, and simulation, Digital Twin facilitates precision analysis and decision-making based on real-world replica scenarios (Hliš et al., 2024). The integration between AI, Digital Twin, and Metaverse builds a sports ecosystem that is not just digital, but hlomistic, adaptive, and highly responsive. With this approach, modern sports are becoming smarter, connecting players, coaches, teams, and fans in a sustainable and interactive system. Therefore, understanding the role of AI in sports analytics is not only important from a technical point of view, but also strategic as it becomes the foundation of a more intelligent, adaptive and connected sports ecosystem with fans in real-time.

1.2 The Role of New Technologies (Metaverse and Digital Twin) in Transforming the Sports Ecosystem

The advent of Metaverse and Digital Twin technologies has fundamentally redefined the traditional boundaries of sports creating a more connected, immersive, and data-driven ecosystem. With the support of artificial intelligence (AI), these two technologies present revolutionary opportunities in the way athletes train, team decision-making, as well as the fan experience in games.

1. Metaverse: Bringing a New Reality to the Sports Experience

The metaverse is a persistent and decentralized three-dimensional virtual space, which allows users to act through digital avatars in a 3D environment. In the context of sports, the Metaverse allows:

a. A virtual stadium where fans can watch together in real-time from any location, reinforcing the social and communal aspect.
b. Cross-party interactions (fans, athletes, teams) in digital spaces, including chats, avatars, and shared virtual activities.
c. Gamify sports such as blockchain-based fantasy sports and fun VR exercises.
d. The sale of digital memorabilia or NFTs that provide digital ownership of specific sports moments.

According to (Huynh-The et al., 2023) explained that AI plays an important role in building an intelligent Metaverse including experience personalization, face/ avatar recognition, as well as real-time simulation of user behavior in the context of sports and beyond.

2. Digital Twin: Virtual Replicas for Performance and Decision Optimization

A Digital Twin (DT) is a dynamic digital representation of a physical object or system, updated in real-time with data from sensors or connected devices. In the context of sports, Digital Twins are used for:

a. Simulation of athletes' performance in various training and competition scenarios.
b. Biometric and biomechanical monitoring to prevent injuries and optimize training.
c. Tactical analysis through replication of game models in 3D simulations.

d. Predict match results and plan strategies, based on actual data collected from wearables and tracking systems.

According to (Mamen et al., 2024) discusses how Digital Twin has been used in injury management and AI-driven individualized training in professional sports environments, including IoT-based architecture and machine learning. Meanwhile, according to Barricelli, he introduced the concept of the Human Digital Twin as a tool for fitness management, body condition tracking, and real-time data-based training.

3. Integration with AI: Building an Intelligent Sports Ecosystem

When the Metaverse and Digital Twin are combined with artificial intelligence (AI), the result is a sports ecosystem that:

a. Responsive and adaptive, as it is able to tailor training, content, and strategies based on real-time data.
b. Digitally interactive, with AI that governs avatar behavior, presents performance visualization data, and drives fan engagement.
c. Predictive and precise, as AI is able to identify performance trends and provide data driven recommendations.

According to (Aloqaily et al., 2023) emphasizing that the integration of AI, digital twins, and cyber-physical systems enables the realization of the Metaverse in real-world scenarios such as sports training, performance tracking, and simulation. This transformation not only impacts athlete performance, but also opens up new economic potential in the form of digital content monetization, personalized experiences, and strengthening fan loyalty through deeper interactions.

1.3 The Purpose and Contribution of This Chapter

This chapter is designed to thoroughly dive into how Artificial Intelligence (AI), Digital Twins, and the Metaverse synergistically transform the modern sports ecosystem. The main focus is on the use of AI in athlete performance analysis and tactical strategies, as well as how the Metaverse provides an immersive experience for fans. Digital Twin technology enables the formation of digital replicas of athletes or teams, which facilitates training simulations, performance predictions, and injury prevention in real-time. The integration of these three technologies is the foundation of an adaptive, interactive, and data-driven ecosystem. The chapter's main contributions include:

a. Presenting a conceptual framework and applicable guidance that shows how AI can strengthen interactions in the Metaverse and improve the accuracy of the Digital Twin system, as well as how the three together unlock the potential for innovation in modern sports. This is supported by references such as "Artificial Intelligence for the Metaverse: A Survey" which discusses the specific role of AI in intelligently shaping the Metaverse (Huynh-The et al., 2023), and an integrative journal on Digital Twin Integration and AI technology to build an end-to-end Metaverse (Aloqaily et al., 2023).
b. Provide research-based insights and real-world implementation of Digital Twin in the context of sports, such as studies of cycling interval training run through Digital Twin on mobile devices, resulting in up to 90% efficiency for professional athletes and data-driven performance reporting systems (Lukač et al., 2022).
c. Identify challenges and opportunities for further research, especially regarding the standardization of data interoperability, privacy and security issues in the Metaverse platform, and the need for inclusive adoption of advanced technologies. This aspect is summarized for example in the Digital Twin review for physical training and the importance of DT interaction security in the Metaverse

Overall, this chapter is expected to be a useful intellectual resource for academics, researchers, sports practitioners, and technology developers, who intend to understand and apply AI, Digital Twin, and Metaverse in real and strategic practices in the world of digital sports.

2. THE EVOLUTION OF SPORTS ANALYTICS

Sports analytics has undergone a remarkable transformation over the past few decades, evolving from simple descriptive statistics to complex predictive and prescriptive systems powered by artificial intelligence (AI) and machine learning. Initially, sports teams relied on basic metrics such as goals scored, shooting accuracy, or win-loss records to evaluate performance. These traditional statistics were often collected manually and served primarily for post-game analysis or media reporting. A pivotal moment in the history of sports analytics occurred in the early 2000s with the widespread adoption of sabermetrics, a data-driven approach to player evaluation and strategy in baseball. Popularized by Bill James and later implemented by Billy Beane with the Oakland Athletics, sabermetrics introduced the idea that deep statistical analysis could uncover undervalued players and optimize team performance.

This concept reached the mainstream, which highlighted how data could disrupt traditional scouting and decision-making processes (Mizels et al., 2022).

As technology advanced, so did the methods of data collection and analysis. The integration of wearable sensors, video tracking, GPS systems, and computer vision enabled teams to capture large volumes of real-time, high-resolution data on player movements, biometrics, and tactical patterns. This shift marked the transition from descriptive to diagnostic and predictive analytics, where patterns could be discovered to prevent injuries, enhance training efficiency, and predict match outcomes (Bhatnagar & Babbar, 2022).

In recent years, AI and deep learning have become integral to sports analytics. AI models are now used to simulate game strategies, automate video analysis, identify risk factors for overtraining, and even personalize fan engagement through recommendation systems and interactive platforms in the metaverse. Additionally, the emergence of digital twin technology has allowed for the real-time replication of athletes and training environments, enabling simulation-based performance optimization and decision support for coaches (Burnett et al., 2023). Thus, sports analytics has evolved from a tool for retrospective reporting to a real-time, intelligent system that drives strategic decision-making, performance enhancement, and immersive fan experiences. The convergence of AI, digital twin, and immersive environments like the metaverse marks the latest frontier in the continuous evolution of this interdisciplinary field.

2.1 A Brief History of Sports Analytics

Sports analytics, as a discipline that combines data and decision-making science in the context of sports, starts from the use of traditional statistics that are descriptive. In the early stages, the data collected is limited to basic metrics such as the number of goals, rebounds, assists, shooting percentage, or win-loss records. This data is usually compiled manually and used for post-match reporting or evaluation by coaches or media analysts. A significant change occurred in the early 2000s, when quantitative approaches began to gain widespread attention in the sports industry, particularly through the concept of sabermetrics in Major League Baseball (MLB). Sabermetrics, popularized by Bill James and implemented in real life by Billy Beane at the Oakland Athletics, emphasizes the importance of utilizing deeper statistical data to objectively and efficiently evaluate player performance (Mizels et al., 2022). This story was popularized in books and movies *Moneyball*, which marked an important turning point in the history of Sports Analytics.

The transition from conventional statistics to an artificial intelligence (AI)-based approach has become evident in the last decade. Advances in sensor technology, position tracking, video processing, and real-time data collection allow for more thorough and precise analysis of athlete performance. AI, especially through machine learning and computer vision, is now used to detect game patterns, measure athlete fatigue, predict injuries, and analyze tactics and strategies in various sports such as football, basketball, and e-sports. According to (Bhatnagar & Babbar, 2022), The evolution of sports analytics has moved from descriptive to predictive and prescriptive, where data not only explains what has happened, but also provides an overview of what will happen and how optimal decisions can be made based on those predictions. This transformation reflects a shift from a reactive to a proactive paradigm in athlete performance management and team strategy. This development is not only limited to elite sports. AI is now also used in personal fitness apps, app-based training, and digital twin-based physical activity tracking, which shows that these technologies are increasingly inclusive and extend to different levels of competition.

2.2 The Need for a Data-Driven Approach in Modern Sport

In modern sports, a datadriven approach has become absolutely essential. Traditional decision-making based on intuition, anecdotal evidence, or static statistics no longer suffices in an era where speed, precision, and performance optimization determine success. Data-driven strategies now inform nearly every aspect of sport management, from training and injury prevention to fan engagement and business operations. A key driver of this shift is the increased availability of real-time data from wearables, GPS tracking, and video analytics, which enable coaches and analysts to monitor athlete performance continuously. For instance, (Jha et al., 2022) demonstrate how video analytics and IoT sensors have revolutionized performance tracking in elite soccer, giving teams unprecedented insight into player positioning, fatigue, and technical execution during matchplay.

Moreover, (S et al., 2022) present a comprehensive survey of data science in organized sports, emphasizing how machine learning and advanced predictive models are used not just to assess past performance but to forecast game outcomes, tailor training regimens, and drive strategic decisions across sports and business contexts. As a result, combining descriptive, diagnostic, predictive, and prescriptive analytics has become standard practice. This progression from historical reporting to actionable insights enables sports programs to react quickly, personalize player development, and maintain a continuous performance loop. Without such a data-driven framework, teams risk losing the competitive edge in environments where fractions of a second or slight efficiency gains can decide outcomes.

2.3 Development of Devices and Sensors in Collecting Data

Over the past few years (2020–2025), sports analytics has increasingly relied on advanced sensors and wearable technologies to generate high-fidelity, real-time data for performance optimization, injury prevention, and immersive fan interactions. These sensing systems have revolutionized the way athletes are monitored and coached, and how performance data is made available for both analysis and spectator engagement.

2.4 Wearable Sensors for Biomechanical and Physiological Monitoring

Commercial wearable devices such as smart shirts, wristbands, and embedded trackers—now capture internal (heart rate, ECG, HRV, SpO_2) and external metrics (acceleration, velocity, muscle activity via EMG) non-invasively. These systems support continuous performance monitoring and real-time feedback during training or competition. Importantly, AI-enabled algorithms process sensor data to assess athlete workload, recovery, and health risk factors efficiently and accurately.

2.5 Positional Tracking and Motion Analysis

Systems such as GNSS/GPS, UWB, RFID, and camera marker tracking allow accurate positional and motion tracking of athletes. Wearables integrate inertial measurement units (IMUs) and biometric sensors to convert complex motions into analyzable digital data. These technologies enable motion recognition, tactical modeling, and Digital Twin creation for training simulations and strategic planning(Seçkin et al., 2023).

2.6 Innovations in Smart-Textiles and Microelectronic Wearables

Next-generation devices embed sensors directly into fabrics (e-textiles), enabling seamless measurement of physiological parameters like heart rate, body temperature, sweat composition, and muscle activity. Such embedded wearables offer increased comfort, minimal intrusiveness, and improved data fidelity for athlete monitoring and simulation systems(L. Liu & Zhang, 2022). To further illustrate the ecosystem of sensing technologies discussed above, Figure 1 presents a conceptual overview of the key categories of devices and how they contribute to data collection in modern AI-powered sports analytics.

Figure 1. Ecosystem of Devices and Sensors in AI-based Sports Analytics

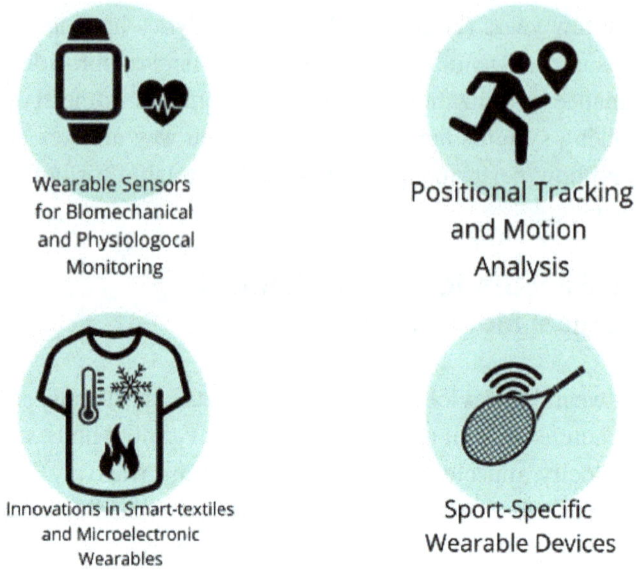

Infographic illustrating the roles of wearable sensors, tracking systems, e-textiles, and embedded IoT devices in modern AI-driven sports analytics ecosystems. This figure depicts the four main categories of sensor and device systems used in data-driven sports environments:

1. Wearable Sensors for Biomechanical and Physiological MonitoringDevices such as smartwatches, chest straps, and wristbands gather data on heart rate (HR), heart rate variability (HRV), oxygen saturation (SpO_2), and movement patterns. These are processed in real-time to assess workload, recovery, and injury risk using AI-based platforms.
2. Positional Tracking and Motion AnalysisTechnologies such as GPS, RFID, and UWB sensors, integrated with video tracking and inertial measurement units (IMUs), provide highly accurate positional and movement data. These support performance optimization and tactical analysis (Seçkin et al., 2023).
3. Smart Textiles and Embedded MicroelectronicsE-textiles embed physiological and biomechanical sensors directly into athletic clothing, enabling seamless, non-invasive data collection during play and practice (Pekgor & Toros, 2024).
4. Sport-Specific Devices and Equipment-Embedded SensorsSpecialized sensors integrated into sporting gear (tennis rackets, smart shoes) collect sport-specific

data like stroke type, impact force, and vibration feedback enhancing technical analysis and player development.

These systems form a foundational layer of Digital Twin models, real-time analytics, and immersive metaverse integrations in contemporary sports ecosystems. This graphic is designed to visualize the ecosystem of devices used in modern sports analytics, particularly in the context of integration with AI, Digital Twins, and the Metaverse. Each element in the infographic reflects the specific contribution of each device type to accurate and sustainable data collection in the smart sports ecosystem.

2.7 Sport Specific Wearable Devices

Novel miniaturized devices like tennis racket dampener sensors provide domain-specific analytics. For example, the smart tennis "Smart Dampener" captures ball speed, stroke classification, and vibration patterns, with high accuracy and minimal interference in play. This demonstrates the growing adoption of ultra-light, sportspecific performer sensors integrated into traditional equipment.

2.8 Data Integration, Edge Computing & IoT

Modern wearables form part of broader systems built with IoT infrastructure: sensor nodes onboard, local edge processing for initial signal processing, and cloud-based ML/AI for advanced analysis. This architecture ensures real-time feedback loops for training or wellness interventions while balancing device autonomy and communication efficiency(Seçkin et al., 2023).

3. ARTIFICIAL INTELLIGENCE IN SPORTS

Arising as a transformative pillar in modern sports, Artificial Intelligence (AI) fundamentally reshapes how athletic performance is measured, managed, and monetized. With advances in machine learning, computer vision, and predictive modeling, AI offers powerful capabilities beyond traditional human-centered analysis. One of the critical domains is performance analysis. AI systems now process massive datasets from wearable devices, optical cameras, and match statistics in real-time. According to sensor-based research, edge-embedded AI monitors physiological and biomechanical signals such as heart rate variability, joint kinematics, and muscle activation and enables instantaneous feedback and injury prevention strategies during training sessions and matches (Rahmani et al., 2024). These models improve athlete readiness, reduce fatigue, and help optimize training workloads. AI is also instrumental in injury risk prediction and rehabilitation management. By analyzing historical injury logs, movement patterns, and training load, AI models can anticipate overuse injuries or biomechanical stress before they manifest. Research shows AI-enabled systems can reduce muscle-related injuries by up to 25% by alerting coaches to fatigue patterns and high-risk scenarios (Mateus et al., 2025). Furthermore, personalized recovery protocols using AI-guided metrics optimize rehabilitation timelines for each athlete.

From a broader perspective, AI contributes to fan engagement and sports business intelligence. Applications include AI-driven content creation like automated highlight reels or real-time statistics and sentiment analysis tools that personalize fan interactions, merchandising, and digital campaigns (Cossich et al., 2023). Virtual assistants and chatbots leverage NLP to answer fan queries in real time, enhancing immersive experiences in stadiums or digital platforms. The market landscape signals rapid expansion. Reports estimate global sports analytics mheavily fueled by AI growing from approximately $58 billion in 2025 to over $243 billion by 2032, underscoring accelerating demand for data-driven decision support and fan analytics tools.

Technological innovations further expand capability. For instance, AI-driven wearable textile systems (smart sportswear with embedded strain sensors) can classify exercise execution and identify biomechanical irregularities with over 92% accuracy, using deep neural networks like ResNet-18 and explainability via Grad-CAM heatmaps (Tang et al., 2025). hese advanced biosensors bridge granular motion tracking with AI classification, optimizing training and rehabilitation through non-intrusive, real-time monitoring. Despite its promise, AI in sports faces challenges: ethical concerns over data privacy, algorithmic bias, and transparency remain pressing especially with sensitive biometric data and recruitment decisions (Kim et al., 2025). Smaller or resource-limited teams may struggle to adopt costly AI systems, raising equity concerns across different levels of sport. In summary, AI in sports has evolved from augmenting analysis to becoming a critical enabler across performance, injuries, strategy, fan experience, and business intelligence. By combining wearable sensor inputs, computer vision, predictive models, and interactive fan platforms, AI transforms the sports industry towards a responsive, data-centric ecosystem. As technology advances, robust ethical frameworks and inclusive infrastructure will be vital to fully harness its potential for all stakeholders.

3.1 AI Algorithms Used in Sports (Machine Learning, Deep Learning, NLP)

The application of Artificial Intelligence (AI) in the world of sports has grown rapidly in recent years, driving significant changes in the way athletes are trained, performance is assessed, and fan experiences are shaped. Behind this transformation are the three main pillars of AI algorithms: machine learning, deep learning, and natural language processing (NLP). All three of these allow data processing that was once just statistics to become a source of deeper tactical, biological, and social insights.

Machine learning (ML) is commonly used for predictive tasks, such as detecting injury risk, classifying movement patterns, and evaluating the effectiveness of exercises. Models such as decision trees, support vector machines, and random forests were trained using data from wearable devices that measure heart rate, speed, or joint pressure. With that data, ML algorithms can identify signs of fatigue before an injury occurs (Pietraszewski et al., 2025). For example, in a study by (Marquina et al., 2023) The ML system based on biomechanical data shows high accuracy in predicting injuries based on the analysis of player movement patterns.

Meanwhile, deep learning (DL) especially convolutional neural networks (CNN) plays a major role in video analysis and visual imagery. In the context of sports, CNN is able to recognize the team's tactical formation, assess the position of the players, and automatically detect the movement of the ball from the match footage. These networks are capable of managing data at scale and detecting complex patterns invisible to the human eye. This not only makes it easier for coaches to evaluate strategies, but also opens up room for automation in scouting and monitoring opponents.

Natural Language Processing (NLP) adds a social dimension to AI in sports. NLP algorithms are used to extract emotions and opinions from social media, fan forums, and live broadcasts. With techniques such as sentiment analysis and topic modeling, clubs and sponsors can understand how fans feel about team performance, referee decisions, or the viewing experience. Research by Boatwright shows that NLP helps clubs adapt digital communications based on fans' real-time preferences and emotions (Du et al., 2024).

These three approaches do not stand alone, but rather integrate with each other to create a smart sports ecosystem. In modern training scenarios, wearable sensors collect data, machine learning processes and provides early warnings, deep learning analyzes motion visualizations, and NLP ensures fans stay emotionally connected with their teams. Together, these algorithms enable personalization in training, efficiency in strategy, and emotional engagement in today's sports experiences. Figure 2 shows the Integration of AI Algorithms in Sports.

Figure 2. Integration of AI Algorithms in Sports

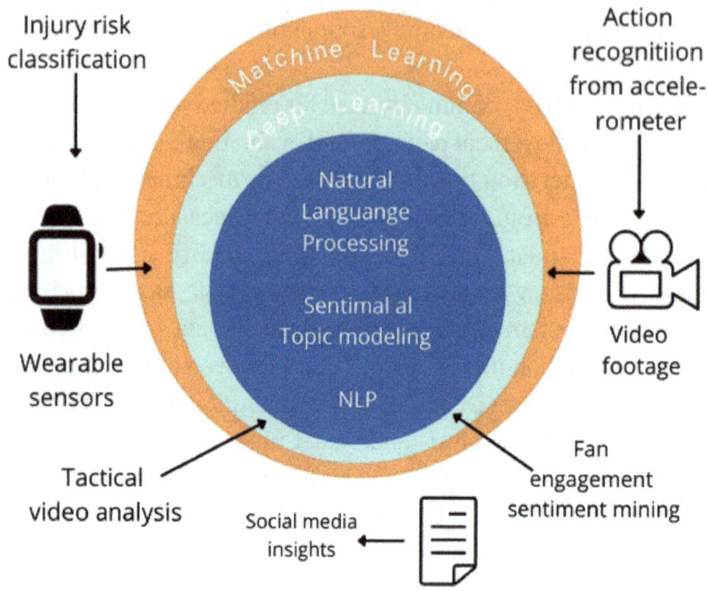

The illustration consists of three main parts:

1. Machine Learning → process wearable data such as speed and heart rate → output in the form of injury predictions. Machine learning includes predictive models such as random forests and decision trees, generating outputs such as injury risk dashboards and motion classification.
2. Deep Learning → analyze match videos → generate tactical analysis and a heatmap of player positions. Deep Learning shows CNN for pose estimation and tactical analysis, offering a heatmap of player positions and prediction of attack patterns.
3. NLP (Natural Languange Processing) → analyzes social media and fan comments → provide insights into fan sentiment and preferences. NLP connects to social media analytics and fan sentiment, providing engagement insights and content recommendations.

All algorithms are directed towards one main goal: a Sport Intelligence System that supports coaches, players, and fans simultaneously. Data arrows flow from source to algorithm and from algorithm to use case such as coaching feedback, team strategy, and fan experience on metaverse platforms.

3.2 AI in Performance Tracking and Injury Prevention

In modern elite sports, Artificial Intelligence (AI) has become essential for monitoring performance and preventing injuries. AI transforms raw data from wearable sensors and tracking systems into actionable insights for trainers and medical teams. One primary application of AI is in performance tracking. Wearable devices record variables such as heart rate, acceleration, and GPS coordinates, providing rich datasets for machine learning models. A study in Sports Medicine Open demonstrated that machine learning algorithms like support vector machines and random forest could predict reinjury risk in football with high accuracy, facilitating proactive intervention strategies (Majumdar et al., 2022). Figure 3 shows the Workflow of the EPTS System with Edge AI and Cloud Analytics.

Figure 3. The Workflow of the EPTS System with Edge AI and Cloud Analytics

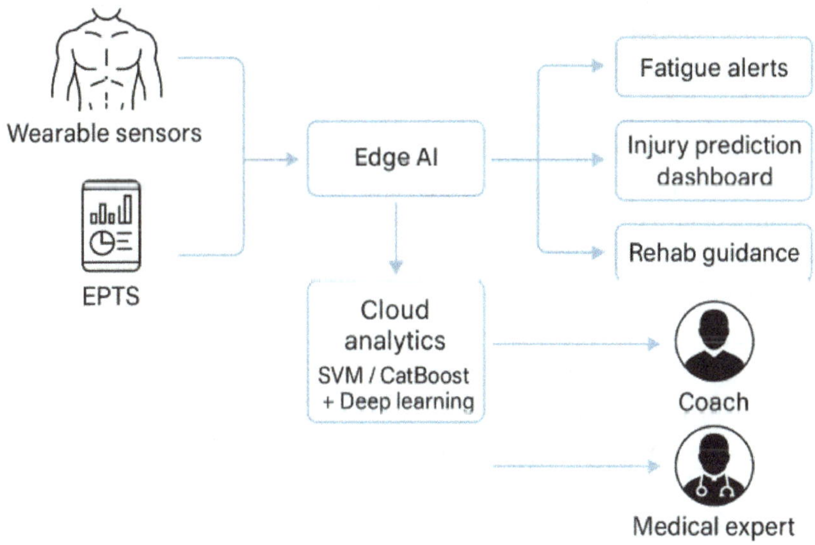

A visual flowchart shows:

Input: wearable sensors (HR, EMG, GPS) dan EPTS (Electronic Performance Tracking System).

Processing: Edge AI for real-time flagging; Cloud analytics implements an ML/DL model.

Outputs: fatigue alerts, injury risk dashboard, and rehabilitation recommendations.

Figure 1 illustrates the data-driven ecosystem enabled by Artificial Intelligence (AI) in the context of athlete performance monitoring and injury prevention. The image outlines a step-by-step pipeline, beginning with various data sources, such as wearable sensors, Electronic Performance Tracking Systems (EPTS), and biometric devices. These inputs capture physiological and biomechanical metrics including heart rate variability, acceleration, electromyography (EMG), and GPS positioning.

Next, the data flows into the processing layer, which is divided into two components: edge AI and cloud-based analytics. Edge AI handles real-time computations on portable or field-side devices, enabling immediate alerts when signs of fatigue or overload are detected. Meanwhile, the cloud processing unit applies machine learning (ML) and deep learning (DL) models such as Support Vector Machines (SVM), Random Forests, or CNNs to analyze patterns and trends across sessions and athletes. The final section shows the output layer, where results are visualized through dashboards, fatigue warnings, and predictive injury maps. These outputs are accessible to coaches, medical teams, and sports scientists, facilitating quick decision-making and individualized intervention. The diagram emphasizes how AI acts as a bridge between raw sensor data and evidence-based action, ultimately enhancing athlete safety and performance sustainability. AI also plays a pivotal role in injury risk prediction. A comprehensive review published in Diagnostics showed how AI systems integrating physiological, biomechanical, and load data enhance predictions for muscle and joint injuries. These models support precision prevention by producing personalized risk profiles and recommendations (Musat et al., 2024).

Beyond prediction, AI guides rehabilitation and return-to-play decision-making. Longitudinal tracking of recovery metrics enables personalized protocols developed from historical trends. Coaches and medical staff receive data-based dashboards instead of subjective estimates, improving safety and performance during return phases. The synergy of machine learning, deep learning, and data fusion transforms how athlete load is analyzed. Machine learning handles structured data for classification; deep learning methods analyze unstructured data like video for movement anomalies; data fusion integrates diverse input sources to build composite models. Together, these approaches enable precise, individualized interventions that were previously unattainable. AI also supports real-time alert systems: when sensor readings indicate fatigue or abnormal stress, edge computing units trigger notifications to trainers, enabling immediate adjustments to training loads or rest plans. This proactive feedback loop reduces overtraining and minimizes the risk of acute or chronic injuries.

Table 1. AI Applications in Performance Tracking & Injury Prevention

Domain	AI Technical/Data Source	Outcame & Benefit
Real-time performance tracking	Wearable sensors+ML (Machine Learning) models (SVM, RF)	Detects fatigue early; adjusts training load
Injury risk prediction	Biomechanical + load data integrated with AI	Personalized injury risk scores; prevents re-injury
Rehabilitation & RTS (Return-To-Play)	Longitudinal recovery data + ML monitoring	Tailored rehab protocols; safer RTP decisions

Table 1 summarizes the main applications of Artificial Intelligence in sports across three key areas: real-time performance tracking, injury risk prediction, and rehabilitation or return-to-play support. In real-time performance tracking, body-based sensors such as accelerometers, GPS, and heart rate monitors generate rich datasets that are analyzed using machine learning algorithms like decision trees and random forests to detect early signs of fatigue or muscle strain, enabling timely training adjustments. Injury risk prediction combines training load data, biomechanical patterns, and physiological variables to estimate the likelihood of injury for each athlete, helping medical teams design more effective prevention strategies. Meanwhile, in rehabilitation, longitudinal data are analyzed through machine learning to monitor recovery progress and develop individualized return-to-play protocols, ensuring that athletes resume activity safely and based on objective, data-driven evidence.

3.3 AI Applications in Tactical and Strategic Analysis

In high-performance sports, tactics and strategy often determine the outcome between victory and defeat, and the increasing complexity of team dynamics, game flow, and opponent behavior has intensified the need for data-driven tactical analysis. Artificial Intelligence (AI), particularly through machine learning (ML), computer vision, and deep learning (DL), has become an essential tool for coaches and analysts aiming to optimize in-game decision-making. AI-powered tactical systems integrate data from video feeds, GPS tracking, and event logs to decode team formations, player positioning, and ball movement patterns. Deep learning models, especially Convolutional Neural Networks (CNNs), are trained to identify team structures, defensive transitions, and pressing schemes, providing a detailed understanding of strategic evolution across matches and seasons. For example, AI can detect spatio-temporal trends such as a team's tendency to create numerical superiority in specific zones or how individual players exploit spaces between defensive lines. Through clustering and unsupervised learning, analysts can categorize offensive build-ups and defensive breakdowns, enhancing tactical preparation. During match planning, AI facilitates large-scale opposition analysis by automatically generating reports that identify behavioral tendencies, such as frequent passing triangles or vulnerabilities to counterattacks after turnovers. These insights are visualized through heatmaps, passing networks, and trajectory maps, transforming complex tactical data into clear, actionable strategies for competitive advantage. Table 2 shows the AI Techniques and Their Applications in Football Strategy and Analysis.

Table 2. AI Techniques and Their Applications in Football Strategy and Analysis

Domain	AI Method/Technique	Use Case/Output
Formation Recognition	Convolutional Neural Networks (CNNs), Video Analysis	Detects team shapes (e.g., 4-3-3, 3-5-2) and transitions during match phases
Spatiotemporal Pattern Detection	Clustering, Unsupervised Learning	Identifies recurring passing networks, spatial control zones, or pressing triggers
Opposition Scouting	Computer Vision + Event Data Integration	Generates opponent heatmaps, passing tendencies, and weakness zones
Tactical Simulation	Deep Reinforcement Learning (DRL), Q-Learning	Simulates alternate strategies for optimal decision-making (e.g., Q-Ball Model)
NLP-based Tactical Mining	Natural Language Processing (NLP) on reports	Extracts insights from scouting reports, commentary, and historical match narratives

AI is also transforming in-game strategy optimization. Real-time data streams can be fed into predictive models that simulate likely outcomes of tactical adjustments. For example, a coach may use AI to assess whether switching to a high press in the 70th minute improves win probability, based on historical data and the opponent's fatigue indicators (Yanai et al., 2022). Moreover, Natural Language Processing (NLP) techniques have been applied to extract tactical information from large textual databases like scouting reports, expert commentary, or historical match notes enhancing the knowledge base with qualitative and contextual layers. As tactical data becomes richer and more granular, AI helps bridge the gap between quantitative complexity and intuitive coaching decisions. Coaches no longer rely solely on intuition or static stats they now have dynamic, evolving models that support scenario-based decision-making. Ultimately, AI fosters a competitive edge by turning raw tactical data into predictive insights. The synergy between human expertise and machine intelligence has started to redefine the art and science of coaching in modern sport.

3.4 AI in Talent Scouting and Player Development

In modern sports, AI is revolutionizing talent identification and player development by providing data-driven insights beyond traditional scouting methods. Conventional approaches, reliant on subjective observation, often led to biased or incomplete evaluations. Today, AI uses large datasets such as biomechanics, match statistics, and video analysis to create comprehensive talent profiles. Through computer vision and machine learning, thousands of athletes can be assessed efficiently, including those at grassroots levels. Automated video analysis is a key application, identifying patterns in player movement, decision-making, and tactical awareness. These insights are benchmarked against elite players to uncover emerging talents and predict long-term potential, including injury risks and skill development. AI also supports recruitment by simulating player adaptability to various tactical systems, reducing the risk of unsuccessful transfers.

For development, AI creates personalized training programs by analyzing biometric and performance data, adjusting plans based on workload, progress, and mental readiness. Youth academies benefit from AI dashboards that track players' growth across physical and tactical metrics. Comparative benchmarking further guides goal setting and progression by continuously evaluating players against established professionals. Some systems also use Natural Language Processing to assess mindset through scouting reports and interviews. Ultimately, AI turns talent scouting into a precise, predictive science, offering continuous, holistic evaluation and development.

Figure 4. AI-Powered Talent Development Cycle in Sports

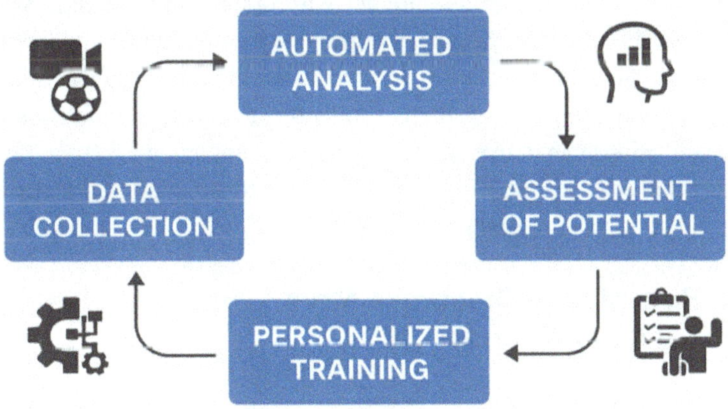

Figure 4 illustrates the flow of an AI-based process used in athletic talent identification and development, showing how Artificial Intelligence (AI) supports a continuous cycle of evaluation and performance improvement from data collection to personalized training design. The process begins with data acquisition, which involves gathering information from match videos, GPS sensors, biometric data, and performance statistics. These datasets are then processed through automated analysis, where computer vision and machine learning algorithms extract behavioral patterns, technical abilities, and physical as well as tactical indicators. The analyzed results feed into a potential assessment stage, where AI systems benchmark individual performance against professional standards and predict career development trajectories using historical and contextual data. Based on this analysis, AI generates personalized training plans tailored to each athlete's specific needs, focusing on strengthening weaknesses, preventing injuries, and enhancing targeted skills. The process operates as a continuous feedback loop, making talent development adaptive, data-driven, and evidence-based. Overall, the visualization demonstrates that AI not only accelerates talent identification but also enhances understanding of long-term athletic potential while empowering coaches to make more informed and strategic decisions.

4. FAN ENGAGEMENT THROUGH IMMERSIVE TECHNOLOGIES

Immersive technologies are transforming how fans experience sports by creating interactive and personalized engagement through Virtual Reality (VR), Augmented Reality (AR), and Metaverse platforms. VR provides 360-degree views of live events, while AR overlays real-time statistics and visuals on broadcasts, enhancing excitement and understanding. Within the Metaverse, fans can attend matches as avatars, explore digital stadiums, interact with others, and purchase virtual merchandise, fostering a stronger sense of community among global audiences. These technologies also enable gamified experiences such as fantasy leagues and live polls, increasing participation and loyalty. By collecting and analyzing fan behavior data, sports organizations can deliver more targeted content and marketing. Overall, immersive technologies are redefining sports as an interactive, emotionally engaging, and globally connected digital ecosystem.

4.1 The Role of AI in Creating a More Personalized Fan Experience

Artificial Intelligence (AI) is transforming fan engagement in sports by delivering personalized, immersive, and data-driven experiences. By analyzing data such as viewing habits, social media activity, purchases, and location, AI tailors content like match highlights, merchandise recommendations, and ticket offers in real time. AI-powered chatbots and virtual assistants enhance interaction by answering questions naturally, while integration with AR and VR lets fans explore virtual stadiums and experience games from unique perspectives. Through these innovations, AI strengthens emotional connections between fans and teams, boosting loyalty, digital engagement, and new revenue opportunities in the sports industry.

4.2 The Use of AI in Social Media Management, Match Predictions, and Avatar Interactions

Artificial Intelligence (AI) is widely used in sports for managing social media, predicting match outcomes, and enabling avatar-based interactions. In social media management, AI tools schedule posts, analyze engagement trends, and generate personalized content to boost fan involvement. For match predictions, machine learning models process historical data, team statistics, and player performance to forecast outcomes with high accuracy. Meanwhile, in virtual environments like the metaverse, AI powers interactive avatars that allow fans to engage in real-time conversations, attend virtual matches, or meet digital versions of their favorite athletes creating more engaging and immersive fan experiences across platforms.

5. DIGITAL TWINS IN SPORTS

Digital twins in sports are virtual replicas of athletes, equipment, or teams that use real-time data to simulate performance for analysis, injury prevention, and strategy optimization. By integrating information from sensors, GPS, video, and biometrics, these models reveal insights into fatigue, movement efficiency, and injury risk. In professional sports, coaches use digital twins to test tactics or predict player responses without physical strain, while medical teams monitor rehabilitation by comparing recovery data to baseline models. Combined with VR and AR, digital twins also enhance fan engagement by visualizing training and performance in real time, making them a transformative tool in modern sports science and management.

5.1 Understanding and Concepts of Digital Twin and the Application of Digital Twin in Athlete Training and Match Simulation

A Digital Twin is a real-time, data-driven virtual replica of a physical object, system, or process that mirrors real-world behavior using continuous input from sensors and connected devices. In sports, Digital Twin technology is transforming athlete performance, training, and strategic planning by integrating biomechanical, physiological, environmental, and performance data into dynamic, interactive models. For athlete training, Digital Twins allow coaches and sports scientists to monitor physical strain, predict fatigue, and adjust training loads in real time, reducing injury risk. The system can simulate various workloads and environmental conditions to forecast how an athlete responds under stress or during recovery, enabling personalized and adaptive training strategies.

In match preparation, Digital Twins simulate game scenarios using real-time and historical data. This helps teams evaluate tactical options, analyze opponent behavior, and optimize player positioning without physically taxing athletes. These digital simulations enhance strategic planning and support smarter decision-making. Overall, Digital Twin technology bridges the physical and digital realms to improve performance, prevent injuries, and refine strategies. It offers a powerful, precise approach to athlete management by allowing continuous analysis, simulation, and optimization of training and gameplay, helping teams and individuals perform at their peak while minimizing risk. Figure 5 shows the concepts of Digital Twin and the application of digital twin in athlete training and match simulation

Figure 5. Digital Twin and the application of digital twin in athlete training and match simulation

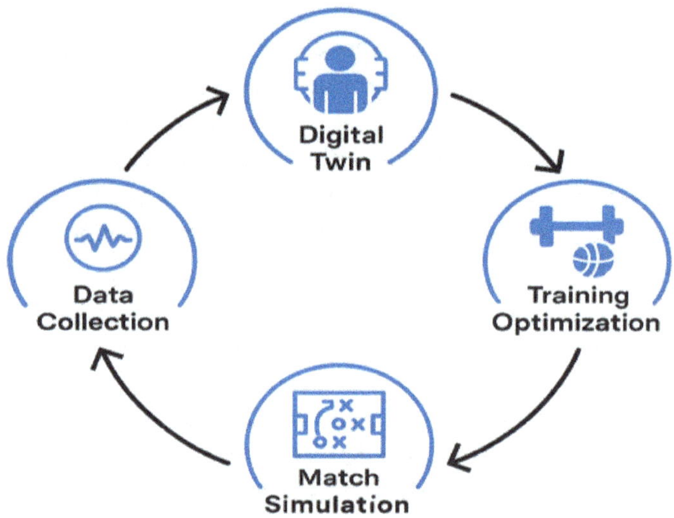

5.2 Integration With Wearable Devices and Biometric Tracking

Integration of Artificial Intelligence (AI) with wearable devices and biometric tracking has transformed performance monitoring in sports. Wearables such as GPS trackers, heart rate monitors, and motion sensors continuously collect real-time data on athletes' movement, physiology, and workload. AI algorithms analyze this biometric data to detect fatigue, predict injury risks, and personalize training programs based on individual needs and performance goals. This integration enables coaches to make data-driven decisions and adapt strategies instantly. It also enhances long-term athlete development by monitoring progress, recovery patterns, and overall health. The seamless connection between wearables and AI creates a responsive, precision-based approach to sports performance management.

6. METAVERSE AND THE FUTURE OF SPORTS EXPERIENCE

In sports, the metaverse is an immersive virtual world using VR/AR and AI where fans engage through avatars, attend matches, and join digital economies. It expands the stadium experience into a limitless online space connecting global communities. Virtual stadiums allow fans to pick seats, explore the venue, socialize, and switch environments like sports bars or press boxes. This creates unique experiences beyond what physical arenas offer, enhancing engagement and accessibility. Avatar-based competitions and eSports are another dimension: fans can play in digital tournaments, train virtually with athlete avatars, or compete in gamified leagues that blend real sport and digital gameplay (Chohan & Schmidt-Devlin, 2024). AI enhances these environments through real-time personalization. Intelligent algorithms curate content, customized highlights, interactive commentary, and dynamic fan-to-fan conversations. In virtual worlds, AI avatars respond conversationally and animate with human-like grace, enriching engagement and emotional connection with the team. Overall, AI and the metaverse coalesce to deliver hyper-personalized, immersive sports experiences. Fans are no longer passive viewers but active participants, sharing the stadium space with avatars, forming communities, and engaging across digital media in real time. Figure 6 shows the Metaverse and the Future of Sports Experience.

Figure 6. Metaverse and the Future of Sports Experience

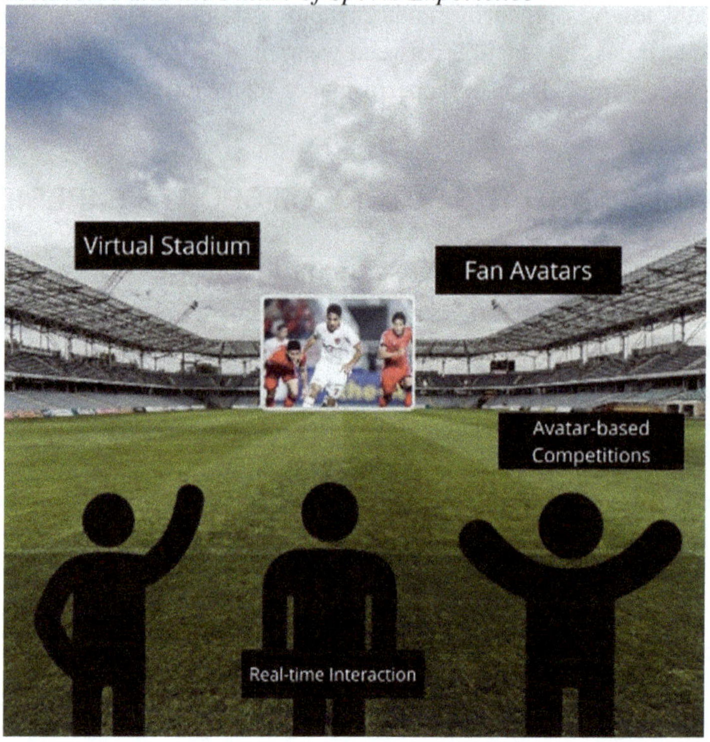

This digital illustration shows a virtual stadium where fan avatars are engaged in watching a live soccer match. Key elements such as avatar-based competitions, real-time interaction, immersive viewing, and virtual stadium highlight the integration of AI and metaverse technologies in transforming the future sports experience.

7. CHALLENGES AND ETHICAL CONSIDERATIONS

The growing use of AI in sports brings significant ethical concerns, particularly around data privacy and security. Athletes and fans produce vast amounts of sensitive data through wearables, apps, and immersive platforms ("Vulnerabilities, Attacks, and Security Aspects on the Internet of Things (IoT)," 2026). Without strong data governance, this information is vulnerable to misuse, breaches, or commercial exploitation without consent posing risks to personal integrity and organizational trust. Another critical issue is algorithmic bias, which can skew results if AI models are trained on unbalanced datasets. This may lead to unfair talent evaluations, recruitment errors, or inaccurate injury predictions, especially for underrepresented groups.

Moreover, over-reliance on automated systems can weaken human decision-making in coaching and medical contexts. Ethical implementation of AI should prioritize transparency and maintain human oversight to ensure that technology supports, rather than replaces, human expertise in sports. Figure 7 shows the Key Challenges and Ethical Considerations in AI-Driven Sports Systems.

Figure 7. Key Challenges and Ethical Considerations in AI-Driven Sports Systems

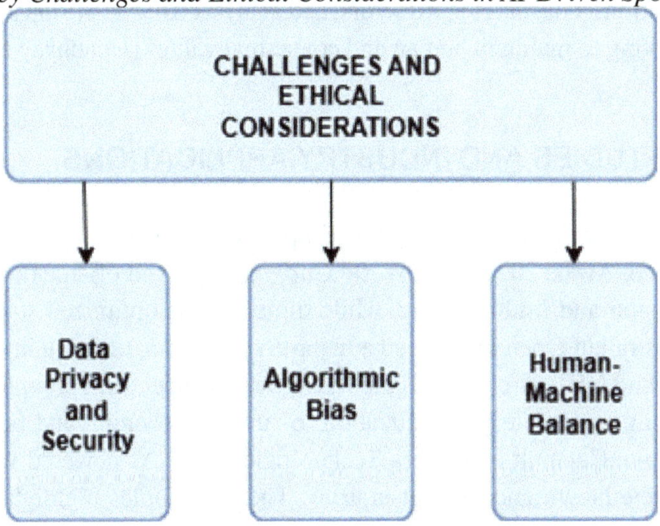

This diagram illustrates three key challenges faced in the application of Artificial Intelligence (AI) in the sports industry, particularly in the context of sports analytics, athlete training, and fan experience. The diagram also aims to simplify the complexity of ethics in sports technology and help readers understand that the application of AI is not only a matter of efficiency, but also of responsibility.

1. Data Privacy and Security

This element refers to the protection of sensitive data collected from athletes and fans. AI technology often relies on biometric data, digital habits, and location, which if not properly maintained can be misused or leaked. Therefore, cybersecurity and privacy policies are important aspects of AI implementation.

2. Algorithmic Bias

This section points out the risk that AI algorithms can generate biased conclusions if trained on unrepresentative data. In sports, this bias can have an impact on player selection, performance analysis, or competitive decisions—ultimately creating injustice and discrimination (Deveci et al., 2023).

3. Human-Machine Balance

This element emphasizes the importance of maintaining a balance between AI-based decisions and human intuition. While AI can provide quick and accurate recommendations, coaches, team doctors, and analysts still need to have authority in decision-making to maintain human and contextual values (Upadhyay et al., 2023).

8. CASE STUDIES AND INDUSTRY APPLICATIONS

Case studies of AI in sports show its impact on performance, operations, and fan experience. At the 2022 FIFA World Cup, AI improved offside decisions with computer vision and limb tracking, while digital twins optimized stadium logistics. The Australian Open introduced a metaverse stadium, offering immersive fan experiences and NFT purchases. In the NBA, Second Spectrum provides real-time player tracking and strategy visualization to support coaching and broadcasting. Companies like Catapult and Zebra Technologies offer AI-powered wearables to monitor athlete health and prevent injuries. These examples highlight how AI is transforming sports into a smarter, more connected ecosystem (Gupta et al., 2023).

8.1 Case Study of AI Use in Sports Clubs/Organizations (FIFA)

FIFA has implemented artificial intelligence (AI) to improve the accuracy of match decisions and the fan experience (Wisnujati et al., 2023). One of the most important examples is the use of AI in the video assistant referee (VAR) system, which involves Computer Vision technology to detect player positions in real-time. This algorithm helps to speed up and enforce offside decisions and fouls, improving the fairness and integrity of matches. In addition, the FIFA Innovation Programme in 2022 reported on the readiness of global football clubs for the adoption of AI, including the modernization of the Electronic Performance Tracking System (EPTS) and smart ball tracking in collecting match data and player performance. The use of AI is also permeating player performance analysis for scouting and strategic decision-making (Rathi et al., 2020). AI improves operational efficiency, from player analysis to fan management, and strengthens the capabilities of clubs and national federation unity. By combining player tracking data, ball tracking, and AI algorithms, FIFA creates an intelligent ecosystem that supports match decisions and optimizes athletes performance. Figure 8 shows the AI Integration in FIFA Operations.

Figure 8. AI Integration in FIFA Operations

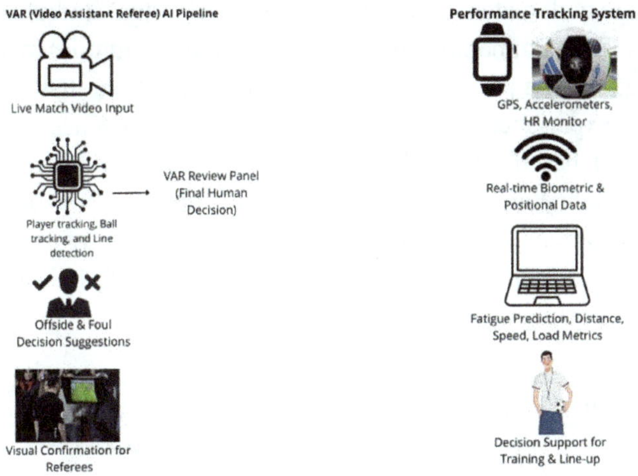

In the image on the left is the VAR (Video Assistant Referee) AI pipeline which consists of: Match camera input (Broadcast Feed), AI processing unit (Computer Vision), decision engine, and output to the referee. Then on the right is performance tracking system consisting of: sensor & smart ball, data transmission, AI analysis dashboard, and coach/analyst review. This diagram explains how FIFA uses AI in two main contexts:

1. On the left side, VAR uses computer vision to automatically detect player positions, fouls and offside situations, before displaying the information back to the referee for confirmation.
2. On the right, AI processes data from wearable sensors and a smart ball to analyze athlete performance. Coaches and analysts use this analysis to make tactical decisions and prevent injuries.

8.2 Metaverse and Digital Twin Initiatives in Major Sporting Events

The integration of Metaverse and Digital Twin technologies in major sporting events is transforming how sports are hosted, experienced, and analyzed. Digital Twin initiatives allow organizers to create real-time replicas of venues, athlete conditions, and event operations. For instance, at the 2022 FIFA World Cup, digital twins were used to simulate stadium crowd flow and security scenarios, ensuring smoother logistics and safety management. These models mirrored physical infrastructure and real-time data, enabling predictive adjustments without disrupting the actual event. Meanwhile, Metaverse platforms have introduced virtual fan zones where users can engage with matches using avatars, explore virtual stadiums, and interact with other fans. These immersive spaces provide new opportunities for broadcasting, merchandising, and fan participation. For example, the Australian Open offered a virtual stadium experience where fans could attend live matches in the metaverse and purchase NFT-based collectibles. Together, these technologies not only enhance operational efficiency and fan experience but also open up new business models for sports organizations, marking a shift toward more interactive, data-driven, and global sporting ecosystems. Figure 9 shows the Integration of Metaverse and Digital Twin in Major Sporting Events.

Figure 9. Integration of Metaverse and Digital Twin in Major Sporting Events

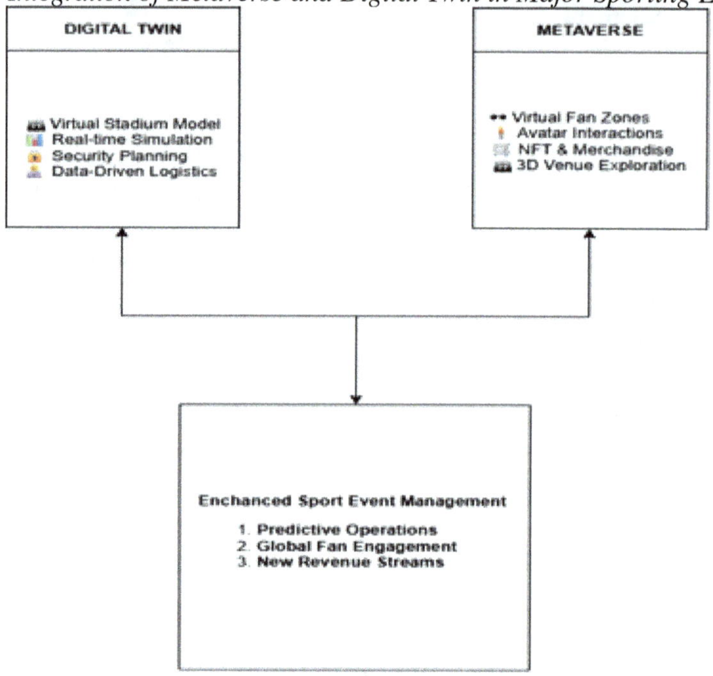

This diagram illustrates how Digital Twin and Metaverse technologies operate in parallel but complementary ways to enhance the management and experience of large-scale sporting events.

1. Digital Twin Side

On the left side of the diagram, the Digital Twin flow represents how event organizers create:

a. Virtual stadium models, that digitally replicate the physical venue.
b. Real-time simulations, used to predict crowd movement, entry/exit flows, and congestion scenarios.
c. Security planning, allowing simulation of emergency scenarios based on live data inputs (Widodo et al., 2025).
d. Data-driven logistics, supporting operational decisions such as scheduling, facility access, and resource deployment using predictive analytics.
   2. Metaverse Side

On the right side, the Metaverse flow showcases innovations in:

a. Virtual fan zones, enabling global fans to attend events virtually from anywhere.
b. Avatar interactions, allowing fans to engage with other fans and even virtual athletes.
c. NFT & digital merchandise, opening up new monetization strategies through blockchain-based assets.
d. 3D venue exploration, offering immersive tours and interactive experiences of sports arenas.
   3. Unified Outcome

At the bottom, both flows converge into a central outcome:

a. Enhanced Sports Event Management, where AI-driven digital twins and immersive metaverse features together support predictive planning, increase fan engagement, and create new business opportunities.

8.3 Collaboration between technology companies and the world of sports

Collaboration between tech companies and the sports industry is revolutionizing athlete performance, fan engagement, and event operations. Partnerships like Microsoft with LaLiga and SAP with Bayern Munich use AI and data dashboards to enhance real-time analysis and training. At global events like the FIFA World Cup, firms such as Intel and IBM provide digital twins, predictive systems, and AI-driven broadcasting tools. Wearable tech companies including Catapult and Whoop enable biometric tracking for injury prevention and recovery. Additionally, immersive technologies like AR, VR, and the Metaverse allow fans to engage through virtual stadiums and digital collectibles. These collaborations not only boost performance but also create new revenue streams and expand global fan reach, positioning technology as a core driver in the future of sports.

These collaborations have also paved the way for long-term innovation pipelines, where technology companies and sports organizations co-develop experimental platforms and pilot programs. For example, AI-powered scouting tools and virtual coaching assistants are being tested to support youth development programs and lower-tier leagues, expanding access to high-performance resources beyond elite teams. This inclusive approach ensures that the benefits of AI and immersive technology extend across all levels of sport, fostering a more connected, data-driven, and equitable athletic landscape (Darwinto et al., 2025).

9. FUTURE DIRECTIONS AND RESEARCH OPPORTUNITIES

Future research in AI-driven sports analytics focuses on advanced predictive models for training and injury prevention, improving AI explainability, and exploring generative AI for simulations and fan content. As Metaverse and Digital Twin adoption grows, studies must address their psychological and commercial impacts. Ethical issues like data privacy and algorithmic fairness also require attention.

9.1 Future Trends in AI and Immersive Sports Tech

AI and immersive tech are shaping the future of sports through virtual stadiums, digital twins, and predictive analytics for personalized training. Generative AI and AR enhance coaching and fan engagement, while NFTs and metaverse platforms offer new monetization models. Ethical research will ensure fair, transparent, and human-centered AI use. (Roumeliotis, n.d.).

9.2 Potential Research in the Field of Human-Computer Interaction in Sports

Potential research in human-computer interaction (HCI) in sports includes developing intuitive interfaces for coaches and athletes, enhancing real-time feedback through AR/VR, and improving gesture or voice-based control systems. Studies may also explore how adaptive AI interfaces affect training outcomes, decision-making, and athlete engagement in immersive environments (Rahaman et al., 2024).

9.3 The Potential for Integrating AI With Neurotechnology, Blockchain, and Smart Contracts

The integration of AI with emerging technologies like neurotechnology, blockchain, and smart contracts is poised to transform sports. AI-powered brain-computer interfaces can monitor mental focus and stress, enabling personalized cognitive training and neurological recovery. Simultaneously, combining AI with blockchain enhances transparency in sports management by automating contract triggers, securing athlete data, and enabling decentralized transactions through smart contracts. This convergence fosters more precise performance optimization, fair compensation, and trusted governance, creating a smarter, more equitable sports ecosystem (Singla et al., 2022).

10. CONCLUSION

10.1 Summary of AI's Contribution to Sports

AI has transformed sports by optimizing athlete performance, enabling injury prediction, and enhancing tactical analysis. It also personalizes fan experiences through immersive technologies and automates event management. These innovations make sports more data-driven, efficient, and interactive, reshaping both on-field performance and off-field engagement across the global sports ecosystem.

10.2 The Future of Sports: Technology, Data, and Immersive Experiences

Future technology will enable athletes to train smarter with real-time biometric tracking and AI-based simulations. Teams will make more accurate tactical decisions through predictive analytics. For fans, the experience becomes more immersive through the metaverse, interactive avatars, and personalized content that enhances emotional and digital engagement in sports.

10.3 Conclusions and Outlook for the Future

This book illustrates how artificial intelligence is beginning to play an important role in the world of sports. In the future, technologies such as digital twins and the metaverse are expected to increasingly support the way athletes train, teams make decisions, and fans enjoy the games. All these developments open up new opportunities to create a more engaging, interactive, and relevant sports experience that evolves with the changing times. These innovations also drive new business models, improve operational efficiency, and strengthen the emotional connection between fans and the sports they love.

REFERENCES

Aloqaily, M., Bouachir, O., Karray, F., Al Ridhawi, I., & El Saddik, A. (2023). Integrating Digital Twin and Advanced Intelligent Technologies to Realize the Metaverse. *IEEE Consumer Electronics Magazine*, *12*(6), 47–55. DOI: 10.1109/MCE.2022.3212570

Bhatnagar, R., & Babbar, M. (2022). A systematic review of sports analytics. *International Journal of Technology Transfer and Commercialisation*, *19*(4), 393. DOI: 10.1504/ijttc.2022.127574

Burnett, B., Keaney, M., & Mcintire, K. (2023). *The Impact of Data Analytics in Basketball. A Case Study from the National Basketball Association Abstract.*

Chohan, R., & Schmidt-Devlin, E. (2024). Sports fandom in the metaverse: Marketing implications and research agenda. *Marketing Letters*, *35*(1), 1–14. DOI: 10.1007/s11002-023-09702-6

Cossich, V. R. A., Carlgren, D., Holash, R. J., & Katz, L. (2023). Technological Breakthroughs in Sport: Current Practice and Future Potential of Artificial Intelligence, Virtual Reality, Augmented Reality, and Modern Data Visualization in Performance Analysis. *Applied Sciences (Switzerland)*, *13*(23). Advance online publication. DOI: 10.3390/app132312965

Darwinto, P. A., Widodo, A. M., Agustina, N. P., Wahyuadnyana, K. D., & Rahaman, M. (2025). Artificial Intelligence (AI) for Autonomous Drones. In *AI Developments for Industrial Robotics and Intelligent Drones* (pp. 55–84). IGI Global Scientific Publishing. https://doi.org/DOI: 10.4018/979-8-3693-2707-4.ch004

Deveci, M., Pamucar, D., Gokasar, I., Köppen, M., & Gupta, B. B. (2023). Personal Mobility in Metaverse With Autonomous Vehicles Using Q-Rung Orthopair Fuzzy Sets Based OPA-RAFSI Model. *Trans. Intell. Transport. Sys.*, *24*(12), 15642–15651. DOI: 10.1109/TITS.2022.3186294

Du, J., Mamo, Y. Z., Floyd, C., Karthikeyan, N., & James, J. D. (2024). Machine Learning in Sport Social Media Research: Practical Uses and Opportunities. *International Journal of Sport Communication*, *17*(January), 97–106. DOI: 10.1123/ijsc.2023-0151

Gupta, B. B., Gaurav, A., Albeshri, A. A., & Alsalman, D. (2023). New paradigms of sustainable entrepreneurship in metaverse: A micro-level perspective. *The International Entrepreneurship and Management Journal*, *19*(3), 1449–1465.

Hayduk, T. (2020). The future of sport data analytics. *Statistical Modelling and Sports Business Analytics*, (May), 159–173. DOI: 10.4324/9780367854454-14

Hliš, T., Fister, I., & Fister, I. (2024). Digital twins in sport: Concepts, taxonomies, challenges and practical potentials. *Expert Systems with Applications*, *258*(June). Advance online publication. DOI: 10.1016/j.eswa.2024.125104

Huynh-The, T., Pham, Q. V., Pham, X. Q., Nguyen, T. T., Han, Z., & Kim, D. S. (2023). Artificial intelligence for the metaverse: A survey. *Engineering Applications of Artificial Intelligence*, *117*, 1–24. DOI: 10.1016/j.engappai.2022.105581

Jha, D., Rauniyar, A., Johansen, H. D., Johansen, D., Riegler, M. A., Halvorsen, P., & Bagci, U. (2022). Video Analytics in Elite Soccer: A Distributed Computing Perspective. *Proceedings of the IEEE Sensor Array and Multichannel Signal Processing Workshop, 2022-June*(ii), 221–225. https://doi.org/DOI: 10.1109/SAM53842.2022.9827827

Kim, J. H., Kim, J., Kang, H., & Youn, B. Y. (2025). Ethical implications of artificial intelligence in sport: A systematic scoping review. *Journal of Sport and Health Science, 14*(MI), 101047. https://doi.org/DOI: 10.1016/j.jshs.2025.101047

Liu, A., Mahapatra, R. P., & Mayuri, A. V. R. (2023). Hybrid design for sports data visualization using AI and big data analytics. *Complex & Intelligent Systems*, *9*(3), 2969–2980. DOI: 10.1007/s40747-021-00557-w

Liu, L., & Zhang, X. (2022). A Focused Review on the Flexible Wearable Sensors for Sports: From Kinematics to Physiologies. *Micromachines*, *13*(8). Advance online publication. DOI: 10.3390/mi13081356 PMID: 36014277

Lukač, L., Fister, I., & Fister, I. (2022). Digital Twin in Sport: From an Idea to Realization. *Applied Sciences (Switzerland)*, *12*(24). Advance online publication. DOI: 10.3390/app122412741

Majumdar, A., Bakirov, R., Hodges, D., Scott, S., & Rees, T. (2022). Machine Learning for Understanding and Predicting Injuries in Football. *Sports Medicine - Open*, *8*(1). Advance online publication. DOI: 10.1186/s40798-022-00465-4 PMID: 35670925

Mamen, A., Kovaçi, S., Montanaro, T., Sergi, I., & Patrono, L. (2024). A Digital Twin Architecture for Minimizing Injuries Risks with Personalized Regimens via IoT and Machine Learning. *2024 9th International Conference on Smart and Sustainable Technologies (SpliTech)*, 1–5. https://doi.org/DOI: 10.23919/SpliTech61897.2024.10612411

Marquina, M., Lozano, D., García-Sánchez, C., Sánchez-López, S., & de la Rubia, A. (2023). Development and Validation of an Observational Game Analysis Tool with Artificial Intelligence for Handball: Handball.ai. *Sensors (Basel)*, *23*(15). Advance online publication. DOI: 10.3390/s23156714 PMID: 37571498

Mateus, N., Abade, E., Coutinho, D., Gómez, M. Á., Peñas, C. L., & Sampaio, J. (2025). Empowering the Sports Scientist with Artificial Intelligence in Training, Performance, and Health Management. *Sensors (Basel)*, *25*(1), 4–6. DOI: 10.3390/s25010139 PMID: 39796930

Mizels, J., Erickson, B., & Chalmers, P. (2022). Current State of Data and Analytics Research in Baseball. *Current Reviews in Musculoskeletal Medicine*, *15*(4), 283–290. DOI: 10.1007/s12178-022-09763-6 PMID: 35486325

Musat, C. L., Mereuta, C., Nechita, A., Tutunaru, D., Voipan, A. E., Voipan, D., Mereuta, E., Gurau, T. V., Gurău, G., & Nechita, L. C. (2024). Diagnostic Applications of AI in Sports: A Comprehensive Review of Injury Risk Prediction Methods. *Diagnostics (Basel)*, *14*(22), 1–23. DOI: 10.3390/diagnostics14222516 PMID: 39594182

Pekgor, M., & Toros, T. (2024). *Wearable Sensors in Sports and Healthcare: Technological Advancements, Applications, and November.*

Pietraszewski, P., Terbalyan, A., Roczniok, R., Maszczyk, A., Ornowski, K., Manilewska, D., Kuli, S., & Zaj, A. (2025). *The Role of Artificial Intelligence in Sports Analytics: A Systematic Review and Meta-Analysis of Performance Trends.* 1–21.

Rahaman, M., Bakkireddygari, S. S., Chattopadhyay, S., Gomez, A. L., Arya, V., & Bansal, S. (2024). Infrastructure and Network Security. In *Metaverse Security Paradigms* (pp. 108–144). IGI Global Scientific Publishing., DOI: 10.4018/979-8-3693-3824-7.ch005

Rahmani, M., Majedi, N., Hemmatinejad, M., & Jamshidi, A. (2024). Application of Artificial Intelligence in the Sports Industry: A Review Article. *AI and Tech in Behavioral and Social Sciences*, *2*(2), 20–27. DOI: 10.61838/kman.aitech.2.2.4

Rathi, K., Somani, P., Koul, A. V., & Manu, K. S. (2020). Applications of Artificial Intelligence in the Game of Football: The Global Perspective. *Research World*, *11*(2), 18–29.

Roumeliotis, K. I. (n.d.). *A Review of Arti cial Intelligence in Sports: Applications.* Ethical Concerns, and Legal Frameworks.

S, S. K., HV, P., & Nandini, C. (2022). *A Survey on the application of Data Science And Analytics in the field of Organised Sports.*

Seçkin, A. Ç., Ateş, B., & Seçkin, M. (2023). Review on Wearable Technology in Sports: Concepts, Challenges and Opportunities. *Applied Sciences (Switzerland), 13*(18). Advance online publication. DOI: 10.3390/app131810399

Singla, A., Gupta, N., Aeron, P., Jain, A., Garg, R., Sharma, D., Gupta, B. B., & Arya, V. (2022). Building the Metaverse: Design Considerations, Socio-Technical Elements, and Future Research Directions of Metaverse. [JGIM]. *Journal of Global Information Management, 31*(2), 1–28. DOI: 10.4018/JGIM.321755

Tang, C., Yi, W., Zhang, Z., Occhipinti, E., Occhipinti, L. G., & Member, S. (2025). *AI-Driven Smart Sportswear for Real-Time Fitness Monitoring Using Textile Strain Sensors*. 1–12.

Upadhyay, U., Kumar, A., Sharma, G., Gupta, B. B., Alhalabi, W. A., Arya, V., & Chui, K. T. (2023). Cyberbullying in the Metaverse: A Prescriptive Perception on Global Information Systems for User Protection. [JGIM]. *Journal of Global Information Management, 31*(1), 1–25. DOI: 10.4018/JGIM.325793

Vulnerabilities, attacks, and security aspects on the Internet of Things (IoT). (2026). In *Internet of Things Security* (pp. 33–59). Elsevier. https://doi.org/DOI: 10.1016/B978-0-44-333759-8.00011-3

Widodo, A. M., Wisnujati, A., Prasetyo, E., & Rahaman, M. (2025). Active-Reconfigurable Intelligent Surfaces for Unmanned Aerial Vehicles: BMS Data Transmission. In *AI Developments for Industrial Robotics and Intelligent Drones* (pp. 187–230). IGI Global Scientific Publishing. https://doi.org/DOI: 10.4018/979-8-3693-2707-4.ch009

Wisnujati, A., Widodo, A. M., Mudjijana, M., Tambunan, K., Rahaman, M., & Chen, H.-C. (2023). Implementation of fuzzy simple additive weighting (Fuzzy-SAW) as decision support system for leave scheduling. *AIP Conference Proceedings, 2865*(1), 060004. DOI: 10.1063/5.0182808

Xu, H., Baniya, A. A., Well, S., Bouadjenek, M. R., Dazeley, R., & Aryal, S. (2025). *Action Spotting and Precise Event Detection in Sports: Datasets, Methods, and Challenges*. 1–15.

Yanai, C., Solomon, A., Katz, G., Shapira, B., & Rokach, L. (2022). Q-Ball: Modeling Basketball Games Using Deep Reinforcement Learning. *Proceedings of the 36th AAAI Conference on Artificial Intelligence, AAAI 2022, 36*, 8806–8813. https://doi.org/DOI: 10.1609/aaai.v36i8.20861

Chapter 8
Improving Engagement in Sacred Sites Through Smart Technology Solutions

Mohammad Badruddoza Talukder
http://orcid.org/0009-0008-1662-9221
International University of Business Agriculture and Technology, Bangladesh

Shuvasree Banerjee
http://orcid.org/0000-0001-5255-2489
Amity University, India

Tonmoy Malaker
http://orcid.org/0009-0002-2042-1833
Daffodil International University, Bangladesh

ABSTRACT

Sacred sites are the destinations of pilgrims and visitors alike because of their significant cultural, spiritual, and historical value. On the other hand, traditional techniques of visitor involvement frequently fail to live up to the standards that contemporary tourists have set for themselves. This chapter investigates how intelligent technological solutions, such as augmented reality (AR), mobile applications, artificial intelligence-driven guides, and Internet of Things-based systems, can improve tourists' experience while protecting the holiness and authenticity of hallowed locations. This chapter discusses the issues associated with technological intrusion, data privacy, and community acceptability. We look at case studies from various sacred places worldwide to highlight successful implementations and

DOI: 10.4018/979-8-3373-4541-3.ch008

lessons gained. The findings highlight the potential for technology to convert holy tourism into a more interactive, inclusive, and meaningful journey for a wide variety of people worldwide.

INTRODUCTION

Religious and cultural heritage involves important features and places of worship including temples, shrines, cathedrals, mosques, historic pilgrimage routes and natural religious characteristics. They are the places where people can meet in groups, conduct religious rituals, practice personal devotion, and support the centuries-old traditions (Talukder, 2020). Based on this, they are luxuries to tourism in most regions that attract millions of tourists annually in pursuit of spiritual comfort, cultural enhancement, or historical insight. The sacred sites also possess an intrinsic value in their spiritual nature, collective memory, and cultural representation in addition to their architectural or historical value. Sacred places are highly important. These locations house intangible heritage including oral histories, rituals, prayers, and practice that are passed down across generations and also contain identities of the respective communities. These ingrained ideologies are at the risk of being washed away during the modern era as more tourists visit, the expectations of the travelers change and the urbanization is taking place at the same time. Conversely, there is an unprecedented growth in the movement of tourists to holy places.

The primary variables driving the growth are global mobility, the desire to explore many cultures, and behavioural patterns towards healing (Rane, N. et al., 2023). The phenomenon is associated with opportunities and challenges that should be handled. Although there are some positive aspects of a community that can be realized through tourism in terms of revenues that can be used to preserve and develop the community, there are other forms of negative impacts it can present in terms of restrictions, stereotyping, and commercialization of spiritual activities. Hence, the crucial factor is to strike a balance between the need to conserve the legacy and the presence of the tourists in a way that is sustainable, meaningful and respectful to their presence. This issue can be resolved through the use of ingenious technology, which is the prerogative of the information era (Mishra et al.,2024). Digital tools are meant to enhance and to extend traditional experiences and not to substitute them.

Here is the purpose of digital tools. These technologies are interactive mobile applications, geofencing, sensor-based infrastructure, multilingual content delivery, augmented reality and virtual reality and artificial intelligence guided tours (Lukita, C., et al., 2023). These experiences are therefore considered more personalized, educative and dynamic. The variety of technologies is used in such experiences, through which one can comprehend them.

TECHNOLOGIES APPLIED IN SACRED SITES

Such places are being equipped with various advanced technology to ensure that the visitors to sacred places do not lose the reverence and authenticity of their visit. Among the most conspicuous ones, one can distinguish the following: With the help of such technologies, visitors can now make part in the rituals that were practiced in the ancient times, take a tour to three-dimensional versions of sacred sites, and observe elements of sacred places that are lost or have lost their relevance over the centuries (Saleem, M., et al., 2024). Some of the technologies in this category are virtual reality (VR) and augmented reality (AR).

Mobile Device Applications: These are compatible with mobile devices and they offer a wide scope of functions, including audio guides, prayer schedules, rituals description, interactive maps and future events push messages. Their data is typically posted in multiple languages to have a high targeting base.

Artificial Intelligence (AI): AI-based chatbots or virtual assistants can give immediate support to tourists, respond to queries, and tailor nearer tours according to the theme interests of users. Crowd tracking, lighting automation, and preventing misuse or damage of sensitive areas are performed by the Internet of Things (IoT) devices. Good examples of Internet of Things devices are smart sensors, beacons, and RFID systems. Two technologies that provide location-based narratives, context-sensitive alerts, as well as virtual boundaries triggers site-specific information when the consumer moves through the space, are called geolocation and geofencing. Such technologies have come to be known as geolocation and geofencing respectively.

The utilization of Quick Response (QR) Codes and Near Field Communication (NFC) Tags: These are strategically located tags and codes that allow visitors to access information on history, religious texts, or multimedia resources in a flash after scanning mobile gadgets. The technologies are helpful to the navigation and understanding and enable site managers to extract information on visitors, predict the most popular periods, and develop superior conservation policies. Such technology can help sacred places aid interpretation, control visitor flow, achieve inclusive interactions and inform viewers without compromising the sanctity of the experience. All these things can be achieved without sacrifices. Sensor-driven works may offer the user narratives that are contextually relevant, which play themselves out as the user traverses the site. Virtual recreation of earlier rites can also help tourists to deepen their spiritual action knowledge without any physical disturbance (Grundner, L., & Neuhofer, B., 2021). Ai-powered back-end technologies and leading data analytics assist site operators with the investigation of behavioral patterns, estimating population flows, and real-time changes made to secure the most important areas. The technologies can also be applied to behavioral patterns.

The purpose of this chapter is to argue about the use of intelligent technology in the context of sacred site tourism to illustrate how this form of technology can be used to provide an engaging, respectful, or educational experience. The chapter looks at the best practice, considers ethical concerns and gives recommendations that would help in implementing it so that technology does not undermine and devalue the spiritual and cultural significance of these sanctuaries. The chapter is meant to safeguard the spiritual and cultural awareness of these places. This can be done with the help of case studies that are looked at in different geographical and cultural realities.

CONCEPTUAL FRAMEWORK

The theoretical structure of this chapter is built of the convergence of three main elements, which are (i) the cultural and spiritual values of the sacred sites; (ii) the transformational nature of the innovative technology in improving the tourism experiences; and (iii) the need to make the implementation process both ethical and sustainable. The chapter is structured based on the convergence of these three important aspects. This framework is to be used to consider how technology may be incorporated in sacred spaces to ensure that the area remains holy but at a higher level of interaction to the visitors.

Sacred Sites as the Examples of Various Approaches to the Spiritual and Cultural Practice

Sacred spaces are not merely geographical space, rather, they are multidimensional spaces comprised of various layers of meaning. Sacred places are not a place only geographically. It is not exceptional to see that area being the center of the identity of the community and it offers a feeling of continuity and belonging to the community that they are part of. Also, they possess the intangible features, e.g., rituals, prayers, oral traditions, and emotional-spiritual experiences, besides the tangible ones, e.g., architecture, relics, and landscapes. Consequently, they are made of tangible and intangible components. The idea of understanding sacred places can be useful in order to make sure that the technology is not introduced as a foreign element but rather incorporated in a fashion enabling to appreciate and improve the naturally occurring attributes of sacred places. This is achievable through the knowledge on how sacred places are cultural and spiritual systems.

An Examination on the Role of Intelligent Technology as a Facilitator

It can be achieved by the use of intelligent technology, which is a tool, to help and enhance the journey of a tourist through sacred places (Correia, P. A. P., 2025). This would be achieved through improving the experience. The traditional readings do not oppose traditional interpretations; on the contrary, they complement each other, in the following ways:

- To empower individuals to access project both in-site and out-site through mobile applications and web tours.
- Not only individualized but also adaptive as in the learning process is contingent on the behavior of the user.
- Creating experiences that can appeal to a wide range of senses and bring history alive by using soundscapes, visualisation and interactive storytelling.
- Providing support to the visitors with varying linguistic backgrounds or abilities will make sure that every visitor can enter the facility.

This is the reason why technology is being depicted as a means of knowledge transfer and storytelling, but not merely as a means of pleasure or productivity. Particularly, this is due to the fact that technology is a facilitator.

Adoption of the Principles of Ethics and Negotiation of Values

Ethical considerations are supposed to be at the frontline when making a decision on whether to intervene or not to intervene in sacred locations. The importance of the fact that technologies should be implemented in the respectful way is the highest, in order to preserve the rights of the local stakeholders and the dignity of the region. The following should be included in ethics implementing:

- With the required actions, it is possible to make sure that the use of technology is not disruptive to rituals or that it does not exceed set limits.
- Inclusion of religious leaders, community elders and cultural custodians in the implementation and execution of the project.
- Protecting against the process of commercializing or misusing content considered sacred.
- The privacy and spiritual sensibilities of a person are being safeguarded.

To enable this discussion, the term cultural mediation will be used to mean the act of using technology to bridge cultural differences between tourists and people who host them. In more specific terms, this is the generation of information that will help tourists to understand the local social practices and customs, the symbolic meaning of various events and destinations.

The Integrative Model and the Critical Evaluation Model intersect in two ways

Likely, the former is viewed by the latter as a partial case of the latter; the latter may, in turn, be considered by the former as a partial case of the former humn intersection of the integrative Model. The Integrative Model and the Critical Evaluation Model overlap in two respects: The Integrative Model is probably treated by the latter as a special case of the latter; the latter may be interpreted by the former as a special case of the former. The integrated model offers a structured process when using intelligent technologies, which is efficient and respectful (Liberato, P., et al., 2023). Each of its basic elements is discussed with detailed explanations as follows:

It is possible to provide authenticity with references to the lived realities, traditions, and spiritual stories of the place (Dogan, S., and Niyet, I. Z., 2024). This is also known as cultural-spiritual anchoring. In the process, inspiration and guidance is available in numerous forms and some of these include attending community workshops, conducting ethnographic research and listening to oral histories. Technologies are being more and more placed not as dominant categories but rather as intermediaries between different points of view.

Its existence enables people living in various regions of the world to communicate with each other, allowing the representatives of the past to communicate with the representatives of the present, and the physical culture to interrelate with the digital innovation (Taoheed, B. K., et al., 2024). Superimposed rituals and historic reconstructions such as augmented reality can help to understand things and at the same time maintain the sanctity of experiences occurring in the actual world (Van Nuenen, T., & Scarles, C., 2021). In order to build trust and relevance, participatory co-design through interaction with stakeholders is essential. There exist numerous forms of participatory approaches, some of which are iterative feedback loops with visitors, collaborative sessions of design with technology developers, focus groups with community members (Suanpang, P., & Pothipassa, P., 2024).

The degree of resistance is minimized and the degree of ownership is increased by employing these techniques. Such a structure as that of a flexing and ever-changing one is highly required in order to achieve success within a broader time frame. Among the approaches that can be adopted to improve technology over time, it is possible to identify the utilization of data analytics, the management of surveys, the collection of feedbacks of the visitors and the analysis of their actions (Setiawan, B.,

2024). This facilitates managing any undesirable outcomes and constant conformity to the spiritual values.

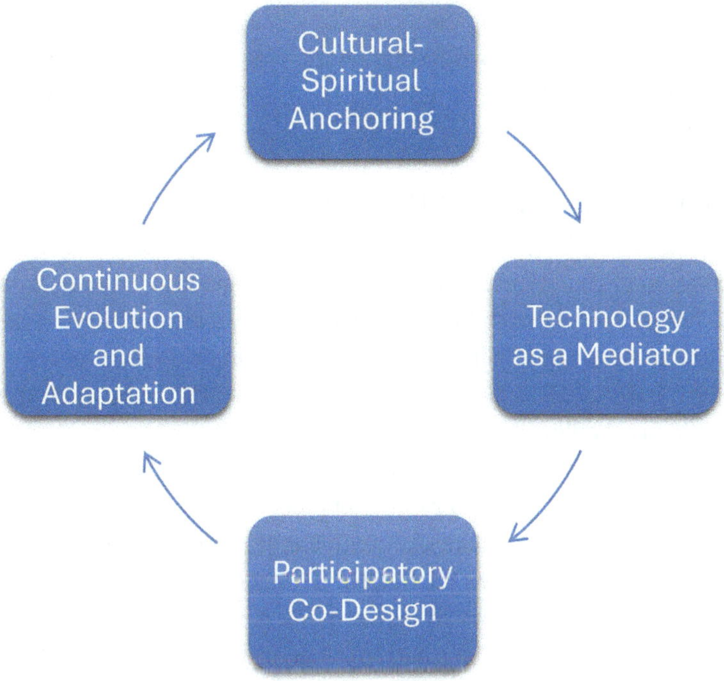

Source: Author's compilation

In Figure 1, the theoretical structure can ensure complete knowledge of the holy site engagement, where technology is used to support rather than substitute for the spiritual, cultural, and emotional aspects of the heritage experience. This interpretation becomes practical as far as the interaction of sacred sites is concerned.

SACRED SITES SMART TECHNOLOGY USAGES

The introduction of smart technology to sacred places would be a game-changer in terms of preserving, understanding, and valuing spiritual and cultural heritage. Properly used new digital technologies can boost engagement, access, and make it possible to manage these places in a sustainable way, which is far less likely to diminish the sanctity of these places (ARICAN, I., 2024). There are critical smart technology applications that are addressed in details below, their features, advantages, and issues in their application in religious contexts.

The Virtual Reality and Augmented One

VR or virtual reality creates computerized realities that can be accessed by consumers using special headsets. People lose the real world and become fully engrossed in a virtual world. Using the technology of augmented reality (AR) glasses, anyone can see some digital content (images, movies, 3D models, and text) overlaid on their real environment (Chaturvedi, R., et al., 2024). It unites the virtual world with the real world.

House of Worship Use and Growth

Conservation of Historical Artifacts: Augmented and virtual reality systems can be used to reconstruct damaged or modified buildings through digital means and allow visitors to understand what a monastery or temple used to look like several centuries ago. Individuals can either browse the ruins of an old church structure or appreciate the vivid colors of a lost painting.

Drown into the past of the History: VR technology is able to take individuals into the past to recreate the sacred place and processions, everyday life, and rituals of the religious ceremony. This creates an unmatched sense of being there and perception of the elusive past. With the help of the interactive overlays of augmented reality apps, pointing a device at a monument, inscription, or an architectural object can provide some background information (Mohamed Saed et al., 2022). This could involve cartoon explanations of complex symbols, historical stories or bilingual writing.

Virtual pilgrimages/remote access: Virtual reality tours may make people experience presence and they can visit the sacred sites virtually, attend online prayers and rituals despite the inability to move to the place. This increases engagement and access in the world.

Educational Resources: AR and VR can be implemented in visitor centers or off-campus to provide people with behind-the-scenes information prior to arrival, providing a frame of reference and increasing their interest in it.

Positive Aspects: Brings detailed information that concerns the situation and visual support which cannot be attained using traditional cues, resulting in more awareness.

More Accessible: Enables physically challenged or mobility-impaired people to access places that were once not accessible to them.

Conserving Intangible Cultural Assets: Making the old and new lifestyles more real in the digital world. This is attractive to the youthful generations since it targets the tech-savvy youth and breaks down complicated ideas such as religion and history. Through non-intrusive learning, the learners can immerse themselves in an event without necessarily disrupting the place of worship.

Considerations

Technical and Financial Competence: The production and maintenance of the best-in-class augmented and virtual reality may be expensive and time consuming. Too high reliance on electronics will threaten to disturb the quiet and reflective atmosphere of a sacred place. Re-creations in cyberspace should be wary to be historically accurate and be culturally sensitive not to lose authenticity.

Convenience to the User: Virtual reality (VR) can cause some individuals to feel nauseous, whereas augmented reality (AR) requires equipment to be held.

Smartphone Apps

Applications that have been designed to work with the mobile devices such as the ones that have features that are specific to the usage in the holy spaces can be downloaded here.

Design and Construction in Houses of Worship

Audio Guides; Guides visitors to guided tours and provide them with interviews, music and sound effects; they can be turned on in certain points with the help of the GPS technology (Fan, Xiaojun, et al., 2022). This could include spiritual narratives, historical narratives and cultural notes.

Maps & Navigation: Have detailed maps of the site showing what is available on the site such as attractions, facilities (like bathrooms and prayer areas), and available routes. They can be used to assist tourists with complex patterns especially in large temple complexes or historical areas.

Provision of Content in an array of Languages: Enhance access to the site by individuals across the globe by means of provision of content in variety of languages.

Description of Rituals and Prayer Times: Fostering respectful interaction, provide real prayer schedules, narrate religious practices and educate on the proper behavior in the sacred space.

Notifications and Alerts: With a push notification, users can be notified about upcoming ceremonies, ceremonial activities, or access change thus enhancing active participation. Facilitate the need to make contributions easily and quickly and enable users to give feedback on their experience to support the maintenance of the sites through special portals.

Advantages

The visitors will be given an opportunity to tailor their experience by watching as they please and choosing content that fits their interests.

Ensure access: Provides the information required by visitors including deaf and hard-of-hearing visitors (text) or visually impaired visitors (audio).

Up-to-the-minute Data: Provides real-time information to the visitor of the changing aspects such as the date and time of events or the sizes of crowds.

Data Collection: Anonymous aggregated visitor path and popular display data can be useful in site management and preservation activities.

Factors to be considered:

Reliable telephones or the internet are not available to all guests, which leads to the digital divide.

- Long usage may rapidly drain the batteries of the gadgets.
- Current app maintenance activities include updating, bug fixing, and content management.
- User Adoption: The visitors to the site might not be easily persuaded to use and install the app.

Artificial Intelligence as a Field

The artificial intelligence (AI) is a system that applies mathematical algorithms to simulate human intellect in many situations, such as learning data, decision-making, natural language understanding and working with tasks.

Use and Proliferation in Houses of Worship: Chatbots and AI-based virtual assistants: Provide real-time responses to the site visitors who may want to find out about the history of the site, rituals, the logistics, or spiritual requirements (Talukder, M. B., & Muhsina, K.,2024). Conversational interfaces enable them to assist visitors by tracking their interests and making individual suggestions to them.

Personalized Itineraries and Content: AI can analyze preferences of visitors (e.g. interest in history, spirituality, appreciation of architecture) and give them a tailored itinerary and content, which gives a more fitting experience. One of the ways site managers can curb the flow of visitors is by reading past visitor data and current inputs (IoT sensors) using predictive analytics provided by AI to forecast fewer visitors or to open up additional entry points to the site (Chiru, C.,2025).

Information Shaving and Recommender Systems: AI will be useful to shape a vast library of religious books, historical books, and multimedia. It might result in an appropriate content being provided to the users according to their interaction patterns (El Archi, Y., et al., 2023).

Greater Security and Surveillance: AI-driven video analytics will manage to signal suspicious activity, understand whether users have followed sacred borders, and warn employees about possible risks.

Positive Aspects

Efficient: A query can be answered fast and it will lessen the workload of human members of staff when posed recurrently.

Hyper-personalization: These generate individual experiences depending on the preferences and needs of individual users. One of the main elements of proactive management is the ability to foresee and address the problem, e.g., congestion or security threat. The processes are optimized, visitor experiences are enhanced, and significant patterns and insights are gained out of huge volumes of data.

Factors to be Considered

Data Privacy: There should be ethical and safe processing of sensitive visitor information.

Algorithmic Bias: The prejudices of the training data of the AI systems may propagate unintentionally. The cost of development of sophisticated AI solutions is accompanied by loads of money and expertise that also contribute to the cost of implementation (Battour, M., et al.,2023).

Keeping the Human Involvement: Finding a Balance between AI Assistance and the Spiritually Important role of Human beings.

World Wide Web (WWW)

A physical network of objects with the ability to sense, and spread the sensed information to other devices and computers via internet.

Homes of Worship Application and Enlargement

Big Crowd Management: Infrared, thermal, and light detector and range sensors are able to scan the density, movement, and the amount of individuals in a specific zone. Third, through this information real-time crowd control policies can be adopted to make sure that people are safe and elimination of bottlenecks.

Preservation-Oriented Environmental Control: The Internet of Things (IoT) sensors have the ability to monitor the air quality, humidity, light exposure, and temperature conditions in sacred spaces or near delicate objects at all times (Bingol, S., and Yang, Y. 2025;Ionescu, A. M., and Sarbu, F. A. 2024). The maintenance of such priceless artwork, textiles, manuscripts and architectural artifacts is based on this information. One of the buildings that embraces the application of IoT technology to manage microclimate is the Sistine Chapel (Reejo, R. J. 2020; Abdurakhmanova, G. K., et al., 2022).

Electricity Saving and Automated Lighting: Smart lighting systems are able to regulate the intensity based on such factors as natural light, visitors and time of the day. In that manner, sacred areas and paintings can be lit in the proper manner without using electricity.

Predictive Maintenance: With our sensors in our infrastructure we can keep track of the health of it and help detect early signs of wear, stress or damage. This will enable us to fix them fast before a bad thing occurs (Jang, W., et al., 2023; Setiawan, B., 2024).

Smart Signage: With the help of the Internet of Things (IoT), digital signs can dynamically change their content based on the number of visitors or weather, and indicate real-time information such as waiting time, adhering to the prayer schedule, or special events (Rahman, E. Z., et al., 2024;Talukder, M. B., et al., 2023).

Positive Aspects:

Real time monitoring makes it possible to make quick decisions with the assistance of constant and accurate data. Augmented Preservation is also involved in preserving notable heritage through environmental legislation and structural management. Resource optimization includes the reduction of the energy consumption, and the process of making most of the human resources available to manage the crowd. It is able to identify threats or security breaches in real time, thus ensuring that there is maximum safety.

Things to Consider

- The initial expenses of the sensors and network equipment can be expensive.
- It is crucial to ensure that an IoT network is not attacked.
- The storage and processing of sensor data into valuable information requires enormous storage and processing power.
- Saving power on many sensors especially those in remote areas.

Identifying and Surrounding Local Region

Description

Geolocation: The geolocation identifies the exact physical position of a user, based on GPS, Wi-Fi, or cellular connection. Through geofencing, it is possible to geofence (virtually) an area. An action or a notification is set to happen every time a device enters or leaves this zone (Talukder, M. B., 2024).

Application and Expansion: Position-Based Storytelling: In some places, audio stories, historical data or spiritual information of the particular location can be triggered as the visitor passes a sacred location or on a pilgrimage path. This generates a contextualized experience that is immersive (Talukder, M. B., et al., 2023). The software can be used to activate context-sensitive notifications to remind the user about etiquette, necessary rules, or additional details upon entering a restricted area, such as a quiet prayer spot or a site of archeological interest.

Geo-fencing of Sensitive Areas: Geo-fencing would be able to define restricted or sacred areas. In case of accidental entry of visitors to such areas, warnings are also elevated to avoid exposing them to sensitive sections of the site (Kumar, S., et al., 2024). Tailor-made Routes: In this feature, users can make their own routes depending on their preference like an Architecture tour, Spiritual Journey and Limited Lessons of history, with turn-by-turn directions and content available.

Visitor Path Analysis: Site managers can utilize the results of aggregated anonymous geolocation to understand the average visitor paths, average time on the site, and possible hotspots of congestion that can be used in future management and planning efforts (Zahidi, F., et al., 2024).

Positive Aspects

Experiences Rich in Context: Provides users with very relevant data where it is most required.

Greater Control over the Visitors: Leads them away, reduces pedestrian traffic and safeguards sensitive sites. Communicates offers and hints without having constant contact with the screen with Subtle Guidance. Efficient operation and preservation planning Provides essential data on movement patterns.

Factors to be Considered

Power Drain: Battery power on devices can easily be significantly evaporated with constant location tracking. In order to overcome privacy issues, there is need to explain everything in a clear and seek permission to gather location information.

Setting up exact geofences and mapping the content to them may be time-consuming, which contributes to the complexity of the initial set up.

Quick Response Codes and Near Field Communication Tags

Description

Quick Response Codes or QR Codes refer to two-dimensional barcodes that can be opened instantly when scanned with a smartphone camera to an online page, text or picture, among other online digital content (Talukder, M. B., et al., 2024). NFC tags, sometimes abbreviated as NFC, are small, passive, chips that activate an event or provide information upon being tapped by the correct smartphone (typically within a few centimetres).

Use and Spread into Houses of Worship

Easy Access to Multimedia: locating a code or an NFC tag in a strategic spot will allow you instant access to a movie which explains a ritual, history of an item, a large religious book, or even a 3D view of a buried treasure.

Interactive Displays: A visitor can touch an NFC tag or scan a QR code to receive instant access to an interactive graphic in order to navigate various parts of the item.

- Offer information in various languages without displaying multiple signs using the multilingual information kiosks.
- The users can be asked to give their thoughts and opinions in one scan itself on a contribution page or a survey.
- Easy accessibility to information on events happening, or easy access to registration.

Near-field communication (NFC) tags or QR codes can also be used as some of the stops of a self-guided tour, and such codes or tags could supply the relevant information about this or that place.

Advantages

Simple to install and cheap: The printing and placement are cheap and the user interface is simple.

Quick Access: Presentation of data in real time without necessarily typing the URLs or using complex lists. With the material that can be modified at will, there need be no physical alteration of a sign that is modified as the electronic content attached to the codes is changed. The level of clutter physically produced is also reduced through the need to have fewer physical markings to maintain the aesthetic and spiritual purity of the area.

A Smartphone: Although a majority of the new phones currently have a QR code reader installed on them, they will still require a smartphone that is able to access the internet.

Degree of engagement: Provides a passive relationship to content; lacks the interactive, immersive characteristics of AR/VR or AI.

Physical Wear and Tear: With time elapsing, the QR codes may be damaged or even defiled.

Although the trend is towards the near field communication (NFC) usage, not all older phones may be compatible with it.

THE BENEFITS OF TECHNOLOGY INTELLIGENCES AT HOLY PLACES IN GENERAL

Besides the special merits of each of the technologies, the advantages to use all of them in sacred places are multiple:

- Interpretation and narrative that is creative and concise assists in making the spiritual accounts, cultural significance, and history of places living.
- This increased accessibility and inclusivity makes the legacy accessible to all people, no matter where they are, language hindrance, or disability due to their accessibility.
- It is especially in the case of peak hours or major occasions when efficient visitor management enables control of the flow of people, congestion, and polite direction of visitors.
- Active preservation contributes to long-term conservation of physical and intangible heritage as it provides the opportunity to monitor the environmental conditions and the structural stability in general.

Sustainable Tourism: Technology will assist in creating more sustainable type of holy site tourism through increasing access to remote locations and managing on-site effects. This will also assist in averaging the preservation needs and the visitors.

Data-Driven Decision Making: The data-driven decision making provides an opportunity to do informed management and development activities because it offers the essential information regarding the visitor behaviour, preferences and the conditions of the site.

Figure 2.

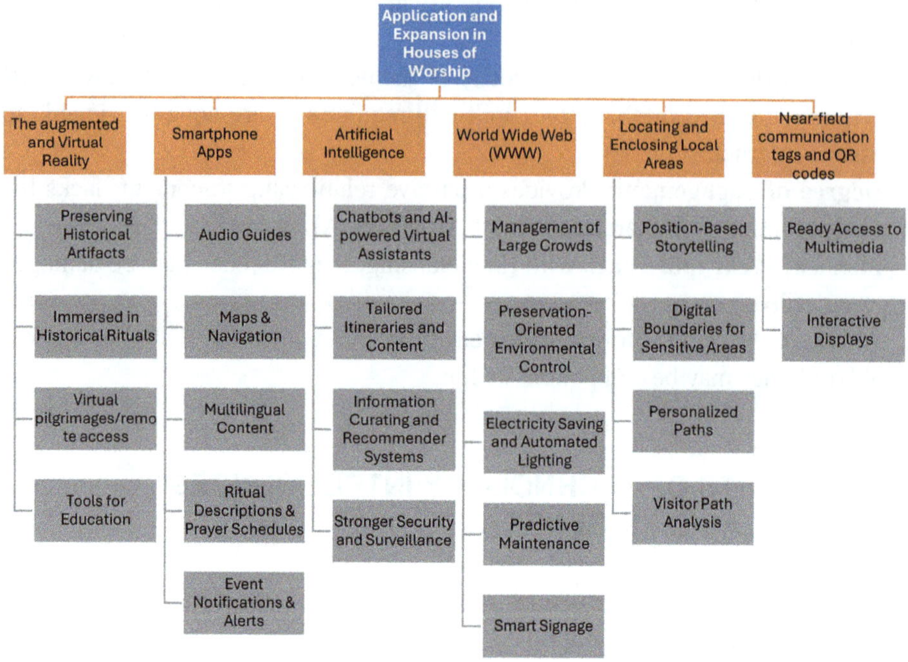

Source: Author's compilation

CHALLENGES AND DETERMINANTS OF ETHICS

The application of new technology to sacred places causes serious ethical concerns and creates challenging issues, although the potential advantages of the new technology are evident:

Maintaining the Authenticity and Spirituality of the Site: It is important to make sure that technology will contribute to the spirituality and authenticity of the site. There is an absolute need to ensure that sacred content should not be over-commercialised or trivialized (Talukder, M. B., et al., 2024).

The fact that not all tourists might have and be acquainted with the use of smart devices could be impractical in some segments of the population, e.g. older individuals or lower income consumer groups, and form a digital divide.

Data Security and Privacy: The privacy issue with gathering information about visitors, including their location, interest as well as activity, exists. The open contact with the visitors and the solid data protection practices are critical.

Ongoing Maintenance and Depreciation: New technology is introduced at an unbelievable rate. Major continuous resources and competencies are needed to upgrade, maintain, and in the end replace systems (Talukder, M. B., et al., 2024). The communities, the religious leaders, and cultural guardians should be actively engaged in the planning and implementation to ensure that there is community acceptance and co-designing. Their feedback plays a key role in making the technology of the site to be in line with the expectations and spiritual values of the community.

Unfortunately, the visitors find themselves in the danger of being overly occupied with their phones and other contemporary gadgets to enjoy the spiritual feel of the location and its subtle beauty. The critical aspect of designing technology is to ensure that it is a guideline and not a point of focus.

Financial Viability: some of these technologies are cheaper but innovative systems that would satisfy all this need demand high initial capital and additional capital investment in upkeep and upgrading.

Modern technology can offer a variety of resources which can enhance the experience of visitors to holy sites. Some of how these technologies could enable churchgoers to bridge the gap between traditional worship and modern expectations are personalized spiritual counsel, historical depth that is contextualized, and simple administrative functionality. Nevertheless, reflection, ethics, and inclusivity are the key elements that should be applied to the issue to emphasize the holiness of the place, genuineness of the experience, and incorporating the indigenous population to ensure success. Well employed innovative technology can offer more audiences in the 21 st century a deeper insight, value, and connection to these particular cultural and spiritual riches (Banerjee, S., & Tyagi, P. K. 2025).

CASE STUDIES

Tirupati Balaji Temple,located in India, in the city of Tirupati.

The Tirupati Balaji Temple in Andhra Pradesh, India, is devoted to Lord Venkateswara and receives tens of millions of people per year, which is why it is currently one of the most holy places on the Earth. This massive influx has also been managed in an innovative way by the temple trust through the use of the state of the art smart technology that does not interfere with the sanctity of the ceremonies or the quality of the experience to the visitors. Some of the projects that had to be carried out were the implementation of biometric queue management systems, advanced mobile applications to schedule, donation, hotel booking and e-darshan (online queue booking to see the deity) (Muruganantham & Patro, 2025).

Impact and Explanation

Through a special web site or mobile application, pilgrims can reserve their time to darshan (sacred seeing of the god). This is called E-Darshan or Online Darshan Queue Booking.

In a Nutshell: After registering online and choosing a convenient time and date, the visitors would be in a position to get an electronic ticket. They can visit it with it, with identification added to it.

Benefits: Previously one-day long lines have been reduced to comparably shorter ones. It also provides the pilgrims with a feeling of routine which enables them to plan their visit better. It is great that traditional lineups are not crowded as much. There is an urgent need to maintain the darshan experience in a more disciplined and polite atmosphere by managing the admission.

Preservation of the Sacred: E-darshan helps pilgrims to come closer to the God with more spiritual concentration and commitment as it reduces physical pain and secluded lines, and instead, makes them weary with long waits.

Biometric Queue management: These systems are used in the darshan complex which scan the fingerprints and other biometric data of the visitors upon entry and exit points. It is expected that the pilgrim undergoes a process of gathering the biometric information including fingerprints data in the different entry points and that data will assist in monitoring the movement of the pilgrim through those entry points without unfair entry, duplication of entry and misuse of passes.

Benefits: This option will make the system transparent, fair, and free in terms of the movement of pilgrims. It does away with touts and intermediaries that would otherwise exploit pilgrims. This real time data on pilgrim movement could be used by the authorities to dynamically adjust the resources.

Darshan and Charity-Booking Mobile Apps: There are a number of additional features in the government temple app other than the making of darshan booking. The application enables pilgrims to donate online (including hundi offerings or specific seva donations), book accommodation at the temple, keep track of rituals and other events, and stream major rituals live.

Its benefits are numerous, such as that it is immeasurably simple to join and stay in touch with fellow believers all around the world. It provides a straight forward and reliable channel through which official communications can flow and enhances openness of financial operations. The integration of these technologies has generally resulted in a revolution in the management of pilgrims at Tirupati. The fact that the location is flexible to meet the existing requirements without losing its profound spiritual heritage is a message to its sanctity and antiqueness. Through adopting digital solutions, the site will be able to reach out to millions of individuals within a spiritual context and at the same time, be efficient.

Shrine of Meiji in Japan

Meiji Jingu is a serene Shinto shrine in a spacious forest within the metropolis city Tokyo that was built in honor of Emperor Meiji and Empress Shoken. It is a very popular tourist attraction and another believed to be a spiritual place of worship (Meiji Japan and The Imperial Rule," 2022). The shrine has integrated a new technology that is not only innovative but also sensitive to allow religious experience of the place and its cultural value to the visitors, particularly those who come in form other countries without spoiling the harmonious environment:

It is possible to access history, prayer guides and audio stories by scanning QR codes using smartphones. Tiny and insignificant QR codes are placed at major points of interest on the vast shrine grounds, such as the massive torii gates, the cleansing springs (temizuya) and some architectural features.

This is the concept that the visitors can scan these QR codes with their phones. The scanning will redirect users to an official application or a mobile-friendly webpage that provides users with digital content that is place-based (Banerjee, S., & Banerjee, T., 2024).

Information Provided

Guides to Prayer: Information on Shinto rites, the etiquette of using the shrine (e.g. how to bow, use the temizuya), and the meaning of various gifts. This will be of great assistance to the non-Japanese tourists who do not understand the Shinto rituals.

Taking a form of classical music or ambient music in most cases to create a more realistic effect, auditory narratives are interesting audio descriptions that allow a level of deeper understanding. The method will enable the visitors to visit the cultural and spiritual context of the shrine at their own time and this will improve their comprehension. They make being on the site more than just a walk, since their knowledge of the historical value of the site, rituals, and architectural symbolism takes the experience to a whole new level of cultural education.

Retaining the Spiritual Aura: What is brilliant with this method is that it does not intervene with things.

Securing the Harmonic Atmosphere of the Shrine: The QR code system does not promote the demonstration of large-scale information display and audio ads, but simply offers the viewer a piece of information in the device without making noise. Nobody can hear you, or see any flashing screens. Tourists can do it on their own time, choosing when and where to see anything to have didactic breaks with peaceful reflection. Simply put, Meiji Jingu can be seen as a reminder of the power of technology to be used creatively to enhance the experience of a tourist without taking away the spiritual meaning of the site. It presents more people to Japanese

Shintoism and makes it more accessible to their knowledge and it further leads to respect and understanding.

Italy's Vatican Museums

The Vatican Museums annually receive millions of visitors to visit the Sistine Chapel and the collection of world-famous art that is located there (Linder-Gaillard, 2021). The artifacts of the Vatican have a religious and artistic meaning, and the problem of preservation and managing the crowd have promoted the state-of-the-art virtual reality (VR) experiences. They allow tourists to immerse themselves in the strata of history and the painstaking restoration works of the Sistine Chapel and provide an incomparable experience in terms of knowledge and faith. The frescoes and holiness of the Sistine Chapel require a very strict regulation of photography and access. Nevertheless, the Vatican Museums offer virtual reality experiences, typically offered in designated spaces or in formal digital resources.

A Brief Overview: Virtual reality (VR) environments are meticulously designed by using high-resolution digital scans and photographic information on the Sistine Chapel, with even details being taken during the restoration work. Using virtual reality glasses, the users can be in a complete digital identity (Yousef, A. B., et al., 2024).

Information and Communication

Virtual reality tends to be people: Just being able to view the paintings by Michelangelo in detail (like Adam creation and the last judgment) a detail that is impossible to do when you are on the floor of the chapel because you are flying over the high-resolution painting.

Note Historical Layers: VRs of different types can digitally reveal the development of the chapel by peeling off paint or moving the viewer through time.

Get a Sense of the Restoration Process: The viewers can obtain a virtual before and after of certain areas and it is one way of underlining the painstaking efforts of the restorers and the amazing vividness of the restored colors. Alongside these graphics usually comes the professional commentary.

This strategy is artfully judged by balancing the competing needs to incorporate detailed information on the instruction but retain the grandeur and sense of awe in the actual Sistine Chapel.

Learning Without Distraction: Virtual reality can allow researchers to conduct in-depth research and engage in a profound study that is not confined to the physical space of the chapel and is not subject to the influence of noise, light, or crowds.

The artistic and spiritual value of the chapel may be better comprehended by visitors as a result of a detailed pre-visit or post-visit experience (Allen, G. 2020).

This will assist them in being more reverent to the chapel and focusing on the overall impression and not attempting to see something through the torturous eyesight. This accessibility feature will no longer allow visitors with mobility problems or difficulties in staring up at the high ceilings to overlook the minute details of the artwork or its historical background. The fact the Vatican Museums uses virtual reality implies that it is very competent in preserving digital artifacts. It can enrich the educational experience of the visitor that does not and cannot rival the solemnity of the physical location, and it aids the necessary preservation activity, all of which eases the intellectual and spiritual awareness of a world-renowned sacral art by the visitor.

In India, Bodh Gaya

Siddhartha Gautama found nirvana and under the Bodhi Tree in Bodh Gaya, Bihar, India, where the Bodhi Tree is regarded as the sacred place of Buddhists all over the world (Ghosh et al., 2024). They have a hard time telling the most profound spiritual tales and historical significance in a manner that is available and open to the varied languages and cultures that pilgrims and visitors represent. In Bodh Gaya, the multimedia story telling and audio tours of the Mahabodhi Tree complex and the sacred Bodhi Tree bring the whole complex to life in a variety of languages.

Impact and Explanation: Digital storytelling is usually demonstrated in the interactive kiosks and mobile applications in the complex, as they display the life and teachings of Buddha in different digital formats. Since the time of his birth as Prince Siddhartha and as late as his renunciation, pursuit of the truth and enlightenment under the Bodhi Tree, the events that occurred in his life are the key aspects of his life. These stories are supplemented by pictures, historical context, and religious meanings. The use of digital storytelling may involve:

Animated process or short videos: To provide an example of what Buddha led. Interactive timelines allow the user to explore different phases of the process they are in.

A summary of critical thinking Buddhism concepts: Helping to comprehend the spiritual doctrines better.

Multi-language hearing aids: These aids can be hired on the site or located inside a particular application on your mobile phone.

Operation: When downloading an app or renting a device, customers select a language of their preference. Game players can be affected by location-based audio stories as they navigate the Mahabodhi Temple complex and explore places including the Vajrasana, Chankramanar, Animeshlochan Chaitya and the Bodhi Tree.

Data Given: There are detailed accounts of the happenings in each location through the audio tours.The historical and religious significance of the numerous trees, stupas and shrines.Training on the code of conduct or behavior when in the altar area.

Staffing an Open and Educational Environment

Overcoming the Language barrier: A site that appeals to the pilgrims of the whole world should contain the material in more than one language, including English, Chinese, Japanese, Korean, Thai, Hindi, etc. Due to this, all people are able to listen to the historical facts and the spiritual message.

A Large Plexus of customers: Be you an inquisitive tourist or a spiritual traveler determined to find spiritual enlightenment, the digital guides provide multiple levels of information so that you can engage at the depth of your preference. Consequently, the visitors develop a stronger attachment to the rich history of the site.

Overall, Bodh Gaya demonstrates how a sacred site can be transformed into a global educational and spiritual source through online narration and multiple language audio-guided tours. Such technological improvements allow Bodh Gaya to be used as a reminder of Buddhist heritage in that complex stories can be presented to many people and made more appreciated, pilgrimage becomes more profound, and the healing process is accelerated.

ETHICAL ISSUES AND PROBLEMS

The use of new technology in sacred places is highly problematic in terms of morality and extremely difficult. Because of the religious, cultural, and historical values that accompany these sites, it is important that development of technology should serve to develop it and not weaken it. These challenges have to be carefully planned and implemented in order to manage them.

The Sanctity vs. Technology Debate is a Debate That Has Been Described in the Way Listed Below

An inherently serene atmosphere of the sacred site, free of time, spiritual and immersed in nature, clashes with the typically contemporary, utilitarian and perhaps distracting facet of technology. Holy spaces have respect, solitude, prayer, and long standing tradition among the attributes. Without taking care of technology, these worship places will become tourism attraction sites.

Commercializing the spiritual experience is one of the major concerns, which would lead to over-commercialization. Unfortunately, religious mission of the site can be destroyed when technology is mainly employed to carry out pushy marketing, intrusive advertisements or desecrate sacred content so that they can make profits.

Building on the Digital Divide and the Accessibility

Even though the potential of innovative technology in terms of accessibility is enormous, it also leads to the development of a digital gap in which other visitors cannot be involved. Considering that all people are familiar with or can access technology may result in an unequal experience.

Smartphone and Internet Access Reliability: Not all visitors of the site will have an access to a reliable internet (data plan or Wi-Fi) or even have cellphones. This is a direct challenge to individuals that cannot afford to acquire or access the necessary devices and internet.

Tech-Savviness and Digital Literacy: Not everyone can use virtual reality headsets, read QR codes, or jump through complex apps, which means that even younger people, as well as those living in the less developed world, can be considered tech-savvy and digitally literate. This may lead to the experience of exclusion and frustration.

Physical and sensory disabilities: Audio support is availed to support visually challenged, and text alternatives are offered to support hearing challenged people who are also assisted. However, customers having dextrality problems will not be able to cope with complicated touchscreen manipulations. People who easily experience nausea or certain visual disturbance may also consider virtual reality a traumatic experience.Consider the possibility of using online resources as the main or only source of finding valuable information or experience. In such an instance, the people on the other side of the digital divide will experience the diminished, less instructively informative, or even frustrating visit. This is what exclusion brings about.

Building on Data Privacy

Whenever sacred places have a high use of AI, smartphone applications, and Internet of Things sensors, information about pilgrims or tourists will inevitably be collected, including:

Demographics: We usually request the age, country and language preferences of the users when they register or leave us feedback.Information gathered in the course of interaction: questions posed to AI chatbots, content visibly observed.Queues and entries are managed using biometric data, e.g. face scans or fingerprints (like at certain busy locations).

Methods to Minimize Risk

Openness to Personal Data Policy: Prepare simply understood privacy statements and clarify the manner of collection, use, storage, and disclosure of your data in detail.

Minimising Data: Only the required data to the specified purpose needs to be collected.

Do not seek personal information of a person unless you need it and you have permission to receive it.

Aggregation and Anonymization: Do not monitor more than necessary individual visitors, for example, where possible, process and analyze aggregated or anonymized data. This can be particularly helpful in the case of the crowd flow research. Obtain opt-in permission of the user before taking any information and especially sensitive or personal information. Ensure privacy settings or opt out are easily accessible to the users.

Ensuring Strong Cybersecurity: To prevent data breaches, the encryption should be robust, secure servers, multi-factor authentication, and security audits should be carried out on a regular basis.

- Sandbox their own information by allowing them to access, edit, and delete information, and offer the option to revoke the consent to process their information.
- Great commitment to cultural sensitivity is needed in the development of technical material because there is a broad range of spiritual and cultural dispositions of holy places.
- Cultural Sensitivity should be elaborated upon by the multidomesticity model. Human Cultural Sensitivity Elaboration- The multidomesticity model should expand on cultural sensitivity.
- Technology must be a polite way of knowing rather than a way of distorting or imposing culture.

Technology must not attempt to dictate its meanings on the site and the related populations and to attempt to normalize various spiritual experiences; rather, it ought to augment and respect their existing cultural scripts, traditions and beliefs.

Potentially Troubling Information: Unvetted digital content can represent the symbols of religious rituals, historical occurrences, or practices in a manner that is offensive or misleading.

Offending Devotees and Local Communities: The content can be sensational, insulting or disrespectful of holy elements and this can be highly offensive. An example of such an experience is a virtual reality experience, which utilizes offensive music, graphic design, or language.

Isolation of Local Communities: Technology developed and put on the ground without consulting with people who control the land and the heritage such as in the cases of religious leaders, community elders and cultural practitioners could be perceived to be invasive, insensitive or even colonial. This may cause resistance and mistrust. Technology can provide a Western-centric account or knowledge of the site and this could result in marginalization of the various spiritual traditions and interpretations of the place.

Criticism of Co-creation: Creating something with the right people is not only a practice it is a moral imperative.

Religious Leaders: These individuals are required to protect the religious wisdom and ritual heritage and such that whatever is said or done protects the religious values and does not displease anybody.

- The living legacy, oral traditions and social context of a place determine its ownership of authentic cultural and community ownership by the local communities.
- Historians and archaeologists need to bring to past tellings scholarship and accuracy.
- Cherish the intangible heritage and take care of it in a respectful manner; this is the task of cultural custodians.

Implementation Strategies

- Stakeholder Collaboration: Cooperation with religious leaders, local governments, technology developers and leaders.
- Pilot Programs: Evaluate the small-scale technological interventions before implementation.
- Training and Capacity Building: Prepare the local guides and staff with the ability to handle and interpret new tools.
- Periodic tests to measure the satisfaction of the visitor, spiritual integrity and technical performance.

CONCLUSION

The adoption of new technology in sacred places is a magical tale of new technology intertwining with the old. However, in spite of the common belief, there is a golden opportunity to introduce spiritual and cultural artifacts to the present day by using digital technologies strategically (Xie, Y. 2024). The chapter investigated the way in which these irreplaceable sites are interacted with by tourists by using a combination of technology like customized apps on smartphones, fully immersive AR/VR experiences, and advanced AI and IoT networks.

The logic behind this is quite straightforward: sacred places can be effectively monetized, and through the careful utilization of innovative technology, can be facilitated more easily, comprehensibly, and to the visitor experience. The case studies of Tirupati Balaji Temple, Meiji Jingu, and the Vatican Museums, and Bodh Gaya show that the tools are useful in dealing with mass tourism, provide a context, and allow participation at a distance and aid in the critical preservation of physical objects and spiritual activities. They provide interactive and customized experiences on top of being mere exhibition items, which can attract different audiences by facilitating the personal interpretation of history and faith. However, the trick to the success of this integration has not only been the adoption of technology but also the deliberate and moral use of the technology.

The sacred sites should also be perceived as multifaceted cultural-spiritual frameworks, and the theoretical perspective developed in this chapter. This dictates that technology should act as a respectful mediator, built in collaboration with religious figures, community and historians and should always have a basis within cultural and spiritual practice. This co-creative approach plays a significant role in determining the accuracy, cultural sensitivity and true reflection of the natural sacredness of individual sites and their unique narratives within online information (Nijjer, S., et al., 2023). It should be prudently balanced and this is what we did in the section of ethical issues and challenges. The solutions should be modest, considerate and attentive to the spiritual atmosphere in order to avoid polluting the innate sanctity of the site or introduce technology that might be obtrusive.

REFERENCES

Abdurakhmanova, G. K., Astanakulov, O. T., Goyipnazarov, S. B., & Irmatova, A. B. (2022, December). Tourism 4.0: Opportunities for applying industry 4.0 technologies in tourism. In *Proceedings of the 6th International Conference on Future Networks & Distributed Systems* (pp. 33-38).

Allen, G. (2020). Understanding AI technology. *Joint Artificial Intelligence Center (JAIC). The Pentagon United States*, *2*(1), 24–32.

Arican, İ. (2024). *Smart destinations: integration of ai in the tourism destinations (akilli destinasyonlar: yapay zekanin turizm destinasyonlarina entegre edilmesi)* (doctoral dissertation, istanbul university).

Banerjee, S., & Tyagi, P. K. (2025). Leveraging Social Media for Tea Destination Branding: Strategies and Impacts. In *Tracking Tourism Patterns and Improving Travel Experiences With Innovative Technologies* (pp. 49-82). IGI Global.

Battour, M., Mady, K., Salaheldeen, M., Elsotouhy, M., Elbendary, I., & Boğan, E. (2023). AI-enabled technologies to assist Muslim tourists in Halal-friendly tourism. *Journal of Islamic Marketing*, *14*(5), 1291–1309.

Bingöl, S., & Yang, Y. (2025). Integrating smart technologies and artificial intelligence to build smart tourism destination ecosystems: A model for smart destination management. *Tourism Management Perspectives*, *58*, 101380.

Chaturvedi, R., Verma, S., Ali, F., & Kumar, S. (2024). Reshaping tourist experience with AI-enabled technologies: A comprehensive review and future research agenda. *International Journal of Human-Computer Interaction*, *40*(18), 5517–5533.

Chiru, C. (2025). AI-DRIVEN VR AND THE IMMERSIVE EXPERIENCE. *The Role of Artificial Intelligence in the Tourism and Hospitality Sector*.

Correia, P. A. P. (2025, April). From Virtual to Reality: Enhancing Cultural Tourism Through AI, VR, and the Metaverse. In *International Conference on Tourism Research* (Vol. 8, No. 1, pp. 47-55). Academic Conferences International Limited.

El Archi, Y., Benbba, B., Kabil, M., & Dávid, L. D. (2023). Digital technologies for sustainable tourism destinations: State of the art and research agenda. *Administrative Sciences*, *13*(8), 184.

Fan, X., Jiang, X., & Deng, N. (2022). Immersive technology: A meta-analysis of augmented/virtual reality applications and their impact on tourism experience. *Tourism Management*, *91*, 104534.

Ghosh, P., Chakravarty, T., & Johari, H. (2024). Bodhgaya, India as a Buddhist Cultural Heritage Site: A Journey from Pilgrimage to Tourism. In Brunn, S. D. (Ed.), *Geography of Time, Place, Movement and Networks* (Vol. 3, pp. 119–134). Springer Nature Switzerland., DOI: 10.1007/978-3-031-58033-8_7

Grundner, L., & Neuhofer, B. (2021). The bright and dark sides of artificial intelligence: A futures perspective on tourist destination experiences. *Journal of Destination Marketing & Management, 19*, 100511.

Ionescu, A. M., & Sârbu, F. A. (2024). Exploring the impact of smart technologies on the tourism industry. *Sustainability, 16*(8), 3318.

Jang, W., Kim, S., Chun, J. W., Jung, A. R., & Kim, H. (2023). Role of recommendation sizes and travel involvement in evaluating travel destination recommendation services: Comparison between artificial intelligence and travel experts. *Journal of Hospitality and Tourism Technology, 14*(3), 401–415.

Kumar, S., Talukder, M. B., & Pego, A. (Eds.). (2024). *Utilizing smart technology and AI in hybrid tourism and hospitality*. IGI Global.

Liberato, P., Pereira, D., Liberato, D., & Lopes, M. C. (2023, November). Technology applications in the competitiveness of tourism destinations. In *International Conference on Tourism, Technology and Systems* (pp. 471-482). Singapore: Springer Nature Singapore.

Linder-Gaillard, I. (2021). Roman Catholic Art after L'Art Sacré and Vatican II. In *I. Linder-Gaillard, Oxford Research Encyclopedia of Religion*. Oxford University Press., DOI: 10.1093/acrefore/9780199340378.013.793

Lukita, C., Pangilinan, G. A., Chakim, M. H. R., & Saputra, D. B. (2023). Examining the impact of artificial intelligence and internet of things on smart tourism destinations: A comprehensive study. [ATT]. *Aptisi Transactions on Technopreneurship, 5*(2sp), 135–145.

Meiji Japan and The Imperial Rule: A Symbiotic Encounter. (2022). *Asian Journal of Research in Education and Social Sciences*. https://doi.org/DOI: 10.55057/ajress.2022.4.1.26

Mishra, D., Das, S., & Patnaik, R. (2024). Application of AI technology for the development of destination tourism towards an intelligent information system. *Economic Affairs, 69*(2), 1083–1095.

Mohamed Saed Mohamed Farahat, E., Ezzat Mohamed, M., & Samir, B. (2022). Artificial intelligence applications and its impact on the competitiveness of the Egyptian tourist destination. *11*(2), 57.

Muruganantham, G., & Patro, U. S. (2025). Role of Technology for Sustainable Growth of Religious Tourism. In Tyagi, P. K., Sharma, N., Singh, P., & Bhatt, V. (Eds.), *Technology and Religious Tourism: Emerging Trends, Cases and Futuristic Perspectives* (pp. 25–48). Emerald Publishing Limited., DOI: 10.1108/978-1-83662-260-420251003

Nijjer, S., Singh, J., Sharma, P., Malhotra, M., & Verma, R. (2023). Unraveling a new age of travel in blockchain based metaverse. In *Mobile Radio Communications and 5G Networks: Proceedings of Third MRCN 2022* (pp. 555-570). Singapore: Springer Nature Singapore.

Rahman, E. Z., Aziz, S., Shah, S. B. A., & Asrifan, A. (2024). The Effect of the Regenerative Tourism Movement on the Global Industry and the Role of Artificial Intelligence. In *The Role of Artificial Intelligence in Regenerative Tourism and Green Destinations* (pp. 165–183). Emerald Publishing Limited.

Rane, N., Choudhary, S., & Rane, J. (2023). Sustainable tourism development using leading-edge artificial intelligence (AI), blockchain, internet of things (IoT), augmented reality (AR) and virtual reality (VR) technologies. *Blockchain, Internet of Things (IoT), Augmented Reality (AR) and Virtual Reality (VR) technologies (October 31, 2023).*

Reejo, R. J. (2020). Adoption of artificial intelligence and augmented reality for smart tourism in Kerala.

Saleem, M., Shah, M. J., Wajid, M., Akhter, M., & Malik, J. A. (2024). A Comprehensive Study of AI and IoT's Impact on Smart Tourism Destinations. *Journal of Computing & Biomedical Informatics.*

Setiawan, B. (2024). The Augmented Reality (AR) Based on Artificial Intellegence (AI) in Integrated Marketing Communication (IMC) in Tourism Villages. *Media Wisata, 22*(2), 341–352.

Suanpang, P., & Pothipassa, P. (2024). Integrating Generative AI and IoT for Sustainable Smart Tourism Destinations. *Sustainability, 16*(17), 7435.

Talukder, M. B. (2020). An Appraisal of the Economic Outlook for the Tourism Industry, Specially Cox's Bazar in Bangladesh. *i-manager's Journal on Economics & Commerce,* 2(1), 23-35. https://doi.org/DOI: 10.26634/jecom.2.1.17285

Talukder, M. B. (2020). The Future of Culinary Tourism: An Emerging Dimension for the Tourism Industry of Bangladesh. I-Manager's. *Journal of Management, 15*(1), 27. DOI: 10.26634/jmgt.15.1.17181

Talukder, M. B. (2024). Implementing artificial intelligence and virtual experiences in hospitality. In *Innovative technologies for increasing service productivity* (pp. 145–160). IGI Global.

Talukder, M. B. (2024). Implementing Artificial Intelligence and Virtual Experiences in Hospitality. In Manohar, S., Mittal, A., Raju, S., & Nair, A. J. (Eds.), *Advances in Hospitality, Tourism, and the Services Industry* (pp. 145–160). IGI Global., DOI: 10.4018/979-8-3693-2019-8.ch009

Talukder, M. B., Kabir, F., Kaiser, F., & Lina, F. Y. (2024). Digital detox movement in the tourism industry: Traveler perspective. In *Business drivers in promoting digital detoxification* (pp. 91–110). IGI Global Scientific Publishing.

Talukder, M. B., Kumar, S., & Das, I. R. (2024). Implications of blockchain technology-based cryptocurrency in the cloud for the hospitality industry. In *Emerging trends in cloud computing analytics, scalability, and service models* (pp. 340–358). IGI Global Scientific Publishing.

Talukder, M. B., Kumar, S., Kaiser, F., & Mia, M. N. (2024). Pilgrimage Creative Tourism: A Gateway to Sustainable Development Goals in Bangladesh. In *Global Trends in Governance and Policy Paradigms* (pp. 285-300). IGI Global.

Talukder, M. B., Kumar, S., Sood, K., & Grima, S. (2023). Information Technology, Food Service Quality and Restaurant Revisit Intention. *International Journal of Sustainable Development and Planning, 18*(1).

Talukder, M. B., & Muhsina, K. (2024). Prospect of Smart Tourism Destination in Bangladesh. In *AI Innovations for Travel and Tourism* (pp. 163–179). IGI Global.

Taoheed, B. K., Olusegun, O. A., & Akanni, O. A. (2024). Transformative Impact of Artificial Intelligence (AI), Virtual Reality (VR) and Augmented Reality (AR) on Tourism Marketing in Lagos State, Nigeria.

Van Nuenen, T., & Scarles, C. (2021). Advancements in technology and digital media in tourism. *Tourist Studies, 21*(1), 119–132.

Xie, Y. (2024). Blockchain Technology and The Future of Tourism: A Critical Analysis of The Positive Impacts of Metaverse on The Tourism Sector. *Journal of Smart Cities, 9*(1), 30–48.

Zahidi, F., Kaluvilla, B. B., & Mulla, T. (2024). Embracing the new era: Artificial intelligence and its multifaceted impact on the hospitality industry. *Journal of Open Innovation, 10*(4), 100390.

Chapter 9

Exploring the Strategic Integration of the Metaverse in Religious Tourism:
Reimagining Tourist Experience and Engagement at the Sanctuary of Fátima

Diogo Fonseca
University of Porto, Portugal

Francisco Campos
University of Porto, Portugal

Gustavo Nogueira
http://orcid.org/0009-0004-6826-1810
University of Porto, Portugal

Gustavo Tarábbia
University of Porto, Portugal

Paulo Andrade
University of Porto, Portugal

Pedro Carvalho
http://orcid.org/0009-0009-0130-9847
University of Porto, Portugal

Belem Barbosa
http://orcid.org/0000-0002-4057-360X
University of Porto, Portugal

ABSTRACT

Digital transformation through emerging technologies is reshaping business operations, influencing products, processes, value chains, networks, and business models. Within this context, the Metaverse introduces innovative ways for businesses and consumers to interact with each other in virtual and interconnected shared spaces. While organizations across industries are increasingly adopting Metaverse technol-

DOI: 10.4018/979-8-3373-4541-3.ch009

ogies, research in this field remains in its early stages, with limited understanding of its implications and opportunities. To address this gap, this study employs a case study approach based on secondary data to conduct a strategic assessment of the Metaverse's application in religious tourism. The Sanctuary of Fátima in Portugal was selected as the focal case. The findings highlight the Metaverse's potential to facilitate new forms of value creation, delivery, and capture, particularly through stakeholder engagement and digital pilgrimage experiences beyond physical destinations

INTRODUCTION

In the past decade, our society has presented a variety of technological advancements that have transformed and innovated the landscape, notably the Metaverse. Virtual Reality (VR) and Augmented Reality (AR) are some of the key components of the ongoing wave of technological advancements, revolutionizing user experiences like never before. The Metaverse is described as a mix of Virtual Reality, Augmented Reality, and the Real World (Aburbeian et al., 2022). This technology is seen as the next disruptive technology that will impact society in the coming years, by enabling immersive experiences converging the physical and digital universe (Buhalis et al., 2023). In line with this, investments in the metaverse are shaping the technology of the future. According to research conducted by McKinsey and Company (2022), the Metaverse could create up to $5 trillion in value by 2030 – an opportunity too significant to overlook. This technology is having an impact on multiple sectors and has significant business potential, with companies in different industries starting to benefit from it (Shin & Kang, 2024).

Tourism is one of the key areas that can benefit from the Metaverse (World Economic Forum, 2022). In recent years, tourism has been increasingly recognized for its vital role in boosting the local economy by creating jobs, stimulating economic growth, and generating wealth (Budovich, 2023). Many tourism companies currently feel the need to incorporate Metaverse technologies into their products and services to meet consumers' demand (Chen, 2024). As Metaverse technology advances, it will become indispensable to the tourism industry, going beyond tourists' horizons (Go & Kang, 2023). As a result, a growing number of companies in the tourism industry are embracing the metaverse to maintain a competitive edge (Chi et al., 2024). Additionally, Metaverse tourism enables visitors to explore the world from their homes (Dwivedi et al., 2022). It eliminates time, space, and physics constraints, allowing users to explore new places without traveling and addressing issues such as mobility restrictions, high costs, and environmental concerns (Chen, 2024). Users can visit famous tourist destinations and attractions, and attend events such as museum tours, conventions, and concerts, with the Metaverse being inserted into the tourism industry.

One of the oldest forms of tourism is travel motivated by religious purposes (Choe, 2024). Religious tourism, encompassing diverse religious minorities, traditional ceremonies, sacred sites, and spiritual experiences, has significant potential to attract both cultural and economic tourists (Budovich, 2023). Thus, this potential needs to be recognized and explored. With the Metaverse being inserted into religious tourism, it could revolutionize the way people experience sacred sites, fostering deeper spiritual connections and accessibility for a global audience.

Although there is growing research on the use of the Metaverse in tourism, current studies do not comprehensively consider the impact of the Metaverse on tourists and the tourism industry, particularly in religious tourism, and they often overlook potential challenges. Therefore, research is needed to explore the possible effects of the Metaverse on religious tourism and effectively address the associated challenges.

The purpose of this study is to explore the transformative potential of the metaverse in the religious tourism field by conducting a strategic analysis to determine whether the specific location should adopt the metaverse to create, deliver, and capture value. A case study research design was followed, with a qualitative approach that relied mostly on secondary data sources. The Sanctuary of Fátima, in Portugal, was chosen as the case study, given both the potential for innovation and the opportunity to revolutionize a deeply traditional niche. Firstly, Fátima is a globally recognized pilgrimage destination with historical and cultural significance, attracting millions of visitors from all over the world annually. Secondly, with religious tourism in the metaverse remaining largely unexplored, Fatima can be positioned as an early adopter in a market with vast potential, offering a unique and immersive spiritual experience to a global audience. And lastly, introducing the metaverse into such a historically traditional setting represents a bold step toward innovation, bridging the past and the future, offering a new way for believers to connect with their spirituality while respecting the essence of religious devotion.

BACKGROUND

This study is guided by the theoretical framework of value creation, delivery, and capture. To create value for their stakeholders, companies and institutions need to capitalize on the use of the metaverse into "concrete strategic advantages". However, it isn't clear how they can do it (Ritala et al., 2024). For example, Meta and Disney reduced their investments in the Metaverse because they had returns lower than what they expected (Ritala et al., 2024; Krüger et al., 2025). This creates questions and doubts about value creation in the metaverse (Krüger et al., 2025).

According to Amit and Zott (2001), a value driver refers to the "sources of a firm's value creation, including all factors that determine and enhance the total value a firm creates". Nevertheless, this traditional definition doesn't apply to Metaverse, because it reveals a shift of focus from the traditional value drivers, representing a space for value co-creation. Krüger et al (2025) consider that Metaverse value drivers prioritize value co-creation, as it is reflected in massive user participation in innovation and broad ecosystem collaboration. Metaverse offers technologies so advanced that users can interact in a virtual world and feel that they are linked to the physical world. For that reason, value drivers need to be treated and analyzed differently for the Metaverse context (Krüger et al., 2025). According to Ritala et al. (2024), new organizational practices and processes that help to create value alongside the developing metaverse technologies would be essential to overcome this intermediate period where value drivers for metaverse are unclear. These can include "virtual economies, exclusive events and connected communities free from the physical limitations of the natural world" (Marabelli & Newell, 2023).

However, noe should not just focus on the digital twins, because the use of metaverse creates value not only for the virtual world, but also for the physical realm (Ritala et al., 2024), giving users the choice of "enjoying" the physical or virtual world at the palm of their hands. This can make learning personalized and adaptive as it allows for tailored simulations based on both realms and leads to more engaging skills and knowledge development. (Ritala et al., 2024). In this way, firms can deliver value to customers (Tomini et al., 2025). This connection can lead to the creation of "new products and innovations that can redefine the very identity of a firm" (Ritala et al., 2024). Hosting events, as well as collaborating with influential people, may facilitate the interaction with existing and potential customers and consequently the integration of the metaverse (Tomini et al., 2025). Having this kind of tailoring to the customer leads to a better understanding of consumer behaviors and patterns (Tomini et al., 2025). So, value delivery is crucial to grant the value for users and customers (Teece, 2010). Delivering value through personalized user experiences is attractive to tech-savvy customers (Tomini et al., 2025).

Whether it is due to pilgrimages, retreats, conferences, or religious festivals, religious tourism is the oldest form of planned travel, having centuries of ethnic and cultural heritage as its drivers (Ohlan & Ohlan, 2024). Additionally, given the numerous interpretations religion has had throughout the years, it is really challenging to define what exactly is religious tourism (Choe, 2024). Yet, it has been historically defined as the practice of travelling aiming to fulfill one's religious needs. The past few years have seen an increase in this segment of cultural tourism as it holds huge socio-political relevance (Ohlan & Ohlan, 2024). Yet not everything in religious tourism is as promising as this trend, as they currently face a series of challenges. Religious tourism is often overcrowded, causing congestion, noise pollution, microclimatic change, damage to fauna (such as water pollution, deforestation), and sometimes even vandalism (Shinde & Olsen, 2022). This is related to the hard task of managing the religious tourism supply chain (Mittal & Sinha, 2021), which currently stands as the hardest challenge for this type of spiritual tourism.

The Metaverse: Definition, advantages, and challenges

The metaverse can be defined as a digital space (Buhalis & Karatay, 2022) that provides an integrated and interoperable network of real-time rendered three dimensional (3D) virtual worlds, which can be experienced synchronously (Ball, 2021) and persistently (Laborde, 2022) by an unlimited number of users that interact through the use of digital avatars (Gursoy et al., 2022). A variety of experiences, assets and environments that exist beyond the world in which we live (Herrman, 2021), made possible thanks to a mixture of technologies, such as AI and/or blockchain (Smaili & de Rancourt-Raymond, 2022), aiming to provide a bridge between digital and physical universes (Buhalis, 2020).

By removing boundaries of space and time, the metaverse has the ability to lead a new industrial revolution in areas as diverse as the economy, education, or tourism (Smaili & de Rancourt-Raymond, 2022). Apart from the fences of time and space, the metaverse can also tear down all prevailing barriers associated with race, gender, physical disability, and/or country of origin, actively promoting accessibility, equality, inclusion, and diversity (Wei, 2023).

Like any newborn technology, the metaverse is also associated with some risks and challenges, mainly related to property, control, fraud, privacy threats, ethics, accountability, and security issues inherent to any transaction made inside the metaverse (Smaili & de Rancourt-Raymond, 2022). The legislation void regarding the metaverse is huge, and that stands as the most important challenge to be solved, mostly as intellectual and ownership property. Additionally, there are several other challenges for the metaverse, namely psychological health and safety, morality and ethics, and data collection and privacy (Mystakidis, 2022). Psychological health and safety are related to the cyberbullying that the users might face, as well as the consequences that might have on their lives outside of the metaverse (Mystakidis, 2022). Morality and ethics have a higher presence in organizations that could behave unethically in the metaverse, because of the nonexistent legal constraints (Smaili & de Rancourt-Raymond, 2022). Finally, data collection and privacy might face different, less restrictive criteria in the digital world (Smaili & de Rancourt-Raymond, 2022).

Metaverse Tourism

This concept can be defined as a form of tourism that eliminates the need for actual travel (Choubey et al., 2025), by providing a digital experience that uses a collection of spatial environments enhanced by multi-sensory information processing (Go & Kang, 2023), accessible through immersive technology, like VR, to create a dynamic (Choubey et al., 2025) convergence of the physical and virtual worlds (Go & Kang, 2023).

As Generation Z and Generation Alpha grew between the real and the virtual world, they are more familiar with the various metaverse experiences (Go & Kang, 2023). Therefore, the metaverse has disrupted the current global tourism environment by creating unparalleled opportunities for immersive engagements (Go & Kang, 2023). The possibility to visit exotic places, interplanetary voyages, and/or explore events inaccessible to tourists is probably the most obvious advantage of tourism in the metaverse (Choubey et al., 2025). Yet, that is hardly the only one. The use of avatars that allow users to immerse themselves in the virtual world is also beneficial for tourists as it provides them with multi-sensory reference points beyond touch and feel.

Another relative advantage over traditional tourism is related to the financial side of travelling. Traditional tourism can be extremely expensive. On the contrary, travelling on the metaverse is much cheaper (not counting the equipment, just talking about software), which can allow tourists to explore destinations way above their pay range (Choubey et al., 2025).

Organizations planning to provide tourism through the metaverse must undergo a series of challenges. Since Metaverse tourism is in the birth stage, there are still some difficulties in understanding how the stakeholders behave and what their preferences are (Fazio et al., 2023). Also, those challenges and barriers are yet to be deeply explored (Choubey et al., 2025). Some of the main challenges are the cost of equipment, in which people may find it too expensive (Buhalis et al., 2023), the way people love to meet and interact with other people physically instead of virtually, and the importance of living the real experience (authentic and full experience), and the need to "feel" the place (Ipsos, 2023). Not only consumer challenges, but also ethical challenges are posed. Harassment and bullying are present in our everyday life, and in the Metaverse, it's no exception; avatars can also be bullied (Choubey et al., 2025). Nevertheless, Metaverse experiences can be helpful to research about expectations and alterations in a tourist's experience journey (Gursoy et al., 2022). Dividing those challenges into three main branches, we can observe usage, value, and risk barriers. The first one refers to the complexity of using Metaverse interfaces, as not everyone is tech-savvy (Choubey et al., 2025). In terms of value, barriers may appear from the tourists' "perception of a lack of benefits" (Choubey et al., 2025).

And finally, there are some risks and worries about security and privacy (Choubey et al., 2025).

In conclusion, although religious tourism is facing some challenges, those can be fixed by introducing the metaverse and its advantages. For example, by offering immersive virtual experiences, the metaverse could reduce the strain on physical locations while still maintaining spiritual engagement. Besides, metaverse tourism offers a cost-effective alternative, enabling individuals to explore religious sites without the financial burden associated with traditional travel.

METHOD

The research employed a case study design that is suitable for exploring complex, contemporary phenomena in their real-life context and addressing how and why questions (Yin, 2018). Rather than aiming for generalization, this approach provides in-depth insights into the unique characteristics of a single instance through intensive and detailed analysis (Clark et al., 2021; Yin, 2018). Although case studies can use various research methods for data collection (e.g. surveys, interviews) (Yin, 2018), they typically prioritize qualitative approaches (Clark et al, 2021; Yin, 2018), which are often associated with the exploration of new phenomena or innovative strategies adopted by organizations.

Case Study Selection

This study considers the Sanctuary of Fátima as the single unit of analysis, to gain a comprehensive understanding of its context and significance, relying primarily on secondary data. Specifically, the case study examines the interplay between digital innovation and religious tourism to assess whether the Metaverse represents a viable investment opportunity and propose a pathway for its implementation.

The case was selected based on its relevance to the research objectives and the availability of sufficient data for analysis (Yin, 2018). The Sanctuary of Fátima is a complex of Catholic religious buildings located in Cova da Iria, Fátima, Portugal, which has evolved over the past century into one of the world's most significant Catholic pilgrimage centers. Its historical legacy and spiritual significance attract millions of pilgrims and tourists annually, establishing it as a prominent religious, cultural, and touristic landmark with international recognition. Furthermore, the emerging Metaverse technology presents a unique opportunity to merge tradition and modernity by creating immersive experiences that can inspire future visits or establish new means of engagement. This innovation can thereby represent a novel approach to value creation in religious tourism.

Data Collection and Analysis

This study primarily relied on secondary data sources to understand the context and strategic potential of integrating Metaverse technology at the Sanctuary of Fátima. Data was gathered from a variety of sources, including:

- The organization's website, reports, press releases, and media coverage, to capture information on strategy, structure, and operational functioning.
- News articles, expert opinion pieces, and industry reports, to gain broader insights into the application of digital innovation in religious tourism.
- Furthermore, the researchers engaged directly with Metaverse applications in non-religious contexts to obtain first-hand knowledge of their functionalities and usability.

The collected data served as the basis for applying essential strategic management tools to assess strategic positioning, formulate strategies, and evaluate outcomes. This methodological approach ensures a holistic examination of the case through rich data generation, synthesis, systematization, and in-depth analysis (Yin, 2018).

POTENTIAL METAVERSE STRATEGIES FOR THE SANCTUARY OF FATIMA

This section presents the results of the strategic assessment, beginning with an analysis of external factors in the broader environment and the competitive landscape surrounding the Sanctuary of Fatima. It then progresses to an internal analysis of the organization's capabilities and resources. Finally, the findings are synthesized into a SWOT matrix, and the TOWS and Ansoff matrices are used to explore potential strategic directions and options for developing a metaverse strategy.

External Analysis

To provide a comprehensive analysis of the external environment for this case study, three strategic management tools were used: PEST analysis, Porter's Five Forces, and Market Analysis.

PEST Analysis

A PEST analysis, sometimes referred to as PESTEL, is essential for analyzing an organization's broader external environment. This framework categorizes four environmental categories: political, economic, technological, and social, each assessed regarding opportunities and threats (Johnson et al., 2020). One key benefit of the PEST tool is that it helps managers and organizations remain alert to macroenvironmental changes and allows them to adjust, accordingly, their decision-making and overall strategy, minimizing unexpected impacts on the organization. For this analysis, the PESTL tool was chosen instead of the PESTEL tool, as there weren't enough relevant factors to create the environmental category. Table 1 provides a detailed view of the external factors related to each category.

Table 1. PESTL Analysis

CATEGORY	FACTORS	DESCRIPTION	O/T	SUPPORTING REFERENCES
Political	Geopolitical Instability	Rising global tensions and conflicts are disrupting country relations at all levels	T	*(Hernández-Morales, 2025)*
	Portugal's Political Crisis and Corruption Issues	Recent political events, including corruption/conflict of interest allegations, have led to a decline in Portugal's Corruption Perception Index, potentially impacting investor confidence	T	*(Transparência Internacional Portugal, 2025)*
	Emerging Influence of New Governance Systems	The increasing influence of new governance models, fueled by the prominence of digital media platforms, is challenging established institutions, influencing and polarizing society	O	*(European Commission, 2022)*
	Government Prioritization of Tourism Growth	The ongoing development of the Portuguese tourism strategy shows the government's commitment to fostering tourism growth	O	*Turismo de Portugal, 2024*
	Strong Economic Outlook Fueling In Portugal, Fueling Consumption	A strong economic outlook is driving consumer spending, creating a favourable market for metaverse-based tourism experiences	O	*(Banco de Portugal, 2024)*
	Lower Consumer Discretionary Spending	Economic pressures are leading to less spending on non-essential experiences, affecting demand for metaverse tourism	T	*(KPMG, 2024)*
	Reduction of inflationary pressures	While inflation is expected to normalize, current high consumer price indices may impact discretionary spending	O	*(Trading Economics, n.d.a)*

continued on following page

Table 1. Continued

CATEGORY	FACTORS	DESCRIPTION	O/T	SUPPORTING REFERENCES
Economic	Increased Exchange Rate Fluctuations	Volatility in exchange rates can impact project funding and travel affordability	T	*(Trading Economics, n.d.-b)*
	Growth In the Portuguese Tourism Sector	The expanding tourism industry in Portugal provides a solid foundation for integrating metaverse experiences into existing offerings	O	*(Turismo de Portugal, 2025)*
	Rapid Growth of Emerging Economies Surpassing Developed Markets	The accelerating economic development of emerging markets presents opportunities for expanding the metaverse's reach and audience	O	*(World Bank Group, 2025)*
	Growing Influence of East and South	The expanding economic and political influence of Eastern and Southern nations creates new markets and partnership opportunities	O	*(European Commission, 2023a)*
	Rising Religious Practices in Asia and Africa	The growth of religious engagement in Asia and Africa presents a significant target audience.	O	*(Llywelyn,, 2022)*
	Portugal's High Safety and Security Ranking	Portugal's reputation as a safe and secure destination enhances its appeal to international visitors and metaverse users	O	*(Institute for Economics and Peace, 2024)*
	Diversification Of Education And Learning	The integration of AI and GenAI enhances the capabilities and interactivity of the metaverse	O	*(European Commission, 2023b)*
Social	Increasing Migration	The growing global migration patterns offer opportunities to connect different religious communities through the metaverse	O	*(European Commission, 2023c)*
	Emergence Of New Spirituality	The rise of new forms of spirituality presents an opportunity to cater to a broader audience seeking meaningful virtual experiences	O	*(Popp-Baier, 2010)*
	Demographic Shift Towards An Aging Population	An ageing population signals the adaptation of the metaverse experience to cater to older users, potentially requiring accessible, simplified interfaces	T	*(Our World in Data, 2025)*
	Declining Religious Engagement Among Younger Demographics	Reduced religious participation among younger generations in the U.S. and Europe requires innovative strategies to attract and engage this demographic	T	*(Pomeroy, 2023)*
Technological	Advancements In VR/ AR	Continued improvements in virtual and augmented reality enhance the immersive Technologies experience of the metaverse	O	*(Edwards, 2025)*
	Hyperconnectivity	The increasing interconnectedness of digital platforms enables seamless integration and accessibility of the metaverse	O	*(European Commission, 2023d)*
	AI And GenAI Development	Open new possibilities in Metaverse development	O	*(Nyhan, 2024)*
	Metaverse As A Tourism Revolution	The metaverse offers transformative potential for the tourism industry, creating new avenues for virtual exploration and engagement	O	*(Calderón-Fajardo et al., 2025)*
	Growing Cybersecurity Concerns	The increasing prevalence of cyberattacks requires robust security measures to protect user data and ensure platform integrity	T	*(Bell, 2023)*
Legal	Data Privacy Compliance	Navigating the evolving regulatory landscape for metaverse technologies presents complexities. Compliance with regulations such as GDPR requires robust management of personal and sensitive data within the metaverse environment.	T	*(GDPR-advisor.com, 2025)*

Source: Developed by the Authors.

Notes: "O" stands for Opportunities, and "T" stands for Threats.

Porter's Five Forces

Porter's Five Forces is a framework for examining five essential forces that shape the competitive landscape of an industry and influence the long-term survival of the organization. It stands as a significant complement to the PEST tool, assisting managers in identifying industry attractiveness and in defining a strategy to tackle industry-specific issues, if needed. Specifically, managers can understand their position in the industry and whether they should protect themselves or influence the five forces in their favor (Johnson et al., 2020). The analysis is summarized in Table 2.

Table 2. Porter's Five Forces Analysis

Force	Description	Conclusion
Threat of New Entrants	• Strong brand loyalty and reputation based on spiritual credibility and institutional trust • Heritage and historical significance	**Low**
Bargaining Power of Buyers	• Devotees prioritize the spiritual experiences, as they are less price sensitive • Organized pilgrimages limit buyer power	**Low to Moderate**
Threat of Substitutes	• Competing metaverse experiences • Traditional tourism and entertainment options	**Low**
Bargaining Power of Suppliers	• Concentrated suppliers (e.g., local governments, tour operators, service providers) • Partnerships mitigate supplier power	**Low**
Competitive Rivalry	• Competition based on **quality of experience** and **authenticity** • Fragmented market (niches like Mecca, Vatican City) • Strategic partnerships with religious institutions	**Moderate**

Source: Developed by the Authors.

The religious tourism industry presents substantial entry barriers, making it challenging for new players to establish themselves. One of the barriers is the historical and cultural significance of pilgrimage sites, such as the Sanctuary of Fátima, the Vatican, or Mecca. These destinations have developed centuries-old reputations that religious followers widely accept and, consequently, enjoy strong brand loyalty, another barrier discouraging possible new entrants (Santuario de Fátima, 2023a). Without official endorsement, newcomers are likely to face legitimacy hurdles. As a result, the threat of new entrants in religious tourism is relatively low.

Regarding key suppliers, religious institutions and local government are the primary suppliers, influencing important aspects including access to the sites, infrastructure, and funding for pilgrimage sites. While service providers, such as tour operators, support the industry, their influence is limited due to the inelastic demand of religious tourism (Iliev, 2020), as devotees prioritize visiting sacred sites regardless of service providers.

Regarding key buyers, and according to Iliev (2020), religious tourism is segmented into three main groups: pilgrims (individual or organized in groups), tourists, and spiritual tourists. Their level of bargaining power fluctuates alongside the motivation for visiting religious sites. Pilgrims and spiritual tourists typically travel for spiritual and faith-based reasons, making them less price-sensitive, while tourists visiting religious sites for historical or architectural interest tend to be more sensitive to price (Collins-Kreiner, 2016). Pilgrimage sites within the same faith offer choice, but strong religious ties limit buyer power.

While religious tourism is unique in its spiritual significance, potential substitutes exist, particularly in traditional cultural tourism and digital experiences. Traditional cultural tourism is a realistic alternative, as some visitors may prefer museums, historical landmarks, or secular heritage sites. Tourists increasingly embrace virtual and digital experiences (Kieanwatana & Vongvit, 2024) with alternatives such as virtual tours, live-streamed religious events, and replicated metaverse environments. Generally, these experiences are less expensive and are highly accessible for individuals facing financial, physical, or geographical constraints. However, for devout pilgrims, on-site visits still offer experiences that digital experiences cannot yet match. Therefore, while digital alternatives may complement physical pilgrimage, they do not pose a high substitution threat.

Religious tourism competition is based on authenticity, experience, and accessibility rather than price sensitivity (Terzidou et al., 2018). Destinations supported by religious institutions or governments often collaborate in order to preserve heritage, which reduces direct competition. However, competition still occurs in three main ways:

- Between sites of the same religious tradition, such as the Sanctuary of Fátima and Lourdes, which attract pilgrims through infrastructure improvements and historical events.
- Regionally, where countries or regions leverage geographic advantages and complementary tourism to stand out.
- Through technological innovation, with the rise of digital experiences, which may appeal to younger, tech-savvy audiences.

While differentiation based on historical and spiritual significance remains a key factor, the push for enhanced visitor engagement and technological adaptation creates a new competitive landscape. Thus, rivalry among existing competitors is moderate, driven by efforts to balance tradition with evolving technology efforts.

Overall, the religious tourism industry remains attractive for current players. Meanwhile, the adoption of technological innovation can present opportunities to foster engagement, offer complementary services, and attract new audiences.

Competitors and Market Analysis

In Portugal, the Sanctuary of Fátima doesn't have serious competitors; the closest is the Sanctuary of Sameiro, in Braga, with other smaller places scattered across the country. In Spain, there are relevant pilgrimage sites, such as Santiago de Compostela, with a record number of over 400,000 pilgrims in 2024 registered through their main routes (Ramonde, 2025). On average, the Sanctuary of Fátima has registered a stable number of visitors over the past 15 years, usually between 5 and 7 million visitors, excluding special occasions such as the hundredth anniversary and visits of the Pope. In 2023, 17% of visitors were young people, a record, driven by the World Youth Day (Santuario de Fátima, 2023a). "Market segmentation is critically important to the success of tourist destinations and tourism and hospitality businesses" (Hajibaba et al., 2019). Tourists are all different; therefore, market segmentation is necessary to have a better understanding of the products and services we should offer.

Unable to access the raw data from the Sanctuary of Fátima, we explored a study from the University of Coimbra that surveyed visitors of the Sanctuary, *Exploring Memorable Sacred Tourism Experiences and Place Attachment.* Of the inquired, the majority were women (56%), with men making up the remaining 44%. Around 50% were aged between 25 and 53 years old. Further research shows that events such as the Blessing of Helmets (attracting 180,000 people, ANSR, 2024) and youth group excursions help attract a younger audience. Almost 90% of the visitors were Portuguese, with the remaining visitors coming in mainly from Latin America and Europe. Over 70% had completed at least the mandatory 12 years of schooling, but only 17,4% earned more than 2001€ per month. Finally, around 95% traveled with family, companions, or friends (Silva et al., 2023).

Expanding more into the religious tourism segment, and relating to Fátima, there are four dimensions in how tourists relate to sacred places: identity, dependence, familiarity and symbolism. Furthermore, their experiences are more memorable when hedonism, novelty, refreshment and meaningfulness, and involvement impact their visits (Silva et al., 2023).

Internal Analysis

To assess potential sources of competitive advantage, two strategic tools were employed: Value Chain Analysis and VRIO Analysis.

Value Chain Analysis

According to Porter (Johnson et al., 2020), the unique bundle of activities performed by an organization is a key determinant of performance. The value chain analysis helps examine the Sanctuary of Fátima's internal activities and identify where the value is created, providing insights into cost structures, product differentiation, and opportunities to improve efficiency. This analysis is summarized in Table 3.

Table 3. Value Chain Analysis

Support Activity	Description
Organization Infrastructure	**Activities:** Overall management, administration, financial planning, facility maintenance, and regulatory compliance. **Value Creation:** A well-organized infrastructure that ensures the sanctuary operates smoothly, maintains its heritage buildings, and efficiently allocates resources to core activities.
Human Resources Management	**Activities:** Recruitment, training, and development of clergy, pastoral staff, guides, and volunteers; fostering a culture aligned with the sanctuary's values. **Value Creation:** Skilled and motivated personnel are essential to deliver the sanctuary's mission effectively and to ensure that every visitor receives a warm, knowledgeable, and inspiring welcome.
Technology Development	**Activities:** Implementation and maintenance of digital platforms (website, social media, online store), and preservation of digital archives and documentation. **Value Creation:** Leveraging technology enhances communication, extends the sanctuary's reach to a global audience, and modernizes visitor engagement while preserving its traditional values.
Procurement	**Activities:** Sourcing of building materials for restoration, liturgical supplies, merchandise for the gift shop, and other essential goods and services. **Value Creation:** Efficient procurement practices help control costs and ensure high-quality inputs that contribute to the overall excellence and authenticity of the sanctuary's offerings. Long-term relationship with institutional authorities, government, and local authorities.
Primary Activity	**Description**
Inbound Logistics	**Activities:** Planning of pilgrimages and visits, assisting with the journey to the Message of Fátima, the Shrine, the activities and services offered. **Value Creation:** A warm reception and personal assistance help visitors fully grasp the spiritual message.
Operations	**Activities:** Organization and conduct of religious activities, including sacraments, liturgical celebrations, pastoral programs, guided tours, and spiritual retreats. **Value Creation:** Delivering a transformative experience at the heart of the sanctuary's mission, engaging pilgrims in the message and meaning of Fátima.
Outbound Logistics	**Activities:** Distribution of informational materials (brochures, media, books, multimedia content), and merchandising through gift and souvenir shops. **Value Creation:** Sharing the sanctuary's message and making spiritual symbols and publications accessible helps broaden its impact.
Marketing & Sales	**Activities:** Promotion of the sanctuary via its website, social and media platforms, public relations, organizing events, and partnerships (e.g., pilgrimage shrine networks). **Value Creation:** Non-commercial spirit.

Source: Developed by the Authors.

In their primary activities, we have the coordination of pilgrims' arrivals, supporting them with transportation and accommodations (such as the retreat houses), the management of different religious ceremonies, such as masses and spiritual services, and the offer of guided tours and spiritual retreats to further deepen the engagement. The organization also offers and sells religious materials, books and digital content to extend the Sanctuary's reach and its impact beyond just a presential visit. To help promote religious tourism, marketing is done through the website and social media, with partnerships with travel agencies also created. The message and mission of the institution are further reinforced through its services and outreach programs. Spiritual guidance (in the Centro de Escuta Lúcia de Jesus (Santuario de Fátima, 2023b), volunteer programs, and charitable initiatives (such as the offering of primary health care for all pilgrims).

The support activities help ensure the Sanctuary's operations and primary activities. Administrative and financial management are essential to ensure the institution's efficiency, as they maintain the facility's upkeep. The recruitment and training of clergy staff and volunteers help keep the established quality service, while technology helps maintain a role in accessibility. The maintenance of digital platforms such as the website, social media, and online store, and the preservation of digital archives and documentation are essential to extend the Sanctuary's reach. The efficient sourcing of liturgical supplies, merchandise for the shops, and other essential goods is also important in controlling costs and ensuring high-quality inputs to maintain the overall excellence and authenticity of the place.

VRIO Analysis

The VRIO framework is used to assess the extent to which a firm's resources meet the criteria for sustained competitive advantage (Knott, 2015). We can assess their value, rarity, inimitability, and organizational support. The analysis is summarized in Table 4.

Table 4. VRIO Analysis

Resource/Capability	V (Valuable)	R (Rare)	I (Inimitable)	O (Organized)	Outcome
Architectural Heritage	✓		–	–	Competitive Parity
Cultural Heritage	✓		–	–	Competitive Parity
Masses and Special Religious Events	✓		–	–	Competitive Parity
History of Fátima	✓	✓	✓	✓	**Sustainable Competitive Advantage**
Brand Reputation	✓	✓	✓	✓	**Sustainable Competitive Advantage**

Resource/Capability	V (Valuable)	R (Rare)	I (Inimitable)	O (Organized)	Outcome
Message of Fátima	✓	✓	✓	✓	**Sustainable Competitive Advantage**
International Anniversary Pilgrimages	✓	✓	✓	✓	**Sustainable Competitive Advantage**

Source: Developed by the Authors.

The Sanctuary can find a sustainable competitive advantage in the history and message of Fátima, its brand reputation, and in the international anniversary pilgrimages, while only finding competitive parity in its architectural and cultural heritage and in its masses and special religious events. The apparitions of Our Lady are an exclusive and documented historical event recognized by the Church (Britannica, 2024). This makes the history of Fátima not only a valuable resource but also a rare and inimitable one. The message of Fátima, and its three secrets conveyed in the apparitions, are also inimitable due to their impact on the catholic faith. Fátima is one of the most recognized Sanctuarys in the world, receiving millions of pilgrims every year. Its 100+ year legacy also builds a not so easily copied reputation. The 13th of May and the 13th of October celebrations are landmarks in the celebration of the apparitions. While other sanctuaries may also hold special events, none embraces this richness like the Sanctuary of Fátima.

The architectural heritage of Fátima, with its two basilicas and its chapels, is, while very rich, neither rare nor inimitable. Sanctuaries across the world have very rich and appealing architectures, such as the Sanctuary of Lourdes or the Vatican. The same logic applies to the cultural heritage of Fátima. While embedded in a very traditional and catholic culture, it is not unique across the globe. Masses and other religious events are also common across several other religious sites.

Discussion of Findings

The main findings were synthesized into a SWOT matrix. Then, to provide insights into their strategic implications, a TOWS analysis and an Ansoff Matrix analysis were conducted.

SWOT Analysis

In strategic planning and management, SWOT analysis is a decision-making technique that identifies an organization's or project's strengths, weaknesses, opportunities, and threats (Johnson et al., 2020).

The Sanctuary of Fatima benefits from significant international recognition, supported by its historical significance, message, and mysticism. It boasts good financial health and appeals to a strong nostalgia market, particularly among emigrants. Its rich cultural and religious heritage (for example, Fátima's museum, which has the crown that contains the bullet) strengthens its global appeal. The organization already demonstrates technological competence through live broadcasts, an online store, and museum virtual experiences. Also, they have a well-structured network that spans associations, sanctuaries, and churches worldwide. Additionally, the Sanctuary is open and free to all, regardless of their beliefs.

However, the Sanctuary suffers from high seasonality, with peak activity around May 13 and October 13. Its audience remains relatively homogeneous, primarily Portuguese and female, limiting broader engagement. Despite a high number of annual visitors, this destination didn't benefit from the tourist boom observed in Portugal in the last 10 years. Moreover, a conservative stance on integrating new technologies hinders innovation. Physical accessibility also presents a challenge, with considerable distances between key sites, discouraging elderly visitors and those with reduced mobility.

Technologies like Virtual Reality, Augmented Reality, and the Metaverse create opportunities for immersive religious experiences. The Metaverse remains largely untapped by Roman Catholic institutions, offering a chance for early leadership. The global economy is shifting towards virtual platforms, with McKinsey and Company (2022) predicting that the Metaverse economy could reach $5 trillion by 2030. Additionally, the growing number of older adults adopting technology, Portugal's booming tourism sector, government investment, and access to European development funds all create favorable conditions. The virtual economy could also stimulate local businesses connected to the Sanctuary.

In terms of threats, political instability in Portugal and globally remains an ongoing concern. More critically, the Sanctuary faces resistance from conservative believers who may view digital experiences as an illegitimate simulation of faith. Reproducing the spiritual and emotional depth of a physical pilgrimage in a virtual space remains a significant challenge. Additionally, cybersecurity risks, such as hacker attacks and privacy breaches, could deter participation. Finally, the Metaverse's current user base skews predominantly male (59%), which may further narrow the audience.

TOWS Matrix

A SWOT analysis is useful, but on its own, it doesn't generate actionable ideas for improvements.

Using a SWOT analysis can give insights into the company's position, but it doesn't give strategies or ideas for improvement. That's where a TOWS comes in. It can very quickly define key focal points for actions. It covers all bases by considering positive and negative influences (Johnson et al., 2020). It is summarized in Table 5.

Table 5. SWOT and TOWS Analysis

		Opportunities	Threats
		• Tourism **• Consumption** **• Elderly Technology Adoption**	**• Politics** **• Conservatism** **• Number of Metaverse Users**
Strengths	• Message • Heritage • Free Access	**SO Strategies** **(Strengths–Opportunities)** • Invest in VR/AR and metaverse technology • Tourism growth and European funds	**ST Strategies** **(Strengths–Threats)** • Invest in cybersecurity
Weaknesses	• Seasonality • Audience • Distances	**WO Strategies** **(Weaknesses–Opportunities)** • Offer all-year-round virtual "pilgrimages" • Attract more tech-savvy elder people	**WT Strategies** **(Weaknesses–Threats)** • Gradually integrate experiences in the metaverse • Use the metaverse as a learning tool

Source: Developed by the Authors.

Strengths-Opportunities (SO): To leverage Fatima's strengths, the Sanctuary can use its financial stability to invest in VR, AR, and Metaverse technology, creating immersive religious experiences. By capitalizing on tourism growth and European development funds, it can build accessible virtual pilgrimages, especially for elderly visitors and those with mobility challenges.

Weaknesses-Opportunities (WO): To address weaknesses, the Sanctuary can reduce seasonality by offering year-round virtual pilgrimages, religious tourism in the Metaverse, and interactive online community events. With older adults increasingly adopting technology, these initiatives could transform accessibility, allowing more people to experience Fatima regardless of physical limitations.

The Metaverse can enhance Fátima's outreach and engagement with younger audiences in the Global South, where most Catholics already live and have increasing purchasing power. This can help balance the decline in religiosity in Western countries.

Strengths-Threats (ST): To defend against threats, Fatima can rely on its global notoriety and strong message to build trust around virtual experiences. Investing in cybersecurity is crucial to ensure the privacy and safety of believers engaging in digital religious activities, creating loyalty and trust in the platform.

Weaknesses-Threats (WT): Overcoming conservative resistance by gradually integrating Metaverse experiences alongside traditional practices can show those against using Metaverse that it is not a replacement but a complement. The Sanctuary can also counter its less diverse audience by using the Metaverse as an educational tool to teach both older and younger generations about faith interactively and engagingly.

Ansoff Matrix Analysis

The Ansoff matrix is a strategic planning tool that provides a framework to help executives and senior managers decide strategies for future business growth by assessing whether an organization should focus on existing or new products and existing or new markets. The four quadrants are Market Penetration, Product Development, Market Development, and Diversification (Johnson et al., 2020).

After determining the current position of the Sanctuary of Fátima and considering the Metaverse as an investment opportunity, we believe that the Metaverse presents a greater potential to create and capture value through experiences outside the physical Sanctuary of Fátima. Since the Metaverse allows the travel journey and experience to be dematerialized and brought into the virtual space, it opens new possibilities. This is particularly appealing for a strategy targeting tech-savvy, Metaverse-oriented consumers, especially younger audiences across the globe. It breaks down geographic, economic, and cultural barriers, expanding Fatima's outreach and enhancing investment viability. Additionally, the Metaverse allows past visitors to relive their physical experiences, fostering ongoing engagement and connection.

Therefore, a market development strategy made possible by an innovative way of offering current products and services is the best option for the organization's growth and initiative sustainability.

SOLUTIONS AND RECOMMENDATIONS

In this section, a plan is presented to implement the Metaverse at the Sanctuary of Fatima.

Strategic Plan

The motto for this proposal is that a metaverse bond can never be broken, especially when that bond was made in God's name. With our proposal, we will create a platform that allows Christian faithful to meet with other Christian faithful through the mystic of Fátima. To make it come to life, we have structured a five year plan. While crafting it, we took careful attention to the reservations that the more conservative voices of the church might have, and so, we specifically designed it in a way that avoids big investments that might lead the Sanctuary to ruin. Thus, financial stability and gradual steady improvement were our focus while formulating the following plan.

2026 – The Holy Sanctuary of Fátima on the Metaverse: Until the beginning of 2026, we plan to develop the Minimum Value Project (MVP) of the project. This basic Metaverse preliminary form is planned to be launched on the 1st of January of 2026 and will include the outside outline of all the Sanctuary's main buildings as well as the inside outline of the *Basilica da Nossa Senhora do Rosário*. This will allow all digital pilgrims to feel Fátima from the comfort of their homes and will be the stepping stone upon which all the other advancements will be built. To put the project on track for profitability, we suggest you establish the main source of revenue right from the start. This will also ease the investment needed for the remaining parts of the plan, as pilgrims will be free to make donations inside the Basilica da *Nossa Senhora do Rosário*, such as lighting a digital candle. Cybersecurity will also be essential in this project, and so we believe there should be a focus on establishing a secure environment right from the start by creating cybersecurity measures. These cybersecurity measures should remain a focus both during the full duration of the plan and beyond its expiration.

2027 – Fátima in the Metaverse: This year will mark the 110th anniversary of the apparitions and to celebrate this very important date, we suggest scaling up Fátima's Metaverse and do the full launch of the program, including all the buildings outside and inside outline, as well as the Via Sacra path. On the 12th of May and 12th of October, a live transmission of the *Procissão das Velas* mass on the Metaverse will also be arranged. This way, the full essence of Fátima will finally be on the Metaverse and available to everyone around the world, disregarding location, race, age, or physical issues. From a financial point of view, we plan to expand the revenue streams, including 10 Fátima's traditional souvenir stores on the metaverse. This will help finance the plan as those stores will pay rent directly into Sanctuary. These stores will sell unofficial NFTs to all the digital pilgrims who visit the Sanctuary. These pilgrims will also have the chance to buy official New Fátima Tokens (The Official Fátima NFTs) through the official stores strategically placed inside the Sanctuary.

2028 – Deepening the experience: To deepen the experience of the Fátima visitors, in 2028, we plan to start the live transmission of all Fátima masses on the metaverse. As we expect to receive digital pilgrims from all over the world, and inclusion and accessibility have always been two of the main values of Fátima, we plan to use Spanish, English, and Portuguese AI-generated subtitles on all the official mass transmissions on the Metaverse.

2029 – The road to Fátima: Fátima has always been more than just the Sanctuary. For decades, people have used Portuguese roads for their pilgrimages. In 2029, we plan to make that accessible for all pilgrims around the world, despite the countries they are from or their health status. To make that come true, we plan to design and launch in the Metaverse the three main pilgrimage routes that lead to the Sanctuary of Fátima: Caminho do Norte, Caminho do Tejo and Caminho do Mar.

2030 – Long-term financial sustainability: By following this plan, we believe we will reach long-term financial sustainability by 2030.

Business Plan

A proposal for the business model is presented in Figure 1. Regarding the business plan, we intend to implement a Freemium model, which consists of a business model that allows the user to participate in the product without paying any fee, but incentivizes them to buy some of the available tokens inside the product. Therefore, our revenue structure will be divided into three dimensions: donations, sales of New Fátima Tokens, and rent from Metaverse stores.

- **Donations**: This will be our main source of revenue right from the start of the project. Each year, thousands of pilgrims visit Fátima and donate physically to the Sanctuary, most of them by lighting a candle in its beautiful churches. The same business model can be applied to the Metaverse, as digital pilgrims could have the chance to light a digital candle inside the *Basilica da Nossa Senhora do Rosário.*
- **Sale of New Fátima Tokens**: NFTs are the souvenirs of the Metaverse. By creating our own souvenir store in the Fátima Metaverse, we are not only assuring an additional source of revenue but also improving the experience of the digital pilgrims, as they will have something to remember from their trip to Fátima. Additionally, all the digital pilgrims will transform into an active source of marketing for the Fátima Metaverse, which will help attract more faithful, not only to the digital version of Fátima, but also to its real version.
- **Rent from Metaverse stores**: just like in the real world, sometimes pilgrims prefer to buy their souvenirs at non-official stores due to price or preference for the products. To cover this wish, we plan to include non-official stores in the Fátima Metaverse. Ideally, those stores will be some of the many that exist in Fátima and, to guarantee their spot, they will pay rent to the Sanctuary, thus varying the revenues of the project.

This stable and varied source of revenue will be essential to partially fund the investment that the project requires, as well as to maintain its profitability after 2030. As gathered from the strategic plan, the cost structure will be based on the technological companies that will not only develop and design but also be responsible for maintaining Fátima on the Metaverse. Apart from this keystone, a firm in charge of cybersecurity will also be needed, so that Fátima remains as pure as it has ever been.

Besides being the centerpiece of the project's cost structure, these companies will also be two of our most important partners. Apart from them, the Fátima Metaverse project we also plan to establish partnership with some Catholic Nursing Homes, namely those run by Santa Casa da Misericórdia. This partnership will be a testimony to the project's social benefits, as we plan to offer 10 VR glasses to each of the Nursing Homes with which the partnership is established. This way, the elder Catholic will have the chance to go to Fátima while being strictly monitored and accompanied by the Nursing Homes caretakers.

Figure 1. Business Model Canvas - Proposal

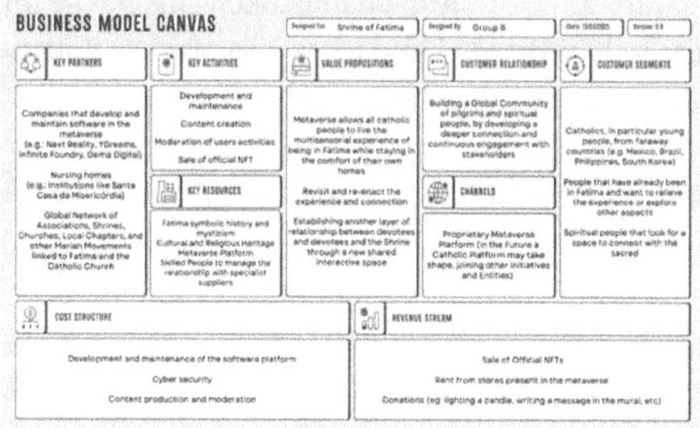

Source: Developed by the Authors.

SAFe Analysis for Evaluating Strategic Options

Johnson et al. (2020) propose a framework with three criteria for evaluating strategic options: Suitability, Acceptability, and Feasibility. Suitability analyses whether the strategy addresses the challenges facing the organization, aligns with its strategic position, and represents the best course of action given its mission and goals. Acceptability focuses on the strategy's expected outcomes in terms of risk, return, and stakeholder reactions. Feasibility examines whether the organization has, or can acquire, the necessary resources and capabilities to effectively implement the strategy. Consequently, strategy evaluation synthesizes these assessments to ensure that only strategies meeting all three previous criteria are pursued, accounting for any conflicting conclusions and ensuring overall consistency. For instance, the best strategy according to the suitability analysis might not be possible to implement. In this case study, an essentially qualitative assessment is conducted based on the analyses that underpinned the formulation of the proposal.

Suitability

Since the scope of the case study is related to research on the potential of the Metaverse applied to the Sanctuary of Fátima, only strategic options concerning its implementation were analyzed. As shown in Table 6, the Market Development option is the only strategic direction capable of effectively responding to the key environmental factors identified, particularly those influencing the Sanctuary's market positioning. This conclusion is reinforced when analyzing the alignment between this option and the organization's Mission and Objectives. By providing physical experiences to those who, for various reasons, cannot visit in person, the metaverse creates value for participants and helps fulfill the Sanctuary's mission while enhancing its outreach. This demonstrates the strong suitability of the proposed strategy.

Table 6. Suitability Analysis

Key Strategic Factor	**Product Development**	**Market Development**
Travel Resilience	☒	☑
Accelerating technological change and hyperconnectivity	☒	☑
Expanding influence of East and South	☒	☑
Increasing influence of new governing systems	?	☑
Ageing population in developed countries	☒	☑
Increasing urbanization and decreasing religiosity	☒	☑
Spiritual Tourism	?	?
Seasonality	?	☑
Portuguese and mature woman	?	☑
Fátima's identity and reputation	☑	☑
Fátima's cultural and religious heritage	☑	☑
Multisensorial Experience	☒	☑
Affordability	☒	☑
Global accessibility	☒	☑
Engagement and interactivity	☒	☑
TOTAL	**-6**	**13**
Mission and Objectives	**Product Development**	**Market Development**
Cultural and Heritage Tourism	3	5
Religious Events	3	4
Pilgrimages and Rituals	2	4
Diffusion of the Message of Fatima	3	4

Key Strategic Factor	Product Development	Market Development
Community Building / Evangelization	1	4
Total	**2.4**	**4.2**

Source: Developed by the Authors.

The primary risk associated with the project lies in the high initial investment and future maintenance costs. This risk could either be mitigated or exacerbated depending on the pace of technological development and the Metaverse's adoption within the economy and society. For this case study, we assume a scenario where the technology continues to accelerate toward creating a new space for social interaction. To manage these risks, we propose a phased development of the Fátima Metaverse features, allowing the organization to gradually build its capabilities while increasing public awareness, familiarity, and access to the technology. Despite this cautious approach, the Minimum Viable Product (MVP) remains ambitious. It should not only include historical and cultural visits, which are essential, but also be sufficient for them. The main value and success factor lies in offering immersive experiences of the Sanctuary's message and spirituality. For this reason, it is crucial that live broadcasts of key religious events and rituals be made available within the Metaverse. The third aspect, involving the establishment of a virtual community, requires special attention and will therefore be the last to be implemented. This is to ensure that the social space created is safe and respectful, requiring robust monitoring, user activity control, and advanced data protection systems.

Moreover, a positive impact is expected on donations, commercial revenue, and the number of physical visitors. This return is anticipated because the Metaverse will allow the Sanctuary of Fátima to expand its activities to new, potentially more lucrative markets, increasing visibility and engagement while offering new revenue streams. As evidenced in the literature, the Metaverse also fosters a desire among users to visit physical locations. Furthermore, Metaverse aims to extend the post-visit experience and enhance visitor loyalty, encouraging repeated engagement whether in the virtual space or through future physical visits.

Acceptatibility

Regarding stakeholder reactions, a mixed response is expected. On one hand, younger devotees and pilgrims may express enthusiasm and recognize the value this new medium provides for access and interaction. On the other hand, more conservative pilgrims and devotees may view the project negatively, as they might perceive it as diminishing the authenticity and meaning of the experience. Older segments may also approach it with skepticism if they do not understand its use or face limited access to the platform. For religious authorities, a neutral reaction is anticipated if Catholic doctrine is respected. Other religious entities connected to Fátima may view the initiative positively, as it allows for a stronger and closer connection. Among the public, the project could generate a positive impact due to its innovative and pioneering nature, positioning Fátima and the Catholic Church within the context of the 21st century. Overall, the entry of Fatima in the Metaverse would drive interest across all shareholders while increasing their power of influence over its activities. Additionally, suppliers of metaverse services will become key strategic stakeholders.

Given these dynamics, it is advisable to involve strategic stakeholders in both the decision-making and implementation processes. This prioritization will enable a more effective response to the needs and concerns of the interested parties while improving communication to foster understanding and the project's overall success.

Feasibility

The implementation of this initiative requires highly specific resources and capabilities that the organization currently does not possess. This is a substantial constraint, but one that is common to most organizations operating within the Metaverse, given that it is an emerging technology controlled by specialized experts. It is crucial to select a Metaverse company with proven capabilities to ensure quality, security, and trust. Additionally, assembling a capable and multidisciplinary content development team is essential to maintain the platform's dynamism. In this regard, the organization should aim to upskill existing staff and/or hire new personnel to ensure greater internal control and sustain the platform's ongoing development.

Considering the characteristics of the project, the feasibility of implementation increases if it is carried out within a framework of formal and informal partnerships and strategic alliances. Given the nature of this niche touristic market, cooperation between Catholic religious destinations could be relatively easy to achieve. For instance, Fátima could play a pioneering role in representing Catholic religious tourism in the Metaverse, especially in terms of religious experiences and pilgrimages. This initiative could align with the Catholic Church's broader commitment, as the Vatican is already developing a project focused on cultural and heritage preservation. The coordination of efforts can promote the development of a broader Metaverse platform where Catholic tourist destinations would be gradually integrated, forming a "Catholic World". Furthermore, within each religious attraction, local tourism information and attractions could also be integrated, encouraging domestic partnerships, enhancing local community impact and engagement.

As an investment opportunity for the Sanctuary of Fátima, the Metaverse does not fully satisfy all three evaluation criteria, particularly in terms of feasibility, resulting in a conditional recommendation, as highlighted in Table 7.

Table 7. SAFe Analysis Conclusion

SAFe Evaluation Criteria	Objectives for the Implementation of the metaverse				Assessment
	Historical and Cultural Heritage	Pilgrimages and Rituals	Message of Fatima	Global Evangelization	
Evaluation Conclusions					
Suitability	Closely aligns with the Sanctuary's mission and objectives, and addresses key environmental factors.				High
Acceptability	Reactions of stakeholders are expected to be mixed; they require proper communication and engagement in development and implementation. Risk-return balance could be negative if not shared.				Low / Medium
Feasibility	Lack of in-house capabilities and resources. Feasible if the organization can form alliances with key stakeholders.				Low
Evaluation	The strategy is viable if all assumptions are met. The Shrine of Fatima could be a fast second mover rather than an early adopter, which may improve acceptability by lowering risk.				Conditional

Source: Developed by the Authors.

To improve this assessment, it is crucial to establish the proposed network of relationships to ensure the critical mass required for the initiative's success. If these partnerships are secured, they will positively impact Acceptability by sharing financial costs and risks, enabling continuous investment in cutting-edge technology to maintain the quality of the experience, essential for the reputation of all involved and user satisfaction. Furthermore, a multilateral initiative could also help gain acceptance from more hesitant stakeholders, reinforcing effective communication and credibility.

FUTURE RESEARCH DIRECTIONS

This study presented several limitations that open avenues for future research. First, alternative investment options beyond the Metaverse were not considered, meaning that potential trade-offs with other strategic investments were not analyzed. This omission could influence the ranking in the suitability criterion of the SAFE analysis if different options were included. Second, the study relied exclusively on secondary data sources, which were mostly collected for other purposes. Therefore, future research should incorporate primary data collection through surveys, focus groups, and stakeholder interviews. Involving the target organization in the research process would contribute to a more rigorous internal assessment, while interviewing pilgrims could assess how they perceive the metaverse in this context.

Therefore, continued research is needed to explore case studies on the application of the Metaverse in religious tourism to identify critical success factors for its implementation. Additionally, it is important to investigate how cooperation between religious organizations and civil society entities could facilitate the development of religious tourism in the Metaverse. For example, collaborations between gyms and the Sanctuary of Fátima could facilitate virtual pilgrimage experiences.

CONCLUSION

This case study shows the potential that the metaverse can bring to the religious tourism segment, more particularly to the Sanctuary of Fátima, a unique and irreplaceable pilgrimage destination. The best-suited strategy to implement the Metaverse in this case is to provide experiences beyond the physical space, not only before and after the visit, but also for continuous engagement. This option for market development should focus on trying to attract a younger audience, while offering the possibility for travel-restricted people to still visit, to ensure a wide spectrum of potential clients and increase the Sanctuary's global outreach.

The external analysis shows there is a favorable external environment for organizations that want to invest in this technology. However, the lack of in-house capabilities and the high investment it would require could prove a major challenge to the ability to quickly establish a satisfying product and take advantage of being an early adopter. The strict rules of the Catholic Church on the Metaverse may also prove to be a challenge to fully take advantage of the Metaverse. For instance, the Church requires physical presence for the sacraments to be valid (Thomas et al., 2024).

Given the importance of tourism to the Portuguese economy (which represented 17,5% of total exports in 2022 (LCG, 2024), it is essential to conduct further research on how to leverage its main destinations and tourist attractions into this new era of the digital world.

REFERENCES

Aburbeian, A. M., Owda, A. Y., & Owda, M. (2022). A Technology Acceptance Model Survey of the Metaverse Prospects. *AI*, *3*(2), 285–302. DOI: 10.3390/ai3020018

Amit, R., & Zott, C. (2001). Value creation in e-business. *Strategic Management Journal*, *22*(6-7), 493–520.

ANSR. (2024). 180 mil motards juntaram-se para a Bênção dos Capacetes. Ansr.pt. http://www.ansr.pt/Noticias/Pages/180-mil-motards-juntaram-se-para-a - B%C3%AAn%C3%A7%C3%A3o-dos-Capacetes.aspx

Ball, M. (2021). Framework for the Metaverse. MatthewBall.co. https://www .matthewball.co/all/forwardtothemetaverseprimer

Banco de Portugal. (2024, December 13). Boletim Económico — Dezembro 2024 | Banco de Portugal. Bportugal.pt. https://www.bportugal.pt/publicacao/boletim -economico-dezembro-2024

Bell, M. (2023, March 20). The Top Five Cybersecurity Concerns. Forbes. https:// www.forbes.com/councils/forbestechcouncil/2023/03/20/the-top-five-cybersecurity -concerns/

Britannica. (2024, October 30). Our Lady of Fatima | Christianity | Britannica. Www .britannica.com. https://www.britannica.com/event/Our-Lady-of-Fatima

Budovich, L. S. (2023). The impact of religious tourism on the economy and tourism industry. *Hervormde Teologiese Studies*, *79*(1), 1–7. DOI: 10.4102/hts.v79i1.8607

Buhalis, D. (2020). Technology in tourism-from information communication technologies to eTourism and smart tourism towards ambient intelligence tourism: A perspective article. *Tourism Review*, *75*(1). Advance online publication. DOI: 10.1108/tr-06-2019-0258

Buhalis, D., & Karatay, N. (2022). Mixed Reality (MR) for Generation Z in Cultural Heritage Tourism Towards Metaverse. *Information and Communication Technologies in Tourism*, *2022*, 16–27. DOI: 10.1007/978-3-030-94751-4_2

Buhalis, D., Leung, D., & Lin, M. (2023). Metaverse as a disruptive technology revolutionising tourism management and marketing. *Tourism Management*, *97*, 104724. DOI: 10.1016/j.tourman.2023.104724

Calderón-Fajardo, V., Puig-Cabrera, M., & Rodríguez-Rodríguez, I. (2025). Beyond the real world: Metaverse adoption patterns in tourism among Gen Z and Millennials. *Current Issues in Tourism*, *28*(8), 1261–1281. DOI: 10.1080/13683500.2024.2330675

Chen, Z. (2024). Beyond boundaries: Exploring the Metaverse in tourism. *International Journal of Contemporary Hospitality Management*. Advance online publication. DOI: 10.1108/ijchm-06-2023-0900

Chi, M., Chen, Y., Xu, Y., & Wu, Y. (2024). Modelling barriers to metaverse adoption in the hospitality and tourism industry. *Information Technology & Tourism*, •••, 1–33. DOI: 10.1016/10.1007/s40558-024-00298-9

Choe, J. (2024). Religious tourism. *Tourism Geographies*, •••, 1–10. DOI: 10.1080/14616688.2024.2423168

Choubey, V., Chakraborty, D., Sharma, A., Khorana, S., & Buhalis, D. (2025). Metaverse in tourism: Tourist involvement as a moderator. *Asia Pacific Journal of Tourism Research*, *30*(1), 1–26. DOI: 10.1080/10941665.2024.2414881

Clark, T., Foster, L., Bryman, A., & Sloan, L. (2021). *Bryman's Social Research Methods* (6th ed.). Oxford University Press.

Collins-Kreiner, N. (2016). The lifecycle of concepts: The case of "Pilgrimage Tourism.". *Tourism Geographies*, *18*(3), 322–334. DOI: 10.1080/14616688.2016.1155077

Dwivedi, Y. K., Hughes, L., Baabdullah, A. M., Ribeiro-Navarrete, S., Giannakis, M., Al-Debei, M. M., & Wamba, S. F. (2022). Metaverse beyond the hype: Multidisciplinary perspectives on emerging challenges, opportunities, and agenda for research, practice and policy. *International Journal of Information Management*, *66*, 102542. DOI: 10.1016/j.ijinfomgt.2022.102542

Edwards, L. (2025, March 24). This Meta Quest 3 update teases some seriously exciting VR upgrades. Digital Trends. https://www.digitaltrends.com/news/this-meta-quest-3-update-teases-some-seriously-exciting-vr-upgrades/

European Commission. (2022, December 9). Increasing influence of new governing systems | Knowledge for policy. Knowledge4policy. https://knowledge4policy.ec.europa.eu/increasing-influence-new-governing-systems_en

European Commission. (2023a, February 8). Expanding influence of East and South | Knowledge for policy. Knowledge4policy. https://knowledge4policy.ec.europa.eu/expanding-influence-east-south_en

European Commission. (2023b, February 13). Accelerating technological change and hyperconnectivity | Knowledge for policy. Knowledge4policy. https://knowledge4policy.ec.europa.eu/accelerating-technological-change-hyperconnectivity_en

European Commission. (2023c, February 15). Diversification of education and learning | Knowledge for policy. Knowledge4policy. https://knowledge4policy.ec.europa.eu/diversification-education-learning_en

European Commission. (2023d, June 26). Increasing significance of migration | Knowledge for policy. Knowledge4policy. https://knowledge4policy.ec.europa.eu/increasing-significance-migration_en

Fazio, G., Fricano, S., Iannolino, S., & Pirrone, C. (2023). Metaverse and tourism development: Issues and opportunities in stakeholders' perception. *Information Technology & Tourism*, *25*(4), 507–528. DOI: 10.1007/s40558-023-00268-7

GDPR-advisor.com. (2025, February 24). GDPR Compliance in the Metaverse: Managing Virtual Identity and Privacy - GDPR Advisor. GDPR Advisor. https://www.gdpr-advisor.com/gdpr-compliance-in-the-metaverse-managing-virtual-identity-and-privacy/

Go, H., & Kang, M. (2023). Metaverse tourism for sustainable tourism development: Tourism agenda 2030. *Tourism Review*, *78*(2), 381–394. DOI: 10.1108/tr-02-2022-0102

Gursoy, D., Malodia, S., & Dhir, A. (2022). The metaverse in the hospitality and tourism industry: An overview of current trends and future research directions. *Journal of Hospitality Marketing & Management*, *31*(5), 527–534. DOI: 10.1080/19368623.2022.2072504

Hajibaba, H., Grün, B., & Dolnicar, S. (2019). Improving the stability of market segmentation analysis. *International Journal of Contemporary Hospitality Management*, *32*(4), 1393–1411. DOI: 10.1108/ijchm-02-2019-0137

Hernández-Morales, A. (2025, March 12). 3 elections in 3 years: Portugal's political crisis explained. POLITICO. https://www.politico.eu/article/portugal-elections-political-crisis-luis-montenegro-spinumviva/

Herrman, J. (2021, July 10). Are We in the Metaverse Yet? The New York Times. https://www.nytimes.com/2021/07/10/style/metaverse-virtual-worlds.html

Iliev, D. (2020). The evolution of religious tourism: Concept, segmentation and development of new identities. *Journal of Hospitality and Tourism Management*, *45*, 131–140. DOI: 10.1016/j.jhtm.2020.07.012

Institute for Economics and Peace. (2024). Global Peace Index 2024: Measuring Peace in a Complex World (p. page 8 and 15). Institute for Economics and Peace. https://www.economicsandpeace.org/wp-content/uploads/2024/06/GPI-2024-web.pdf

Ipsos. (2023). The Metaverse And The Future Of Travel. https://www.ipsos.com/sites/default/files/ct/news/documents/2023-10/The%20Metaverse%20and%20the%20future%20of%20travel%20-%205%20things%20to%20consider%20about%20travel%20in%20the%20Metaverse.pdf

Johnson, G., Whittington, R., Scholes, K., Angwin, D., & Regner, P. (2020). *Exploring Corporate Strategy: Text and Cases* (12th ed.). Pearson Education.

Kieanwatana, K., & Vongvit, R. (2024). Virtual reality in tourism: The impact of virtual experiences and destination image on the travel intention. *Results in Engineering*, *24*, 103650. DOI: 10.1016/j.rineng.2024.103650

Knott, P. J. (2015). Does VRIO help managers evaluate a firm's resources? *Management Decision*, *53*(8), 1806–1822. DOI: 10.1108/md-08-2014-0525

KPMG. (2024, June 20). Discretionary spending hit as household cost pressures continue to mount. KPMG. https://kpmg.com/uk/en/media/press-releases/2024/06/discretionary-spending-hit-as-household-cost-pressures-continue-to-mount.html

Krüger, K., Weking, J., Fielt, E., Böttcher, T., Kowalkiewicz, M., & Krcmar, H. (2025). Value drivers for Metaverse business models: A complementor perspective. *Journal of Management Information Systems*, *42*(1), 143–173.

Laborde, O. (2022, March 25). 3 raisons de vous intéresser au métavers - Harvard Business Review France. HBR France. https://www.hbrfrance.fr/innovation/3-raisons-de-vous-interesser-au-metavers-45420

LCG. (2024). TravelBI by Turismo de Portugal - Tourism Receipts. Turismodeportugal.pt. https://travelbi.turismodeportugal.pt/en/tourism-in-portugal/tourism-receipts/

Llywelyn, D. (2022, April 30). Global Christianity: the Future of the Catholic Church. Institute for Advanced Catholic Studies at USC. https://dornsife.usc.edu/iacs/2022/04/30/global-christianity/

Marabelli, M., & Newell, S. (2023). Responsibly strategizing with the metaverse: Business implications and DEI opportunities and challenges. *The Journal of Strategic Information Systems*, *32*(2), 101774. DOI: 10.1016/j.jsis.2023.101774

McKinsey & Company. (2022, August 17). What is the metaverse and where will it lead next? Www.mckinsey.com

McKinsey & Company. https://www.mckinsey.com/featured-insights/mckinsey-explainers/what-is-the-metaverse

Mittal, R., & Sinha, P. (2021). Framework for a resilient religious tourism supply chain for mitigating post-pandemic risk. *International Hospitality Review*, *36*(2). Advance online publication. DOI: 10.1108/ihr-09-2020- 0053

Mystakidis, S. (2022). *Metaverse. Encyclopedia*, *2*(1), 486–497. DOI: 10.3390/encyclopedia2010031

Nyhan, P. (2024, December 5). 6 AI trends you'll see more of in 2025. Microsoft. https://news.microsoft.com/source/features/ai/6-ai-trends-youll-see-more-of-in-2025/

Ohlan, R., & Ohlan, A. (2024). Religious tourism scholarship: Current state and future research directions. *Journal of Islamic Marketing*, *15*(3), 800–818. DOI: 10.1108/jima-05-2023-0152

Our World in Data. (2025). How old are you compared to most people? Our World in Data. https://ourworldindata.org/grapher/median-age?time=1950.latest&country=~OWID_WRL

Pomeroy, R. (2023, August 29). A surprising explanation for the global decline of religion. Big Think. https://bigthink.com/the-present/a-surprising-explanation-for-the-global-decline-of-religion/ Popp-Baier, U. (2010). From Religion to Spirituality—Megatrend in Contemporary Society or Methodological Artefact? A Contribution to the Secularization Debate from Psychology of Religion. Journal of Religion in Europe, 3(1), 34–67. https://doi.org/DOI: 10.1163/187489209x478337

Ramonde, T. (2025, January 30). The Camino de Santiago Statistics for 2024. Follow the Camino. https://followthecamino.com/en/camino-de-santiago-statistics- 2024/

Ritala, P., Ruokonen, M., & Kostis, A. (2024). The metaverse flywheel: Creating value across physical and virtual worlds. *California Management Review*, *66*(4), 80–101. DOI: 10.1177/00081256241252700

Santuario de Fátima. (2023a). Santuario de Fátima |Santuário de Fátima acolheu 6,8 milhões de peregrinos nas celebrações em 2023. Santuário de Fátima. https://www.fatima.pt/pt/news/santuario-de-fatima-acolheu-68-milhoes-de-peregrinos-nas-celebracoes-em-2023

Santuario de Fátima. (2023b, June 15). Santuario de Fátima |Em Fátima "temos um colo de mãe, e eu penso que a Igreja, independentemente do tempo que atravessa, tem de ser este colo." Santuário de Fátima. https://www.fatima.pt/pt/news/em-fatima-temos-um-colo-de-mae-e-eu-penso-que-a-igreja-independentemente-do-tempo-que-atravessa-tem-de-ser-este-colo-2023-06-15

Shin, H., & Kang, J. (2024). How does the metaverse travel experience influence virtual and actual travel behaviors? Focusing on the role of telepresence and avatar identification. *Journal of Hospitality and Tourism Management*, *58*, 174–183. DOI: 10.1016/j.jhtm.2023.12.009

Shinde, K. A., & Olsen, D. H. (2022). Reframing the Intersections of Pilgrimage, Religious Tourism, and Sustainability. *Sustainability*, *15*(1), 461. DOI: 10.3390/su15010461

Silva, C., Luís, J., & Reis, M. (2023). Exploring Memorable Sacred Tourism Experiences and Place Attachment. International Journal of Religious Tourism and International Journal of Religious Tourism and Pilgrimage Pilgrimage, 11. https://doi.org/DOI: 10.21427/38P9-MC74

Smaili, N., & de Rancourt-Raymond, A. (2022). Metaverse: Welcome to the new fraud marketplace. *Journal of Financial Crime*, *31*(1), 188–200. DOI: 10.1108/jfc-06-2022-0124

Teece, D. J. (2010). Business Models, Business Strategy and Innovation. *Long Range Planning*, *43*(2-3), 172–194. DOI: 10.1016/j.lrp.2009.07.003

Terzidou, M., Scarles, C., & Saunders, M. N. K. (2018). The complexities of religious tourism motivations: Sacred places, vows and visions. *Annals of Tourism Research*, *70*, 54–65. DOI: 10.1016/j.annals.2018.02.011

Thomas, J., Kuhail, M. A., & AlBeyahi, F. (2024). The Metaverse, Religious Practice and Wellbeing: A Narrative Review. *Cyberpsychology, Behavior, and Social Networking*, *27*(1), 57–63. DOI: 10.1089/cyber.2023.0003

Tomini, N., Brenk, K., Kanbach, D. K., Stubner, S., & Bernhard, F. (2025). From hype to impact: How companies can leverage the metaverse technology for business models. *International Journal of Entrepreneurship and Innovation*, *26*(1), 12–22. DOI: 10.1177/14657503241258934

Trading Economics. (n.d.-a). Portugal Consumer Price Index (CPI). Tradingeconomics.com. https://tradingeconomics.com/portugal/consumer-price-index-cpi

Trading Economics. (n.d.-b). Portugal Inflation Rate. Tradingeconomics.com. https://tradingeconomics.com/portugal/inflation-cpi

Transparência Internacional Portugal. (2025, February 11). Índice de Perceção da Corrupção 2024. https://transparencia.pt/indice-de-percecao-da-corrupcao-2024/

Turismo de Portugal. (2024). Estratégia Turismo 2035. Turismodeportugal.pt. https://www.turismodeportugal.pt/pt/Turismo_Portugal/Estrategia/estrategia-turismo - 2035/Paginas/default.aspx

Turismo de Portugal. (2025, February 26). Visão geral. Www.turismodeportugal .pt. https://www.turismodeportugal.pt/pt/Turismo_Portugal/visao_geral/Paginas/default.aspx

Wei, W. (2023). A buzzword, a phase or the next chapter for the Internet? The status and possibilities of the metaverse for tourism. Journal of Hospitality and Tourism Insights. https://doi.org/DOI: 10.1108/jhti-11-2022-0568

World Bank Group. (2025, January). Global Economic Prospects. World Bank. https://www.worldbank.org/pt/publication/global-economic-prospects

World Economic Forum. (2022, May 26). How the metaverse can be a force for good in an uncertain world. https://www.weforum.org/stories/2022/05/how-metaverse-can-be-a-force-for-good-in-an-uncertain-world/

Yin, R. K. (2018). *Case Study Research and Applications: Design and Methods* (6th ed.). Sage Publications.

Compilation of References

Abdellatif, G., Alexandre, P., Fouad, B. A., & Christophe, J. (2025, June). Knowledge Management in the metaverse for sustainable supply chains. In IAMOT 2025.

Abdurakhmanova, G. K., Astanakulov, O. T., Goyipnazarov, S. B., & Irmatova, A. B. (2022, December). Tourism 4.0: Opportunities for applying industry 4.0 technologies in tourism. In *Proceedings of the 6th International Conference on Future Networks & Distributed Systems* (pp. 33-38).

Aburbeian, A. M., Owda, A. Y., & Owda, M. (2022). A Technology Acceptance Model Survey of the Metaverse Prospects. *AI*, *3*(2), 285–302. DOI: 10.3390/ai3020018

Achuthan, K., Gupta, B. B., & Raman, R. (2025). Bridging cybersecurity with digital twin technology: A thematic analysis. *International Journal of Information Security*, *24*(5), 207. DOI: 10.1007/s10207-025-01115-y

Adapa, S., Fazal-E-Hasan, S., Makam, S., Azeem, M., & Mortimer, G. (2020). Examining the antecedents and consequences of perceived shopping value through smart retail technology. *Journal of Retailing and Consumer Services*. Advance online publication. DOI: 10.1016/J.JRETCONSER.2019.101901

Adel, A., & Alani, HS, N. (2024). Human Centric Collaboration and Industry 5.0 Framework in Smart Cities and Communities: Fostering Sustainable Development Goals 3, 4, 9, and 11 in Society 5.0. *Smart Cities*, *7*(4), 1723–1775. DOI: 10.3390/smartcities7040068

Afolabi, J., Olatoye, F., Eboigbe, E., Abdul, A., & Daraojimba, H. (2023). REVOLUTIONIZING RETAIL: HR TACTICS FOR IMPROVED EMPLOYEE AND CUSTOMER ENGAGEMENT. *International Journal of Applied Research in Social Sciences*. https://doi.org/DOI: 10.51594/ijarss.v5i10.635

Agrawal, R., & Wankhede, V. A. (2025). Breaking the virtual wall: Analysing barriers to metaverse adoption in manufacturing industries. *The International Journal of Organizational Analysis*. Advance online publication. DOI: 10.1108/IJOA-07-2024-4676

Ajzen, I. (1991). The theory of planned behaviour. *Organizational Behavior and Human Decision Processes*, *50*(2), 179–211.

Al Kfairy, M., Alrabaee, S., Alfandi, O., Mohamed, A. T., & Khaddaj, S. (2025). Navigating ethical dimensions in the metaverse: Challenges, frameworks, and solutions. *IEEE Access : Practical Innovations, Open Solutions*, *13*, 79996–80018. DOI: 10.1109/ACCESS.2025.3564498

Alexander, B., Blazquez, M., Chrimes, C., & Boardman, R. (2024). The role of immersive spaces on the customer experience: An exploration of fashion metaverses. *Psychology and Marketing*. Advance online publication. DOI: 10.1002/mar.22140

Ali, M. H., Suleiman, N., Khalid, N., Tan, K. H., Tseng, M. L., & Kumar, M. (2021). Supply chain resilience reactive strategies for food SMEs in coping to COVID-19 crisis. *Trends in Food Science & Technology*, *109*, 94–102.

Ali, O., Ally, M., Dwivedi, Y. K., & Rana, N. P. (2023). A review of the key challenges of non fungible tokens. *Technological Forecasting and Social Change*, *190*, 122248. DOI: 10.1016/j.techfore.2022.122248

Alkaeed, M., Qayyum, A., & Qadir, J. (2024). Privacy preservation in artificial intelligence and extended reality (AI XR) metaverses: A survey. *Journal of Network and Computer Applications*, *231*, 103989. DOI: 10.1016/j.jnca.2024.103989

Allen, G. (2020). Understanding AI technology. *Joint Artificial Intelligence Center (JAIC). The Pentagon United States*, *2*(1), 24–32.

Aloqaily, M., Bouachir, O., Karray, F., Al Ridhawi, I., & El Saddik, A. (2023). Integrating Digital Twin and Advanced Intelligent Technologies to Realize the Metaverse. *IEEE Consumer Electronics Magazine*, *12*(6), 47–55. DOI: 10.1109/MCE.2022.3212570

Amit, R., & Zott, C. (2001). Value creation in e-business. *Strategic Management Journal*, *22*(6-7), 493–520.

An, M., & Han, S. (2020). Effects of experiential motivation and customer engagement on customer value creation: Analysis of psychological process in the experience-based retail environment. *Journal of Business Research*, *120*, 389–397. DOI: 10.1016/j.jbusres.2020.02.044

ANSR. (2024). 180 mil motards juntaram-se para a Bênção dos Capacetes. Ansr.pt. http://www.ansr.pt/Noticias/Pages/180-mil-motards-juntaram-se-para-a - B%C3%AAn%C3%A7%C3%A3o-dos-Capacetes.aspx

Arican, İ. (2024). *Smart destinations: integration of ai in the tourism destinations (akilli destinasyonlar: yapay zekanin turizm destinasyonlarina entegre edilmesi)* (doctoral dissertation, istanbul university).

Asad, U., Khan, M., Khalid, A., & Lughmani, W. A. (2023). Human-Centric Digital Twins in Industry: A Comprehensive Review of Enabling Technologies and Implementation Strategies. In Sensors (Vol. 23, Issue 8). MDPI. https://doi.org/ DOI: 10.3390/s23083938

Attaran, M., & Celik, B. G. (2023). Digital Twin: Benefits, use cases, challenges, and opportunities. *Decision Analytics Journal*, *6*, 100165. DOI: 10.1016/j.dajour.2023.100165

Bagdare, S., & Jain, R. (2013). Measuring retail customer experience. *International Journal of Retail & Distribution Management*, *41*, 790–804. DOI: 10.1108/IJRDM-08-2012-0084

Balaji, M., & Roy, S. (2017). Value co-creation with Internet of things technology in the retail industry. *Journal of Marketing Management*, *33*, 31–37. DOI: 10.1080/0267257X.2016.1217914

Balcerzak, A. P., Nica, E., Rogalska, E., Poliak, M., Klieštik, T., & Sabie, O. M. (2022). Blockchain technology and smart contracts in decentralized governance systems. *Administrative Sciences*, *12*(3), 96. DOI: 10.3390/admsci12030096

Ball, M. (2021). Framework for the Metaverse. MatthewBall.co. https://www .matthewball.co/all/forwardtothemetaverseprimer

Ball, M. (2022). *The metaverse: And how it will revolutionize everything*. Liveright Publishing.

Banco de Portugal. (2024, December 13). Boletim Económico — Dezembro 2024 | Banco de Portugal. Bportugal.pt. https://www.bportugal.pt/publicacao/boletim -economico-dezembro-2024

Banerjee, S., & Tyagi, P. K. (2025). Leveraging Social Media for Tea Destination Branding: Strategies and Impacts. In *Tracking Tourism Patterns and Improving Travel Experiences With Innovative Technologies* (pp. 49-82). IGI Global.

Bascur, C., & Rusu, C. (2020). Customer Experience in Retail: A Systematic Literature Review. *Applied Sciences (Basel, Switzerland)*. Advance online publication. DOI: 10.3390/app10217644

Battour, M., Mady, K., Salaheldeen, M., Elsotouhy, M., Elbendary, I., & Boğan, E. (2023). AI-enabled technologies to assist Muslim tourists in Halal-friendly tourism. *Journal of Islamic Marketing*, *14*(5), 1291–1309.

Behnam, M., Hollebeek, L., Clark, M., & Farabi, R. (2021). Exploring customer engagement in the product vs. service context. *Journal of Retailing and Consumer Services*, *60*, 102456. DOI: 10.1016/J.JRETCONSER.2021.102456

Bell, M. (2023, March 20). The Top Five Cybersecurity Concerns. Forbes. https://www.forbes.com/councils/forbestechcouncil/2023/03/20/the-top-five-cybersecurity-concerns/

Berry, L. L., Carbone, L. P., & Haeckel, S. H. (2002). Managing the total customer experience. *MIT Sloan Management Review*, *43*(3), 85.

Bhatnagar, R., & Babbar, M. (2022). A systematic review of sports analytics. *International Journal of Technology Transfer and Commercialisation*, *19*(4), 393. DOI: 10.1504/ijttc.2022.127574

Bibri, S. E., & Allam, Z. (2022). The metaverse as a virtual form of data driven smart urbanism: On post pandemic governance through the prism of the logic of surveillance capitalism. *Smart Cities*, *5*(2), 715–727. DOI: 10.3390/smartcities5020037

Bilyk, I., Kindii, M., & Kurylo, S. (2024). PERSONALIZATION OF MARKETING AS A TOOL TO INCREASE SALES AND CUSTOMER LOYALTY. *Eastern Europe: economy, business and management*. https://doi.org/DOI: 10.32782/easterneurope.45-7

Bingöl, S., & Yang, Y. (2025). Integrating smart technologies and artificial intelligence to build smart tourism destination ecosystems: A model for smart destination management. *Tourism Management Perspectives*, *58*, 101380.

Bokhtiar Al Zami, M., Shaon, S., Khanh Quy, V., & Nguyen, D. C. (2025a). Digital Twin in Industries: A Comprehensive Survey. *IEEE Access : Practical Innovations, Open Solutions*, *13*, 47291–47336. DOI: 10.1109/ACCESS.2025.3551532

Boopathy, P., Deepa, N., Maddikunta, P. K. R., Victor, N., Gadekallu, T. R., Yenduri, G., Wang, W., Pham, Q.-V., Huynh-The, T., & Liyanage, M. (2025). The Metaverse for Industry 5.0 in NextG Communications: Potential Applications and Future Challenges. *IEEE Open Journal of the Computer Society*, *6*, 4–24. DOI: 10.1109/OJCS.2024.3497335

Bowden, J., & Mirzaei, A. (2021). Consumer engagement within retail communication channels: An examination of online brand communities and digital content marketing initiatives. *European Journal of Marketing*. Advance online publication. DOI: 10.1108/EJM-01-2018-0007

Boyce, C., & Neale, P. (2006). *Conducting in-depth interviews: A guide for designing and conducting in-depth interviews for evaluation input.* Pathfinder International.

Bozkurt, A., Altay, M., Karadeniz, A., & Koçdar, S. (2021). Digital equity and inclusion in the metaverse. *Open Praxis*, *13*(3), 235–246. DOI: 10.5944/openpraxis.13.3.136

Bradley, M. M., Miccoli, L., Escrig, M. A., & Lang, P. J. (2008). The pupil as a measure of emotional arousal and autonomic activation. *Psychophysiology*, *45*(4), 602–607. DOI: 10.1111/j.1469-8986.2008.00654.x

Braun, V., & Clarke, V. (2006). Using thematic analysis in psychology. *Qualitative Research in Psychology*, *3*(2), 77–101.

Britannica. (2024, October 30). Our Lady of Fatima | Christianity | Britannica. Www .britannica.com. https://www.britannica.com/event/Our-Lady-of-Fatima

Brodie, R. J., Hollebeek, L. D., Jurić, B., & Ilić, A. (2011). Customer engagement: Conceptual domain, fundamental propositions, and implications for research. *Journal of Service Research*, *14*(3), 252–271.

Brodie, R. J., Hollebeek, L. D., Jurić, B., & Ilić, A. (2013). Customer engagement in a virtual brand community: An exploratory analysis. *Journal of Business Research*, *66*(1), 105–114. DOI: 10.1016/j.jbusres.2011.07.029

Bruni, R., & Piccarozzi, M. (2022). Industry 4.0 enablers in retailing: A literature review. *International Journal of Retail & Distribution Management*. Advance online publication. DOI: 10.1108/ijrdm-07-2021-0314

Bucci, I., Fani, V., & Bandinelli, R. (2025). Towards Human-Centric Manufacturing: Exploring the Role of Human Digital Twins in Industry 5.0. In Sustainability (Switzerland) (Vol. 17, Issue 1). Multidisciplinary Digital Publishing Institute (MDPI). https://doi.org/DOI: 10.3390/su17010129

Budovich, L. S. (2023). The impact of religious tourism on the economy and tourism industry. *Hervormde Teologiese Studies*, *79*(1), 1–7. DOI: 10.4102/hts.v79i1.8607

Bughin, J., Seong, J., Manyika, J., Chui, M., & Joshi, R. (2018). Notes from the AI frontier: Modeling the impact of AI on the world economy. *McKinsey Global Institute*. https://www.mckinsey.com/featured-insights/artificial-intelligence

Buhalis, D. (2020). Technology in tourism-from information communication technologies to eTourism and smart tourism towards ambient intelligence tourism: A perspective article. *Tourism Review*, *75*(1). Advance online publication. DOI: 10.1108/tr-06-2019-0258

Buhalis, D., & Karatay, N. (2022). Mixed Reality (MR) for Generation Z in Cultural Heritage Tourism Towards Metaverse. *Information and Communication Technologies in Tourism*, *2022*, 16–27. DOI: 10.1007/978-3-030-94751-4_2

Buhalis, D., Leung, D., & Lin, M. (2023). Metaverse as a disruptive technology revolutionising tourism management and marketing. *Tourism Management*, *97*, 104724. DOI: 10.1016/j.tourman.2023.104724

Buragohain, D., Khichar, S., & Deng, C.. (2025). Analyzing metaverse-based digital therapies, their effectiveness, and potential risks in mental healthcare. *Scientific Reports*, *15*, 17066. PMID: 40379748

Burnett, B., Keaney, M., & Mcintire, K. (2023). *The Impact of Data Analytics in Basketball. A Case Study from the National Basketball Association Abstract.*

Bustamante, J., & Rubio, N. (2017). Measuring customer experience in physical retail environments. *Journal of Service Management*, *28*, 884–913. DOI: 10.1108/JOSM-06-2016-0142

Butt, A. S., Alghababsheh, M., & Awan, U. (2025a). Barriers to the adoption of the Metaverse in digital supply chains. *Journal of Enterprise Information Management*. Advance online publication. DOI: 10.1108/JEIM-09-2024-0500

Calderón-Fajardo, V., Puig-Cabrera, M., & Rodríguez-Rodríguez, I. (2025). Beyond the real world: Metaverse adoption patterns in tourism among Gen Z and Millennials. *Current Issues in Tourism*, *28*(8), 1261–1281. DOI: 10.1080/13683500.2024.2330675

Chaffey, D. (2019). *Digital marketing: Strategy, implementation and practice.* Pearson UK.

Chandra, S., Verma, S., Lim, W., Kumar, S., & Donthu, N. (2022). Personalization in personalized marketing: Trends and ways forward. *Psychology and Marketing*. Advance online publication. DOI: 10.1002/mar.21670

Chaturvedi, R., Verma, S., Ali, F., & Kumar, S. (2024). Reshaping tourist experience with AI-enabled technologies: A comprehensive review and future research agenda. *International Journal of Human-Computer Interaction*, *40*(18), 5517–5533.

Chaudhuri, A., & Holbrook, M. B. (2001). The chain of effects from brand trust and brand affect to brand performance: The role of brand loyalty. *Journal of Marketing*, *65*(2), 81–93. DOI: 10.1509/jmkg.65.2.81.18255

Chen, Z. (2024). Beyond boundaries: Exploring the Metaverse in tourism. *International Journal of Contemporary Hospitality Management*. Advance online publication. DOI: 10.1108/ijchm-06-2023-0900

Chhabria, S., Gupta, S., & Gupta, H. (2023). A Study on the Impact of "Personalized Marketing" on Customer Satisfaction and Loyalty in Retail Fashion in 2023. *International Journal of Computer Applications*. Advance online publication. DOI: 10.5120/ijca2023922707

Chi, M., Chen, Y., Xu, Y., & Wu, Y. (2024). Modelling barriers to metaverse adoption in the hospitality and tourism industry. *Information Technology & Tourism*, •••, 1–33. DOI: 10.1016/10.1007/s40558-024-00298-9

Chiru, C. (2025). AI-DRIVEN VR AND THE IMMERSIVE EXPERIENCE. *The Role of Artificial Intelligence in the Tourism and Hospitality Sector*.

Choe, J. (2024). Religious tourism. *Tourism Geographies*, •••, 1–10. DOI: 10.1080/14616688.2024.2423168

Chohan, R., & Schmidt-Devlin, E. (2024). Sports fandom in the metaverse: Marketing implications and research agenda. *Marketing Letters*, *35*(1), 1–14. DOI: 10.1007/s11002-023-09702-6

Choubey, V., Chakraborty, D., Sharma, A., Khorana, S., & Buhalis, D. (2025). Metaverse in tourism: Tourist involvement as a moderator. *Asia Pacific Journal of Tourism Research*, *30*(1), 1–26. DOI: 10.1080/10941665.2024.2414881

Christensen, C. M., Raynor, M. E., & McDonald, R. (2016). What is disruptive innovation? *Harvard Business Review*, *93*(12), 44–53.

Clark, T., Foster, L., Bryman, A., & Sloan, L. (2021). *Bryman's Social Research Methods* (6th ed.). Oxford University Press.

Colicev, A. (2023). How can non-fungible tokens bring value to brands. *International Journal of Research in Marketing*, *40*(1), 30–37. DOI: 10.1016/j.ijresmar.2022.07.003

Collins-Kreiner, N. (2016). The lifecycle of concepts: The case of "Pilgrimage Tourism.". *Tourism Geographies*, *18*(3), 322–334. DOI: 10.1080/14616688.2016.1155077

Connell, C., Marciniak, R., Carey, L., & McColl, J. (2019). Customer engagement with websites: A transactional retail perspective. *European Journal of Marketing*. Advance online publication. DOI: 10.1108/EJM-10-2017-0649

Correia, P. A. P. (2025, April). From Virtual to Reality: Enhancing Cultural Tourism Through AI, VR, and the Metaverse. In *International Conference on Tourism Research* (Vol. 8, No. 1, pp. 47-55). Academic Conferences International Limited.

Cossich, V. R. A., Carlgren, D., Holash, R. J., & Katz, L. (2023). Technological Breakthroughs in Sport: Current Practice and Future Potential of Artificial Intelligence, Virtual Reality, Augmented Reality, and Modern Data Visualization in Performance Analysis. *Applied Sciences (Switzerland)*, *13*(23). Advance online publication. DOI: 10.3390/app132312965

Cummings, J. J., & Bailenson, J. N. (2016). How immersive is enough? A meta-analysis of the effect of immersive technology on user presence. *Media Psychology*, *19*(2), 272–309. DOI: 10.1080/15213269.2015.1015740

Darwinto, P. A., Widodo, A. M., Agustina, N. P., Wahyuadnyana, K. D., & Rahaman, M. (2025). Artificial Intelligence (AI) for Autonomous Drones. In *AI Developments for Industrial Robotics and Intelligent Drones* (pp. 55–84). IGI Global Scientific Publishing. https://doi.org/DOI: 10.4018/979-8-3693-2707-4.ch004

Davenport, T. H., & Harris, J. G. (2007). *Competing on analytics: The new science of winning*. Harvard Business Press.

Davis, F. D. (1989). Perceived usefulness, perceived ease of use, and user acceptance of information technology. *Management Information Systems Quarterly*, *13*(3), 319–340. DOI: 10.2307/249008

De Giovanni, P. (2023). Sustainability of the Metaverse: A Transition to Industry 5.0. *Sustainability (Switzerland)*, *15*(7). Advance online publication. DOI: 10.3390/su15076079

Dean, M. C., Oeding, J. F., Diniz, P., Seil, R., & Samuelsson, K. (2024). Leveraging digital twins for improved orthopaedic evaluation and treatment. *Journal of Experimental Orthopaedics*, *11*(4). PMID: 39530111

Deveci, M., Pamucar, D., Gokasar, I., Köppen, M., & Gupta, B. B. (2023). Personal Mobility in Metaverse With Autonomous Vehicles Using Q-Rung Orthopair Fuzzy Sets Based OPA-RAFSI Model. *Trans. Intell. Transport. Sys.*, *24*(12), 15642–15651. DOI: 10.1109/TITS.2022.3186294

Dhole, K. D. (2022). Lessons from Digital India for the right to internet access. arXiv.

Di Pasquale, V., Fantini, P., Peruzzini, M., & Pellicciari, M. (2024). Immersive virtual reality training for assembly and disassembly operations: A systematic review. *Machines (Basel)*, *12*(8), 528. DOI: 10.3390/machines12080528

Domínguez Jiménez, J. A., Campo Landines, K. C., Martínez Santos, J. C., Delahoz, E. J., & Contreras Ortiz, S. H. (2020). A machine learning model for emotion recognition from physiological signals. *Biomedical Signal Processing and Control, 55*, 101646. DOI: 10.1016/j.bspc.2019.101646

Donovan, T. (2023). Implementation costs of hospital-based computerised decision support systems: A systematic review of costing analyses. *Implementation Science : IS, 18*(1), 27. PMID: 37420284

Draper, A. K. (2004). The principles and application of qualitative research. *The Proceedings of the Nutrition Society, 63*(4), 641–646.

Du, J., Mamo, Y. Z., Floyd, C., Karthikeyan, N., & James, J. D. (2024). Machine Learning in Sport Social Media Research: Practical Uses and Opportunities. *International Journal of Sport Communication, 17*(January), 97–106. DOI: 10.1123/ijsc.2023-0151

Dunmoye, I. K., Rukangu, S., May, A., & Das, D. (2024). Social presence and cognitive engagement in collaborative virtual reality learning environment: A mixed methods approach. *Computers and Education: X Reality, 5*, 100054. DOI: 10.1016/j.cexr.2024.100054

Dwivedi, Y. K., Hughes, D. L., & Baabdullah, A. M.. (2022). Metaverse beyond the hype: Multidisciplinary perspectives on emerging challenges, opportunities and agenda for research, practice and policy. *International Journal of Information Management, 66*, 102542. DOI: 10.1016/j.ijinfomgt.2022.102542

Edelman, D. C., & Singer, M. (2015). Competing on customer journeys. *Harvard Business Review, 93*(11), 88–100.

Edwards, L. (2025, March 24). This Meta Quest 3 update teases some seriously exciting VR upgrades. Digital Trends. https://www.digitaltrends.com/news/this-meta-quest-3-update-teases-some-seriously-exciting-vr-upgrades/

Ejjami, R., & Rahim, N. (2024). *Retail 5.0: Creating Resilient and Customer-Centric Shopping Experiences through Advanced Technologies.* International Journal For Multidisciplinary Research., DOI: 10.36948/ijfmr.2024.v06i04.25930

El Archi, Y., Benbba, B., Kabil, M., & Dávid, L. D. (2023). Digital technologies for sustainable tourism destinations: State of the art and research agenda. *Administrative Sciences, 13*(8), 184.

European Commission. (2022, December 9). Increasing influence of new governing systems | Knowledge for policy. Knowledge4policy. https://knowledge4policy.ec.europa.eu/increasing-influence-new-governing-systems_en

European Commission. (2023a, February 8). Expanding influence of East and South | Knowledge for policy. Knowledge4policy. https://knowledge4policy.ec.europa.eu/expanding-influence-east-south_en

European Commission. (2023b, February 13). Accelerating technological change and hyperconnectivity | Knowledge for policy. Knowledge4policy. https://knowledge4policy.ec.europa.eu/accelerating-technological-change-hyperconnectivity_en

European Commission. (2023c, February 15). Diversification of education and learning | Knowledge for policy. Knowledge4policy. https://knowledge4policy.ec.europa.eu/diversification-education-learning_en

European Commission. (2023d, June 26). Increasing significance of migration | Knowledge for policy. Knowledge4policy. https://knowledge4policy.ec.europa.eu/increasing-significance-migration_en

Fang, M., Yang, W., Kuijper, A., Štruc, V., & Damer, N. (2024). Fairness in face presentation attack detection. *Pattern Recognition*, *147*, 110002. DOI: 10.1016/j.patcog.2023.110002

Fan, X., Jiang, X., & Deng, N. (2022). Immersive technology: A meta-analysis of augmented/virtual reality applications and their impact on tourism experience. *Tourism Management*, *91*, 104534.

Fazio, G., Fricano, S., Iannolino, S., & Pirrone, C. (2023). Metaverse and tourism development: Issues and opportunities in stakeholders' perception. *Information Technology & Tourism*, *25*(4), 507–528. DOI: 10.1007/s40558-023-00268-7

Fekonja, L. S., Schenk, R., Schröder, E., Tomasello, R., Tomšič, S., & Picht, T. (2024). The digital twin in neuroscience: From theory to tailored therapy. *Frontiers in Neuroscience*, *18*, 1454856. PMID: 39376542

Fernandez-Carames, T. M., & Fraga-Lamas, P. (2024). Forging the Industrial Metaverse for Industry 5.0: Where Extended Reality, IIoT, Opportunistic Edge Computing, and Digital Twins Meet. *IEEE Access : Practical Innovations, Open Solutions*, *12*, 95778–95819. DOI: 10.1109/ACCESS.2024.3422109

Feroz, A. K., Zo, H., Eom, J., & Chiravuri, A. (2023). Identifying organizations' dynamic capabilities for sustainable digital transformation: A mixed methods study. *Technology in Society*, *73*, 102257. DOI: 10.1016/j.techsoc.2023.102257

Flavián, C., Ibáñez Sánchez, S., Orús, C., & Barta, S. (2024). The dark side of the metaverse: The role of gamification in event virtualization. *International Journal of Information Management*, *75*, 102726. DOI: 10.1016/j.ijinfomgt.2023.102726

GDPR-advisor.com. (2025, February 24). GDPR Compliance in the Metaverse: Managing Virtual Identity and Privacy - GDPR Advisor. GDPR Advisor. https://www.gdpr-advisor.com/gdpr-compliance-in-the-metaverse-managing-virtual-identity-and-privacy/

Ghobakhloo, M., Iranmanesh, M., Tseng, M. L., Grybauskas, A., Stefanini, A., & Amran, A. (2023). Behind the definition of Industry 5.0: A systematic review of technologies, principles, components, and values. *Journal of Industrial and Production Engineering*, *40*(6), 432–447. DOI: 10.1080/21681015.2023.2216701

Ghosh, P., Chakravarty, T., & Johari, H. (2024). Bodhgaya, India as a Buddhist Cultural Heritage Site: A Journey from Pilgrimage to Tourism. In Brunn, S. D. (Ed.), *Geography of Time, Place, Movement and Networks* (Vol. 3, pp. 119–134). Springer Nature Switzerland., DOI: 10.1007/978-3-031-58033-8_7

Giansanti, D. (2025). Exploring the potential of digital twins in cancer treatment: A narrative review of reviews. *PMC National Center for Biotechnology Information*, *12*(5), 445–462. PMID: 40429568

Gleim, M. R., McCullough, H., Gabler, C., Ferrell, L., & Ferrell, O. C. (2025). Examining the customer experience in the metaverse retail revolution. *Journal of Business Research*, *186*, 115045. DOI: 10.1016/j.jbusres.2024.115045

Go, H., & Kang, M. (2023). Metaverse tourism for sustainable tourism development: Tourism agenda 2030. *Tourism Review*, *78*(2), 381–394. DOI: 10.1108/tr-02-2022-0102

Goldenberg, B. (2023). Gucci's metaverse makeover: A case study on fashion innovation. Retrieved from https://ismguide.com/gucci-xr-metaverse-case-study/

Gralka, P., Müller, C., Geringer, S., Reina, G., & Weiskopf, D. (2025). Quantifying energy reduction of foveated volume visualization. In *Proceedings of the 2025 Symposium on Eye Tracking Research and Applications (ETRA '25)*. ACM. DOI: 10.1145/3715669.3725881

Grewal, D., Gauri, D., Roggeveen, A., & Sethuraman, R. (2021). Strategizing Retailing in the New Technology Era. *Journal of Retailing*, *97*, 6–12. DOI: 10.1016/J.JRETAI.2021.02.004

Grewal, D., Levy, M., & Kumar, P. (2009). Customer Experience Management in Retailing: An Organizing Framework. *Journal of Retailing*, *85*, 1–14. DOI: 10.1016/J.JRETAI.2009.01.001

Grewal, D., & Roggeveen, A. (2020). Understanding Retail Experiences and Customer Journey Management. *Journal of Retailing*, *96*, 3–8. DOI: 10.1016/j.jretai.2020.02.002

Grewal, D., Roggeveen, A. L., & Nordfält, J. (2020). The future of retailing. *Journal of Retailing*, *96*(1), 86–95.

Grewal, D., Roggeveen, A., Benoit, S., Andrade, M., Wetzels, R., & Wetzels, M. (2025). A new era of technology-infused retailing. *Journal of Business Research*. Advance online publication. DOI: 10.1016/j.jbusres.2024.115095

Grewal, D., Roggeveen, A., & Nordfält, J. (2017). The Future of Retailing. *Journal of Retailing*, *93*, 1–6. DOI: 10.1016/J.JRETAI.2016.12.008

Grewal, D., Roggeveen, A., Sisodia, R., & Nordfält, J. (2017). Enhancing Customer Engagement Through Consciousness. *Journal of Retailing*, *93*, 55–64. DOI: 10.1016/J.JRETAI.2016.12.001

Grundner, L., & Neuhofer, B. (2021). The bright and dark sides of artificial intelligence: A futures perspective on tourist destination experiences. *Journal of Destination Marketing & Management*, *19*, 100511.

Guidotti, R., Monreale, A., Ruggieri, S., Turini, F., Pedreschi, D., & Giannotti, F. (2019). A survey of methods for explaining black box models. *ACM Computing Surveys*, *51*(5), 93. Advance online publication. DOI: 10.1145/3236009

Guo, S., Zhang, J., Jiang, Q., & Zhang, B. (2022). Surface integrity in high-speed grinding of Al6061T6 alloy. *CIRP Annals*, *71*(1), 281–284. DOI: 10.1016/j.cirp.2022.03.002

Gupta, B. B., Gaurav, A., Albeshri, A. A., & Alsalman, D. (2023). New paradigms of sustainable entrepreneurship in metaverse: A micro-level perspective. *The International Entrepreneurship and Management Journal*, *19*(3), 1449–1465.

Gupta, B. B., Gaurav, A., Arya, V., & Alhalabi, W. (2024). Data science in sustainable entrepreneurship: A multidisciplinary field of applications. *Technological Forecasting and Social Change*, *209*, 123798. DOI: 10.1016/j.techfore.2024.123798

Gupta, B. B., Gaurav, A., Arya, V., Waheeb Attar, R., Bansal, S., Alhomoud, A., & Chui, K. T. (2025). Sustainable supply chain security through BEART-based fake news detection on supplier practices. *Enterprise Information Systems*, *19*, 2462972. DOI: 10.1080/17517575.2025.2462972

Gursoy, D., Malodia, S., & Dhir, A. (2022). The metaverse in the hospitality and tourism industry: An overview of current trends and future research directions. *Journal of Hospitality Marketing & Management, 31*(5), 527–534. DOI: 10.1080/19368623.2022.2072504

Hagberg, J., Jonsson, A., & Egels-Zandén, N. (2017). Retail digitalization: Implications for physical stores. *Journal of Retailing and Consumer Services, 39*, 264–269. DOI: 10.1016/J.JRETCONSER.2017.08.005

Hajibaba, H., Grün, B., & Dolnicar, S. (2019). Improving the stability of market segmentation analysis. *International Journal of Contemporary Hospitality Management, 32*(4), 1393–1411. DOI: 10.1108/ijchm-02-2019-0137

Hamari, J., Koivisto, J., & Sarsa, H. (2014). Does gamification work? A literature review of empirical studies on gamification. In *47th Hawaii International Conference on System Sciences*, 3025–3034. IEEE.

Hang, F., Duan, S., Li, Y., Zou, Y., & Gao, L. (2024). End-to-end deep-learning-based classification of three-dimensional flow state in virtual reality using electroencephalography signals. *Sensors (Basel), 24*(6), 1894. DOI: 10.3390/s24061894

Har, L., Rashid, U., Chuan, L., Sen, S., & Xia, L. (2021). Revolution of Retail Industry: From Perspective of Retail 1.0 to 4.0. **, 1615-1625. https://doi.org/DOI: 10.1016/j.procs.2022.01.362

Hassoun, A., Jagtap, S., Trollman, H., Garcia-Garcia, G., Duong, L. N. K., Saxena, P., Bouzembrak, Y., Treiblmaier, H., Para-López, C., Carmona-Torres, C., Dev, K., Mhlanga, D., & Aït-Kaddour, A. (2024a). From Food Industry 4.0 to Food Industry 5.0: Identifying technological enablers and potential future applications in the food sector. In Comprehensive Reviews in Food Science and Food Safety (Vol. 23, Issue 6). John Wiley and Sons Inc. https://doi.org/DOI: 10.1111/1541-4337.70040

Hayduk, T. (2020). The future of sport data analytics. *Statistical Modelling and Sports Business Analytics*, (May), 159–173. DOI: 10.4324/9780367854454-14

Hemmati, A., Aliyari, M., & Chobar, A. P. (2025). In Nozari, H. (Ed.), *AIoE-Powered Supply Chain Optimization for Smart Agriculture BT - Artificial Intelligence of Everything and Sustainable Development* (pp. 223–240). Springer Nature Singapore., DOI: 10.1007/978-981-96-7202-8_13

Hemphill, T. A. (2023). The metaverse and the challenge of responsible standards development. *Journal of Responsible Innovation, 10*(1), 2243121. DOI: 10.1080/23299460.2023.2243121

Hernández-Morales, A. (2025, March 12). 3 elections in 3 years: Portugal's political crisis explained. POLITICO. https://www.politico.eu/article/portugal-elections-political-crisis-luis-montenegro-spinumviva/

Herrman, J. (2021, July 10). Are We in the Metaverse Yet? The New York Times. https://www.nytimes.com/2021/07/10/style/metaverse-virtual-worlds.html

Hliš, T., Fister, I., & Fister, I. (2024). Digital twins in sport: Concepts, taxonomies, challenges and practical potentials. *Expert Systems with Applications*, *258*(June). Advance online publication. DOI: 10.1016/j.eswa.2024.125104

Hollebeek, L. D., Srivastava, R. K., & Chen, T. (2019). S-D logic–informed customer engagement: Integrative framework, revised fundamental propositions, and application to CRM. *Journal of the Academy of Marketing Science*, *47*(1), 161–185. DOI: 10.1007/s11747-016-0494-5

Hui, P. (2023). Exploring the potential of metaverse in education: A case study of MetaHKUST. https://cei.hkust.edu.hk/en-hk/event/exploring-potential-metaverse-education-case-study-metahkust

Hu, X., Wu, X., Ma, M., Xu, X., Gu, Y., Wang, G., Xu, Y., Meng, X., & Wang, L. (2025). Efficient VR rendering: Survey on foveated, stereo, cloud, and low-power rendering techniques. *Virtual Reality & Intelligent Hardware*, *7*(5), 421–452. DOI: 10.1016/j.vrih.2025.08.003

Huynh-The, T., Pham, Q. V., Pham, X. Q., Nguyen, T. T., Han, Z., & Kim, D. S. (2023). Artificial intelligence for the metaverse: A survey. *Engineering Applications of Artificial Intelligence*, *117*, 1–24. DOI: 10.1016/j.engappai.2022.105581

Iliev, D. (2020). The evolution of religious tourism: Concept, segmentation and development of new identities. *Journal of Hospitality and Tourism Management*, *45*, 131–140. DOI: 10.1016/j.jhtm.2020.07.012

Institute for Economics and Peace. (2024). Global Peace Index 2024: Measuring Peace in a Complex World (p. page 8 and 15). Institute for Economics and Peace. https://www.economicsandpeace.org/wp-content/uploads/2024/06/GPI-2024-web.pdf

Ionescu, A. M., & Sârbu, F. A. (2024). Exploring the impact of smart technologies on the tourism industry. *Sustainability*, *16*(8), 3318.

Ipsos. (2023). The Metaverse And The Future Of Travel. https://www.ipsos.com/sites/default/files/ct/news/documents/2023-10/The%20Metaverse%20and%20the%20future%20of%20travel%20-%205%20things%20to%20consider%20about%20travel%20in%20the%20Metaverse.pdf

Isharyani, M., Sopha, B., Wibisono, A., & Tjahjono, B. (2023). Retail Technology Adaptation in Traditional Retailers: A Technology-to-Performance Chain Perspective. *Journal of Open Innovation*. Advance online publication. DOI: 10.1016/j.joitmc.2023.100204

Jagabathula, S., Mitrofanov, D., & Vulcano, G. (2022). Personalized Retail Promotions Through a Directed Acyclic Graph-Based Representation of Customer Preferences. *Operations Research*, *70*, 641–665. DOI: 10.1287/opre.2021.2108

Jang, W., Kim, S., Chun, J. W., Jung, A. R., & Kim, H. (2023). Role of recommendation sizes and travel involvement in evaluating travel destination recommendation services: Comparison between artificial intelligence and travel experts. *Journal of Hospitality and Tourism Technology*, *14*(3), 401–415.

Japutra, A., Utami, A., Molinillo, S., & Ekaputra, I. (2020). Influence of customer application experience and value in use on loyalty toward retailers. *Journal of Retailing and Consumer Services, 102390*. Advance online publication. DOI: 10.1016/j.jretconser.2020.102390

Jha, D., Rauniyar, A., Johansen, H. D., Johansen, D., Riegler, M. A., Halvorsen, P., & Bagci, U. (2022). Video Analytics in Elite Soccer: A Distributed Computing Perspective. *Proceedings of the IEEE Sensor Array and Multichannel Signal Processing Workshop, 2022-June*(ii), 221–225. https://doi.org/DOI: 10.1109/SAM53842.2022.9827827

Jin, H. S., & Song, E. J. (2021). A study on the future development direction of the virtual world metaverse industry. In *Proceedings of the Korean Institute of Information and Communication Sciences Conference*, 432–433.

Johnson, G., Whittington, R., Scholes, K., Angwin, D., & Regner, P. (2020). *Exploring Corporate Strategy: Text and Cases* (12th ed.). Pearson Education.

Juárez-Varón, D., & Juárez-Varón, M. Á. (2024). SEO vs. UX in Web Design: Are Companies' Digital Marketing Strategies Correct? A Neurotechnological Study. [IJSSCI]. *International Journal of Software Science and Computational Intelligence*, *16*(1), 1–26. DOI: 10.4018/IJSSCI.342127

Jung, T., Dieck, M., Moorhouse, N., & Jung, T. (2018). Technological Innovations Transforming the Consumer Retail Experience: A Review of Literature. **, 133-143. https://doi.org/DOI: 10.1007/978-3-319-64027-3_10

Jyeniskhan, N., Shomenov, K., Ali, M. H., & Shehab, E. (2024). Exploring the integration of digital twin and additive manufacturing technologies. *International Journal of Lightweight Materials and Manufacture*, *7*(6), 860–881. DOI: 10.1016/j.ijlmm.2024.06.004

Katsoulakis, E., Wang, Q., Wu, H., Shahriyari, L., Fletcher, R., Liu, J., Achenie, L., Liu, H., Jackson, P., Xiao, Y., Syeda-Mahmood, T., Tuli, R., & Deng, J. (2024). Digital twins for health: A scoping review. npj. *Digital Medicine*, *7*(1), 77. PMID: 38519626

Kaur, S. (2024). Adidas: Pioneering digital innovation. Retrieved from https://www.slideshare.net/slideshow/adidas-pioneering-digital-innovation-mrk634ztt/273345128

Kaushik, M., & Sharma, M. (2023). *Personalization in Marketing: Customizing the Customer Experience for Greater Engagement*. International Journal For Multidisciplinary Research., DOI: 10.36948/ijfmr.2023.v05i06.11194

Khamaj, M., & Ali, S. (2024). Adapting user experience with reinforcement learning. *Alexandria Engineering Journal*, *90*, 925–934. DOI: 10.1016/j.aej.2024.03.045

Kieanwatana, K., & Vongvit, R. (2024). Virtual reality in tourism: The impact of virtual experiences and destination image on the travel intention. *Results in Engineering*, *24*, 103650. DOI: 10.1016/j.rineng.2024.103650

Kim, J. H., Kim, J., Kang, H., & Youn, B. Y. (2025). Ethical implications of artificial intelligence in sport: A systematic scoping review. *Journal of Sport and Health Science*, *14*(MI), 101047. https://doi.org/DOI: 10.1016/j.jshs.2025.101047

Kim, Y. (2025). Not just for play: Why the metaverse should be leveraged for cocreation. *Business Horizons*, *68*(1), 45–54. DOI: 10.1016/j.bushor.2023.11.002

Kim, Y., & Xiong, S. (2022). The pseudo haptic button for mid air interaction with virtual content in mixed reality. *International Journal of Human-Computer Studies*, *164*, 102907. DOI: 10.1016/j.ijhcs.2022.102907

Klaus, P. (2013). The case of Amazon.com: Towards a conceptual framework of online customer service experience (OCSE) using the emerging consensus technique. *Journal of Services Marketing*, *27*(6), 443–457.

Klaus, P., & Kuppelwieser, V. (2022). A glimpse of the future retail customer experience – Guidelines for research and practice. *Journal of Retailing and Consumer Services*. Advance online publication. DOI: 10.1016/j.jretconser.2022.103205

Knott, P. J. (2015). Does VRIO help managers evaluate a firm's resources? *Management Decision*, *53*(8), 1806–1822. DOI: 10.1108/md-08-2014-0525

Kosiba, J., Boateng, H., Amartey, A., Boakye, R., & Hinson, R. (2018). Examining customer engagement and brand loyalty in retail banking. *International Journal of Retail & Distribution Management*. Advance online publication. DOI: 10.1108/IJRDM-08-2017-0163

Kotler, P., & Keller, K. L. (2019). *Marketing management* (15th ed.). Pearson.

Kour, R., Karim, R., Venkatesh, S. N., & Kumar, U. (2025). Metaverse in industrial contexts: A comprehensive review. *Frontiers in Virtual Reality*, *6*, 1488926. DOI: 10.3389/frvir.2025.1488926

KPMG. (2024, June 20). Discretionary spending hit as household cost pressures continue to mount. KPMG. https://kpmg.com/uk/en/media/press-releases/2024/06/discretionary-spending-hit-as-household-cost-pressures-continue-to-mount.html

Krüger, K., Weking, J., Fielt, E., Böttcher, T., Kowalkiewicz, M., & Krcmar, H. (2025). Value drivers for Metaverse business models: A complementor perspective. *Journal of Management Information Systems*, *42*(1), 143–173.

Kshetri, N. (2022). The economics of the metaverse: Business models, technological developments, and challenges. *IT Professional*, *24*(1), 62–67.

Kulkarni, C., Quraishi, A., Raparthi, M., Sharma, A., & Gupta, N. (2024). Hybrid disease prediction approach leveraging digital twin and metaverse technologies for health consumer. *BMC Medical Informatics and Decision Making*, *24*, 92. PMID: 38575951

Kumar, S., Talukder, M. B., & Pego, A. (Eds.). (2024). *Utilizing smart technology and AI in hybrid tourism and hospitality*. IGI Global.

Kumar, V., Aksoy, L., Donkers, B., Venkatesan, R., Wiesel, T., & Tillmanns, S. (2021). Undervalued or overvalued customers: Capturing total customer engagement value. *Journal of Service Research*, *24*(2), 220–239. DOI: 10.1177/1094670517709588

Kye, B., Han, N., Kim, M., Park, Y., & Jo, S. (2021). Educational applications of metaverse: Possibilities and limitations. *Journal of Educational Evaluation for Health Professions*, •••, 18.

Laborde, O. (2022, March 25). 3 raisons de vous intéresser au métavers - Harvard Business Review France. HBR France. https://www.hbrfrance.fr/innovation/3-raisons-de-vous-interesser-au-metavers-45420

Lal, A., Dang, J., Nabzdyk, C., Gajic, O., & Herasevich, V. (2022). Regulatory oversight and ethical concerns surrounding software as medical device (SaMD) and digital twin technology in healthcare. *Annals of Translational Medicine*, *10*(18), 950. PMID: 36267783

Lambillotte, L., Magrofuoco, N., Poncin, I., & Vanderdonckt, J. (2022). Enhancing playful customer experience with personalization. *Journal of Retailing and Consumer Services*. Advance online publication. DOI: 10.1016/j.jretconser.2022.103017

Lavie, N. (2005). Distracted and confused? Selective attention under load. *Trends in Cognitive Sciences*, *9*(2), 75–82. DOI: 10.1016/j.tics.2004.12.004

LCG. (2024). TravelBI by Turismo de Portugal - Tourism Receipts. Turismodeportugal.pt. https://travelbi.turismodeportugal.pt/en/tourism-in-portugal/tourism-receipts/

Lee, L.-H., Braud, T., Zhou, P. Y., Wang, L., Xu, D., Lin, Z., Kumar, A., Bermejo, C., & Hui, P. (2021). All one needs to know about metaverse: A complete survey on technological singularity, virtual ecosystem, and research agenda. 14(8), 1–64. https://doi.org/DOI: 10.13140/RG.2.2.11200.05124/8

Lee, Z., Chan, T., Chong, A., & Thadani, D. (2019). Customer engagement through omnichannel retailing: The effects of channel integration quality. *Industrial Marketing Management*. Advance online publication. DOI: 10.1016/J.INDMARMAN.2018.12.004

Lemon, K. N., & Verhoef, P. C. (2016). Understanding customer experience throughout the customer journey. *Journal of Marketing*, *80*(6), 69–96.

Libby, W. L., Lacey, B. C., & Lacey, J. I. (1973). Pupillary and cardiac activity during visual attention. *Psychophysiology*, *10*(3), 270–294. DOI: 10.1111/j.1469-8986.1973.tb00526.x

Liberato, P., Pereira, D., Liberato, D., & Lopes, M. C. (2023, November). Technology applications in the competitiveness of tourism destinations. In *International Conference on Tourism, Technology and Systems* (pp. 471-482). Singapore: Springer Nature Singapore.

Li, L.-F., Wang, X., Hu, W.-J., Xiong, N. N., Du, Y.-X., & Li, B.-S. (2020). Deep Learning in Skin Disease Image Recognition: A Review. *IEEE Access : Practical Innovations, Open Solutions*, *8*, 208264–208280. DOI: 10.1109/ACCESS.2020.3037258

Lim, J. Z., Mountstephens, J., & Teo, J. (2020). Emotion recognition using eye tracking: Taxonomy, review and current challenges. *Sensors (Basel)*, *20*(8), 2384. DOI: 10.3390/s20082384

Linder-Gaillard, I. (2021). Roman Catholic Art after L'Art Sacré and Vatican II. In *I. Linder-Gaillard, Oxford Research Encyclopedia of Religion*. Oxford University Press., DOI: 10.1093/acrefore/9780199340378.013.793

Ling, A., & Butakov, S. (2024). Trust framework for self-sovereign identity in metaverse healthcare applications. *Data Science and Management*, *7*(4), 304–313. DOI: 10.1016/j.dsm.2024.04.003

Liu, A., Mahapatra, R. P., & Mayuri, A. V. R. (2023). Hybrid design for sports data visualization using AI and big data analytics. *Complex & Intelligent Systems*, *9*(3), 2969–2980. DOI: 10.1007/s40747-021-00557-w

Liu, L., & Zhang, X. (2022). A Focused Review on the Flexible Wearable Sensors for Sports: From Kinematics to Physiologies. *Micromachines*, *13*(8). Advance online publication. DOI: 10.3390/mi13081356 PMID: 36014277

Liu, M., Fang, S., Dong, H., & Xu, C. (2021). Review of digital twin about concepts, technologies, and industrial applications. *Journal of Manufacturing Systems*, *58*, 346–361. DOI: 10.1016/j.jmsy.2020.06.017

Li, Y., Gunasekeran, D. V., & Chandran, N. R.. (2023). The next generation of healthcare ecosystem in the metaverse. *Biomedical Journal*, *47*(3), 100679. PMID: 38048990

Llywelyn, D. (2022, April 30). Global Christianity: the Future of the Catholic Church. Institute for Advanced Catholic Studies at USC. https://dornsife.usc.edu/iacs/2022/04/30/global-christianity/

Lu, H., Cheng, H., Tzou, J., & Chen, C. (2023). Technology roadmap of AI applications in the retail industry. *Technological Forecasting and Social Change*. Advance online publication. DOI: 10.1016/j.techfore.2023.122778

Lukač, L., Fister, I., & Fister, I. (2022). Digital Twin in Sport: From an Idea to Realization. *Applied Sciences (Switzerland)*, *12*(24). Advance online publication. DOI: 10.3390/app122412741

Lukita, C., Pangilinan, G. A., Chakim, M. H. R., & Saputra, D. B. (2023). Examining the impact of artificial intelligence and internet of things on smart tourism destinations: A comprehensive study. [ATT]. *Aptisi Transactions on Technopreneurship*, *5*(2sp), 135–145.

Lusch, R. F., Vargo, S. L., & O'Brien, M. (2007). Competing through service: Insights from service-dominant logic. *Journal of Retailing*, *83*(1), 5–18. DOI: 10.1016/j.jretai.2006.10.002

Lu, Y., Liu, C., Wang, K. I. K., Huang, H., & Xu, X. (2020). Digital Twin driven smart manufacturing: Connotation, reference model, applications and research issues. *Robotics and Computer-integrated Manufacturing*, *61*, 101837. DOI: 10.1016/j.rcim.2019.101837

M.Mandaliya, D. (2025). Digital Marketing Strategies and Customer Engagement in the Online Retail Industry. *International Journal on Science and Technology*. https://doi.org/DOI: 10.71097/ijsat.v16.i1.2494

Maathuis, C., Cidota, M. A., Datcu, D., & Marin, L. (2025). Integrating explainable artificial intelligence in extended reality environments: A systematic survey. *Mathematics*, *13*(2), 290. DOI: 10.3390/math13020290

Majumdar, A., Bakirov, R., Hodges, D., Scott, S., & Rees, T. (2022). Machine Learning for Understanding and Predicting Injuries in Football. *Sports Medicine - Open*, *8*(1). Advance online publication. DOI: 10.1186/s40798-022-00465-4 PMID: 35670925

Ma, M., Li, Y., & Gao, L.. (2023). The need for digital health education among next-generation health workers in China: A cross-sectional survey on digital health education. *BMC Medical Education*, *23*, 541. PMID: 37525126

Mamen, A., Kovaçi, S., Montanaro, T., Sergi, I., & Patrono, L. (2024). A Digital Twin Architecture for Minimizing Injuries Risks with Personalized Regimens via IoT and Machine Learning. *2024 9th International Conference on Smart and Sustainable Technologies (SpliTech)*, 1–5. https://doi.org/DOI: 10.23919/SpliTech61897.2024.10612411

Manshad, M. S., & Brannon, D. (2021). Haptic-payment: Exploring vibration feedback as a means of reducing overspending in mobile payment. *Journal of Business Research*, *122*, 88–96. DOI: 10.1016/j.jbusres.2020.08.049

Marabelli, M., & Newell, S. (2023). Responsibly strategizing with the metaverse: Business implications and DEI opportunities and challenges. *The Journal of Strategic Information Systems*, *32*(2), 101774. DOI: 10.1016/j.jsis.2023.101774

Mariana, C. D., Husodo, Z. A., Ekaputra, I. A., & Fahlevi, M. (2025). The advancement of digital payment ecosystem in metaverse: A literature review. *Computers in Human Behavior Reports*, *17*, 100570. DOI: 10.1016/j.chbr.2024.100570

Marquina, M., Lozano, D., García-Sánchez, C., Sánchez-López, S., & de la Rubia, A. (2023). Development and Validation of an Observational Game Analysis Tool with Artificial Intelligence for Handball: Handball.ai. *Sensors (Basel)*, *23*(15). Advance online publication. DOI: 10.3390/s23156714 PMID: 37571498

Martínez-Gutiérrez, A., Díez-González, J., Perez, H., & Araújo, M. (2024). Towards industry 5.0 through metaverse. *Robotics and Computer-integrated Manufacturing*, *89*, 102764. https://doi.org/https://doi.org/10.1016/j.rcim.2024.102764

Mateus, N., Abade, E., Coutinho, D., Gómez, M. Á., Peñas, C. L., & Sampaio, J. (2025). Empowering the Sports Scientist with Artificial Intelligence in Training, Performance, and Health Management. *Sensors (Basel)*, *25*(1), 4–6. DOI: 10.3390/s25010139 PMID: 39796930

Mathôt, S. (2018). Pupillometry: Psychology, physiology, and function. *Journal of Cognition*, *1*(1), 16. Advance online publication. DOI: 10.5334/joc.18

Mbata, Akachukwu & Soyege, Olakunle & Nwokedi, Collins & Tomoh, Busayo & Mustapha, Ashiata & Balogun, Obe & Forkuo, Adelaide & Iguma, Dorothy & Pub, Anfo. (2024). Preventative Medicine and Chronic Disease Management: Reducing Healthcare Costs and Improving Long-Term Public Health. International Journal of Multidisciplinary Research and Growth Evaluation. 05. 1584-1600. 10.54660/.IJMRGE.2024.5.6.1584-1600.

McAlexander, J. H., Schouten, J. W., & Koenig, H. F. (2002). Building brand community. *Journal of Marketing*, *66*(1), 38–54.

McKinsey & Company. (2022, August 17). What is the metaverse and where will it lead next? Www.mckinsey.com

McKinsey & Company. (2024, June 7). Digital transformation: Health systems' investment priorities. https://www.mckinsey.com/industries/healthcare/our-insights/digital-transformation-health-systems-investment-priorities

McKinsey & Company. https://www.mckinsey.com/featured-insights/mckinsey-explainers/what-is-the-metaverse

Mehra, P., & Kansra, P. (2024). Fostering gratifying customer experiences through the art of visual content and storytelling. In Shukla, R., & Pal, S. (Eds.), *Multidisciplinary applications of extended reality for human experience* (pp. 401–423). IGI Global., DOI: 10.4018/978-1-6684-9886-4.ch016

Meiji Japan and The Imperial Rule: A Symbiotic Encounter. (2022). *Asian Journal of Research in Education and Social Sciences*. https://doi.org/DOI: 10.55057/ajress.2022.4.1.26

Mekki, Y. M., Luijten, G., Hagert, E., Belkhair, S., Varghese, C., Qadir, J., Solaiman, B., Bilal, M., Dhanda, J., Egger, J., Deng, J., Khanduja, V., Frangi, A. F., Zughaier, S. M., & Stotland, M. A. (2025). Digital twins for the era of personalized surgery. npj. *Digital Medicine*, *8*(1), 283. PMID: 40374901

Meyer, C., & Schwager, A. (2007). Understanding customer experience. *Harvard Business Review*, *85*(2), 116–126.

Mishra, D., Das, S., & Patnaik, R. (2024). Application of AI technology for the development of destination tourism towards an intelligent information system. *Economic Affairs*, *69*(2), 1083–1095.

Mittal, B., & Lassar, W. (1996). The role of personalization in service encounters. *Journal of Retailing*, *72*, 95–109. DOI: 10.1016/S0022-4359(96)90007-X

Mittal, R., & Sinha, P. (2021). Framework for a resilient religious tourism supply chain for mitigating post-pandemic risk. *International Hospitality Review*, *36*(2). Advance online publication. DOI: 10.1108/ihr-09-2020- 0053

Mizels, J., Erickson, B., & Chalmers, P. (2022). Current State of Data and Analytics Research in Baseball. *Current Reviews in Musculoskeletal Medicine*, *15*(4), 283–290. DOI: 10.1007/s12178-022-09763-6 PMID: 35486325

Mogili, R., & Natarajan, T. (2021). Online Retailing and Customer Engagement. **, 184-195. https://doi.org/DOI: 10.4018/978-1-7998-3919-4.CH010

Mohamed Saed Mohamed Farahat, E., Ezzat Mohamed, M., & Samir, B. (2022). Artificial intelligence applications and its impact on the competitiveness of the Egyptian tourist destination. *11*(2), 57.

Molinillo, S., Aguilar-Illescas, R., Anaya-Sánchez, R., & Carvajal-Trujillo, E. (2021). The customer retail app experience: Implications for customer loyalty. *Journal of Retailing and Consumer Services*. Advance online publication. DOI: 10.1016/j.jretconser.2021.102842

Monferrer, D., Moliner, M., & Estrada, M. (2019). Increasing customer loyalty through customer engagement in the retail banking industry. *Spanish Journal of Marketing - ESIC*. Advance online publication. DOI: 10.1108/sjme-07-2019-0042

Moslehpour, M., Dwikesumasari, P. R., Pappachan, P., Lin, P.-K., Sakina, N., & Rahaman, M. (2024). Incorporating Web Semantics, the Technology Acceptance Model, and the Theory of Planned Behavior for Analyzing User Intentions on Dating Apps. [IJSWIS]. *International Journal on Semantic Web and Information Systems*, *20*(1), 1–20. DOI: 10.4018/IJSWIS.356388

Mourtzis, D. (2023). Digital twin inception in the Era of industrial metaverse. *Frontiers in Manufacturing Technology*, *3*, 1155735. DOI: 10.3389/fmtec.2023.1155735

Mourtzis, D. (2023b). The Metaverse in Industry 5.0: A Human-Centric Approach towards Personalized Value Creation. *Encyclopedia, 3*(3), 1105–1120. DOI: 10.3390/encyclopedia3030080

Mourtzis, D. (2024). 15 - Outlook, trends, and future directions toward Industry 5.0. In Mourtzis, D. (Ed.), *Manufacturing from Industry 4.0 to Industry 5.0* (pp. 465–492). Elsevier., https://doi.org/https://doi.org/10.1016/B978-0-443-13924-6.00015-6

Mourtzis, D., & Angelopoulos, J. (2023). Development of an Extended Reality-Based Collaborative Platform for Engineering Education: Operator 5.0. *Electronics (Switzerland), 12*(17). Advance online publication. DOI: 10.3390/electronics12173663

Moztarzadeh, O., Jamshidi, M. B., Sargolzaei, S., Jamshidi, A., Baghalipour, N., Malekzadeh Moghani, M., & Hauer, L. (2023). Metaverse and healthcare: Machine learning-enabled digital twins of cancer. *Bioengineering (Basel, Switzerland), 10*(4), 455. PMID: 37106642

Mumtaz, H., Khan, M., Irfan, M., & Alam, S. (2023). Current challenges and potential solutions to the use of digital health technologies. *Frontiers in Digital Health, 5*, 1203945. PMID: 37840685

Muniz, A. M., & O'Guinn, T. C. (2001). Brand community. *The Journal of Consumer Research, 27*(4), 412–432. DOI: 10.1086/319618

Muposhi, A., Dhurup, M., Surujlal, J., & Maramura, T. C. (2015). Thematic content analysis of customer experience in shopping malls. *Journal of Contemporary Management, 12*(1), 445–467.

Muruganantham, G., & Patro, U. S. (2025). Role of Technology for Sustainable Growth of Religious Tourism. In Tyagi, P. K., Sharma, N., Singh, P., & Bhatt, V. (Eds.), *Technology and Religious Tourism: Emerging Trends, Cases and Futuristic Perspectives* (pp. 25–48). Emerald Publishing Limited., DOI: 10.1108/978-1-83662-260-420251003

Musat, C. L., Mereuta, C., Nechita, A., Tutunaru, D., Voipan, A. E., Voipan, D., Mereuta, E., Gurau, T. V., Gurău, G., & Nechita, L. C. (2024). Diagnostic Applications of AI in Sports: A Comprehensive Review of Injury Risk Prediction Methods. *Diagnostics (Basel), 14*(22), 1–23. DOI: 10.3390/diagnostics14222516 PMID: 39594182

Musso, F., & Adam, R. (2020). Retailing 4.0 and Technology-Driven Innovation. **, 338-354. https://doi.org/DOI: 10.4018/978-1-7998-1412-2.ch015

Mystakidis, S. (2022).. . *Metaverse. Encyclopedia, 2*(1), 486–497.

Naranjo, J. E., Sanchez, D. G., Robalino Lopez, A., Robalino Lopez, P., Alarcon Ortiz, A., & Garcia, M. V. (2020). A scoping review on virtual reality based industrial training. *Applied Sciences (Basel, Switzerland), 10*(22), 8224. DOI: 10.3390/app10228224

Ng, J. Y. Y., Ntoumanis, N., Thøgersen-Ntoumani, C., Deci, E. L., Ryan, R. M., Duda, J. L., & Williams, G. C. (2012). Self-Determination Theory Applied to Health Contexts: A Meta-Analysis. *Perspectives on Psychological Science*, *7*(4), 325–340. PMID: 26168470

Nijjer, S., Singh, J., Sharma, P., Malhotra, M., & Verma, R. (2023). Unraveling a new age of travel in blockchain based metaverse. In *Mobile Radio Communications and 5G Networks: Proceedings of Third MRCN 2022* (pp. 555-570). Singapore: Springer Nature Singapore.

Nowak, K. L., & Fox, J. (2018). Avatars and computer-mediated communication: A review of the definitions, uses, and effects of digital representations. *Review of Communication Research*, *6*, 30–53.

Nyhan, P. (2024, December 5). 6 AI trends you'll see more of in 2025. Microsoft. https://news.microsoft.com/source/features/ai/6-ai-trends-youll-see-more-of-in-2025/

OECD. (2023). [OECD Indicators. Organisation for Economic Co-operation and Development.]. *Health at a Glance*, •••, 2023.

Ohlan, R., & Ohlan, A. (2024). Religious tourism scholarship: Current state and future research directions. *Journal of Islamic Marketing*, *15*(3), 800–818. DOI: 10.1108/jima-05-2023-0152

Oliver, R. L. (1999). Whence consumer loyalty? *Journal of Marketing*, *63*(4), 33–44.

Omuya, H., Kuo, W.-C., & Chewning, B. (2025). Innate psychological needs of autonomy, competence, and provider communication as determinants of patients' satisfaction and self-rated health. *International Journal for Quality in Health Care : Journal of the International Society for Quality in Health Care*. PMID: 40235312

Oró, E., Taddeo, P., & Salom, J. E. (2019). Waste heat recovery from urban air cooled data centres to increase energy efficiency of district heating networks. *Sustainable Cities and Society*, *45*, 522–542. DOI: 10.1016/j.scs.2018.12.012

Osello, A., Manera, U., Rimella, N., Bin, C., Vasta, R., Masala, E., Shields, J. A. E., Tarantola, G., & Chiò, A. (2024). A Metaverse Between Technical and Humanistic Domains to Reach Society 5.0. *2024 IEEE International Humanitarian Technologies Conference (IHTC)*, 1–6. https://doi.org/DOI: 10.1109/IHTC61819.2024.10855137

Our World in Data. (2025). How old are you compared to most people? Our World in Data. https://ourworldindata.org/grapher/median-age?time=1950.latest&country=~OWID_WRL

Ozcan, S., Homayounfard, A., Simms, C., & Wasim, J. (2021). Technology Roadmapping Using Text Mining: A Foresight Study for the Retail Industry. *IEEE Transactions on Engineering Management, 69*, 228–244. DOI: 10.1109/TEM.2021.3068310

Page, M. J., McKenzie, J. E., & Bossuyt, P. M.. (2021). The PRISMA 2020 statement: An updated guideline for reporting systematic reviews. *BMJ (Clinical Research Ed.), 372*(71). PMID: 33782057

Pahl, J., Rieger, I., Möller, A., Wittenberg, T., & Schmid, U. (2022). Female, white, 27? Bias evaluation on data and algorithms for affect recognition in faces. In *Proceedings of the 2022 ACM Conference on Fairness, Accountability, and Transparency (FAccT '22)* (15 pages). Association for Computing Machinery. DOI: 10.1145/3531146.3533159

Panda, D. K., Panigrahi, P. K., Attar, R. W., & Gupta, B. B. (2024). Open Source Adoption for Digital Transformation and Data Management During the COVID-19 Crisis. [JDM]. *Journal of Database Management, 35*(1), 1–26. DOI: 10.4018/JDM.360708

Pansari, A., & Kumar, V. (2017). Customer engagement: The construct, antecedents, and consequences. *Journal of the Academy of Marketing Science, 45*(3), 294–311. DOI: 10.1007/s11747-016-0485-6

Pantano, E., Pizzi, G., Scarpi, D., & Dennis, C. (2017). Competing during a pandemic? Retailers' ups and downs during the COVID-19 outbreak. *Journal of Business Research, 116*, 209–213. DOI: 10.1016/j.jbusres.2020.05.036

Pantano, E., & Priporas, C. (2016). The effect of mobile retailing on consumers' purchasing experiences: A dynamic perspective. *Computers in Human Behavior, 61*, 548–555. DOI: 10.1016/j.chb.2016.03.071

Pantano, E., & Vannucci, V. (2019). Who is innovating? An exploratory research of digital technologies diffusion in retail industry. *Journal of Retailing and Consumer Services, 49*, 297–304. DOI: 10.1016/j.jretconser.2019.01.019

Parihar, P., Dawra, J., & Sahay, V. (2019). The role of customer engagement in the involvement-loyalty link. *Marketing Intelligence & Planning*. Advance online publication. DOI: 10.1108/MIP-11-2017-0318

Pekgor, M., & Toros, T. (2024). *Wearable Sensors in Sports and Healthcare: Technological Advancements, Applications, and. November.*

Perumal, S., Qing, Y., & Jaganathan, M. (2022). Factors influencing attitudes and intentions towards smart retail technology. *International Journal of Data and Network Science*. https://doi.org/DOI: 10.5267/j.ijdns.2021.11.005

Petermans, A., Janssens, W., & Cleempoel, K. (2013). A Holistic Framework for Conceptualizing Customer Experiences in Retail Environments. *International Journal of Design*, •••, 7.

Peteva, V. (2023). *The Personalization in Modern Retailing*. Izvestia Journal of the Union of Scientists - Varna. Economic Sciences Series., DOI: 10.56065/ijusv-ess/2023.12.3.62

Peteva, V. (2024). *The Personalization in Retailing - Problems and Challenges*. Izvestia Journal of the Union of Scientists - Varna Economic Sciences Series., DOI: 10.56065/ijusv-ess/2024.13.2.69

Phattanaviroj, T., Moslehpour, M., Pappachan, P., Cajes, N. C., Gupta, B. B., & Rahaman, M. (2026). A novel predictive framework for green transportation and EV policy towards sustainable mobility and emission reduction. *Green Technologies and Sustainability*, *4*(1), 100260. DOI: 10.1016/j.grets.2025.100260

Pietraszewski, P., Terbalyan, A., Roczniok, R., Maszczyk, A., Ornowski, K., Manilewska, D., Kuli, S., & Zaj, A. (2025). *The Role of Artificial Intelligence in Sports Analytics: A Systematic Review and Meta-Analysis of Performance Trends*. 1–21.

Pine, B. J., & Gilmore, J. H. (2011). The experience economy (Updated ed.). Harvard Business Review Press.

Pine, B. J., & Gilmore, J. H. (1998). Welcome to the experience economy. *Harvard Business Review*, *76*(4), 97–105. PMID: 10181589

Piskorski, J., Stefanovitch, N., Da San Martino, G., & Nakov, P. (2023, July). SemEval-2023 task 3: Detecting the category, the framing, and the persuasion techniques in online news in a multi-lingual setup. In *Proceedings of the 17th International Workshop on Semantic Evaluation (SemEval-2023)*, 2343–2361.

Pomeroy, R. (2023, August 29). A surprising explanation for the global decline of religion. Big Think. https://bigthink.com/the-present/a-surprising-explanation-for-the-global-decline-of-religion/ Popp-Baier, U. (2010). From Religion to Spirituality—Megatrend in Contemporary Society or Methodological Artefact? A Contribution to the Secularization Debate from Psychology of Religion. Journal of Religion in Europe, 3(1), 34–67. https://doi.org/DOI: 10.1163/187489209x478337

Porter, M. E. (1985). *Competitive advantage: Creating and sustaining superior performance*. Free Press.

Prabadevi, B., Deepa, N., Victor, N., Reddy Gadekallu, T., Kumar, P., Maddikunta, R., Yenduri, G., Wang, W., Pham, V., Huynh-The, T., Liyanage, M., & Huynh, T. (2023). Metaverse for Industry 5.0 in NextG Communications: Potential Applications and Future Challenges.

Puccinelli, N., Goodstein, R., Grewal, D., Price, R., Raghubir, P., & Stewart, D. (2009). Customer Experience Management in Retailing: Understanding the Buying Process. *Journal of Retailing*, *85*, 15–30. DOI: 10.1016/J.JRETAI.2008.11.003

Purkayastha, D., & Sharma, R. (2023). Consumer-centric innovation in the metaverse: Personalization and value creation. *Journal of Marketing Trends*, *10*(1), 55–70.

Rahaman, M., Chappu, B., Jana, S., Haque, A., Firmansyah, G., & Chattopadhyay, S. (2025). Security Benefits in Small Medium Business Enterprise Through Cloud Adoption. In N. Nedjah, G. Martinez Perez, & B. B. Gupta (Eds.), *International Conference on Smart Systems and Advanced Computing (SysCom 2022)* (pp. 168–180). Springer Nature Switzerland. https://doi.org/DOI: 10.1007/978-3-031-40905-9_18

Rahaman, M., Chattopadhyay, S., & Anwar, N. (2022). *A Case Study: Physical Layer Security Analysis for Internet of Vehicle (IoV)*. 283–291.

Rahaman, M., Lin, C. Y., Rachmat, I., Bansal, R., & Prayitno. (2024). Secure Health Features: Implementing Hyperledger Fabric in Blockchain-Driven Healthcare Management Systems. In *Digital Forensics and Cyber Crime Investigation*. CRC Press.

Rahaman, M., Bakkireddygari, S. S., Chattopadhyay, S., Gomez, A. L., Arya, V., & Bansal, S. (2024). Infrastructure and Network Security. In *Metaverse Security Paradigms* (pp. 108–144). IGI Global Scientific Publishing., DOI: 10.4018/979-8-3693-3824-7.ch005

Rahaman, M., Cajes, N., Gupta, B. B., Chui, K. T., & Nedjah, N. (2025). Defending against smishing attacks: State-of-the-art techniques, challenges, limitations, and future directions. *Computer Networks*, *273*, 111758. DOI: 10.1016/j.comnet.2025.111758

Rahartomo, A., Merino, L., & Ghafari, M. (2025). Metaverse security and privacy research: A systematic review. *Computers & Security*, *157*, 104602. DOI: 10.1016/j.cose.2025.104602

Rahman, E. Z., Aziz, S., Shah, S. B. A., & Asrifan, A. (2024). The Effect of the Regenerative Tourism Movement on the Global Industry and the Role of Artificial Intelligence. In *The Role of Artificial Intelligence in Regenerative Tourism and Green Destinations* (pp. 165–183). Emerald Publishing Limited.

Rahmani, M., Majedi, N., Hemmatinejad, M., & Jamshidi, A. (2024). Application of Artificial Intelligence in the Sports Industry: A Review Article. *AI and Tech in Behavioral and Social Sciences*, *2*(2), 20–27. DOI: 10.61838/kman.aitech.2.2.4

Rajput, D., Singh, S. K., Kumar, S., Vashisht, H., Chui, K. T., & Gupta, B. B. (2024). SentinelMet: Enhancing Metaverse Security through Deep Learning Techniques in 6G. In *2024 IEEE International Conference on Advanced Networks and Telecommunications Systems, ANTS 2024* (International Symposium on Advanced Networks and Telecommunication Systems, ANTS). https://doi.org/DOI: 10.1109/ANTS63515.2024.10898831

Ramonde, T. (2025, January 30). The Camino de Santiago Statistics for 2024. Follow the Camino. https://followthecamino.com/en/camino-de-santiago-statistics- 2024/

Rane, N. L., Choudhary, S., & Rane, J. (2023, November 28). Metaverse for enhancing customer loyalty: Effective strategies to improve customer relationship, service, engagement, satisfaction, and experience. SSRN Electronic Journal. https://doi.org/DOI: 10.2139/ssrn.4624197

Rane, N., Choudhary, S., & Rane, J. (2023). Sustainable tourism development using leading-edge artificial intelligence (AI), blockchain, internet of things (IoT), augmented reality (AR) and virtual reality (VR) technologies. *Blockchain, Internet of Things (IoT), Augmented Reality (AR) and Virtual Reality (VR) technologies (October 31, 2023).*

Ranjan, K. R., & Read, S. (2021). An ecosystem perspective synthesis of co creation research. *Industrial Marketing Management*, *99*, 79–96. DOI: 10.1016/j.indmarman.2021.10.002

Rathi, K., Somani, P., Koul, A. V., & Manu, K. S. (2020). Applications of Artificial Intelligence in the Game of Football: The Global Perspective. *Research World*, *11*(2), 18–29.

Rawat, D. B. alami, H. El, & Hagos, D. H. (2024). Metaverse Survey & Tutorial: Exploring Key Requirements, Technologies, Standards, Applications, Challenges, and Perspectives. https://arxiv.org/abs/2405.04718

Reejo, R. J. (2020). Adoption of artificial intelligence and augmented reality for smart tourism in Kerala.

Ren, Z., Tian, J., Kang, S., Tang, M., & Tian, J. (2024). Personalized pricing versus showrooming: Competition between online and offline retailers. *International Transactions in Operational Research*, *31*, 3371–3442. DOI: 10.1111/itor.13444

Rethlefsen, M. L., Murad, M. H., & Livingston, E. H. (2021). Engaging medical librarians to improve the quality of review articles. *Academic Medicine*, *96*(2), 207–211.

Richter, S. M., & Richter, A. (2023). What is novel about the Metaverse? *International Journal of Information Management*, *74*, 102684. DOI: 10.1016/j.ijinfomgt.2023.102684

Riegger, A., Klein, J., Merfeld, K., & Henkel, S. (2021). Technology-enabled personalization in retail stores: Understanding drivers and barriers. *Journal of Business Research*, *123*, 140–155. DOI: 10.1016/j.jbusres.2020.09.039

Ritala, P., Ruokonen, M., & Kostis, A. (2024). The metaverse flywheel: Creating value across physical and virtual worlds. *California Management Review*, *66*(4), 80–101. DOI: 10.1177/00081256241252700

Riva, G., Wiederhold, B. K., & Mantovani, F. (2021). Neuroscience of virtual reality: From virtual exposure to embodied medicine. *Cyberpsychology, Behavior, and Social Networking*, *22*(1), 82–96.

Romero, P. M., & Park, H. (2025, January 15). Exploring the impact of brand narrative engagement and social presence in branded virtual worlds. *International Textile and Apparel Association Annual Conference Proceedings*, 81(1). https://doi.org/DOI: 10.31274/itaa.18646

Roozen, I., & Katidis, P. (2019). The Importance of the Service and Shopping Customer Experience in a Retail Environment. *Journal of Relationship Marketing*, *18*, 247–279. DOI: 10.1080/15332667.2019.1619064

Roumeliotis, K. I. (n.d.). *A Review of Arti cial Intelligence in Sports: Applications*. Ethical Concerns, and Legal Frameworks.

Roy, S., Fellowa, R., Balaji, M., Sadeque, S., Nguyen, B., & Melewar, T. (2017). Constituents and consequences of smart customer experience in retailing. *Technological Forecasting and Social Change*, *124*, 257–270. DOI: 10.1016/J.TECHFORE.2016.09.022

Roy, S., Gruner, R., & Guo, J. (2020). Exploring customer experience, commitment, and engagement behaviours. *Journal of Strategic Marketing*, *30*, 45–68. DOI: 10.1080/0965254X.2019.1642937

Roy, S., Singh, G., Sadeque, S., Harrigan, P., & Coussement, K. (2023). Customer engagement with digitalized interactive platforms in retailing. *Journal of Business Research*. Advance online publication. DOI: 10.1016/j.jbusres.2023.114001

Rudek, M., Valle, A. P. R., & Bertolin, R. (2025). Building Realistic Environment from Computer Vision Approach Applied to Manufacturing Simulation in the Digital Twin Context. In Dassisti, M., Madani, K., & Panetto, H. (Eds.), *Innovative Intelligent Industrial Production and Logistics* (pp. 223–235). Springer Nature Switzerland.

Rust, R. T., Lemon, K. N., & Zeithaml, V. A. (2004). Return on marketing: Using customer equity to focus marketing strategy. *Journal of Marketing*, *68*(1), 109–127. DOI: 10.1509/jmkg.68.1.109.24030

S, S. K., HV, P., & Nandini, C. (2022). *A Survey on the application of Data Science And Analytics in the field of Organised Sports.*

Sachdeva, I., & Goel, S. (2015). Retail store environment and customer experience: A paradigm. *Journal of Fashion Marketing and Management*, *19*, 290–298. DOI: 10.1108/JFMM-03-2015-0021

Saini, M., Kumar, S., Singh, S. K., Bansal, A., Han, C., Gupta, B. B., & Psannis, K. (2025). Transforming User Experience in the Metaverse Through Emotional Intelligence and Affective Computing. In Gupta, B. (Ed.), *Unveiling Social Dynamics and Community Interaction in the Metaverse* (pp. 303–332). IGI Global Scientific Publishing., DOI: 10.4018/979-8-3693-8628-6.ch015

Saksena, N. (2024). Hyper-Personalization in Retail: Leveraging Data Science and Real-Time Streaming. *International Journal of Scientific Research in Computer Science, Engineering and Information Technology*. https://doi.org/DOI: 10.32628/cseit241061179

Saleem, M., Shah, M. J., Wajid, M., Akhter, M., & Malik, J. A. (2024). A Comprehensive Study of AI and IoT's Impact on Smart Tourism Destinations. *Journal of Computing & Biomedical Informatics.*

Salem, S., & Alanadoly, A. (2023). Driving customer engagement and citizenship behaviour in omnichannel retailing: Evidence from the fashion sector. *Spanish Journal of Marketing - ESIC*. Advance online publication. DOI: 10.1108/sjme-10-2022-0220

Santuario de Fátima. (2023a). Santuario de Fátima |Santuário de Fátima acolheu 6,8 milhões de peregrinos nas celebrações em 2023. Santuário de Fátima. https://www.fatima.pt/pt/news/santuario-de-fatima-acolheu-68-milhoes-de-peregrinos-nas-celebracoes-em-2023

Santuario de Fátima. (2023b, June 15). Santuario de Fátima |Em Fátima “temos um colo de mãe, e eu penso que a Igreja, independentemente do tempo que atravessa, tem de ser este colo.” Santuário de Fátima. https://www.fatima.pt/pt/news/em-fatima-temos-um-colo-de-mae-e-eu-penso-que-a-igreja-independentemente-do-tempo-que-atravessa-tem-de-ser-este-colo-2023-06-15

Scholdra, T., Wichmann, J., & Reinartz, W. (2023). Reimagining personalization in the physical store. *Journal of Retailing*, *99*(4), 563–579. DOI: 10.1016/j.jretai.2023.11.001

Seçkin, A. Ç., Ateş, B., & Seçkin, M. (2023). Review on Wearable Technology in Sports: Concepts, Challenges and Opportunities. *Applied Sciences (Switzerland)*, *13*(18). Advance online publication. DOI: 10.3390/app131810399

Sekti, B. A. (2025). Machine learning and artificial intelligence (AI) in manufacturing. In *Integrating Digital Innovation and Integrated Frameworks in Manufacturing* (pp. 255–292). https://doi.org/DOI: 10.4018/979-8-3373-1082-4.ch011

Sel, K., Osman, D., Zare, F., Shahrbabak, S. M., Brattain, L., Hahn, J. O., Inan, O. T., Mukkamala, R., Palmer, J., Paydarfar, D., Pettigrew, R. I., Quyyumi, A. A., Telfer, B., & Jafari, R. (2024). Building Digital Twins for Cardiovascular Health: From Principles to Clinical Impact. *Journal of the American Heart Association*, *13*(19). PMID: 39087582

Selvam, D. (2024, August). Securing digital identities: The synergy of information technology security, trust, and privacy. International Journal of Computer Science [IJCSEIT]. *Engineering and Information Technology*, *14*(5), 1–14. DOI: 10.5121/i

Setiawan, B. (2024). The Augmented Reality (AR) Based on Artificial Intellegence (AI) in Integrated Marketing Communication (IMC) in Tourism Villages. *Media Wisata*, *22*(2), 341–352.

Sheth, J. (2020). Impact of COVID-19 on consumer behavior: Will the old habits return or die? *Journal of Business Research*, *117*, 280–283. DOI: 10.1016/j.jbusres.2020.05.059

Shinde, K. A., & Olsen, D. H. (2022). Reframing the Intersections of Pilgrimage, Religious Tourism, and Sustainability. *Sustainability*, *15*(1), 461. DOI: 10.3390/su15010461

Shin, H., & Kang, J. (2024). How does the metaverse travel experience influence virtual and actual travel behaviors? Focusing on the role of telepresence and avatar identification. *Journal of Hospitality and Tourism Management*, *58*, 174–183. DOI: 10.1016/j.jhtm.2023.12.009

Sicilia, M., & Palazón, M. (2023). Developing customer engagement through communication consistency and channel coordination. *Spanish Journal of Marketing - ESIC*. Advance online publication. DOI: 10.1108/sjme-02-2022-0022

Silva, C., Luís, J., & Reis, M. (2023). Exploring Memorable Sacred Tourism Experiences and Place Attachment. International Journal of Religious Tourism and International Journal of Religious Tourism and Pilgrimage Pilgrimage, 11. https://doi.org/DOI: 10.21427/38P9-MC74

Sim, J. K., Xu, K. W., Jin, Y., Kim, J., Lee, J., & Choi, H. (2024). Designing an educational metaverse: A case study of NTUniverse. *Applied Sciences (Basel, Switzerland)*, *14*(6), 2559. DOI: 10.3390/app14062559

Simunaniemi, A. M., & Muhos, M. (2017). Thematic analysis of microenterprise growth constraints in the start-up and stabilization phases. *International Journal of Entrepreneurship and Small Business*, *31*(1), 30–55.

Sinek, S. (2009). *Start with why: How great leaders inspire everyone to take action*. Penguin.

Singh, S. K., Gupta, S., Kumar, S., Gupta, B. B., Alhalabi, W., Arya, V., & Zhang, J. (2024). A novel Cumulative Indicator score using Indicator averaging for optimizing local business websites of enterprise systems. *Enterprise Information Systems*, *18*(2), 2301658. DOI: 10.1080/17517575.2023.2301658

Singh, S. K., Kumar, S., Goyal, S., Arya, V., Attar, R. W., Gupta, B. B., Alhomoud, A., & Chui, K. T. (2025). Leveraging AI and Machine Learning for Enhanced Data Analytics and Visualization in Database Management With Digital Twins. [JDM]. *Journal of Database Management*, *36*(1), 1–29. DOI: 10.4018/JDM.388135

Singla, A., Gupta, N., Aeron, P., Jain, A., Garg, R., Sharma, D., Gupta, B. B., & Arya, V. (2022). Building the Metaverse: Design Considerations, Socio-Technical Elements, and Future Research Directions of Metaverse. [JGIM]. *Journal of Global Information Management*, *31*(2), 1–28. DOI: 10.4018/JGIM.321755

Slater, M., & Wilbur, S. (2006). A framework for immersive virtual environments (FIVE): Speculations on the role of presence in virtual environments. *Presence (Cambridge, Mass.)*, *6*(6), 603–616. DOI: 10.1162/pres.1997.6.6.603

Smaili, N., & de Rancourt-Raymond, A. (2022). Metaverse: Welcome to the new fraud marketplace. *Journal of Financial Crime*, *31*(1), 188–200. DOI: 10.1108/jfc-06-2022-0124

Smith, C. H.. (2025). The challenges of consent in a decentralised metaverse: A study of autonomy, disclosure, and design. *Frontiers in Virtual Reality, 1401073*. Advance online publication. DOI: 10.3389/frvir.2025.1401073

So, K., King, C., Sparks, B., & Wang, Y. (2016). Enhancing customer relationships with retail service brands: The role of customer engagement. *Journal of Service Management*, *27*, 170–193. DOI: 10.1108/JOSM-05-2015-0176

Sombultawee, K., & Tansakul, T. (2022). The customer experience in Thailand's multichannel retail environments. *Asia-Pacific Journal of Business Administration*. Advance online publication. DOI: 10.1108/apjba-08-2021-0427

Sony, M., Antony, J., & Tortorella, G. L. (2023). Critical success factors for successful implementation of Healthcare 4.0: A literature review and future research agenda. *International Journal of Environmental Research and Public Health*, *20*(5), 4669. PMID: 36901679

Sprevak, M., & Smith, R. (2023). An Introduction to Predictive Processing Models of Perception and Decision-Making. *Topics in Cognitive Science*. Advance online publication. DOI: 10.1111/tops.12704

Stauffert, J. P., Niebling, F., Latoschik, M. E., & Steinicke, F. (2020). Latency and cybersickness: Impact, causes, and measures. A review. *Frontiers in Virtual Reality*, *1*, 582204. DOI: 10.3389/frvir.2020.582204

Stephenson, N. (2003). *Snow crash*. Random House Publishing Group. (Original work published 1992)

Suanpang, P., & Pothipassa, P. (2024). Integrating Generative AI and IoT for Sustainable Smart Tourism Destinations. *Sustainability*, *16*(17), 7435.

Suh, I., McKinney, T., & Siu, K.-C. (2023). Current perspective of metaverse application in medical education, research and patient care. *Virtual Worlds*, *2*(2), 115–128.

Supriya, Y., Bhulakshmi, D., Bhattacharya, S., Gadekallu, T. R., Vyas, P., Kaluri, R., Sumathy, S., Koppu, S., Brown, D. J., & Mahmud, M. (2024). Industry 5.0 in Smart Education: Concepts, Applications, Challenges, Opportunities, and Future Directions. *IEEE Access : Practical Innovations, Open Solutions*, *12*, 81938–81967. DOI: 10.1109/ACCESS.2024.3401473

Tallat, R., Hawbani, A., Wang, X., Al-Dubai, A., Zhao, L., Liu, Z., Min, G., Zomaya, A. Y., & Alsamhi, S. H. (2024a). Navigating Industry 5.0: A Survey of Key Enabling Technologies, Trends, Challenges, and Opportunities. *IEEE Communications Surveys and Tutorials*, *26*(2), 1080–1126. DOI: 10.1109/COMST.2023.3329472

Talukder, M. B. (2020). An Appraisal of the Economic Outlook for the Tourism Industry, Specially Cox's Bazar in Bangladesh. *i-manager's Journal on Economics & Commerce,* 2(1), 23-35. https://doi.org/DOI: 10.26634/jecom.2.1.17285

Talukder, M. B., Kumar, S., Kaiser, F., & Mia, M. N. (2024). Pilgrimage Creative Tourism: A Gateway to Sustainable Development Goals in Bangladesh. In *Global Trends in Governance and Policy Paradigms* (pp. 285-300). IGI Global.

Talukder, M. B. (2020). The Future of Culinary Tourism: An Emerging Dimension for the Tourism Industry of Bangladesh. I-Manager's. *Journal of Management, 15*(1), 27. DOI: 10.26634/jmgt.15.1.17181

Talukder, M. B. (2024). Implementing artificial intelligence and virtual experiences in hospitality. In *Innovative technologies for increasing service productivity* (pp. 145–160). IGI Global.

Talukder, M. B. (2024). Implementing Artificial Intelligence and Virtual Experiences in Hospitality. In Manohar, S., Mittal, A., Raju, S., & Nair, A. J. (Eds.), *Advances in Hospitality, Tourism, and the Services Industry* (pp. 145–160). IGI Global., DOI: 10.4018/979-8-3693-2019-8.ch009

Talukder, M. B., Kabir, F., Kaiser, F., & Lina, F. Y. (2024). Digital detox movement in the tourism industry: Traveler perspective. In *Business drivers in promoting digital detoxification* (pp. 91–110). IGI Global Scientific Publishing.

Talukder, M. B., Kumar, S., & Das, I. R. (2024). Implications of blockchain technology-based cryptocurrency in the cloud for the hospitality industry. In *Emerging trends in cloud computing analytics, scalability, and service models* (pp. 340–358). IGI Global Scientific Publishing.

Talukder, M. B., Kumar, S., Sood, K., & Grima, S. (2023). Information Technology, Food Service Quality and Restaurant Revisit Intention. *International Journal of Sustainable Development and Planning, 18*(1).

Talukder, M. B., & Muhsina, K. (2024). Prospect of Smart Tourism Destination in Bangladesh. In *AI Innovations for Travel and Tourism* (pp. 163–179). IGI Global.

Tang, C., Yi, W., Zhang, Z., Occhipinti, E., Occhipinti, L. G., & Member, S. (2025). *AI-Driven Smart Sportswear for Real-Time Fitness Monitoring Using Textile Strain Sensors*. 1–12.

Tang, Y., Xu, J., Liu, Q., Hu, X., Xue, W., Liu, Z., Lin, Z., Lin, H., Zhang, Y., Zhang, Z., Ma, X., Wang, J., Zhong, J., Wang, D., Jiang, H., & Ma, Y. (2024). Advancing haptic interfaces for immersive experiences in the metaverse. *Device, 2*(6), 100365. DOI: 10.1016/j.device.2024.100365

Taoheed, B. K., Olusegun, O. A., & Akanni, O. A. (2024). Transformative Impact of Artificial Intelligence (AI), Virtual Reality (VR) and Augmented Reality (AR) on Tourism Marketing in Lagos State, Nigeria.

Tarnowski, P., Kołodziej, M., Majkowski, A., & Rak, R. J. (2020). Eye-tracking analysis for emotion recognition. *Computational Intelligence and Neuroscience, 2020*, 2909267. Advance online publication. DOI: 10.1155/2020/2909267

Tartaglione, A., & Granata, G. (2019). Retail Customer Engagement. *Advances in Marketing, Customer Relationship Management, and E-Services*. Advance online publication. DOI: 10.4018/978-1-5225-7856-7.CH001

Teece, D. J. (2007). Explicating dynamic capabilities: The nature and microfoundations of sustainable enterprise performance. *Strategic Management Journal, 28*(13), 1319–1350. DOI: 10.1002/smj.640

Teece, D. J. (2010). Business Models, Business Strategy and Innovation. *Long Range Planning, 43*(2-3), 172–194. DOI: 10.1016/j.lrp.2009.07.003

Temperino, E. (2023). The perks of being digital: Nikeland—a case study. In Fashion and communication in digital age: Proceedings of the FACTUM 23 Conference, Pisa, Italy, 88–95. Springer. https://doi.org/DOI: 10.1007/978-3-031-38541-4_9

Terhörst, P., Kolf, J. N., Damer, N., Kirchbuchner, F., & Kuijper, A. (2020). Post comparison mitigation of demographic bias in face recognition using fair score normalization. *Pattern Recognition Letters, 140*, 332–338. DOI: 10.1016/j.patrec.2020.11.007

Terzidou, M., Scarles, C., & Saunders, M. N. K. (2018). The complexities of religious tourism motivations: Sacred places, vows and visions. *Annals of Tourism Research, 70*, 54–65. DOI: 10.1016/j.annals.2018.02.011

Thomas, J., Kuhail, M. A., & AlBeyahi, F. (2024). The Metaverse, Religious Practice and Wellbeing: A Narrative Review. *Cyberpsychology, Behavior, and Social Networking, 27*(1), 57–63. DOI: 10.1089/cyber.2023.0003

Tirinzoni, M., & Mcgale, V. (2025). Reimagining identity, healing, and equality through extended reality: A societal revolution of virtual worlds. In García-Peñalvo, A., & Conde-González, J. A. (Eds.), *Impacts of sensetech on society* (pp. 149–186). IGI Global., DOI: 10.4018/978-1-6684-9155-1.ch007

Tomini, N., Brenk, K., Kanbach, D. K., Stubner, S., & Bernhard, F. (2025). From hype to impact: How companies can leverage the metaverse technology for business models. *International Journal of Entrepreneurship and Innovation, 26*(1), 12–22. DOI: 10.1177/14657503241258934

Trading Economics. (n.d.-a). Portugal Consumer Price Index (CPI). Tradingeconomics.com. https://tradingeconomics.com/portugal/consumer-price-index-cpi

Trading Economics. (n.d.-b). Portugal Inflation Rate. Tradingeconomics.com. https://tradingeconomics.com/portugal/inflation-cpi

Transparência Internacional Portugal. (2025, February 11). Índice de Perceção da Corrupção 2024. https://transparencia.pt/indice-de-percecao-da-corrupcao-2024/

Tu, J., Malakuti, S., Telg, J., Xiong, J., & El Saddik, A. (2023). Digital twins in extended reality: The TwinXR system for scalable production of XR-enabled digital twins. *Frontiers in Virtual Reality*, *4*, 1019080. DOI: 10.3389/frvir.2023.1019080

Turismo de Portugal. (2024). Estratégia Turismo 2035. Turismodeportugal.pt. https://www.turismodeportugal.pt/pt/Turismo_Portugal/Estrategia/estrategia-turismo - 2035/Paginas/default.aspx

Turismo de Portugal. (2025, February 26). Visão geral. Www.turismodeportugal .pt. https://www.turismodeportugal.pt/pt/Turismo_Portugal/visao_geral/Paginas/default.aspx

Tyrväinen, O., Karjaluoto, H., & Saarijärvi, H. (2020). Personalization and hedonic motivation in creating customer experiences and loyalty in omnichannel retail. *Journal of Retailing and Consumer Services*, *57*, 102233. DOI: 10.1016/j.jretconser.2020.102233

Upadhyay, U., Kumar, A., Sharma, G., Gupta, B. B., Alhalabi, W. A., Arya, V., & Chui, K. T. (2023). Cyberbullying in the Metaverse: A Prescriptive Perception on Global Information Systems for User Protection. [JGIM]. *Journal of Global Information Management*, *31*(1), 1–25. DOI: 10.4018/JGIM.325793

Valette, E., Bril El-Haouzi, H., & Demesure, G. (2023). Industry 5.0 and its technologies: A systematic literature review upon the human place into IoT- and CPS-based industrial systems. *Computers & Industrial Engineering*, *184*, 109426. DOI: 10.1016/j.cie.2023.109426

Van Nuenen, T., & Scarles, C. (2021). Advancements in technology and digital media in tourism. *Tourist Studies*, *21*(1), 119–132.

van Vulpen, P., Siu, J., & Jansen, S. (2024). Governance of decentralized autonomous organizations that produce open source software. *Blockchain: Research and Applications*, *5*(1), 100166. DOI: 10.1016/j.bcra.2023.100166

Vargo, S. L., & Lusch, R. F. (2004). Evolving to a new dominant logic for marketing. *Journal of Marketing*, *68*(1), 1–17. DOI: 10.1509/jmkg.68.1.1.24036

Vashisht, D. (2023). Engaging and entertaining customers: Gamification in interactive marketing. In Menon, A. R. R., & Vargo, S. L. (Eds.), *The Palgrave handbook of interactive marketing* (pp. 807–835). Springer., DOI: 10.1007/978-3-030-89505-4_27

Verhoef, P. C., Broekhuizen, T., Bart, Y., Bhattacharya, A., Dong, J. Q., Fabian, N., & Haenlein, M. (2021). Digital transformation: A multidisciplinary reflection and research agenda. *Journal of Business Research*, *122*, 889–901. DOI: 10.1016/j.jbusres.2019.09.02

Verhoef, P. C., Kannan, P. K., & Inman, J. J. (2015). From multi-channel retailing to omnichannel retailing: Introduction to the special issue on multi-channel retailing. *Journal of Retailing*, *91*(2), 174–181. DOI: 10.1016/j.jretai.2015.02.005

Vulnerabilities, attacks, and security aspects on the Internet of Things (IoT). (2026). In *Internet of Things Security* (pp. 33–59). Elsevier. https://doi.org/DOI: 10.1016/B978-0-44-333759-8.00011-3

Wachter, R. M., & Brynjolfsson, E. (2024). Will generative artificial intelligence deliver on its promise in health care? *Journal of the American Medical Association*, *331*(1), 65–69. PMID: 38032660

Wang, D., Guo, Y., Liu, S., & Zhang, Y., & collaborators. (2019). Haptic display for virtual reality: Progress and challenges. *Science China. Information Sciences*, *62*, 060101. DOI: 10.3724/SP.J.2096-5796.2019.0008

Wedel, M., Bigné, E., & Zhang, J. (2020). Virtual and augmented reality: Advancing research in consumer marketing. *International Journal of Research in Marketing*, *37*(3), 443–465. DOI: 10.1016/j.ijresmar.2020.04.004

Weech, S., Kenny, S., & Barnett-Cowan, M. (2019). Presence and cybersickness in virtual reality are negatively related: A review. *Frontiers in Psychology*, *10*, 158. DOI: 10.3389/fpsyg.2019.00158

Wei, W. (2023). A buzzword, a phase or the next chapter for the Internet? The status and possibilities of the metaverse for tourism. Journal of Hospitality and Tourism Insights. https://doi.org/DOI: 10.1108/jhti-11-2022-0568

Wetzlinger, W., Auinger, A., Kindermann, H., & Schönberger, W. (2017). Acceptance of Personalization in Omnichannel Retailing., 114-129. https://doi.org/DOI: 10.1007/978-3-319-58484-3_10

Widodo, A. M., Wisnujati, A., Prasetyo, E., & Rahaman, M. (2025). Active-Reconfigurable Intelligent Surfaces for Unmanned Aerial Vehicles: BMS Data Transmission. In *AI Developments for Industrial Robotics and Intelligent Drones* (pp. 187–230). IGI Global Scientific Publishing. https://doi.org/DOI: 10.4018/979-8-3693-2707-4.ch009

Wiese, A., Kellner, J., Lietke, B., Toporowski, W., & Zielke, S. (2012). Sustainability in retailing: A summative content analysis. *International Journal of Retail & Distribution Management, 40*(4), 318–335. DOI: 10.1108/09590551211211792

Wisnujati, A., Widodo, A. M., Mudjijana, M., Tambunan, K., Rahaman, M., & Chen, H.-C. (2023). Implementation of fuzzy simple additive weighting (Fuzzy-SAW) as decision support system for leave scheduling. *AIP Conference Proceedings, 2865*(1), 060004. DOI: 10.1063/5.0182808

World Bank Group. (2025, January). Global Economic Prospects. World Bank. https://www.worldbank.org/pt/publication/global-economic-prospects

World Economic Forum. (2022, May 26). How the metaverse can be a force for good in an uncertain world. https://www.weforum.org/stories/2022/05/how-metaverse-can-be-a-force-for-good-in-an-uncertain-world/

Xie, Y. (2024). Blockchain Technology and The Future of Tourism: A Critical Analysis of The Positive Impacts of Metaverse on The Tourism Sector. *Journal of Smart Cities, 9*(1), 30–48.

Xu, H., Baniya, A. A., Well, S., Bouadjenek, M. R., Dazeley, R., & Aryal, S. (2025). *Action Spotting and Precise Event Detection in Sports: Datasets, Methods, and Challenges*. 1–15.

Yakhlef, A. (2015). Customer experience within retail environments. *Marketing Theory, 15*, 545–564. DOI: 10.1177/1470593115569016

Yanai, C., Solomon, A., Katz, G., Shapira, B., & Rokach, L. (2022). Q-Ball: Modeling Basketball Games Using Deep Reinforcement Learning. *Proceedings of the 36th AAAI Conference on Artificial Intelligence, AAAI 2022, 36*, 8806–8813. https://doi.org/DOI: 10.1609/aaai.v36i8.20861

Yin, R. K. (2018). *Case Study Research and Applications: Design and Methods* (6th ed.). Sage Publications.

Yi, Y., & Jeon, H. (2003). Effects of loyalty programs on value perception, program loyalty, and brand loyalty. *Journal of the Academy of Marketing Science, 31*(3), 229–240.

Yuan, X., Liu, J., Sun, S., Lin, X., Fan, X., Zhao, W., & Kosonen, R. (2025). Data center waste heat for district heating networks: A review. *Renewable & Sustainable Energy Reviews, 219*, 115863. DOI: 10.1016/j.rser.2025.115863

Zahid, A., Ferraro, A., Petrillo, A., & De Felice, F. (2025). Exploring the Role of Digital Twin and Industrial Metaverse Technologies in Enhancing Occupational Health and Safety in Manufacturing. *Applied Sciences (Basel, Switzerland)*, *15*(15), 8268. DOI: 10.3390/app15158268

Zahidi, F., Kaluvilla, B. B., & Mulla, T. (2024). Embracing the new era: Artificial intelligence and its multifaceted impact on the hospitality industry. *Journal of Open Innovation*, *10*(4), 100390.

Zaidi, S. M. H., Iqbal, R., Alharbi, A., Zuberi, H. H., Ahmed, A., & Sheikh, M. U. (2025). Intelligent Process Automation Using Artificial Intelligence to Create Human Assistant. [IJSSCI]. *International Journal of Software Science and Computational Intelligence*, *17*(1), 1–19. DOI: 10.4018/IJSSCI.371761

Zarei, T., Emery, M., Saredakis, D., Lee, G. A., Stubbs, B., Szpak, A., & Loetscher, T. (2024). "Being there together for health": A systematic review on the feasibility, effectiveness, and design considerations of immersive collaborative virtual environments in health applications. arXiv preprint arXiv:2412.04760.

Zeithaml, V. A. (1988). Consumer perceptions of price, quality, and value: A means-end model and synthesis of evidence. *Journal of Marketing*, *52*(3), 2–22.

Zhang, X., Park, Y., Park, J., & Zhang, H. (2024). Demonstrating the influencing factors and outcomes of customer experience in omnichannel retail. *Journal of Retailing and Consumer Services*. Advance online publication. DOI: 10.1016/j.jretconser.2023.103622

Zhang, Y., Li, T., Li, Z., Pondo, J.-M., Wang, X., & An, P. (2025). Affective response dataset for virtual workspaces: Based on color stimuli and multimodal physiological signals. *Sensors (Basel)*, *25*(24), 7461. DOI: 10.3390/s25247461

Zheng, X., & Zhang, L. (2020). Risk assessment of supply-chain systems: A probabilistic inference method. *Enterprise Information Systems*, *14*(6), 858–877.

Zhou, F., Zhang, N., Li, X., Han, C., & Gupta, B. B. (2025). Managing inter-organizational dependencies operation for discovering digital business model innovation in corporate innovation ecosystem. *Operations Management Research*, *18*(2), 574–590.

Zhou, L., Shao, X., & Mao, Q. (2021). A survey of micro-expression recognition. *Image and Vision Computing*, *105*, 104043. DOI: 10.1016/j.imavis.2020.104043

Zuboff, S. (2019). *The age of surveillance capitalism: The fight for a human future at the new frontier of power*. PublicAffairs.

About the Contributors

Brij B. Gupta received the PhD degree from Indian Institute of Technology (IIT) Roorkee, India (One of the oldest technical institutes in Asia). In more than 19 years of his professional experience, he published over 500 papers in journals/ conferences including 40 books and 10 Patents with over 30000 citations. He has received numerous national and international awards including 2022 Best researcher award from Asia University, Taiwan (2022), Canadian Commonwealth Scholarship (2009), Govt. of Canada, Visvesvaraya Faculty Research Fellowship Award (2017), MeitY, Govt of India, IEEE GCCE outstanding and WIE best paper awards and Best Faculty Award (2018 & 2019), NIT KKR, India respectively. Prof Gupta is also serving as Distinguished Research Scientist with LoginRadius Inc., USA which is one of leading cybersecurity companies in the world, especially in the field of customer identity and access management (CIAM). He has been recognized as a Clarivate Web of Science Highly Cited Researcher in Computer Science (top 0.1% researchers globally) consecutively in 2022 and 2023 and has been included in Stanford University's ranking of the world's top 2% scientists consecutively in 2020, 2021, 2022, and 2023. He is also a visiting/adjunct professor with several universities (i.e. Temple University, Macquarie University, Yamaguchi University, University of Murcia, Deakin University, Staffordshire University, Swinburne University of Technology, etc) worldwide. He is also an IEEE Senior Member (2017) and also selected as 2021 Distinguished Lecturer in IEEE CTSoc. Dr Gupta is also serving as Member-in-Large, Board of Governors, IEEE Consumer Technology Society (2022-2024). Prof. Gupta is also leading IJSWIS, IJSSCI and IJCAC, IGI Global, as Editor-in-Chief. Moreover, he is also serving as lead-editor of Book Series with CRC, World Scientific and IET press. He also served as TPC members and organized/special session chairs in ICCE 2021, GCCE 2014-2021 and TPC Chair in 2018 INFOCOM:CCSNA Workshop, Publicity Co-chair in 2020 ICCCN, etc. Dr Gupta is also serving/served as Associate/Guest Editor of IEEE TII, IEEE TITS, IoT, IEEE Big Data, ASOC, FGCS, etc. At present, Prof. Gupta is working as Director,

International Center for AI and Cyber Security Research and Innovations, and Distinguished Professor with the Department of Computer Science and Information Engineering (CSIE), Asia University, Taiwan. His research interests include cyber security, cloud computing, artificial intelligence, intrusion detection, blockchain technologies, cyber physical systems, social media and networking.

Yuk Ming Tang is currently the Senior Lecturer in the Department of Industrial and Systems Engineering at The Hong Kong Polytechnic University. He is the Lab-in-charge of the Integrated Product Design Laboratory, Deputy Lab-in-charge of Ng Tat Lun Digital Factory, a key and initiating member of the Joint Research Centre for Immersive Learning and Educational Technology (CILME), and Co-PI of the Non-PAIR Research Centre for Assistive Technology. Additionally, Dr. Tang is the President of the Institute of Industrial and Systems Engineers (IISE) - Hong Kong and a Member of The Hong Kong Institution of Engineers (MHKIE). His achievements have been highly recognized, as evidenced by his receipt of the Faculty Award for Outstanding Achievement in Teaching (Individual), Faculty Merit Award in Teaching (Individual) and Service (Team), Distinguished Educator Award, Best Researcher Award, among others. Additionally, he has been nominated for the UGC Teaching Award in the General Faculty Members category. Dr. Tang's research interests include Artificial Intelligence (AI), Virtual Reality (VR), Internet of Things, Digital Twin, blockchain, sustainable technology in Industry 4.0, and healthcare applications. In the span of three years, Dr. Tang has published over 80 internationally referred journal articles, 10 book chapters, edited 4 books, and received 2 patents. His publications are mainly published in top-ranked journals such as Computers & Education (C&E), Expert Systems with Applications (ESWA), Information Sciences, Engineering Applications of Artificial Intelligence, and others. He serves as an editor in several renowned journals, including Internet of Things and Journal of Industrial Information Integration. He was a speaker at the Hospital Authority Convention and was interviewed in the episodes of “香港故事_創科夢工場:活在元宇宙” and “Innovation GPS” (創科導航), television programs on local channels RTHK and TVB, respectively.

***

Adetunji Oludele Adebayo is an experienced cybersecurity and information security expert with pioneering skills at the intersection of technology and governance. As a GenAI GRC Lead, he specialises in managing complex security environments, from IoT and third-party supply chain security to comprehensive operational resilience and risk management. He is a digital futurist proficient in utilising artificial intelligence to enhance and streamline data protection and NIST

CSF, PCI DSS compliance frameworks. His expertise is validated by top industry certifications, including CISM and ISO 27001/22301/27000 Lead Implementer, supported by two Master of Science degrees in Cybersecurity and Technology Management. As a recognised leader, conference speaker, and author, he is dedicated to promoting secure and resilient business operations in the digital era.

Paulo Andrade is currently pursuing a Master of Economics and Business Strategy at the School of Economics and Management, University of Porto. His research interests include business economics and business strategy.

Shuvasree Banerjee is a Asst. Professor with over nine years of teaching experience in Tourism and Hotel Management Institutes. She holds a Bachelor of Business Administration (BBA) in Tourism and Hospitality from Burdwan University, West Bengal, followed by a Post Graduate Diploma in Management (PGDM) in Travel & Tourism Management from the Indian Institute of Tourism and Travel Management (IITTM) Bhubaneswar, an autonomous body under the Ministry of Tourism, Government of India. Additionally, she has completed a Master of Business Administration (MBA) in Tourism and Hospitality from the National Institute of Tourism and Hospitality Management (NITHM), Hyderabad, under affiliation with Jawaharlal Nehru Technological University, Hyderabad. She is awarded a PhD degree in Tourism and Hospitality from Chandigarh University. As an active research scholar, she has presented papers at 14 international conferences from 2022 to 2025 and has 16 publications to their credit. Her scholarly contributions include one paper published in a Scopus Q1 journal and 8 book chapters, with 2 paper and 8 chapters indexed in Scopus.

Belem Barbosa received her PhD in Business and Management Studies – Specialisation in Marketing and Strategy from the University of Porto, Portugal. She is an Associate Professor at the School of Economics and Management of the University of Porto. She is a full researcher at CEF.UP Center for Economics and Finance at the University of Porto. Her research interests lie primarily in the areas of digital marketing and consumer behavior.

Francisco Campos is currently pursuing a Master of Economics and Business Strategy at the School of Economics and Management, University of Porto. His research interests include business economics and business strategy.

Pedro Carvalho is a second-year Master's student in Economics and Business Strategy at the School of Economics and Management, University of Porto. He holds a Bachelor's degree in Business Administration from the same institution. His research interests include strategic firm behavior and business planning.

Sudhanshu Chandra is an Assistant Professor (Academic Coordinator) at Manuu Law School, Maulana Azad National Urdu University Hyderabad A Central University Established by an Act of Parliament in 1988, Accredited with Grade A+ by NACC, (Hyderabad Telangana) -500032. He Completed his B.A.LLB(Hons)-Dr. Ram Manohar Lohiya National Law University Lucknow(U.P) LLM-National Law University Jodhpur (Rajasthan), Cleared UGC-NET, Ph.D. in Law from Gautam Buddha University Greater Noida(U.P.) Authored Three Books- The Menace and Implications of Narcotic Drug Abuse and Alcoholism in India: A Socio- Legal Study (Singhal Law Publication-2022), The Effect of Intellectual Property Rights and Conservation on Biodiversity Law in India (Associated Publishing House-2023), Custodial Violence by Police in India: Analysis of Judicial Decisions 2010-2020 (Associated Publishing House-2023).Also taken Copyright of work Custodial Violence by Police in India: Analysis of Judicial Decisions 2010-2020 Registration No-L-124572/2023 Dated-09/06/2023.Judged Several Moot Court Competition. Published More than 20 Research Papers in International/National/Scopus/UGC-Care Listed Journals.

Devaraj E is Passionate and well-versed in Polymer Materials Engineering. Proficient Mechanical Engineer with a robust foundation in new product development to secure a role in an innovative academic institution and currently working as Assistant professor in CMR University. Dr,Devaraj E is specialized in development and characterization of composite materials.

Diogo Fonseca is currently pursuing a Master of Economics and Business Strategy at the School of Economics and Management, University of Porto. His research interests include business economics and business strategy.

Syed Hassan Imam Gardezi is an accomplished business leader and strategist currently serving as the Executive Director and Board Member at Union Investments LLC, based in Ras Al Khaimah, United Arab Emirates. With extensive experience in corporate governance, investment management, and organizational leadership, Dr. Gardezi has played a pivotal role in driving the company's growth and diversification across multiple sectors. His expertise spans strategic planning, financial oversight, and sustainable business development. Renowned for his visionary leadership and commitment to excellence, Dr. Gardezi continues to contribute significantly to the advancement of Union Investments LLC and the broader business community in the UAE.

Akshat Gaurav is a Senior IEEE Member and a recognized researcher listed in the Stanford–Elsevier Top 2% Scientists (Single-Year 2024) in Artificial Intelligence and Image Processing. He is currently a cyber security researcher at International

Center for AI and Cyber Security Research and Innovations, Asia University, Taiwan. His research spans cybersecurity, AI-driven attack detection, phishing prevention, semantic web technologies, and intelligent IoT systems. He has authored an extensive body of research published in leading venues including IEEE Transactions, Elsevier, Springer, IGI Global, and ACM. His work has earned multiple accolades, such as Best Paper Awards at IEEE/ACM Cluster, Cloud and Internet Computing, International AI & IoT conferences, and Best Oral Presentation at GCCE 2025. Mr. Gaurav also plays active leadership roles in the research community. He served as Session Chair at IEEE GLOBECOM 2025 and previously as Session Co-Chair at IEEE GCCE 2022. In addition, he contributes as a Technical Program Committee (TPC) member and reviewer for premier venues, including IEEE INFOCOM, GLOBECOM, ICC, ICCE, ANTS, and several high-impact IEEE Transactions and ACM journals.

Nidhi Jhawar is an Associate Professor at IPS Academy, Institute of Business Management & Research, Indore, with over 14 years of teaching experience at the postgraduate level. She has an extensive academic and research background, published several research papers in reputed journals. Dr. Jhawar has actively participated in numerous national and international conferences, including those held at esteemed institutions such as MDI Gurgaon, Nirma University, Ahmedabad, IIM Indore & Raipur, IIT Indore & Dhanbad. She has also been involved in a wide range of academic enrichment programs, including seminars, workshops, and faculty development programs, organized by prestigious institutions such as IIT Bombay. Her consistent engagement in academic and professional development activities reflects her commitment to excellence in teaching and research.

Shweta Kaur Khalsa is an Associate Professor in the MBA Department at the School of Commerce and Business Studies, Dayananda Sagar University. She demonstrates rich consulting experience in the fields of marketing and human resource. Her research interests lies in the landscape of marketing and human resource. She is also a successful founder of Amitiel Consultants which is a 5 + years old start up into internet marketing services along with her experience in academia.

Vivek Singh Kushwaha is the Director of the Institute of Business Management & Research (IBMR), IPS Academy, Indore, and a renowned academician with a visionary approach to management education. He also leads the Ph.D. Research Centre in Management, where he has successfully guided 25 scholars to the award of their doctoral degrees. With over 31 years of legacy, IBMR—Central India's first private management institute—has flourished under his dynamic leadership. He has cultivated a vibrant learning environment that blends rigorous academics with experiential learning, industry engagement, and student-led initiatives. His unwavering focus on innovation, inclusivity, and value-based education continues to position IBMR as a premier institution for nurturing future-ready professionals and responsible leaders.

Arun M. R. completed his BE, ME and PhD from Anna University, Chennai. He completed PG Diploma (PGDEEM) from Annamalai University, M.Sc. Counselling Psychology from TNOU University, M.A. Public Administration from Madras University and B.Lib.Sc. from Alagappa University. He is in the Teaching Profession for the past 17 years, Published around 115 papers in Journals, Patents and Conferences, Active participant crossing more than 200 events and internationally networked through various Professional bodies. He is skilled and technically proficient in various simulation Softwares associated to Research in Engineering. He Organized and Coordinated around 15 events in working Institution. Authored more than 15 Books, 20 Book Chapters and he has been technically integrated in various international journals as an Editorial Board Member and Reviewer. His area of interest includes Video Processing, Remote Automation, Wireless Communication, IoT Sensors, Quantum Computing, Machine Learning & Artificial Intelligence.

Durga Madhab Mahapatra is an Associate Professor in the Department of Commerce at North-Eastern Hill University (NEHU), Shillong, India. With a distinguished academic career spanning over two decades, Dr. Mahapatra has made significant contributions to the fields of commerce, business strategy, and socio-economic development. He holds a Ph.D. in Commerce and has developed a strong research portfolio that bridges theory and practice, particularly in the areas of marketing management, consumer behaviour, rural entrepreneurship, and sustainable development. Dr. Mahapatra is widely recognised for his interdisciplinary approach and has published extensively in national and international peer-reviewed journals. His current research interests include digital transformation in commerce, tribal entrepreneurship, inclusive business models, and the socio-economic dynamics of the North-Eastern region of India. He has also actively participated in national conferences and UGC-sponsored seminars and has contributed chapters to edited volumes on contemporary issues in commerce and development. An advocate for community-based research and academic outreach, Dr. Mahapatra frequently collaborates with NGOs and government agencies to promote grassroots entrepreneurship and capacity-building initiatives. He is committed to advancing indigenous knowledge systems and fostering educational excellence in underserved regions.

Tonmoy Malaker is an accomplished author, researcher and Lecturer of the Department of "Tourism and Hospitality Management" of Daffodil International University, Dhaka, Bangladesh with a strong academic background in BBA and MBA majoring in Management Information Systems (MIS) from the University of Dhaka. His passion lies in exploring the intersection of business and emerging technologies. His diverse areas of interest include AI, Business analytics, IoT, Blockchain Technology, ERP. Through his extensive research and insightful writing, he sheds light on the intricate connections between his diverse areas of interests and real life. His work not only enriches the field of MIS but also inspires readers to engage with the world around them in meaningful and responsible ways.

Meena Malik is currently working as an associate professor at the Department of Computer Science & Engineering, Chandigarh University, Punjab, India. She received a Ph.D. from Maharishi Dayanand University, Rohtak, Haryana, India, in 2019. She has teaching experience of more than 14 years and efficiently published more than 35 papers in various peer-reviewed SCI and Scopus journals and international and national conferences. She has been a reviewer and session chair for various conferences. She has delivered expert talks in various colleges and universities. Her research interests include blockchain, cybersecurity, IoT security, and network and cloud security.

Pratap Chandra Mandal is an Assistant Professor (Marketing) at Indian Institute of Management, Shillong, India. He has completed graduate degree from the reputed Indian Institute of Technology, Kharagpur (IIT Kharagpur), India (Bachelor of Technology in Mechanical Engineering), post-graduate degree from Vinod Gupta School of Management, IIT Kharagpur (Masters in Business Adminstration), PhD (Marketing) from Vinod Gupta School of Management, IIT Kharagpur. His research concerns customer relationship management, customer satisfaction, services marketing, marketing intelligence, and qualitative methods in management. He is the editor-in-chief of two international journals and is on the editorial board of journals like Journal of Global Marketing. Pratap has won several prestigious scholarships and awards throughout his academic career.

T.C. Manjunath was born on 6th February 1967. He did his B.E. from RV College of Engg. in 1989 (B'lore Univ), M.E. in Robotics & Automation from Govt.'s LD College of Engg., (Gujarat Univ., Ahmedabad) in 1992 with FCD-First Rank & PhD in Systems & Control Engg. from IIT Bombay in the year 2007, got best research scholar award for the entire IITB. He is currently working as the Dean Research (R & D) and as Professor in Dept. of Computer Science & Engg. with specialization in IoT, Cyber Security, Blockchain Technology in Rajarajeswari

College of Engineering, Bengaluru, Karnataka. He has got a teaching (academic), research & administrative experience of more than 35+ years (10 years as Principal & 8 years as HoD, 1 year as Dean Research & rest as faculty) and has published more than 1500+ research papers in various national & international journals & conferences, with 175+ patents, 100+ book-chapters, 25 awards, 100s of Keynote talks and also published 25 text books in various field of science, engineering & technology, completed projects worth Rs. 9 Crores till date & guided 10 PhD scholars in VTU. He is a member of 30 Professional Society Chapters and is a fellow of IE, IETE, AMIEE, Sr. Member of IEEE and a chartered engineer.

Dhanashree Nagar is Associate Professor at IPS Academy, Institute of Business Management & Research (IBMR), Indore. She has eighteen plus years of teaching experience at under graduate and post graduate level. She has more than forty five research papers published in peer reviewed, referred journals, including few in UGC CARE/Listed, SCOPUS and ABDC publications. She has also actively participated and presented various National & International Conferences including IIM Ahmedabad, IIM Indore and Nirma University to name a few. She has received the Best Research Paper Award in 2018 at 30 th Association of Indian Management Schools (AIMS) Convention, Bangalore and also has accolade with Gold Medal She has also received 'Best Research Paper Runner Up' award for the paper in 14 th International Conference 2020 at Prestige Institute of Management Research, Indore. She has been the member of Organizing Committee of three National Conferences and Co-convener of one International Conference. Her research interest as well as teaching area includes Advertising, Retail Management, Marketing Management, Marketing Strategies, Consumer Behaviour, Sales Promotion, Service Marketing, Branding, CRM, Business Communication and Entrepreneurship. Currently she is recognized as a Ph.D. supervisor at Devi Ahilya Vishwavidyala, Indore and four scholars are pursuing Ph.D. under her supervision.

Gustavo Nogueira is currently pursuing a Master of Economics and Business Strategy at the School of Economics and Management, University of Porto. His research interests include business economics and business strategy.

P. Selvakumar is currently an Associate Professor in the Department of Science and Humanities at Nehru Institute of Technology, Coimbatore, Tamil Nadu, India. Prior to joining Nehru Institute of Technology, he held positions as an Assistant Professor in the Department of Science and Humanities various engineering colleges in Coimbatore, Tamil Nadu, India, spanning from 2011 to 2023. Dr.P. Selvakumar's academic and research interests lie primarily in the field of phytochemistry. He has made significant contributions to his field, with an impressive record that includes

30 journal publications, 12 patents, and 20 conference papers. Additionally, he has organized 5 seminars and conferences, further demonstrating his commitment to academic and scientific exchange. Throughout his career, Dr. P.Selvakumar has been recognized for his dedication and excellence in teaching, having been honored with several awards, including the Best Teacher Awards. He holds a prominent position in the academic community, contributing actively to research.

Yash Pandey is a Ph.D. student in Electrical & Electronic Engineering at Shizuoka University, Japan, specializing in hybrid renewable energy microgrids and sustainable rural electrification. His research employs HOMER Pro simulations, MATLAB analysis, and regression-based modeling to develop practical, scalable energy solutions for underserved communities. Yash completed his master's degree at Shizuoka University in September 2025 as a recipient of the ABP Full Scholarship, focusing on optimal capacity planning for rural electrification across diverse load variability and climatic zones. He earned his B.Tech. in Electrical Engineering from KIIT University, India, and holds an Advanced Diploma in Industrial Safety. Currently serving as a Research Assistant under Prof. Hitoshi Haga, Yash has published multiple peer-reviewed papers on sustainable energy systems, including works in Wiley Publications, Elsevier's e-Prime, and IEEE Xplore. His research addresses critical challenges in PV-BESS capacity estimation and renewable energy transitions toward net-zero emissions. With international research experience spanning Japan, Taiwan, and India, Yash has presented at numerous conferences and contributes as a freelance consultant for energy corporations. He is affiliated with the International Association of Advanced Materials (IAAM) and serves as a research assistant at Shizuoka University.

Jitendranath Patri is a seasoned business leader with nearly 30 years of experience in retail management, marketing, customer relationship management, academia, entrepreneurship, and retail technology. At Future Group, he headed marketing and customer loyalty for Central and Brand Factory, spearheading strategies that enhanced customer engagement and drove significant business growth. Passionate about the intersection of retail and technology, Jitendranath collaborates with tech startups such as Swirl, Arbeit Nexus, Xeno, and others. He is a trusted advisor who helps founders scale and achieve sustainable growth. He brings to these partnerships his understanding of the retail industry, marketing analytics, customer experience, and retail tech innovation. He teaches entrepreneurship and marketing as an adjunct faculty member at the School of Commerce and Management Studies (PG and the Executive MBA Program). He leads the COPE in Entrepreneurship, which inspires the next generation of innovators.

Alya Nurul Qolbi is a researcher with a strong interest in artificial intelligence and emerging technologies. Her work focuses on exploring innovative digital solutions and their applications in education, data systems, and smart environments. She is passionate about advancing research that bridges technology, human interaction, and sustainable development. Alya continues to expand her academic and practical contributions in the field of intelligent systems and technological innovation.

Mosiur Rahman, a Research Assistant at the International Center for AI and Cyber Security Research and Innovations (CCRI) at Asia University, Taiwan, holds a PhD in Computer Science and Information Engineering and master's degrees in Business Management and Computer Science and Engineering. With prior roles as a Research Assistant in AI and an Assistant Professor in Computer Science, he has extensive experience in academia. Dr. Rahman has been actively involved in international conferences, serving in significant roles, and is a part-time lecturer in Humanities and Social Science. His research interests include AI, Neural Networks, and Security, and he is a dedicated peer reviewer for over 50 journals, showcasing his commitment to research and academic excellence.

Nithin Subba Rao, as a distinguished manufacturing excellence leader with over 15 years of experience in the automotive industry, has established himself as a transformational force in operational optimization and cost reduction. He holds a Master's degree in Mechanical Engineering from Michigan Technological University and an MBA in Operations Management, combining technical expertise with strategic business acumen. As a Six Sigma Black Belt with 10+ approved patents in manufacturing process improvement, Nithin Subba Rao has demonstrated exceptional capability in driving operational transformation and delivering measurable results. His track record includes delivering over $80 million in combined cost savings and restructuring benefits while implementing Industry 4.0 technologies across multiple manufacturing facilities. Nithin Subba Rao's expertise spans digital transformation, lean manufacturing, ERP integration, and the development of sustainable continuous improvement cultures that drive long-term competitive advantage. His personal philosophy of continuous improvement – symbolized by naming his daughter "Aarohi," meaning continuous improvement / ascending – reflects his deep commitment to daily progress and systematic excellence. He firmly believes that consistency beats intensity, working toward his goals one step at a time with a target of 1% daily improvement, a principle that has delivered miraculous results in both his personal and professional life.

K. S. Shibani Shankar Ray is a scholar-practitioner at the intersection of strategy, policy, and behavioural science. With an MBA from IIM Indore and a doctoral research in Marketing Management, his research explores heuristics in strategic decision-making, stakeholder engagement in sustainability, and digital health systems. He has taught across premier institutions and delivered flagship programs on women's financial leadership and rural entrepreneurship. Shibani has worked with I-PAC, Udaan, Byju's, and Hindustan Coca-Cola, bringing rich field insights into his classrooms and publications. His writing appears in Empirical Economics Letters, Technology in Society, and IGI Global volumes on AI, blended learning, and sustainable e-commerce. A recipient of multiple national awards, Shibani combines academic rigour with on-ground impact, driven by a commitment to inclusive development and transformative pedagogy.

José De Jesús Reyes-Sánchez, Ph.D. in senior management, has six master's degrees, in education, in management, professional soccer technique, in physical preparation, in professional soccer, in physical rehabilitation sciences, in sports sciences, as well as in coaching and integral well-being, who is a research professor at the TECNM Instituto Tecnológico Superior De Fresnillo, with more than 20 years of teaching experience, PRODEP profile and coordinator of the academic body with vast experience in conferences and workshops, currently novelist and writer.

Pamarthi Satyanarayana, specialize in Constitutional Law and Legal Order, focusing my research on the interface between individual rights and public policy, with a strong emphasis on civil liberties, social justice, and the right to privacy. Over the past 36 months, I have served as an Assistant Professor of Law at Vel Tech Rangarajan Dr. Sagunthala R&D Institute of Science and Technology in Chennai, Tamil Nadu. Here, I teach courses such as Constitutional Law, Legal Research and Writing, and both Civil and Criminal Law. My passion for teaching and in-depth subject knowledge have earned me recognition as a dedicated educator. In addition to my academic role, I actively engage with the community, partnering with legal clinics to provide pro bono services to underprivileged individuals. Looking forward, I aim to expand my research into emerging legal issues in the digital age, especially in privacy rights, while guiding aspiring law students and future legal scholars.

Amrik Singh is working as Professor in the School of Hotel Management and Tourism at Lovely Professional University, Punjab, India. He obtained his Ph.D. degree in Hotel Management from Kurukshetra University, Kurukshetra. He started his academic career at Lovely Professional University, Punjab, India in the year 2007. He has published more than 40 research papers in UGC and peer-reviewed and Scopus/Web of Science) journals. He has published 12 patents and 01 patent has been granted in the inter-disciplinary domain. Dr. Amrik Singh participated and acted as a resource person in various national and international conferences, seminars, research workshops, and industry talks. His area of research interest is accommodation management, ergonomics, green practices, human resource management in hospitality, waste management, AR VR in hospitality, etc. He is currently guiding 8Ph.D. scholars and 2 Ph.D. scholars have been awarded Ph.D.

Mohammad Badruddoza Talukder is an Associate Professor & Chairman at the College of Tourism and Hospitality Management at the International University of Business Agriculture and Technology (IUBAT) in Dhaka, Bangladesh. Holding a PhD from Lovely Professional University, India, he is renowned for his innovative integration of cutting-edge technologies such as Artificial Intelligence (AI), the Internet of Things (IoT), and Blockchain into tourism and hospitality management. His research explores the transformative impact of these technologies on smart tourism, cloud kitchens, and the broader industry landscape. As a prolific author, Dr. Talukder has published numerous scholarly articles and books, with forthcoming titles that address AI innovations in hospitality, the evolution of cloud kitchens, and the enhancement of digital literacy within hospitality education. His work shapes contemporary tourism and hospitality practices, skillfully marrying technological advancements with practical industry applications. Since 2008, Dr. Talukder has imparted his knowledge through a diverse array of courses in tourism and hospitality across various universities in Bangladesh.

Gustavo Tarábbia is currently pursuing a Master of Economics and Business Strategy at the School of Economics and Management, University of Porto. His research interests include business economics and business strategy.

Suyash Thakur is an undergraduate student in Mechanical Engineering at the National Institute of Technology Hamirpur, with a strong interest in product management, marketing, and technology. His research focuses on neuromarketing, consumer behaviour, and digital product strategies.

Agung Mulyo Widodo received a PhD in Computer Science and Information Engineering, Asia University, Taiwan, in 2022, and currently works as a lecturer and researcher at the Faculty of Computer Science, Esa Unggul University, Jakarta, Indonesia. He has worked as a research assistant to his advising professor while a PostDoc Research Fellow at the Artificial Intelligence and Information Security Laboratory, Department of Computer Science and Information Engineering (CSIE), Asia University, Taiwan. Recently, he has worked as a Postdoc Research Fellow at the Intelligent Technology Sustainability Center, National Kaohsiung University of Science and Technology (NKUST), Kaohsiung, Taiwan. His previous projects were with Caltex Pacific Indonesia (CPI), Siemens-Telecommunications, Nokia Siemens Networks (NSN). Currently, his research focuses on wireless communications technologies, including NOMA, OMA, NB-IoT, backscatter systems, cognitive radio, smart antennas, artificial intelligence, and information security.

Index

W

www.ingramcontent.com/pod-product-compliance
Lightning Source LLC
LaVergne TN
LVHW080902300926
849162LV00003B/529